FOURTH EDITION

Language Arts Activities for Children

Donna E. Norton
Texas A & M University

Saundra E. Norton

Merrill, an imprint of Prentice Hall
Upper Saddle River, New Jersey
Columbus, Ohio

Library of Congress Cataloging-in-Publication Data

Norton, Donna E.
    Language arts activities for children / Donna E. Norton, Saundra E.
Norton.—4th ed.
        p.   cm.
    Includes bibliographical references and index.
    ISBN 0-13-913005-5
    1. Language arts.   2. Education, Elementary—Activity programs.
3. Computer-assisted instruction.   I. Norton, Saundra E.
II. Title.
LB1576.N844 1999
372.6—dc21

98-33598
CIP

Cover Art: ©H. Armstrong Roberts
Editor: Bradley J. Potthoff
Production Editor: Mary M. Irvin
Design Coordinator: Diane C. Lorenzo
Cover Designer: Tanya Burgess
Production Manager: Pamela D. Bennett
Production Coordination and Design: Carlisle Publishers Services
Director of Marketing: Kevin Flanagan
Marketing Manager: Suzanne Stanton
Advertising/Marketing Coordinator: Krista Groshong

This book was set in Usherwood by Carlisle Communications, Ltd., and was
printed and bound by Banta Company. The cover was printed by Banta Company.

 ©1999 by Prentice-Hall, Inc.
Simon & Schuster/A Viacom Company
Upper Saddle River, New Jersey 07458

Earlier editions ©1994 by Macmillan College Publishing Company; ©1985, 1980 by
Merrill Publishing Company.

Printed in the United States of America

10 9 8 7 6 5 4 3 2 1

ISBN: 0-13-913005-5

Prentice-Hall International (UK) Limited, *London*
Prentice-Hall of Australia Pty. Limited, *Sydney*
Prentice-Hall of Canada, Inc., *Toronto*
Prentice-Hall Hispanoamericana, S. A., *Mexico*
Prentice-Hall of India Private Limited, *New Delhi*
Prentice-Hall of Japan, Inc., *Tokyo*
Simon & Schuster Asia Pte. Ltd., *Singapore*
Editora Prentice-Hall do Brasil, Ltda., *Rio de Janeiro*

Preface

Bringing effective language arts instruction into the classroom is an exciting experience for both children and teachers. Stimulating activities add sparkle to the environment and enrich children's learning experiences. However, we are living in a time when educators are facing criticism about the effectiveness of instruction, the development of language arts competencies in the classroom, and the ability of schools to meet the needs of a diverse school population. Unfortunately, adding stimulation and enrichment to the environment and effectively meeting competency needs in language arts may be considered opposing goals. This activities book illustrates how teachers can use effective teaching methods and strategies to build children's language arts skills as well as create a stimulating, enriched environment.

The activities in this book include many opportunities for the integration of the language arts across the curriculum. Because of the growing demand for literature-based instruction, most of the activities include selections of children's literature that may be used to focus the lesson and to expand interest in and knowledge of children's literature. These activities also emphasize the importance of oral and written language in the development of language arts capabilities.

This is a very practical book—all activities are developed in a lesson plan format. All of the activities have been tested in school environments, with in-service teachers, and in teacher education classrooms. We found that effective teaching requires a model for lesson plan development, clearly stipulated objectives, and step-by-step development of the lesson. We also discovered that peer teaching, student teaching, and in-service classroom teaching improved when the methods stressed in language arts classes were demonstrated through lesson plan development. The lesson plans in the multicultural section were developed, implemented, and evaluated as part of a multicultural research project designed to improve students' language arts abilities. The lesson plans in the literature and composition sections were developed, implemented, and evaluated as part of literature and writing research projects. The plans can be implemented directly by the teacher, modified for individual needs, or used as a model for additional activities.

A new section in this edition develops literacy activities around technology and computers. This new chapter, entitled "Technology and the Language Arts," explores some of the ways that language arts teachers may effectively use computers and the Internet to assist instruction.

ACKNOWLEDGMENTS

This book would not be possible without interaction with children, teachers, and undergraduate students. We wish to thank all of the school systems that have provided opportunities for consultation, in-service, and workshops; the undergraduate students who enthusiastically tried ideas; and the children who provided the final evaluation. We sincerely hope that you, the teacher or the future teacher, will have equally exciting teaching experiences when you use the activities developed in this book.

We appreciate the insights and comments we received from the reviewers of the manuscript: Ward A. Cockrun, Northern Arizona University; Leslie Marlow-Inman, Northwestern State University; and Linda J. Marriott, Southern Utah University.

Brief Contents

Activity Contents

2   Oral Language and Cognitive Development Activities

3   Listening Activities

4   Writing Activities

*STA = short-term activity; LTA = long-term activity; LC = learning center

Contents

*STA = short-term activity; LTA = long-term activity; LC = learning center

5   Activities for the Mechanics of Language

6   Activities for Literature

*STA = short-term activity; LTA = long-term activity; LC = learning center

7   Media Activities

*STA = short-term activity; LTA = long-term activity; LC = learning center

8   Multicultural Activities

*STA = short-term activity; LTA = long-term activity; LC = learning center

9 Technology and the Language Arts

*STA = short-term activity; LTA = long-term activity; LC = learning center

1

Creative
Language Arts

Do the terms *motivation, stimulation, creativity, enriched environments, effective lesson plans,* and *effective teaching techniques* mean anything in the development of an effective language arts curriculum? All of these factors should be visible in the elementary classroom environment. We should see how these factors influence the development of children's communication skills and affect what children produce during language arts instruction. We should see positive changes in children's attitudes toward communication skills, and we should see how these factors influence the teaching strategies the classroom teacher uses.

If we were to walk into a classroom that ignores these powerful educational tools, we would probably find ourselves in a sterile environment—the room would contain no colorful bulletin boards showing children's creative writing, and there would be no learning centers or library corners for stimulating children's creative thinking and individual growth. In this sterile environment, the teacher would lead no motivational periods or stimulating discussions before assigning tasks. Students would not be stimulated by the thoughts of others and would have few opportunities for developing oral language abilities, creative written expression, or love for books. The materials used in this sterile classroom would reflect lack of creativity, motivation, and attention to individual needs. Children may feel little motivation to answer factual questions or clarify and extend ideas. The teacher would not interact with the children as they wrote; would not provide opportunities for children to read and listen to a variety of stories; would not motivate oral and written expression; would not use knowledge of children's needs to develop instructional tasks; and would not organize the classroom to make use of individual, small-group, and large-group activities.

In contrast, a rich learning environment gives children many opportunities to experience the environment, work at stimulating learning centers, and interact purposefully with classmates and teacher. Children's interests are used to help them select literature. Their interests are also used to stimulate other children to explore reading interests with others in a recreational reading group or literature learning center. In such an environment, teachers assign research projects that are compatible with the students' interests and abilities. Teachers provide vital stimulation before asking children to write. During the writing process, the teacher and students interact frequently, and the teacher helps to clarify ideas and provides instruction when necessary. Children's interests in the media are used to motivate development of reading, writing, and critical evaluation skills, as well as creative oral expression. The teacher in this environment understands the need to read and tell stories to children every day and inspires a love for literature while stimulating appreciative listening skills. The teacher understands the scope and sequence of the language arts curriculum and provides opportunities for children to develop all of the communication skills.

Both teachers and students require stimulating instruction. It is not an easy task to develop the enriched environment and instructional tasks that stimulate and motivate effective communication skills. Preparing and planning creative activities requires time, and finding this extra time in teachers' busy schedules is often difficult. The purpose of this book is to provide ideas and complete lesson plans for the preservice and in-service teacher to use as suggested, to adapt for individual needs, or to use the ideas for developing additional activities.

CONSIDERATIONS IN ORGANIZING LANGUAGE ARTS INSTRUCTION

Before discussing how to use the activities in this book, let us review some of the considerations for effective and efficient classroom organization and instruction. Teachers should adapt language arts instruction to meet individual needs.

Providing for the individual needs of a whole classroom, however, requires considerable instructional, organizational, and management ability. First, the students' language arts abilities need to be evaluated so that instruction can be geared toward their actual needs. After evaluating the students, the teacher must provide instruction that meets the discovered needs. Grouping students into flexible categories is the most efficient way to meet the language arts needs of all of the students. Without flexible groupings, the language arts teacher has an almost impossible task. At one extreme is complete individualization of instruction for all students; at the other extreme is identical instruction for the whole class. Neither of these alternatives allows for the best use of instructional time. Besides, these alternatives would not meet the special requirements of the various language arts. Development of many of the oral language skills would be inconceivable on an individual basis. Can you imagine a one-person discussion or a one-person creative dramatization? To meet both the children's needs and the requirements of the various language arts, the classroom must provide opportunities for children to work individually, in pairs, in small groups, and with the whole class.

The following checklist will help the teacher evaluate effective and efficient instructional practices. Are each of the following factors included in language arts planning, instruction, and classroom organization?

Questions to Answer for Planning Effective and Efficient Language Arts Instruction

	Always	*Sometimes*	*No*
1. Do I evaluate students' language arts abilities?	___	___	___
2. Do I provide opportunities for children to work in appropriate groupings?	___	___	___
a. individual instruction?	___	___	___
b. assignments that can be completed individually?	___	___	___
c. assignments that can be completed in pairs?	___	___	___
d. small-group instruction?	___	___	___
interest groups?	___	___	___
research groups?	___	___	___
ability groups?	___	___	___
special-needs groups?	___	___	___
e. whole-class instruction when appropriate?	___	___	___
3. Do I provide students with opportunities to work in motivating learning centers?	___	___	___
4. Do I provide adequate instructional time for all of the language arts skills?	___	___	___
a. oral communications?	___	___	___
b. written communications?	___	___	___
c. listening?	___	___	___
d. reading?	___	___	___
e. spelling?	___	___	___
f. literature?	___	___	___
g. grammar, usage?	___	___	___
h. handwriting?	___	___	___
i. media?	___	___	___

5. Do I balance the language arts subjects so that listening, creative writing, literature, oral expression, and media are all emphasized? _____ _____ _____

6. Do I use both formal and informal methods of instruction? _____ _____ _____

7. Do I have a balance between oral and written work? _____ _____ _____

8. Do I consider motivation and stimulation in language arts lesson planning? _____ _____ _____

9. Do I develop and include multicultural literature and other related activities? _____ _____ _____

10. Do I use flexible room arrangements so that students can work in groups, pairs, and individually? _____ _____ _____

Most educators would agree that the teacher is the most important element in an effective educational program. Lipson (1990) states that the assessment of the literacy environment must evaluate the role of the teacher. She maintains that the assessment must examine the teacher's use of time in the classroom; for example, how much time is spent on such tasks as interacting with literature, teacher- and student-initiated talk, student reading of connected text, and management?

The current emphasis on literature-based instruction across the curriculum provides opportunities for additional teacher self-evaluation. Our experiences with literature-based programs show that teachers frequently benefit from completing self-evaluation inventories in which they assess their own behaviors and analyze how well these behaviors enrich a literature-based curriculum and help students understand and appreciate literature. The following self-evaluation inventory has been used by many teachers to help them clarify and identify behaviors that should enrich a literature-based curriculum (Norton, 1992, p. 103).

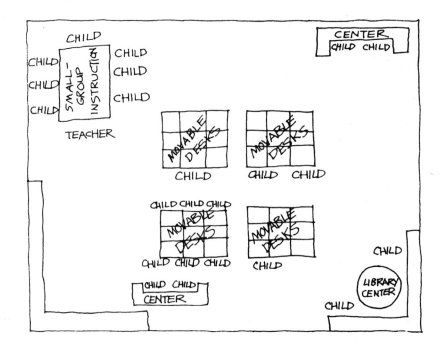

Teachers can use such inventories to brainstorm ways to improve their literature-based curricula. School librarians also can develop self-evaluation inventories and join the teachers in their brainstorming.

Self-Evaluation Inventory of Teacher Behaviors Associated with Literature-Based Curricula.

1. I create an attractive environment that encourages students to read and enjoy literature.
   (List examples of attractive literature environments.)
2. I frequently read aloud to the students from a wide range of literary genres.
   (List examples of books read orally.)
3. I am a role model because I show my students how important reading is to me.
   (List examples of behaviors.)
4. I provide opportunities for students to share their enthusiasm for books with other students through such activities as students reading to students, students discussing books with other students, and students working together on literature-related projects.
   (List examples of sharing enthusiasm.)
5. I develop literature-related activities in which I model how students should think through the literature.
   (List examples of modeling activities.)
6. I encourage my students to give personal responses to the literature.
   (List examples of personal responses.)
7. I try to discover what my students know about the literature, genre, or setting before I expect them to read, analyze, and respond to literature.
   (List examples of discovering background information.)
8. I consider recreational reading to be important. I encourage students to do recreational reading, and I plan school time for recreational activities.
   (List examples of recreational reading activities.)
9. I know the needs of my students and prepare minilessons that teach them about elements of literature and other techniques that readers and writers need to know.
   (List examples of minilessons.)
10. I integrate literature into the total curriculum. I use literature when teaching the various content areas.
    (List examples of integrating literature into the curriculum.)
11. I consider literature to be central to the curriculum and not just something to be added once in a while for enrichment.
    (List examples of integrating literature into the curriculum.)
12. I use additional ways to develop my students' understanding of and appreciation for literature.
    (List examples of additional ways.)

AREAS OF THE LANGUAGE ARTS DEVELOPED IN THIS TEXT

Effective instruction should be broad enough to include all areas of the language arts. For this reason, the activities in this text include oral language, cognitive development, listening, language experience, writing, media, grammar, usage, spelling, handwriting, punctuation, and literature. Because language arts skills are interrelated, many of the activities are designed to improve more than one language arts skill. The current emphasis on literature-based instruction is also highlighted within these lesson plans. Literature-based instruction is becoming a dominant curricular practice within many school districts. For example, the national trust for accelerated schools as envisioned and developed by researchers from Stanford University emphasizes using primary-source literature across the curriculum. The Accelerated Schools Project, as described by MacCormick (1992), includes numerous instructional activities and curricular practices that enrich the environment, encourage active and discovery learning, emphasize literature-based instruction across the curriculum, and enhance opportunities for critical thinking for all students.

The activities not only cover a wide variety of areas but also demonstrate diversity for grouping practices. Many of the activities are easily adaptable for whole-class, group, or individual instruction. For example, many writing activities suggest motivational periods for stimulating whole classes or large groups. These motivational periods are followed by individual writing sessions during which the teacher interacts with each student.

To help the teacher provide motivating learning centers, the text includes activities for use with a learning center format. The listening section, for example, includes several "Listening Post" activities, complete with suggestions for taped listening lessons and self-correcting activity cards.

To provide greater flexibility of instruction, some of the activities can be completed within a short period of time, whereas others involve whole units of study. As an example of this flexibility, the literature section contains storytelling and literature activities that students can complete in one instructional session. The same section contains a unit on historical fiction that could provide students with several weeks of stimulating social studies instruction. Because literature also offers marvelous stimulation for developing learning centers, learning center activities are suggested for fairytales, picture books, and historical fiction.

Because sensitivity toward the contributions and needs of people from different cultures is very important, this book contains activities that focus on positive themes in multicultural literature. The activities provide examples of ways that language arts skills may be taught while children learn to respect and understand their own culture and the cultures of other groups of people from different ethnic backgrounds.

HOW ARE THE ACTIVITIES PRESENTED?

Each activity in this text is designed for maximum usefulness to the teacher. The purposes of the activity are listed first and describe the various language arts skills that will be developed by the activity. Without an understanding of the activity's purpose, the teacher cannot decide whether children need the activity or whether they have actually benefited from instruction. In addition, because communication skills are interrelated, many activities are designed so that students can develop several language arts skills at once. Let us consider, for example, language experience activity 2–1, titled "Sammy Circle's Colors." The purposes for this activity are as follows:

1. To involve students in a motivational activity resulting in oral discussion and a dictated story
2. To identify colors illustrated in a rebus chart story
3. To match colors on cardboard circles with colors on a rebus chart story

These purposes describe the skills and objectives stated in most language arts scope and sequence charts for early elementary grades. If children can already identify colors by both concrete color example and printed words, they will not need to spend time on this activity.

Each activity is also coded according to the *type* of activity and the *term* of the activity, as in the following example:

TYPE	TERM
● CLASS	● STA
● GROUP	○ LTA
● IND	○ LC

Both effective classroom management and effective teaching require instructional activities that allow the teacher to work with the whole class, small groups, and individual children. Many of the activities in the text may be adapted for each of these groups. In our example, "Sammy Circle's Colors," the teacher can use the activity with the whole class if the class needs reinforcement in identifying colors or reading color labels. If, however, only a small group or an individual student needs this instruction or review, the activity may be used with that group or individual child. The additional reinforcement activities listed for the activity also suggest other group and individual activities designed to strengthen color identification. The second coding of each activity refers to the time required to complete the activity: STA means that the activity is a short-term activity that can be completed in one or two instructional sessions; LTA means that the activity is a longer-term activity that can be developed over several sessions or even weeks; LC indicates that the activity is developed in learning center format. The activity "Sammy Circle's Colors" is coded as a short-term activity because it can be completed in one session, although follow-up reinforcement activities may require additional time.

A list of materials necessary to complete the activity appears after the purposes section. These materials are specific, including the names of books, references, suggestions for pictures, motivational activities, media, charts, or stipulations for art or other supplies. All suggestions for charts, paragraphs, games, and so forth are developed fully in the procedural section of the activity. In our example, "Sammy Circle's Colors," the materials include Sammy Circle drawn in each of the basic colors; chart story, "Sammy Circle's Colors"; chart paper for dictated story; and art supplies for individual pictures.

In this activity the motivational chart story is developed as follows:

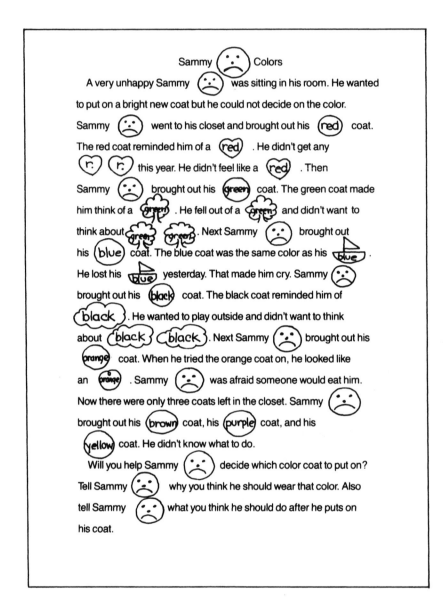

Each activity designates the approximate grade-level range appropriate for the activity (lower elementary, middle elementary, upper elementary, or middle school) rather than a specific grade. Approximations are more useful because children's needs, interests, and abilities vary greatly. Teachers may adapt many of the activities to the needs of younger or older students by rewording the directions and changing the motivating activity. Our example, "Sammy Circle's Colors," has a grade designation of kindergarten and first grade. Although students usually learn the names of colors at this grade level, the activity may be used with older students requiring remedial assistance.

If the activity includes the use of literature, there is a summary of the books to be used. This summary may include several books because the activity frequently includes books that provide background information as well as books that may be used to extend an activity.

Finally, each activity gives step-by-step procedures for developing the activity with children. If the activity demands reading a literature selection, specific directions for using the selection are provided. If the activity requires a motivational chart, paragraph, or game to share with children, the chart is developed, the paragraph is included, or the game board is illustrated and directions included. The procedures in our example, "Sammy Circle's Colors," include the following activities:

1. Lead an oral discussion about Sammy Circle and his problems with colors. Begin the discussion by introducing "Sammy Circle." Draw Sammy on a card or sheet but do not color in the circle. Explain that Sammy Circle is unhappy because he wants to be colorful but cannot decide which color he wants to be. He wants the children to "read" the chart story "Sammy Circle's Colors," which describes his problems. After they "read" the story along with their teacher, he wants them to draw a picture illustrating the solution to his problem and dictate a short story telling about the picture.
2. Introduce the story "Sammy Circle's Colors," which has been printed on large sheets of tagboard or newsprint. Encourage the children to follow along as you read. Allow them to "read" the rebus pictures. Read the story a second time and encourage the children to "read" with you.
3. Discuss the color choices Sammy Circle has for his coat. Encourage the children to discuss advantages and disadvantages for choosing each color. Which color did they choose? Why? What would they feel like if they were wearing a brown, purple, or yellow coat? What would they do after they chose their coat?
4. Have the students dictate a language experience chart story that solves Sammy's problem.

Because the purpose of this activity is to reinforce students' color identification, oral language, and written language skills, it includes five exercises designed to provide additional practice with color identification. These exercises are as follows:

1. Have the students match the Sammy Circles drawn on colored paper with the appropriate rebus drawing on the chart story.
2. Randomly name colors depicted on the chart story. Have children point to the appropriate color on the chart.
3. Ask students to draw a picture of "Sammy Circle's Colors" or their choice of the final color for Sammy's coat and the activities he would engage in after he dressed in his coat. Encourage them to dictate individual stories after they finish their pictures.
4. Match colored felt circles on the flannel board.
5. Have children who are ready match the printed word with the corresponding color circle.

USING THE ACTIVITIES

The teacher's purpose may determine the way the language arts activities can be used. The text can be used effectively by several different groups of preservice and in-service teachers. At the undergraduate level, the activities may be used to supplement the main text in the language arts methods course. Because this activities book covers the major areas of the language arts, it can be used as a supplementary text for any of the language arts methods texts. As a supplementary text, this activities book illustrates, through the complete development of lesson plans, the research findings and methods presented in the main methods book used in the course. The activities are completely developed for use as stipulated by college students during practicum sessions, student-teaching experiences, or peer-teaching experiences. The materials may also be adapted for individual needs or may be used to stimulate the development of other language arts activities. The activities also represent a file of ideas and lessons that teachers may use throughout their teaching careers.

In-service teachers who have already covered the language arts research and methods will be able to use this activities book immediately as a source of ideas and lesson plans with their students. Again, the activities may be used directly from the book, or they may be changed to meet the individual needs of the classroom teacher. It is also hoped that the ideas presented will stimulate the development of other language arts activities in the classroom.

Language arts curriculum specialists will find many uses for this activity book. The text illustrates effective language arts methods for in-service teachers; in-service teachers may participate in the activities during in-service or workshop presentations and may use the activities in their own classrooms. The book can also serve as a guide to help in-service teachers prepare additional language arts instructional plans.

The activities in this text have been used to teach children and demonstrate effective instructional procedures to preservice and in-service teachers and curriculum specialists. I developed and used the activities during my experiences as a classroom teacher, a language arts curriculum specialist for public schools, a director for a university language arts/reading clinic, and a university professor. I hope the activities will stimulate both children and teachers in the areas of the language arts.

Let us now assume that you have evaluated the needs of your class and wish to use these activities to provide language arts instruction. How should you approach this task? First, look at the way the activities are grouped in this book. There are sections for oral language and cognitive development, listening, language experience, writing, mechanics of language, literature activities, media, and multicultural education. Read the activities you are considering. What is the stated purpose of each activity? Does that purpose correspond with the instructional needs of your students? Check the recommended materials. Do you have the materials? Should you prepare any materials, such as a chart or tape, before you begin the lesson? Look at the grade levels given for the activity. Do you need to make any adaptations for your students? Read the step-by-step procedures for the activity. Do you want to use the activity with a large group, a small group, or an individual child? Do you need to make any modifications for your grouping? Do you want to use a short-term activity that can be completed in one session or a long-term activity that may take several sessions to complete? Do you want to develop a whole unit of study? Do you want to develop a learning center dealing with that subject? Do you need to make any modifications because of these requirements? (Many short-term activities can be developed into learning center or unit activities. Likewise, many of the activities listed under learning centers can be used as short-term activities without developing a total unit or learning center.)

REFERENCES

Lipson, M. Y. (1990). Evaluating the reading context. *The Reading Teacher, 44,* 330–332.

MacCormick, S. (1992, October). Training session for accelerated schools. College Station, TX: Texas A&M University.

Norton, D. E. (1992). *The Impact of literature-based reading.* New York: Merrill/ Macmillan.

2

Oral Language and Cognitive Development Activities

The development of oral language skills is one of the most crucial and exciting parts of the language arts curriculum. Oral language instruction includes the development of creative thinking and interpretation through creative drama, puppetry, pantomime, and group discussions. A child's oral skills are essential for success in every part of life, both at school and at home.

Loban's studies (1976, 1986) point out the need for oral language instruction that helps each child organize ideas and illustrate complex generalizations. The teacher needs to use instructional activities that help children develop discussion skills, questioning techniques, and creative thinking abilities.

The activities in this chapter offer numerous stimuli for oral language development. The activities use sensory experiences, familiar objects, pictures, and literature to motivate oral discussion. Several activities expand language and organizational abilities by requiring students to identify multiple labels for pictures and categorize pictures or words into groups. Ysseldyke and Algozzine (1995) conclude that using concrete examples is particularly important when teaching children with special needs.

Activities that develop vocabulary skills through webbing promote language development. Research conducted by Johnson and Pearson (1984) and Toms-Bronowski (1983) shows how valuable webbing is for enhancing vocabulary development. The webbing activities in this chapter illustrate how the technique may be used to increase understanding of vocabulary found in nonfiction information books.

Many of the activities developed in this section relate to the development of critical thinking. Fitzpatrick (1994) found that teaching students critical thinking strategies improves reading comprehension. Some of the strategies identified by Fitzpatrick include asking higher-order questions, having students discuss books and stories they have read and ask each other questions about their readings, using story maps that assist students in understanding organization after a story is read, dramatizing incidents from stories, publishing classroom newspapers, publishing original stories written by students, and brainstorming words related to a specific word or phrase. All of these strategies are developed in either this chapter or subsequent chapters in this book.

Group discussion skills that help children organize ideas and solve problems can best be developed through brainstorming discussion groups and role-playing activities. Role playing also helps children learn and refine interviewing skills. Dramatic interactions provide purposes for children to use their oral language and develop crucial thought processes. Purves, Rogers, and Soter (1990) recommend that teachers enhance responses to literature by having students use their imaginations to role-play interesting and challenging situations from literature. Segedy and Roosevelt (1986) recommend that teachers adapt a courtroom trial format in working with certain types of literature. An oral debate that may be used in a courtroom trial format is developed in this section using Avi's *Nothing But the Truth: A Documentary Novel* (1991).

Choral reading and speaking stimulate oral language activity. Choral reading and speaking choirs were used by the ancient Greeks; minstrels and churchmen used choral speaking choirs during the Middle Ages and the Renaissance. This oral language technique is as useful and enjoyable today as it was long ago. Children enjoy choral activities that allow them to participate in groups and cooperatively develop an enjoyable rendition of a poem, story, or song. Choral exercises may help shy children to practice speaking and reading skills in a nonthreatening environment. Kay (1991) maintains that choral reading is an excellent approach for increasing children's interaction with literature both at school and at home.

Teachers may use the pantomime activities included in this section to heighten students' sensitivity to body actions and gestures. Using actions alone, the pantomimist dramatizes the ideas and emotions that would normally be conveyed by the spoken word. The section concludes with a series of activities that stimulate students to analyze and create television plots.

Activity 2-1:
SAMMY CIRCLE'S COLORS

TYPE	TERM
● CLASS	● STA
● GROUP	○ LTA
● IND	○ LC

Purpose:

1. To participate in a motivational activity resulting in oral discussion and a dictated story
2. To identify colors illustrated in a rebus chart story
3. To match colors on cardboard circles with colors on a rebus chart story

Materials:

Sammy Circle drawn in each of the basic colors; chart story, "Sammy Colors";

chart paper for dictated story; art supplies for individual pictures; literature that can be used to reinforce understanding of colors: Eric Carle's *My Very First Book of Colors* (1974) and Tana Hoban's *Of Colors and Things* (1989).

Grade level:

Kindergarten and first grade

Motivational activity:

Begin the discussion by introducing "Sammy Circle." Draw Sammy on a card or sheet but do not color in the circle.

Explain that Sammy Circle is unhappy because he wants to be colorful but cannot decide which color he wants to be. He wants the children to "read" the chart story

"Sammy Colors," which describes his problems. After they "read" the story along with their teacher, he wants them to draw a picture illustrating the solution to his problem and dictate a short story describing the picture. You may use the following chart story:

Procedures:

1. Lead an oral discussion about Sammy Circle and his problems with colors.

2. Introduce the story "Sammy 😞 Colors," which has been printed on large sheets of tagboard or newsprint. Encourage the children to follow along as you read. Allow them to "read" the rebus pictures. Read the story a second time, encouraging the children to "read" with you.

3. Discuss the color choices Sammy Circle has for his coat. Encourage the children to discuss advantages and disadvantages for choosing each color. Which color did they choose? Why? What would they feel like if they were wearing a brown, purple, or yellow coat? What would they do after they chose their coat?

4. Have the students dictate a language experience chart story that solves Sammy's problem.

Reinforcement:

1. Have the students match the Sammy Circles drawn on colored paper with the appropriate rebus drawings on the chart story.

2. Randomly name colors depicted on the chart story. Have children point to the appropriate color on the chart.

3. Ask students to draw a picture of "Sammy Colors" or their choice of the final color for Sammy's coat and the activities he would engage in after he dressed in his coat. Encourage them to dictate individual stories after they finish their pictures.

4. Match colored felt circles on the flannel board.

5. Have children who are ready match the printed word with the corresponding colored circle.

6. Read one of the books about colors and encourage students to identify the colors.

Activity 2–2:
DEVELOPING VOCABULARY SKILLS
THROUGH WEBBING—PART I

	TYPE		TERM
	● CLASS		● STA
	● GROUP		○ LTA
	○ IND		○ LC

Purpose:
1. To develop and expand vocabulary
2. To develop and expand cognitive abilities
3. To develop a vocabulary web motivated by a book
4. To relate language arts and social studies
5. To discuss the meanings of vocabulary words as these words relate to the Native American context of the book
6. To develop critical thinking

Materials: Marcia Sewall's *People of the Breaking Day* (1990) and additional books with a Native American content.

Grade level: Lower and middle elementary

Book summary: *People of the Breaking Day* presents the life of the Wampanoag nation of southwestern Massachusetts before the arrival of the English settlers. The book is divided into sections that discuss "Our Tribe" and "A Family." Numerous illustrations, a glossary, and a dictionary of terms add to the book's usefulness.

Procedures:
1. Webbing and discussing the important vocabulary from a book are appropriate for any grade level. The vocabulary and text vary with the level. When developing a webbing activity, place the title of the book in the center of the web. Extend the vocabulary words on spokes drawn from the center of the web. If the web is used as a prereading or prelistening activity, ask students to identify and discuss definitions, descriptions, synonyms, or even phrases that they think are related to each of the words. As the book is read, students may verify the correctness of these terms. If the web is a follow-up activity, students can identify and discuss related meanings after reading or listening to the text. It is easy to combine these two approaches by using the initial web as a prereading or listening activity to discover what the students know about the vocabulary. During reading, the students can add to or even change the terms on the web.

2. On the center of the web place the title of the book: *People of the Breaking Day*. On the spokes extending from the center, identify vocabulary words that you believe are necessary for developing understandings related to the Native American content of the book. For example, the important words for this book might include *tribe, Great Spirit, celebrate, warriors, survive,* and *Sachem*.

3. Lead a discussion in which the students provide their understandings of these terms as they relate to Native American people. Fill in as much information as possible on the web. Tell the students that they will have an opportunity to change and add to any of the meanings.

4. Read *People of the Breaking Day,* complete the web, and discuss all of the meanings. Encourage the students to discuss and change any of the meanings that were incorrect on the prereading web. The following web was developed with the assistance of third-grade students:

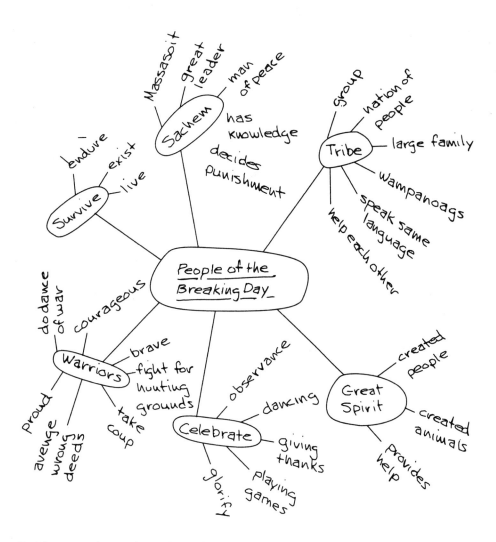

5. After completing the web, students may read additional books with Native American content and compare the meanings of the words, if found, in these additional books.

Activity 2–3:
DEVELOPING VOCABULARY SKILLS
THROUGH WEBBING—PART II

TYPE	TERM
● CLASS	● STA
● GROUP	○ LTA
○ IND	○ LC

Purpose:

1. To develop and expand vocabulary
2. To develop and expand cognitive abilities
3. To develop a vocabulary web motivated by a book
4. To discuss the meanings of vocabulary words as these words relate to science
5. To develop critical thinking

Materials:

Patricia Lauber's *Volcano: The Eruption and Healing of Mount St. Helens* (1986) and other books about volcanic eruptions such as Nick Clifford's *Incredible Earth* (1996).

Grade level:

Upper elementary and middle school

Book summary:

This book is an excellent photographic essay in which the photographs and text follow the progress of the eruption of Mount St. Helens and the changes that have taken place since. The contents include "The Volcano Wakes," "The Big Blast," "Survivors and Colonizers," "Links and More Links," and "Volcanoes and Life." An index increases the book's usefulness.

Procedures:

1. To web the vocabulary for this book, follow the directions presented in the previous webbing activity for lower and elementary grades.
2. The vocabulary chosen for this activity should relate to the science content associated with volcanoes. For example, in the center of the web, place either the term *volcanoes* or the title of the book: *Volcano: The Eruption and Healing of Mount St. Helens.* On the arms that extend from the web place vocabulary words that are important for developing understanding of the concepts related to volcanoes. For example, *earthquake, eruption, magma, geologists, avalanche, pressure,* and *lava* are all important terms. Before reading the book, students can discuss the meanings of the words and explore their understandings. These meanings can be placed in the web. After reading the book, encourage students to make changes, additions, and corrections in the web. If necessary, they can look at additional sources to fill in information about volcanoes. The following web was completed with the help of sixth-grade students:

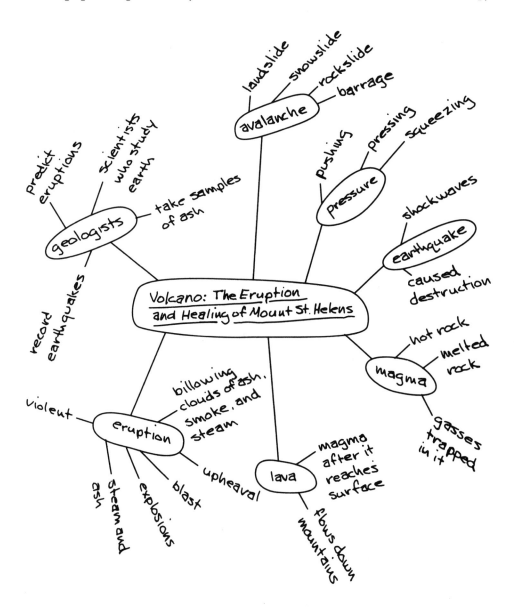

Activity 2–4:
PICTURES STIMULATE DISCUSSION

TYPE	TERM
● CLASS	● STA
● GROUP	○ LTA
● IND	○ LC

Purpose:

1. To participate in a discussion
2. To develop creative thinking skills
3. To develop oral descriptive skills

Materials:

File of pictures and sources of picture books illustrating a variety of subjects that suggest vivid descriptions and topics for creative stories. Sources for illustrated books that can accompany each of these activities include (a) bears: Downs Matthews's *Polar Bear Cubs* (1989) and John Schoenherr's *Bear* (1991); (b) flowers and trees: Lois Ehlert's *Red Leaf, Yellow Leaf* (1991) and Anita Lobel's *Alison's Zinnia* (1990); (c) deserted buildings: Jan Pienkowski's *Haunted House* (1979); (d) musical instruments: Neil Ardley's *Music* (1989); (e) nature: Denise Fleming's *In the Tall, Tall Grass* (1991), Ron Hirschi's *Loon Lake* (1991), and Lisa Westberg Peters's *The Sun, the Wind, and the Rain* (1988); (f) people: Dav Pilkey's *The Paper Boy* (1996); (g) recreational sports: Lillian Morrison's *At the Crack of the Bat* (1992).

Grade level:

Lower and middle elementary

Book summaries:

Each of these books was selected because of the quality of the pictures for motivating discussion, creative thinking, and oral descriptive skills. *Polar Bear Cubs* includes numerous photographs of adult and cub bears as they play, explore, and learn to hunt with their mother in the polar regions. *Bear* follows a young bear as he roams his Alaskan setting. *Red Leaf, Yellow Leaf* tells the story of a maple tree from the time it is planted until it becomes a sapling. *Alison's Zinnia* is an alphabet book that illustrates flowers from *A* (amaryllis) to *Z* (zinnia). *Haunted House* is a pop-up book that illustrates the interiors of an old house. *Music* includes both illustrations and descriptions of musical instruments from early times to the present. *In the Tall, Tall Grass* presents a toddler's view of what can be seen in the grass. *Loon Lake* is illustrated with photographs of northern settings. *The Sun, the Wind, and the Rain* presents, through illustrations, the histories of two mountains. One is a real mountain influenced by the weather and the other is a child's pile of sand that is also influenced by the weather. *The Paper Boy* includes illustrations in which various people perform jobs. *At the Crack of the Bat* presents illustrated poems depicting various aspects of playing baseball.

Procedures:

1. Teachers may repeat this activity using a variety of pictures. The pictures may be used to stimulate large-group, small-group, or individual discussion and oral stories. For example:

   a. A picture of a mother bear in a clearing with a baby cub at the edge of the woods could stimulate an oral story:

My father and I were out in the woods hunting all day. My dad wanted a bearskin to put on the floor of his den. We came upon a clearing and we saw a huge bear right in the middle of the meadow. My dad started to raise his gun when I saw something move. I yelled "Don't shoot."

Have the students look at the picture, tell why the child yelled "Don't shoot," and suggest endings for the story.

The photographs and illustrations in *Polar Bear Cubs* and *Bears* might motivate an oral story about going on a photographic safari through Alaska and the Arctic, living the life of a bear, or developing vivid descriptions of these two areas.

b. Flower pictures encourage children to describe the colors, shapes, sizes, textures, and emotions suggested by flowers. A child might pretend he or she is one of the flowers, starting as a seed warming in the soil, sprouting through the earth, then growing and stretching until he or she is a rose, daisy, thistle, or the like.

c. Pictures of deserted buildings suggest many stories. Who lived in the house? What did they do when they lived there? Why did they leave? Pretend you are going for a walk and come upon a deserted house. Do you go in? What happens if you do?

d. Using pictures of musical instruments, ask each student to select a musical instrument, pretend to be a musical instrument salesperson, and convince the class that this instrument is the best one to buy. Have older students research the musical instruments they choose and ask them to give oral reports to the class. Ask each student to pretend he or she is one of the instruments in the picture file and describe what it would be like to be that instrument, what it feels like to be part of an orchestra or band, and the music he or she likes to play. Have the student tell about his or her most interesting experience as an instrument. Have the student pantomime the instrument while others in the class guess its identity.

e. Divide the students into pairs and give each child a nature picture. Have one child describe the picture to a second child, who draws the picture from the other's description without being told the identity of the picture. Have the students compare the pictures and drawings. For another activity, have the students pretend the picture is a setting for a story or movie. Ask them to describe the setting, suggest a title for the story, and tell the story or movie. Ask them to describe the setting, suggest a title for the story, and tell the story that might take place there. A third activity could require children to compare the descriptions of grass, leaves, stones, twigs, bark, trees, and so forth that would be developed from a picture with the descriptions of the same items from real life.

f. Have each student choose a picture of a person, describe the person in the picture, choose a name for that person, and tell a story about what he or she thinks might be happening to the person. Divide the students into small groups and give each student in the group a picture of a person. Have the group create an oral story using all of the characters in the pictures or, as in *The Paper Boy,* have the students act out the delivery of the paper from the time it leaves the publisher until it is delivered to various people. Ask the group to create an oral story to accompany each of these segments. *The Paper Boy* could also be used to motivate a discussion about the various jobs and people who are required to complete the responsibilities that benefit our daily lives. Divide the students into small groups and have each group create an oral story in which the members follow a specific person and his or her job.

g. Divide the class into pairs, allow each pair of children to select a recreational sports picture, and have one student pretend to be a sportscaster while the other is being interviewed for a TV show. Allow each child to select a picture and describe how he or she feels when doing the activity. Divide the class into two teams and use the pictures to stimulate the activities for a game of charades. The first player draws a picture from the recreation file and acts out the sport for his or her own team. The team is allowed one minute to guess what the student is doing. Using the poems in *At the Crack of the Bat* as stimulation, ask the team members to select poems and to act out the contents of the poems.

Activity 2–5:
THE TELEPHONE

	TYPE	TERM
	o CLASS	● STA
	● GROUP	o LTA
	o IND	o LC

Purpose:
1. To make a play telephone and have a conversation with someone
2. To practice conversational skills

Materials:
Two paper cups, long strings, a nail, and two buttons for each child-made phone; toy phones; or walkie-talkies.

Grade level:
Lower elementary

Procedures:
1. Ask the children whether they enjoy talking on the telephone. Discuss the purpose of the telephone and have them list reasons for talking on the telephone. Tell the children that they are going to make their own phones and that they will have a chance to talk to their friends on their phones.

2. You may make one phone for the group to share, a phone for every two children, or have each child make his or her own phone so each will have one to take home. Directions for making the phones are as follows:

   Carefully poke a hole in the bottom of each paper cup. Put a long piece of string through the hole and tie a button onto the end of the string inside the cup. Attach the string in the same way to the second cup. Stretch the two cups apart so the string is held tight. Have one partner hold the cup to his or her ear while the other speaks into the cup. Use the child-made phones for conversations.

3. Provide toy telephones and allow children to practice talking on the phone. Some suggested roles include the following:

   Talking to a friend about things that happened in school
   Calling your mother or father to ask for a ride home because it is raining
   Calling a friend to ask if the friend may stay overnight
   Calling a friend to ask if the friend may accompany your family to the zoo, to a museum, or on some other outing
   Calling the police in an emergency
   Calling the fire department in an emergency
   Calling mother's or father's office or home to ask one of them to pick you up from school because you are sick

Activity 2-6:

STORYTELLING FROM LOST-AND-FOUND ADVERTISEMENTS

TYPE	TERM
● CLASS	● STA
● GROUP	○ LTA
○ IND	○ LC

Purpose:

1. To participate in an oral discussion
2. To tell a creative story motivated by humorous or unusual lost-and-found advertisements
3. To expand the imagination

Materials:

Collection of humorous or unusual lost-and-found advertisements; newspapers containing lost-and-found advertisements.

Grade level:

All grades; lost-and-found advertisements can be read to younger children

Procedures:

1. Search the lost-and-found advertisements and select thought-provoking ads.

2. Introduce lost-and-found ads to the children by discussing the kinds of things people might lose and how they might try to get the items back. Ask the students if any of them has ever lost anything, why the items were lost, and how they tried to find them.

3. Talk about the newspaper's lost-and-found section. Show it to the group and explain that people often lose items. Read some of the ads aloud and allow students to speculate about how the item was lost, what happened when it was lost, who found the item, whether there was a reward offered, how the owner would try to find the item, and what the students would do with a reward if they earned it.

4. Allow children to select a specific lost-and-found ad and develop a creative story related to that ad. Some examples include the following:

Lost: Two male Dobermans in vicinity of the University campus. Answer to the names of Ringo and Savage.	*Lost:* Northgate Cinema, man's wedding ring. Gold with 3 small diamonds. Sentimental value, substantial reward.
Found: Black cat, about 12 months old, wearing flea collar, front paw in cast.	*Lost:* Boy's 20″ Sears motocross bike, black and yellow. Reward from unhappy boy.
$500 REWARD For return or information on 20-ft camper last seen in Westgate Mall Shopping Center.	

5. Divide the class into smaller groups and allow students to tell their stories to their own groups.

6. Design a lost-and-found bulletin board. Put the lost-and-found ads and the illustrations of the stories on the bulletin board.

7. Lost-and-found ads may easily be used to motivate creative writing.

Activity 2–7:
CATEGORY DETECTIVES

TYPE	TERM
○ CLASS	● STA
● GROUP	○ LTA
● IND	○ LC

Purpose:
1. To expand oral vocabulary
2. To develop critical thinking
3. To identify the relationship among several objects or pictures, select the object that does not belong to the group, name other objects that belong to the category, and tell why objects do or do not belong to the category
4. To analyze categories used by authors in picture books and to develop picture books that are divided according to categories

Materials:
Objects or pictures of objects that can be categorized. Picture books in which the authors divide various things according to categories or develop their whole books according to specific categories: Janet and Allan Ahlberg's *The Baby's Catalogue* (1982); Rebecca Emberley's *City Sounds* (1989); Tana Hoban's *Round & Round & Round* (1983), *Circles, Triangles, and Squares* (1974), and *Shapes, Shapes, Shapes* (1986); and Anne Rockwell's *First Comes Spring* (1985).

Grade level:
Many grades; the objects for grouping can be selected according to the children's ability levels and needs

Book summaries:
The Baby's Catalogue categorizes objects that might be associated with a baby such as toys, carriages, lunches, pets, and moms and dads. *City Sounds* includes pictures of various objects and their accompanying sounds that might be found in a city. *Round & Round & Round* includes photographs of many types of objects that are round. *Circles, Triangles, and Squares* shows common shapes in everyday objects. *Shapes, Shapes, Shapes* depicts shapes such as circles, rectangles, and ovals. *First Comes Spring* categorizes working and playing activities according to the four seasons.

Procedures:
1. Provide a collection of concrete items, pictures of items, or lists of words that can be categorized into ever-narrowing categories. (Use concrete items with younger children so they can visualize the items being grouped and discussed.) Explain that you have grouped items into categories of things that are alike but that each group contains an object that does not belong to the group. The students will play "category detectives" by trying to figure out the final definition of the category. The following objects may be used:
   a. Final Category: Fruits That Grow on Trees
      (1) Category: Things to Eat

orange   apple   peach   ball   plum

What do the items have in common? Which item does not belong with the other items? Why? Describe each item. Look at the next group of items. Do you still think your category is correct?

(2) Category: Fruits

orange   apple   peach   plum   stringbean

Now what item does not belong? Why? What do the other items have in common? What would you call this group in order to exclude the item that does not belong? Look at the next group. Are you right?

(3) Category: Fruits That Grow on Trees

orange   blueberries   apple   peach   plum

Proceed with the same questioning and discussion strategy until students have identified the category.

(4) Ask the students to suggest other items that could be placed in the final category.

b. Final Category: Clothes Worn by Girls
(1) Category: Things to Wear
shoes, slacks, *camera,* coat, stockings
(2) Category: Things to Wear (excluding accessories)
ring, shoes, slacks, coat, stockings
(3) Category: Clothes Worn by Girls
shoes, slacks, coat, stockings, dress

c. Final Category: Wooden Furniture in the Bedroom
(1) Category: Furniture
chair, table, desk, *doll,* stool
(2) Category: Furniture Made from Wood
chair, table, desk, stool, *sofa*
(3) Category: Furniture Made from Wood and Found in the Bedroom
chair, table, desk, stool, bed

d. Final Category: Dangerous Jungle Animals
(1) Category: Animals
lion, snake, *boy,* tiger, elephant
(2) Category: Jungle Animals
lion, snake, tiger, elephant, *sheep*
(3) Category: Jungle Animals That Can Be Dangerous to People
lion, snake, tiger, elephant, crocodile

2. After students have categorized various concrete objects, tell them that authors and illustrators frequently develop books around objects that are of one category or objects that can be divided into several categories. Share any of the books on the materials list. Ask students to observe the illustrations and to decide what categories the author and illustrator are using in these books. Have the students identify the categories and explain why certain objects in the pictures are in each of those categories. You may divide the students into small groups and ask each group to observe and discuss one of the books. After students have observed and discussed the categories in the books, ask them to create their own illustrated books in which they develop meanings for any of the categories through the illustrations.

Activity 2–8:
CAMPBELL'S 59ERS

TYPE	TERM
● CLASS	○ STA
● GROUP	● LTA
○ IND	○ LC

Purpose:
1. To interact orally with a group and find workable answers to a problem
2. To develop creative thinking skills
3. To identify the responsibilities of each member of a discussion group
4. To develop respect for other students' opinions

Materials:
Suggested topics for discussion and problem solving; newspaper articles that suggest problems requiring solutions.

Grade level:
Middle and upper elementary, middle school

Procedures:
1. Explain to the students that groups often need a number of ideas or must solve problems in creative ways. One way to gather a lot of ideas before groups try to solve a problem is a "buzz session." During a buzz session, everyone quickly presents ideas and suggestions. All ideas are written down; none are criticized or judged as either appropriate or inappropriate. After several ideas have been chosen for investigation as workable solutions to the problem, each idea will be discussed in greater detail. The whole class may form a large buzz session, with the teacher acting as secretary and moderator, or the class may be divided into smaller groups that are allowed a limited time to generate ideas and suggestions before reporting back to the larger group. (The choice depends on the children's experience and ability.) In this latter type of buzz session, known as the "Phillips 66 Buzz Session," students are divided into groups of six and allowed to generate ideas rapidly for six minutes. The teacher may choose any combination of numbers and minutes. For example, buzz sessions carried on in Anthony Campbell's fifth-grade room might group five students and discuss rapidly for nine minutes; the class might name itself "Campbell's 59ers." If the teacher is not the secretary for the whole group, each group should appoint someone to write down the ideas.
2. Present a problem to the groups that will stimulate students' thinking. The problem should be important to the group so that the children can empathize with it. The problem should also be phrased in such a way that the solution is not limited by the wording of the problem. Students may suggest problems they feel strongly about, or the teacher can use some of the following problems:

   How can we eliminate the long time spent in the school cafeteria?
   How can we earn money to go on a class trip at the end of the year?
   How can we make our school grounds more attractive?
   How can we make the playground more usable and fun at recess?
   How can we make the streets safer when we walk or ride our bikes to school?
   How can we improve our school newspaper?
   How can we show our parents what we have learned when they come to open house?
   How can we get the minicourses we want, and how can we get the teachers for them?

3. After children's ideas have been stimulated in the buzz session, tell the students that they will have an opportunity to try to really solve the problem through a longer problem-solving discussion session. Tell them that every person in the discussion group has a responsibility to solve the problem. Ask the students to suggest responsibilities they believe would be necessary for solving the problem. List these responsibilities; review the following example:

IN A PROBLEM-SOLVING DISCUSSION GROUP, EVERY MEMBER HAS RESPONSIBILITIES

1. Identify the problem.
2. Collect the facts you need to know so that you can contribute to the discussion.
3. Understand the causes of the problem and any characteristics the solution must have.
4. Participate in the discussion.
5. Be a good listener to other people's ideas.
6. Keep your mind open for other people's viewpoints.
7. Show respect for all ideas.
8. Keep in mind that your main purpose is to find the best solution to the problem, not to sell your idea.

---

4. Give the students an opportunity to gather facts on the problem and then divide the class into smaller discussion groups. Choose a chairperson or discussion leader for each group. Prepare the discussion leaders for their responsibilities:
   a. Study the problem.
   b. Prepare a series of questions that stimulate thinking: what, why, who, how?
   c. Open the discussion by explaining the purpose of the group.
   d. Guide the thinking of the group by asking questions and summarizing points.
   e. Ask for examples and support for ideas and suggestions.
   f. Get everyone involved in the discussion.
   g. Summarize ideas.
   Allow the groups to meet and provide guidance when necessary.

5. Provide an opportunity for all discussion groups to share their solutions with the whole class. Discuss the recommendations and try to reach a joint agreement.

6. The newspaper is another source of topics for problem-solving discussion groups. Find examples of stories related to local, state, national, or world problems and have discussion groups tackle the problems. Advice columns such as those by Ann Landers also provide topics for problem-solving discussions.

Activity 2–9:

SOLVING PROBLEMS THROUGH ROLE-PLAYING

TYPE	TERM
● CLASS	● STA
● GROUP	○ LTA
○ IND	○ LC

Purpose:
1. To solve real problems through role-playing
2. To develop oral communication skills through a spontaneous activity
3. To develop tolerance for others' viewpoints and feelings
4. To role-play situations motivated by plots and conflicts in literature

Materials:
Conflict situations that are important to the group. Books in which there are conflicting situations such as Kevin Henkes's *Lilly's Purple Plastic Purse* (1996), Amy Hest's *The Purple Coat* (1986), and Peggy Rathmann's *Ruby the Copycat* (1991) for lower elementary; Beverly Cleary's *Ramona and Her Father* (1977) and Ellen Howard's *Edith Herself* (1987) for middle elementary; and Marion Dane Bauer's *On My Honor* (1986), Paula Fox's *One-Eyed Cat* (1984), and Jerry Spinelli's *Wringer* (1997) for upper elementary and middle school.

Grade level:
All grades; determining factor is subject matter of the role-playing problem

Book summaries:
Lilly's Purple Plastic Purse is a humorous story in which Lilly experiences traumas associated with school but then learns to overcome her problems. *The Purple Coat* presents conflict when the daughter wants a purple coat, but her mother thinks that navy blue would be more practical and appropriate. *Ruby the Copycat* is a personality development story in which a child discovers that she does not need to copy a classmate because she has her own creative resources. *Ramona and Her Father* provides numerous situations as Ramona tries to help her father after he has lost his job. *Edith Herself,* which is set in an earlier time period, develops sensitivity to feelings as a girl with epilepsy faces misunderstandings. *On My Honor* develops numerous choices and conflicts when a boy disobeys his father and as a consequence his best friend drowns. *One-Eyed Cat* presents a boy's conflicts of guilt and inability to confess to his father when the boy shoots a gun and wounds a cat. *Wringer* discusses the conflicts that arise when a boy does not want to take part in a town activity.

Procedures:
General procedures for use with all levels of role-playing are presented first. These general procedures are followed by some specific role-playing conflicts for different grade levels.

1. Present a situation involving conflict that is important to the students. You may describe the conflict in story format and end the story when the conflict is clearly stated. At that point, ask the group members what they would do in the situation described.
2. Encourage a short discussion of the problem. Ask for volunteers to role-play the parts. The group may role-play the situation several times with different volunteers. Prepare the listeners for the activity so they can contribute to the discussion after the role-playing or take the part of actors in the next activity.
3. Have the group act out the role spontaneously without any staging or other props. The emphasis is on resolving the problem, not on acting.
4. The group members evaluate their role-playing experience. The teacher asks questions to clarify the ideas and solutions. Was the problem solved? Would the solution cause any other problems? Are there any other ways to solve the problem?

Examples:

Lower Elementary

a. New crayons have been taken from a child's desk—Jennifer is a first-grade child who is very excited because she has a brand-new box of crayons. The crayons in her first box were all broken, and her mom has bought her the biggest box in the store. The box even has a crayon sharpener! Jennifer likes the gold and silver colors and shows the class the beautiful pictures she can make. After recess, Jennifer opens her desk to take out her new box of crayons, and they are gone. Jennifer looks around the room and sees that Jackie is coloring with crayons that look just like Jennifer's. When Jennifer asks Jackie about the crayons, Jackie says they belong to her. Jennifer does not believe Jackie and is sure the crayons are the new ones she had brought that morning. How should they solve this problem? What should Jennifer do? What should Jackie do? What should the teacher do?

b. Sharing on the playground (this can be developed into many role-playing situations since there are numerous items on a playground that cause conflict)—There are only three swings, and the same three children always run to the swings and stay on them all recess, not allowing anyone else to swing; there is only one jump rope, and several students refuse to share it; one child always pushes ahead in the line and takes several turns on the slide before the rest of the waiting children get their turns.

Middle to Upper Elementary

a. Sharing responsibility in group work—A class has been divided into groups to do reports on Native Americans, countries, animals, weather, and so forth, depending on the subject in that grade. Jim, Sandy, Christie, and Greg are doing a report together. They must present their findings to the class on Friday. They have planned to show slides that one of the children's parents took while on vacation. They will talk about the slides, demonstrate a Mexican folk dance, show a map of the country and talk about its physical characteristics, and show a piñata and other hand-crafted items from that country. Sandy, Christie, and Greg have done all of the work, but Jim wants to take most of the credit by showing and talking about the slides. How should they solve this problem? What should they say to Jim? What should they have him do? Should they talk to the teacher? If they do, what should the teacher say and do?

b. Cliques, ostracizing a friend—Several girls have a slumber party but decide not to invite Vickie's best friend because Susie does not like her. Both Vickie and her best friend feel hurt and angry. How would you solve this problem?

c. Have students suggest role-playing situations that are meaningful to them.

5. Continue the role-playing activity by using books to motivate situations for role-playing. Read any of the books on the materials list and allow students to choose situations that would be appropriate for role-playing. For example, after reading *Lilly's Purple Plastic Purse,* students can role-play the discussions among Lilly, her parents, and the teacher. After reading *The Purple Coat,* they could role-play the discussion between Gabby and her mother as each tries to convince the other of the worthiness of purple or navy blue as coat colors. They can also role-play the possible discussions after grandfather finds a way for Gabby to have the purple coat. After reading *Ruby the Copycat,* students can role-play possible conversations between Ruby and the other students in her class or her teacher. Numerous situations can be role-played in *Ramona and Her Father* as the students consider ways that they might have Ramona help her father. Role-playing the characters in *Edith Herself* helps students understand the need to be sensitive toward others' needs. *On My Honor, One-Eyed Cat,* and *Wringer* lend themselves to extensions as students role-play possible conversations that might have developed among the characters.

Activity 2–10:
INTERVIEWING

	TYPE		TERM
● CLASS		○ STA
● GROUP		● LTA
○ IND		○ LC

Purpose:

1. To identify the purpose and audience for an oral interview
2. To develop and practice interviewing skills through role-playing
3. To obtain information from another person using interviewing techniques
4. To use literary characters and plots as motivation for interviewing

Materials:

Lists of role-playing suggestions for interviewing; newspaper help-wanted ads that can be used to motivate an interviewing session. References containing directions for interviewing may be included for older children. Books that can motivate interviewing: modern fiction such as Lois Lowry's *Anastasia's Chosen Career* (1987); nonfiction informational books such as William Jaspersohn's *Magazine: Behind the Scenes at* Sports Illustrated (1983); and biographies that could motivate role-playing interviews such as Russell Freedman's *Franklin Delano Roosevelt* (1990), *The Wright Brothers: How They Invented the Airplane* (1991), and *Out of Darkness: The Story of Louis Braille* (1997).

Grade level:

This activity can be adapted to almost all levels. Lower elementary students can interview teachers, parents, brothers, and sisters. Interviewing can become more sophisticated in the upper grades, and students can interview various professional people as well as practice interviewing skills that will benefit them throughout their lives.

Book summaries:

Anastasia's Chosen Career is a humorous look at various challenges as a girl tries to investigate and write about a chosen career. *Magazine: Behind the Scenes at* Sports Illustrated provides an in-depth look at the requirements for publishing a magazine. There is considerable emphasis on the importance of interviewing. *Franklin Delano Roosevelt* traces Roosevelt's life, with special emphasis on his years as president. *The Wright Brothers: How They Invented the Airplane* provides significant background information on the history of early flight. *Out of Darkness: The Story of Louis Braille* includes Braille's struggle to communicate through written words. These biographies provide numerous opportunities for role-playing interviews.

Procedures:

1. Show the words *conversation* and *interview* to the students. Suggest that both words describe a means of oral communication; however, the purposes and methods of these two types of communication are quite different. Ask students if they know the difference between having a conversation with someone and having an interview. Lead the students into the conclusion that a *conversation* is an informal talk or exchange of ideas in which the topics may include anything that interests the people talking. In contrast, an *interview* has a predetermined goal; the interviewer asks for specific information and avoids many topics he or she may consider unimportant.

2. Develop a list of purposes or needs for interviewing. For example:

PEOPLE INTERVIEW

1. Doctors interview patients to find out why the patients are sick.
2. Managers interview job applicants to decide whom they will hire.
3. Reporters interview people to gather information for a newspaper story.
4. Authors interview people to acquire information for a book or story.
5. Teachers interview students about problems in school.
6. Teachers interview parents about students' problems or work at home.
7. Parents interview teachers about their children's work at school.
8. Lawyers interview clients to learn how to help the clients.
9. College admissions officers interview high school students to decide if they should be admitted or receive a scholarship.
10. Police interview suspected criminals to learn about their actions.
11. Detectives interview people to learn facts for an investigation.
12. Television news reporters interview people for the TV news.
13. Talk-show hosts interview famous people to learn about their lives.
14. High school students interview different professionals to learn about careers.
15. Company managers interview employees to learn about problems or to decide whether the employee should be promoted.

---

3. Discuss the different purposes for interviewing and the definite goals of the interviews as suggested by the purpose. Ask students if they believe interviewing skills are important to both the interviewer and the interviewee. Have them explain why.

4. Develop a list of interviewing do's and don'ts. Older students may refer to management references to gain some tips suggested by people who frequently interview personnel.

INTERVIEWING

Do

1. Prepare for the interview and know what you want to ask or anticipate what you will be asked
2. Encourage the interviewee to talk
3. Have a friendly facial expression
4. Be a careful listener
5. Keep the interview on the subject
6. Ask open questions that allow the interviewee to respond with sufficient information
7. Be polite
8. Keep the interview within the present time limits
9. Dress attractively

Don't

1. Ramble off the topic
2. Criticize the interviewer or interviewee
3. Argue with the interviewer or interviewee
4. Show nervousness or discourtesy by tapping the table or chewing gum
5. Ask closed questions that have a single yes or no answer
6. Dress sloppily

---

5. Divide the students into small groups so they can role-play different interviewing circumstances. Have the groups suggest questions they would like to have answered or topics covered for some of the purposes identified for interviewing. For example, a newspaper reporter interviewing the winner of a gold medal at the Olympics might ask the following:

> Why did you decide to enter the Olympics?
> What kind of training did you do to become a winner?
> How did you feel when you knew you had won?
> What other athletic events do you participate in?
> Do you eat anything special like they show on TV? If you do, what do you eat?
> What advice could you give to other young people who also want to be winners in sports?
> What do you want to do when you get back home?

Have the students in the small groups role-play several different interviews. Have other students in the group observe the effectiveness of the interview and ask them to suggest changes. Allow all students in each small group to play the part of both the interviewer and the interviewee. Then have them discuss their experiences in both capacities. Did they feel differently when they were being interviewed than when they were the one doing the interviewing? If so, why was there a difference?

6. Find help-wanted ads or stories from the newspaper and have students pretend they want a job or want to learn more about a subject. Divide the class into small groups and have them role-play both the interviewer and the interviewee. For some subjects, both interviewer and interviewee will need to do some reference work to prepare for the interview. For example:

HELP WANTED	
Help Wanted: Teenager to babysit with 6-year-old after school, 5 days a week. Must be reliable, apply in person.	**We Are Looking for Engineers** Major oil company in Arabia seeks petro chemical engineers. Excellent fringe benefits, high pay for high-risk job. Send résumé to Desert Oil representative, Oil Tower, Houston, Texas.
Help Wanted: Fast food restaurant needs summer help. We will train you for the position.	
Join Our Team We are hiring men and women sales representatives. We offer you a demonstration car, insurance plan, paid vacation, and opportunity for advancement. Call Friendly Car Company for top-paying job in car sales.	

STORIES IN THE NEWS

**Fireman Wins Medal
for Saving Child**

Five-year-old Danny Delong owes his life to fireman Douglas Collins, who risked his own life to pull Danny from the seventh floor of Park Tower Apartments.

**Popular TV Stars to Appear
at Auditorium**

A special children's show involving the *Electric Company* cast will be presented Saturday afternoon at 2:00. Two lucky children will be chosen to have lunch with the stars before the show.

**Camping Family Found after
Four Nights on the Mountain**

An early blizzard on Rabbit Ears Pass stranded a family on the mountainside. Mr. and Mrs. Frankline, 10-year-old Amy, and 7-year-old Todd faced four nights in freezing cold after an early storm separated them from their camper.

---

7. Ask students to watch a TV talk show, to identify the interviewing techniques they see, and to plan a TV talk show of their own. Ask them to choose the guests they wish to interview and the kinds of information they would like to know. Have them do research work to find out about the guests. This activity can focus on themes and can be related to subjects studied in content areas. For example:

>   Phil Phox Presents the Greatest Scientists of Our Time
>   Mike Monroe Interviews the First Astronauts on the Moon
>   Walter Wallace Talks to Lewis and Clark
>   Diana Dufflebag Brings You Cinderella, Snow White, Huck Finn, and Jack and the Beanstalk

8. After students have role-played several situations, allow them to try their interviewing skills in real situations. A school newspaper, a study of occupations, a study of the school personnel, and a story of the neighborhood could all stimulate the need for an oral interview followed by a report back to the class. After the general subject for the interviewing has been selected, have the students list the people they would like to interview and the questions they would like to ask each person. One interview topic might be People Who Run Our School. Students might interview the principal, teachers, secretaries, coaches, librarians, janitors, cooks, the nurse, or bus drivers. Another topic might be Foods Liked and Disliked in the Cafeteria and Why, for which the students could interview other students, teachers, cooks, and anyone who eats in the cafeteria. The interviewers can compile charts showing what they have learned.

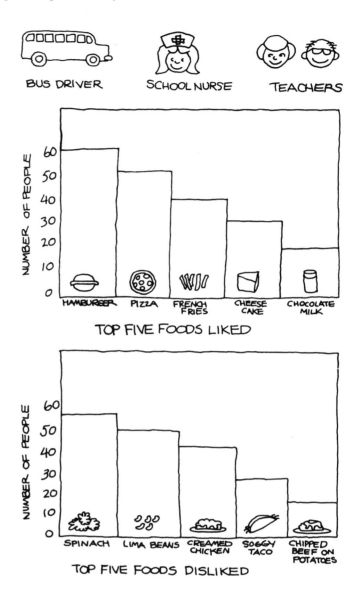

BUS DRIVER   SCHOOL NURSE   TEACHERS

TOP FIVE FOODS LIKED

TOP FIVE FOODS DISLIKED

9. The literature selections may be used to motivate interviewing or role-playing interviewing that is stimulated by information provided in the text. For example, after reading *Anastasia's Chosen Career,* students could choose their own career and interview people to decide if that career is one that they would really like. After reading *Magazine: Behind the Scenes at* Sports Illustrated, students can discuss the importance of interviewing when developing magazine stories. Students can discuss such quotes as the following: "Getting the interesting quotes and offbeat details for a story is part of every *Sports Illustrated* writer's job, and it often requires a great deal of traveling and interviewing. For a long piece on the Boston Red Sox, for example, staff writer Steve Wulf and reporter Bob Sullivan traveled off and on for two weeks with the team, interviewing everyone from manager Ralph Houk to former catcher Carlton Fisk to the grounds-crewmen who operate the left-field scoreboard. 'In any piece I write,' says Steve Wulf, 'I'm after perspective' '' (p. 22). After discussing the complicated process for getting interviews and writing the story, students can choose their own stories, conduct interviews, and write the magazine or newspaper entry. After reading *Franklin Delano Roosevelt, Out of Darkness: The Story of Louis Braille,* or *The Wright Brothers: How They Invented the Airplane,* students can choose interesting instances in the people's lives and role-play interviews that might have taken place.

Activity 2–11:
IN THE ROUND

TYPE	TERM
● CLASS	● STA
● GROUP	○ LTA
○ IND	○ LC

Purpose:

1. To develop appreciation of choral speaking
2. To develop cooperation in the round-choral speaking choir

Materials:

This introductory activity uses familiar verses known to the children; no reading materials are required.

Grade level:

All grades

Procedures:

1. Have the students say or read a short piece or verse. Ask the class to listen carefully and help you divide the voices into light, medium, and heavy voices. Group the students according to voice quality.

2. Have the students try their voice choir using several verses they know. For example, try some familiar rounds in which the light voices begin, then the middle voices are added, and then the heavy voices join in. The following verses in the round are enjoyable:

   a. Light Voices: Row, row, row your boat

   Light Voices: Gently down the stream
   Medium Voices: Row, row, row your boat

   Light Voices: Merrily, merrily, merrily, merrily
   Medium Voices: Gently down the stream
   Heavy Voices: Row, row, row your boat

   Light Voices: Life is but a dream
   Medium Voices: Merrily, merrily, merrily, merrily
   Heavy Voices: Gently down the stream

   (continue for three rounds)

   b. "Three Blind Mice"
   c. "Frère Jacques"

3. Try the same choral speaking groups but use familiar nursery rhymes.

Activity 2–12:
PAT-SI-OO-REE-OO-REE-AY

	TYPE		TERM
	● CLASS		● STA
	● GROUP		○ LTA
	○ IND		○ LC

Purpose:
1. To refine speaking, reading, interpreting, and listening skills
2. To develop cooperation through a group activity
3. To increase enjoyment in reading through a cumulative choral speaking verse
4. To interpret a piece of folk music written in the 1840s

Materials: Copies of the folk song "Pat-si-oo-ree-oo-ree-ay."

Grade level: Middle to upper elementary

Procedures:
1. Background information to share with students: In the 1840s, the first railroads were built in the United States. Much of the work was done by immigrants from Ireland who came to the United States because of the potato famine in their own country. The Irish workers used picks, shovels, and wheelbarrows to build the rail beds for the railroads. This folksong tells the tale of the hardworking railroad laborer.

2. Discuss the background of the song with the students. Talk about the Irish immigration to the United States and the reasons many of the immigrants worked on the railroad. Ask the students if they think it would be an easy job to work on the railroad. Have them read the words of the folk song and decide what kind of a job working on a railroad would actually be. Ask the students to find sentences and phrases that support their ideas about the way the workers felt about their jobs.

3. Divide the class into seven groups. Read the folk song as a cumulative choral reading. In this type of choral group, the first stanza is read by group 1, the second is read by groups 1 and 2, and so forth, until the reading is completed. (Since this folk song is developed around a time sequence, voices are added to increase the volume from the years 1841–1847.) This folk song may be divided in the following way:

Group 1:	In eighteen hundred and forty-one I put my corduroy breeches on. I put my corduroy breeches on To work upon the railroad.
Groups 1 and 2:	In eighteen hundred and forty-two I left the old world for the new. I left the old world for the new To work upon the railroad.
Groups 1, 2, and 3:	In eighteen hundred and forty-three 'Twas then I met sweet Biddy Magee. An elegant wife she's been to me While working on the railroad.
Groups 1, 2, 3, and 4:	In eighteen hundred and forty-four I landed on Columbia's shore. I landed on Columbia's shore To work upon the railroad.

Groups 1, 2, 3, 4, and 5:	In eighteen hundred and forty-five I found myself more dead than alive. I found myself more dead than alive From working on the railroad.
Groups 1, 2, 3, 4, 5, and 6:	In eighteen hundred and forty-six I changed my trade to carrying bricks. I changed my trade to carrying bricks From working on the railroad.
Groups 1, 2, 3, 4, 5, 6, and 7:	In eighteen hundred and forty-seven Sweet Biddy Magee she went to heaven. If she left me one she left me eleven To work upon the railroad.
Groups 1, 2, 3, 4, 5, 6, and 7:	Pat-si-oo-ree-oo-ree-ay Pat-si-oo-ree-oo-ree-ay Pat-si-oo-ree-oo-ree-ay To work upon the railroad.

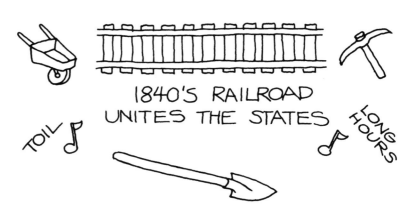

Activity 2–13:
LOW BRIDGE, EVERYBODY DOWN

	TYPE	TERM
	● CLASS	● STA
	● GROUP	○ LTA
	○ IND	○ LC

Purpose:

1. To refine speaking, reading, interpreting, and listening skills
2. To promote cooperation through a group activity
3. To increase enjoyment in reading, speaking, and listening through a refrain choral arrangement
4. To interpret a piece of folk music written to depict the towpath and the workers who pulled boats along the Erie Canal

Materials:

Copies of the folk song "Low Bridge, Everybody Down."

Grade level:

All grades

Procedures:

1. Background information to share with students: In 1817 New York State started to build a canal to connect Albany with Buffalo, on the Great Lakes. The 340-mile canal was opened in 1825. By the year 1845, about four thousand boats were carrying supplies on the canal. These boats were pulled along the canal by mules or horses, which traveled approximately three miles an hour. The mule driver had to watch out for low bridges over the canal and then warn the boat passengers to duck.

2. Discuss the need for a canal, due to western expansion. On a map, show the students the location of the Erie Canal. Ask the students to imagine what it would be like to drive boat-pulling mules along a towpath next to a canal. Have the students imagine they are mule drivers and pantomime their actions. Then have them pretend they are riding the boats on the canal and need to watch out for low bridges. Finally, have the students read or listen to the words of the folk song and describe what it would be like to be a mule driver.

3. Discuss how a refrain choral reading is accomplished. The teacher or student may be the leader, and the rest of the students join in for the chorus or refrain. For example:

Leader: I've got a mule and her name is Sal,
Fifteen miles on the Erie Canal.
She's a good old worker and a good old pal.
Fifteen miles on the Erie Canal.
We've hauled some barges in our day
Filled with lumber, coal, and hay,
And we know every inch of the way
From Albany to Buffalo.

All: Low bridge! Everybody down!
Low bridge! We're coming to a town.
You'll always know your neighbor;
You'll always know your pal
If you've ever navigated on the Erie Canal.

Leader: We'd better get on our way, old pal!
Fifteen miles on the Erie Canal.

You can bet your life I'd never part with Sal,
Fifteen miles on the Erie Canal.
Get us there, Sal, here comes a lock;
We'll make Rome before six o'clock.
One more trip and back we'll go,
Right back home to Buffalo.

All: Low bridge! Everybody down!
Low bridge! We're coming to a town.
You'll always know your neighbor;
You'll always know your pal
If you've ever navigated on the Erie Canal.

Activity 2–14:

YANKEE DOODLE

TYPE	TERM
● CLASS	● STA
● GROUP	○ LTA
○ IND	○ LC

Purpose:

1. To refine speaking, reading, interpreting, and listening skills
2. To promote cooperation through a group activity
3. To increase enjoyment in reading, speaking, and listening through an antiphonal choral arrangement
4. To interpret a piece of folk music written in the 1700s that describes the Revolutionary War

Materials:

Copies of the folk song "Yankee Doodle."

Grade level:

All grades

Procedures:

1. Background information to share with students: The British brought the song "Yankee Doodle" to America. During the Revolutionary War, however, the colonial soldiers adopted the song as one of the symbols for the American struggle for independence.

2. Discuss the significance of the folk song "Yankee Doodle." Allow children to share their knowledge of the Revolutionary War period. Clarify any misconceptions. Have the students read the words to the song. Discuss items such as *hasty pudding, Yankee Doodle Dandy, Captain Washington, slapping stallion, swamping gun, horn of powder, a nation louder, little keg,* and *stabbing iron.*

3. Divide the students into two groups. Boy and girl groupings work well for this song, since the verses may pertain more to a boy's version of the war, while the chorus sounds as if it is a response to a masculine experience. Other groupings, such as high voices and low voices, however, are equally effective. This folk song may be divided in the following manner:

Boys, or Group 1:	Father and I went down to camp,
	Along with Captain Gooding;
	And there we saw the men and boys
	As thick as hasty pudding.
Girls, or Group 2: (chorus)	Yankee Doodle keep it up,
	Yankee Doodle Dandy,
	Mind the music and the step,
	And with the girls be handy.
Boys, or Group 1:	And there we saw a thousand men,
	As rich as Squire David;
	And what they wasted every day,
	I wish it could be saved.
Girls, or Group 2:	*Repeat chorus*
Boys, or Group 1:	And there was Captain Washington
	Upon a slapping stallion,
	A giving orders to his men;
	I guess there was a million.
Girls, or Group 2:	*Repeat chorus*

Boys, or Group 1:	And then the feathers on his hat,
	They looked so very fine, ah!
	I wanted peskily to get
	To give to my Jermima.
Girls, or Group 2:	*Repeat chorus*
Boys, or Group 1:	And there I see a swamping gun,
	Large as a bag of maple,
	Upon a mighty little cart;
	A load for father's cattle.
Girls, or Group 2:	*Repeat chorus*
Boys, or Group 1:	And evertime they fired it off,
	It took a horn of powder;
	It made a noise like father's gun,
	Only a nation louder.
Girls, or Group 2:	*Repeat chorus*
Boys, or Group 1:	And there I saw a little keg.
	Its head all made of leather,
	They knocked upon it with little sticks,
	To call the folks together.
Girls, or Group 2:	*Repeat chorus*
Boys, or Group 1:	The troopers too, would gallop up
	And fire right in our faces;
	It scared me almost half to death
	To see them run such races.
Girls, or Group 2:	*Repeat chorus*
Boys, or Group 1:	It scared me so I hoofed it off,
	Nor stopped, as I remember,
	Nor turned about till I got home,
	Locked up in Mother's Chamber.
Girls, or Group 2:	*Repeat chorus*

Activity 2–15:
THE OLD CHISHOLM TRAIL

TYPE	TERM
● CLASS	● STA
● GROUP	○ LTA
○ IND	○ LC

Purpose:

1. To refine speaking, reading, interpreting, and listening skills
2. To develop cooperation through a group activity
3. To increase enjoyment in reading through the presentation of a line-a-child choral speaking arrangement
4. To interpret a piece of folk music written about the great age of the cowpuncher, during the 1870s to the 1890s

Materials:

Copies of the folk song "The Old Chisholm Trail"

Grade level:

Middle to upper elementary

Procedures:

1. Background information to share with students: The Old Chisholm Trail of the late 1800s was used to move cattle from San Antonio, Texas, to the railroad at Dodge City, Kansas, where some cattle were shipped to the eastern part of the United States. Other cattle continued on the trail to Cheyenne, Wyoming, or to Montana and the Dakotas. The rich pastures were used to fatten the cattle before they were sold. The trip up the Chisholm Trail often included several thousand cattle in one herd and required four or five months of horseback riding to manage the herd. The cowboy's life was hard; he encountered dust from the cattle, storms, long hours in the saddle, sleeping on the ground, and monotonous food. To overcome their boredom and to tell about their hardships, the cowboys sang songs such as "The Old Chisholm Trail."

2. Discuss the background for the folk song. Have students find the location of the Chisholm Trail on a U.S. map. Ask them to pretend they are cowboys in the Old West. Do they think this would be an easy life? What would they like about it? What would be hard? After they have presented their ideas, have them read the words to "The Old Chisholm Trail." Ask them to look for support for their views in the words of the folk song.

3. Using a line-a-child method, ask each child to read a different line, and have all of the children read the chorus. For example:

Child 1:	Come along boys and listen to my tale,
	And I'll tell you of my troubles on the Old Chisholm Trail.
All:	Come a ti yi yippy yippy yi yippi yea,
	Come a ti yi yippy yippy yea.
Child 2:	With a ten-dollar horse and a forty-dollar saddle
	I'm going down to Texas for to punch them cattle.
All:	*Repeat chorus*
Child 3:	I woke up one morning on the Old Chisholm Trail,
	A rope in my hand and a cow by the tail.
All:	*Repeat chorus*
Child 4:	I started up the trail October twenty-third
	I started up the trail with the 2-U Herd
All:	*Repeat chorus*

Child 5:	I'm in my saddle before daylight And before I sleep the moon shines bright.
All:	*Repeat chorus*
Child 6:	It's cloudy in the West, a-looking like rain, And my old slicker's in the wagon again.
All:	*Repeat chorus*
Child 7:	The wind began to blow, the rain began to fall, It looked like we were going to lose them all.
All:	*Repeat chorus*
Child 8:	I jumped in the saddle and grabbed hold the horn, Best cowpuncher ever was born.
All:	*Repeat chorus*
Child 9:	Oh, it's bacon and beans most every day I'd as soon be eating prairie hay.
All:	*Repeat chorus*
Child 10:	There's a stray in the herd and the boss said kill it. So I shot him with the handle of a skillet.
All:	*Repeat chorus*
Child 11:	My feet in the stirrup and my hand on the horn, I'm the best cowboy ever was born.
All:	*Repeat chorus*
Child 12:	I went to the boss to draw my roll, He figured me out nine dollars in the hole.
All:	*Repeat chorus*
Child 13:	A-roping and a-tying and a-branding all day, I'm working mighty hard for mighty little pay.
All:	*Repeat chorus*
Child 14:	So I went to the boss and we had a little chat, And I hit him in the face with my big slouch hat.
All:	*Repeat chorus*
Child 15:	So the boss says to me, "Why, I'll fire you, Not only you, but the whole crew."
All:	*Repeat chorus*
Child 16:	So I rounded up the cowboys and we had a little meeting We all took a vote and the boss took a beating.
All:	*Repeat chorus*
Child 17:	So we organized a union and it's going mighty strong. The boss minds his business and we all get along.
All:	*Repeat chorus*
Child 18:	With my knees in the saddle and my seat in the sky, I'll quit punching cows in the sweet by and by.
All:	*Repeat chorus*

Activity 2–16:
WHAT IT IS LIKE TO BE A RAG DOLL

TYPE	TERM
● CLASS	● STA
● GROUP	○ LTA
○ IND	○ LC

Purpose:
1. To develop body control and communication skills
2. To relax the body and develop the ability to respond creatively to the environment

Materials:
Descriptions of warm-up activities; teacher and student suggestions for warm-ups that allow students to loosen up their muscles. No props are necessary, but space should be available so students can move freely.

Grade level:
All grades; vary complexity of the warm-up with the children's age level

Procedures:

1. Discuss with students how an actor or any person shows actions, emotions, and feelings with the body. Let them try to talk with partners without moving their hands or other parts of their bodies. Discuss how difficult this activity is. Introduce the term *pantomime* and tell the group members that they will be trying some of the activities used by pantomimists such as Marcel Marceau. Tell the group that actors need warm-up periods just like athletes; body control is just as important to an actor as it is to a football or tennis player.

2. Have the students stand in a space that is free of obstacles so they can move freely; at this point, they are developing independent movement.

3. Suggest that the students do loosening-up exercises. For example:
   a. Stand with your feet apart and try to reach as high as you can; the sun is in the sky, and you are trying to catch that beautiful yellow ball. Now look down at the ground. See that four-leaf clover about three feet in front of your right foot? You want that clover but you cannot move. Stretch way down and try to pick it. Oh look, a butterfly is flying by your left ear. The butterfly is just beyond your arm's length. Try to reach out gently and hold the butterfly.
   b. How many of you have ever had a Raggedy Ann or Raggedy Andy doll? Pretend you are a rag doll and try to follow each suggestion: You are lying in the toy box and hoping someone will take you out and play with you. All of a sudden you hear a footstep; you try to listen very hard. The footsteps stop, and a hand reaches into the toy box. The hand grabs you by the hair and pulls you straight up out of the toy box. You stop quickly when you are even with your owner's face. Your owner looks carefully at you, and you stare back. What is going to happen to you? Your owner asks you if you would like to play in the apple tree in the backyard. You are excited and try to shake your head "yes." It is hard, though, because your owner is still holding you by the hair. Your owner makes a quick decision and lowers you rapidly. Your owner lets go of your hair and takes you by the arm. You can feel your head falling toward your side. The room looks funny from this view. Your owner is in a hurry, and you can feel your body moving up and down as your owner runs down the stairs with you. Wow! That was a rough ride. At last you are out in the yard. Just feel that beautiful sunshine. It makes you feel good all over. Oh no, your owner is going to climb up into the apple tree and take you along. Bounce, bounce, bounce, you are hitting the trunk of the tree. That hurts! At last you are sitting on a big tree limb. It feels good to be still. You look down, and the ground looks like it is a long way away. You sit very still because you do not want to fall.

After you have been there awhile, your owner starts to climb down. You realize you have been forgotten; you try to look down and get your owner's attention. Oh! you can feel yourself falling, down, down. All of a sudden you stop, but the stop did not hurt you. Your owner caught you before you hit the ground. You are happy because your owner loves you and takes care of you. Your owner carries you carefully up the steps and puts you back in the toy box. You are happy to stay there for the rest of the day and think about what will happen tomorrow.

4. Have students suggest other exercises to use for warm-ups.

Activity 2–17:
A WALK THROUGH IMAGINATION

TYPE	TERM
● CLASS	● STA
● GROUP	○ LTA
○ IND	○ LC

Purpose:

1. To interpret various actions and emotions through pantomime
2. To develop movement that corresponds with a musical presentation
3. To develop group interaction and cooperation through a group-developed pantomime

Materials:

Descriptions of actions for students to pantomime; recordings that suggest movements or a musical instrument, such as a piano, that can be used to suggest movement; folk stories to read to the group.

Grade level:

All grades; vary complexity and subject matter to correspond with the students' grade levels

Procedures:

1. These activities may be done in various orders and on different days. Some of the activities are whole-group activities, in which children move independently from one another, and others are small-group activities, in which children must plan their movement cooperatively and then move as a group to express the action. Following are examples of activities to help children develop believable actions.
   a. This pantomime activity requires children to change actions on a walk, if the actions are to be believable. Your description might go like this:

   Today we are going to take an imaginary walk through a new attraction at Disney World (name any theme park that the children are familiar with). The attraction is called "A Walk through Imagination." During this walk you will experience many different conditions that require you to walk or move in different ways. You must try to make your actions as believable as you can. Listen as I guide you through the attraction with my voice. Pretend you are actually going through "A Walk through Imagination" and move your body as if you were really there. Here you are at Disney World. You are excited about going into "A Walk through Imagination," and you hurry up to the ticket window. The ticket taker tells you that you can enter in about ten minutes. You stand there waiting impatiently. As you stand there, you look at the other people who will be going in with you. Some are taller than you are, and some are shorter than you are. At last the ten minutes are up, and you hurry to the entrance. The entrance looks odd. Is that a tunnel? The only way to enter is to crawl on your hands and knees. As you go through the tunnel, a bat swoops down toward your head. You hurry faster because you see a room ahead. You're there. It feels good to stand up again. You stretch. All of a sudden, a high wind hits you, and you grab for the wall. The wall opens and you find yourself in a room of ice. You try to walk across the slippery, smooth ice. You think it would be fun to slide across the ice. You fall; the ice is cold. You are almost to the other side of the room, so you crawl to the door. The next room looks different. Could this be a dungeon? You look around. You will need to be careful here. The path winds through a torture chamber. The first torture is a floor of very hot coals. You must walk across these hot, hot coals. You are across, but it looks like sand ahead. You carefully put your foot down. You hear a sucking noise as your foot goes down, down into the sand. You try to pull it out, because this must be quicksand. At last, you make it. You shake the sand off of your shoe and look at the sand. It is only about three feet wide. You know you can jump across. You move back and leap across the quicksand. To get out of the dungeon, you must walk across a narrow board over the moat. You look down and see crocodiles in the moat. You walk very, very carefully so you do not lose your balance. The next room has craters all over the surface. As you enter, you feel funny—as if you are floating in space. This must be the moon. You decide to experiment on the weightless surface. You leap in the air; you jump; you run. It is wonderful; you have never been able to move so easily. You are as light as a feather. You are just about across the moon. The only way off the moon is to climb down a ladder. You go down, down, down. As you climb down, you see beautiful stars and moving comets. All of a sudden, you find yourself back on earth. You are in a beautiful green meadow. You want to skip through the grass and wildflowers. You see a lovely yellow buttercup and stop to smell it. The grass feels so good that you want to roll in the meadow. You roll toward the door and see a pile of autumn leaves from last year. You jump up and decide to walk through them. It is fun to jump in the leaves and hear them crunching and crackling. The sun is out, and the birds are singing. You finish your walk by enjoying this warm spring day. As you leave "A Walk through Imagination," you are surprised. You did not realize how many different ways your body could move.

b. Provide music, such as "The Nutcracker Suite," with different tempos and movements. Have the students sit on the floor in a gymnasium or other large space. Ask them to close their eyes and listen to the music and think about what the music is trying to say. Tell them that they will be able to interpret the music any way they choose as long as the movement is believable when it is matched with the music. After they have listened to a selection, have them spread out in the space and listen to the music a second time while they move independently to the sound of the music. Finally, allow them to talk about what each section of the music represented to them.

c. Folk stories and nursery rhymes also provide sound stimulation for developing believable actions. Select a folktale or nursery rhyme with strong characterization and action. Have the students sit on the floor with their eyes closed. As you read a folktale to them, have them imagine the characters and actions that are taking place. Ask them to describe what they "see." Read the story a second time, allowing the students the opportunity to pantomime each character in the story. The following nursery rhymes are good for young children to pantomime.

> Jack be nimble,
> Jack be quick,
> Jack jumped over the candlestick.

Select a partner and pantomime

> Jack and Jill went up the hill
> To fetch a pail of water.
> Jack fell down,
> And broke his crown,
> And Jill came tumbling after.

Divide into groups of four and pantomime

> Three little kittens, they lost their mittens,
> And they began to cry,
> "Oh, mother dear, we sadly fear
> That we have lost our mittens."
> "What! Lost your mittens, you naughty kittens!
> Then you shall have no pie."
> Mee-ow, mee-ow, mee-ow.
> Then you shall have no pie.
> The three little kittens, they found their mittens,
> And they began to cry,
> "Oh, mother dear, see here, see here,
> For we have found our mittens."
> "Put on your mittens, you silly kittens,
> And you shall have some pie."
> Purr-r, purr-r, purr-r
> Oh, let us have some pie."

and

> Old Mother Hubbard
> Went to the cupboard,
> To fetch her poor dog a bone;
> But when she got there
> The cupboard was bare
> And so the poor dog had none.
>
> She took a clean dish
> To get him some tripe;
> But when she came back
> He was smoking a pipe.
>
> The dame made a curtsey,
> The dog made a bow;
> The dame said, "Your servant,"
> The dog said, "Bow-wow."
>
> She went to the tailor's
> To buy him a coat;
> But when she came back
> He was riding a goat.
>
> She went to the hatter's
> To buy him a hat;

But when she came back
He was feeding the cat.

She went to the barber's
To buy him a wig;
But when she came back
He was dancing a jig.

Have the students choose a partner

Little Miss Muffet
Sat on a tuffet
Eating her curds and whey;

Along came a spider,
And sat down beside her
And frightened Miss Muffet away.

The following folktales are enjoyable for pantomime: The Three Little Pigs, The Three Billy Goats Gruff, Red Riding Hood, and The Three Bears. This pantomime activity may also be done as a guessing game. Divide the class into small groups. Allow each group to select a rhyme or story and practice doing it in pantomime. Then ask the students to present it to the remainder of the students, who will try to guess the name of the story or rhyme.

d. Provide children with opportunities to pantomime various feelings and emotions. This activity can be played as a game, with children choosing cards on which various emotions are written. Ask the children to portray the emotions in pantomime. The other members of the group guess what emotion is being portrayed. Vary the emotion words with the children's grade level. For example:

Happiness
You have just received the birthday present you want.

Sadness
You dropped your ice cream cone in the dirt.

Surprise
You opened a present and a toy snake jumps out.

Fear
You are riding your bicycle across the street and a car suddenly comes toward you.

Worry
Your homework is due and you can't find it.

Embarrassment
You fell asleep in class and the teacher wakes you up and scolds you in front of the whole class.

Anger
Your little brother took your new watch apart and it won't work.

Jealousy
Your mother gives your sister a new sweater and you don't get anything.

Contentment
You are lying in a hammock listening to the birds sing.

Activity 2–18:
A SOFTBALL GAME WITHOUT A BALL

TYPE	TERM
● CLASS	● STA
● GROUP	○ LTA
○ IND	○ LC

Purpose:
1. To observe various actions and emotions and interpret them through pantomime
2. To develop group interaction and cooperation through pantomime
3. To develop creative imagination and empathy

Materials:
Opportunities to observe various people, activities, and inanimate objects; films can also be used for observational purposes.

Grade level:
All grades; observational opportunities will vary with grade level

Procedures:
1. Discuss with children the fact that actors must portray many different kinds of people in different situations. Ask them how they think an actor might prepare himself or herself to be an old person, a tennis player, a firefighter, or a musician. Would these four people move alike and behave in the same way? How can we find out more about the actions of other people? (Suggest to the children that they can learn a lot about people, their actions, and reactions by observing various groups of people.) The following activities help children to develop observational skills and creative imagination:
   a. Observing sports activities: Assign the students to watch a particular sports activity, such as a school softball, basketball, football, soccer, or volleyball game. Ask them to observe the actions of the players. How do the players move? How do they catch or throw the ball? What are they doing when they do not have the ball? How do they stand? How do they run, jump, or slide? After they have seen the sports activity, have students discuss their observations. Then divide the students into appropriate-sized teams and have them pantomime the actions of the sport. For example, two teams could pantomime a softball game with pitcher, batter, catcher, basemen, and so forth. At the same time, other students could pantomime the actions of the spectators.

b. Observing a musician, band, or orchestra: Assign the students to watch a particular musician, band, or orchestra. (Elementary students could watch the middle school or high school band or orchestra. Another alternative would be to ask several guest musicians to come to class so that students can observe the actions of someone playing a wind instrument, a string instrument, or a percussion instrument.) After they have observed the musical activity, have students discuss the actions of each type of musician. How did they sit or stand? How did they hold their instruments? How did they play their instruments? What expressions did they show on their faces? How did the conductor act? How did they know he or she was the leader of the group? How did the conductor show pleasure or displeasure with the band or orchestra? Finally, divide the class into various segments of the band or orchestra, select a conductor, and ask the children to pantomime a musical selection.

c. Observing chores completed by family members: Discuss with children the various chores that they and other members of the family perform. Using a brainstorming format (children rapidly provide oral suggestions), have the students list as many household chores as they can that require different bodily actions; ironing a shirt, washing dishes, filling a dishwasher, vacuuming a rug, sewing on a button, dusting a table, mowing the lawn, baking a cake, painting a wall, cleaning a bathtub, watering plants, making a bed, setting the table, scrubbing a floor, sweeping a floor, washing windows, answering the telephone, feeding the dog, building a fire in the fireplace, frying hamburgers, hanging a picture, and switching on a light are all examples.

Assign the students the task of observing and completing several of these chores. Have them observe carefully all of the required movements. After they have made their observations, have them pantomime their household chores in class while the rest of the group identifies and analyzes the chore and its corresponding movements.

d. Observing hobbies and nonteam sports: Discuss with children the various hobbies and nonteam sports that people participate in. Using a brainstorming technique, have students list hobbies and sports that are characterized by distinctive movements; paddling a canoe, fishing, taking a picture, bicycling, changing a bicycle tire, hiking, boxing, playing tennis, swimming, bowling, golfing, playing archery, wood carving, painting a picture, camping, weaving a rug, playing chess, and riding a horse are all examples.

Assign students to observe someone participating in a hobby or sport and then ask them to pantomime the hobby or sport for the rest of the group.

e. Observing inanimate objects: Show children various inanimate objects and discuss the characteristics of the objects: Have them explore the objects with their senses to describe the color, size, texture, weight, smell, sound, and use of the object. After they have observed various objects, have students pantomime an object for the group to guess. Assign students the task of observing inanimate objects outside of the classroom and then pantomime the objects in class; lightbulb, vacuum cleaner, eggbeater, tennis racket, clock, glass, feather, balloon, rubber ball, mirror, chair, knife, candle, and driftwood are all examples.

f. Observing machines and pantomiming the actions in a group activity: Discuss with children that a machine usually has several moving parts that must work together. If the parts do not work together, the machine will not work correctly. Have the children observe several machines in class. Ask them to look at the moving parts and observe their locations, sounds, and rhythms. Examples of machines to observe in the school include a typewriter, car traveling by, telephone, electric mixer (in the cafeteria), blender (in the cafeteria), piano, bicycle, television, dishwasher (in the cafeteria), and electric or gas stove (in the cafeteria).

Divide the students into small groups, have them choose a machine, and ask them to cooperatively pantomime the machine for the rest of the class.

Activity 2–19:

ORAL DEBATE: WHO IS THE LEADING CONSERVATIONIST?

TYPE	TERM
● CLASS	○ STA
● GROUP	● LTA
○ IND	○ LC

Purpose:

1. To develop and expand research skills
2. To develop oral language ability through debate
3. To select and argue the most important points in a debate

Materials:

Jean Fritz's *Bully for You, Teddy Roosevelt!* (1991) and Nancy Whitelaw's *Theodore Roosevelt Takes Charge* (1992); various library reference materials on the roles of John Muir, John James Audubon, and Henry David Thoreau as leading conservationists; current articles about national forests, game preserves, national parks, and national monuments.

Grade level:

Upper elementary and middle school

Book summaries:

Both biographies emphasize the role that Theodore Roosevelt played as a naturalist and a conservationist. Fritz's biography is written for slightly younger audiences than is Whitelaw's.

Procedures:

1. Lead a discussion in which you ask students to define the meanings of *naturalist* and *conservationist*. Show pictures of various national parks, forests, and monuments. Ask the students to speculate about the importance of these areas to people living in the world. Ask the students the following: "How do you think areas such as these were protected so that people from around the world could enjoy them?" "Who do you think made the enjoyment of these areas possible?" "Is it still important today to consider the protection of these areas? Why or why not?"

2. Tell students that they will be reading biographies about one of the leading naturalists and conservationists of his time. Introduce one or both of the biographies about Theodore Roosevelt and explain to the students that the books describe a former president who lived from 1858 to 1919. Background information about the United States during this time would also provide perspective.

3. After students have read one of the biographies, lead a discussion in which they identify the role of Theodore Roosevelt as he becomes a naturalist and a conservationist. Ask the following: "Why did Roosevelt become a conservationist?" "What influence did his conservationist attitudes have on the United States?" "Do you believe that these conservationist attitudes are still important today? Why or why not?"

4. After this discussion, read and discuss the following quote from Jean Fritz's biography:

   At every opportunity, he tried to educate the public to the dangers of waste and pollution, and it is no wonder that he became known as the "Conservation President." During his time in the White House he established 150 national forests, the first fifty-five bird and game preserves, and five national parks. Under the National Monuments Act he set aside the first eighteen "national monuments," including Devil's Tower in Wyoming, the Grand Canyon, California's Muir

Woods, Arizona's Petrified Forest, and Washington's Mount Olympus. Indeed, Theodore Roosevelt deserves much of the credit for teaching Americans to respect what nature has given them. When the National Wildlife Federation established a Conservation Hall of Fame in 1965, Theodore Roosevelt was given first place. John Muir came in second, John James Audubon fifth, and Henry David Thoreau sixth. (p. 112)

5. Ask the students to pretend that they are sitting on the committee for the 1965 Conservation Hall of Fame. Ask them to choose one of the people who made or could have made placement in the Hall of Fame. After students have chosen their candidate, ask them to do research on the contributions of the candidate and to present their arguments in the form of a debate. Who would the class select as number one and so forth? Why would they place that person in that position? Who are the current people that they would place in the Conservation Hall of Fame? Again, ask the students to present and argue the cases for their nominees.

6. Students can also debate the role of a naturalist and a conservationist versus the role of an industrialist. Do the two positions need to be contrary to each other? Why or why not?

7. Students can locate a current environment issue and debate the issue as if one group were representing the ideals of Theodore Roosevelt and the other group were representing the ideals of the opposing forces.

Activity 2–20:

ORAL DEBATE: THE TRUTH AND NOTHING BUT THE TRUTH

TYPE	TERM
● CLASS	● STA
● GROUP	● LTA
● IND	○ LC

Purpose:
1. To identify and defend a position through oral language
2. To come to conclusions based on evidence found in literature
3. To role-play situations motivated by plots and conflicts in literature
4. To develop tolerance for others' viewpoints and feelings
5. To develop critical thinking

Materials: Avi's *Nothing But the Truth: A Documentary Novel* (1991).

Grade level: Middle school

Book summary: *Nothing But the Truth* is a fictional novel written in documentary format. At Harrison High School a faculty rule requires students to stand at "respectful, silent attention" during the playing of the national anthem during homeroom. When ninth grader Philip Malloy hums and breaks this rule, English teacher Margaret Narwin sends him to the vice principal's office. After Philip is suspended from school, community members, school officials, and the national media become involved in charges and countercharges regarding patriotism, respect, and freedom of speech. Margaret Narwin is then asked to leave her teaching position. This book presents different interpretations of the same incident and encourages readers to discover for themselves who is telling the truth and nothing but the truth.

Procedures:
1. This activity is designed to help students take, defend, and support a position through oral language. It is also designed to help students define, for themselves and the class, the elements of truth. They gain insights into how emotions define and distort the truth.

2. Introduce the book so that students are interested in the topic and motivated to do the activity. For example, ask the following: "Have you ever had an experience in which one version of an incident differed from another version of the same incident?" "Have you and a teacher or parent ever interpreted an experience in two completely different ways?" "Have you ever argued about who is to blame for an incident involving another person?" "Have you ever listened to two news reports and received different interpretations of the same incident?" "Have you ever listened to two opposing lawyers as they argue the same case?" "When you read Avi's *Nothing But the Truth* you will have an opportunity to read different interpretations of the same incident, but the author never tells you who he believes is right and who he believes is wrong. It is up to you, the reader, to come to your own conclusion."

3. Because this book is written in a format that is different from most novels, it is important to discuss the format with students before they read the novel. Explain that the author is trying to document various reactions to the same incident through the use of memos, letters, diary pages, discussions, phone and personal conversations, speeches, and telegrams. Ask students what kind of information could be found in each of these documents and why the author would include

each of these types of documents. Because the students will be the ones to decide who is telling the truth at the end of the novel, emphasize that they should pay particular attention to details. They will use information found in the documents to come to their own conclusions.

4. After students have read the novel, lead a discussion in which they consider what happened to each character as a consequence of the story. Have them decide which character changes the most and which character is most harmfully influenced by the conclusion of the actions. Have students debate the accuracy of the various interpretations and the emotional responses generated by the conflict.

5. This activity may be developed as an oral debate in which students, divided according to position, debate whether the English teacher or the student is telling the truth. This activity may also be developed as a mock trial in which students volunteer or are chosen to play different characters from the novel. Other students would be chosen for the positions of judge, Margaret Narwin's attorney, Philip Malloy's attorney, and the jury. The judge and jury make the final decision, based on the evidence, of who is telling the truth. For example, a student in the role of Philip Malloy would take the stand and present his version of the truth. Students role-playing Philip's parents, his neighbor, and members of the school board or media who support his position would each take the stand and present their versions of the truth. After these characters have made their statements, they would each be cross-examined by Margaret Narwin's attorney. Margaret Narwin would then take the stand and make a statement presenting her version of the truth. The coach and students who support her position would each take the stand and present their versions of the situation. After these characters have made their statements they would be cross-examined by Philip Malloy's attorney.

6. Students may also write their responses to the various documents included in the book and to what happened to the teacher and the boy.

Activity 2–21:

PUTTING ON OUR OWN TV SHOW—PART I

	TYPE		TERM
●	CLASS	○	STA
●	GROUP	●	LTA
○	IND	○	LC

Purpose:

1. To observe television shows and identify the kinds of shows that could be created in the classroom
2. To develop oral language, creative imagination, and creative dramatization skills

Materials:

No materials are necessary, although students should (with parental consent) observe the different types of shows so they can suggest classroom "television" programs they would like to produce.

Grade level:

All grades; there is an adequate variety of formats for young children (especially educational TV) and older students

Procedures:

1. If this activity follows a study of television personnel, students are probably anxious to experiment with their own creative products. If students have not yet studied television shows and the people who create and appear on them, explain that the class is going to try something very exciting. They will have the opportunity to put on their own TV shows in class. (If video equipment is available you may explain to the group that they can actually see themselves on TV.) Ask them to list the kinds of programs that are shown on TV. Discuss what the students feel are different requirements for the programs.

2. Ask the students to observe the different kinds of programs on television, the format of the programs, and the requirements of the programs. Vary this assignment according to grade level; kindergarten and first-grade children might, for example, be asked to watch a segment of *Sesame Street, The Electric Company,* or *Mr. Rogers' Neighborhood* to observe the actors in the program and what they do and to listen for sound effects and the kinds of material that are presented. At the other extreme, upper elementary and middle school children might be asked to observe all types of programs; to identify specific requirements for each kind of program; to identify the type of material presented; to identify any specific oral language requirements on the part of the actors and announcers; and to identify the format of the television presentation, including station breaks and commercials.

3. After they have watched various programs, have the children expand their original list of programs and discuss the nature of the programs, any special requirements, the purpose of the programs, and the audience for the programs. The discussion might cover the following:

Program	Purpose	Audience
Sesame Street	To educate and entertain	Children
Children's Classic	To entertain and develop enjoyment of books	Families
Storytelling Hour	To entertain and develop enjoyment of stories	Children

News, Weather	To inform people	Everyone
Cooking Show	To demonstrate a cooking skill	People interested in cooking
Nature or Animal Show	To inform and entertain	People interested in nature and animals
Game Show	To entertain	People who like game shows
Comedy Show	To entertain	Families
Variety Show	To entertain	Families
Consumer Programs	To inform	Adults
Dramas	To entertain	Adults

4. Discuss the type or types of television shows the children would like to create and perform. Discuss both the staff and performing requirements for each type of production. List the TV shows the class decides it would like to create.

Activity 2–22:

PUTTING ON OUR OWN TV SHOW—PART II

TYPE	TERM
● CLASS	○ STA
● GROUP	● LTA
○ IND	○ LC

Purpose:

1. To develop oral language, creative imagination, and creative dramatization skills
2. To create a group or class TV show and present the show to an audience
3. To develop cooperation by working with a group

Materials:

Sound effects, props, music, or other materials needed for the specific kinds of TV show or shows the group chooses.

Grade level:

All grades; change sophistication of presentation and format according to grade level

Procedures:

1. You have already prepared the background for this activity if your students have investigated the production staff for a television show, observed and discussed the characteristics of various types of programs, and discussed the type or types of TV shows they would like to create.

2. Divide the class into workable groups and help the groups plan a creative oral television presentation with appropriate staff responsibilities, performers, background music or sound effects, and commercials or public service announcements (see media section). For example:

   a. Have a class of young children put on a show with a format similar to that of *Sesame Street* or *The Electric Company.* The whole class can work on the production, but smaller groups can each develop a creative presentation featuring puppets such as Big Bird, Ernie, and the Cookie Monster. Some groups can develop creative stories while other groups think of creative jingles or dialogue to present facts they are learning in school. The *Sesame Street* show should be presented several times so that all children have opportunities to be both performers and technicians. This activity is also effective with older remedial reading or special education groups. These students can develop an *Electric Company* production that includes creative use of some of the skills they are learning and present it to a group of younger children.

   b. News, Weather, and Sports? We've Got Them All! Divide the class into groups to prepare the news, weather, and sports segments of the show. Have other groups work on the technical production, announcements, or advertisements. This TV show can present the news, weather, and sports that are of interest to the class. Students can use their interviewing skills (see Activity 2–10, "Interviewing") to acquire information for the news broadcast, science and map-reading skills to predict the weather, and observational reporting skills to present the sports news.

c. The 40¢ Pyramid. A game-show format can be used with any grade level; the questions or tasks required of the students can be developed for any level. Divide the class into groups according to MC, contestants, writers of questions or creators of stunts, judges for answers or evaluators of stunts, announcers, prize committee members, and technicians. Have the whole group choose a theme for their game show. Young children can prepare activities requiring physical coordination, knowledge of nursery rhymes, listening skills, knowledge of fairytales, and so forth. Older children might choose to have questions about their content fields, questions about a topic that all of the children would research, a musical answer game, or a sports quiz. All of the students should review the subject areas for the questions. Provide any necessary assistance for the writers of the questions or the developers of the stunts so they are appropriate for children of that ability level. This activity is also excellent for remedial reading and many special education groups. A great deal of learning takes place when children are researching information to develop questions for other children to answer, and children are usually very attentive if they know they are responsible for the information because other students will ask them questions about it.

PICK YOUR CATEGORY		
A Literature	**B** Music	**C** Science
D Sports	**E** History	**F** Listening

d. How To? We Can Tell You! Using a brainstorming technique, have the children list their hobbies or other interests that could be demonstrated to an audience. Since many TV shows demonstrate how to cook fish, raise a garden, collect stamps, sew, and the like, tell the students they will have an opportunity to demonstrate something they can do in a TV show format. Discuss the information they must include if they are going to show their audience how to do something. Act out two examples for the students—one in which the presentation is rapid and confused and another in which the demonstration is clear, sequentially developed, and slow enough to follow. Paper-folding and kite-making activities are ideal for this purpose. Have the students try each activity as you demonstrate it and then discuss which demonstration was effective and why one was more effective than the other. Next, divide the class into groups, according to hobbies or other skills they would like to demonstrate. Have each group prepare a TV demonstration to be shown to the rest of the class. Interact with the groups to provide necessary assistance and advice.

HOW TO? WE CAN TELL YOU!

Announcer: Introduces program
Station Break: Commercial message
Announcer: Introduces first demonstration
First Demonstration: How to make balloon animals
Station Break: Commercial message
Announcer: Introduces second demonstration
Second demonstration: How to dance the hokey pokey
Station Break: Commercial message
Announcer: Introduces third demonstration
Third demonstration: How to frost a cake
Announcer: Thanks audience for listening, signs off

e. A Story! A Story! Creative stories and interpretations of literature selections are presented in many different formats on television. Stories are read and told on children's programs such as *Captain Kangaroo.* Children's classics including *Winnie the Pooh, Pinocchio,* and *Beauty and the Beast* are dramatized by puppeteers, cartoonists, and human actors. Both historical fiction and nonfiction are presented in drama form. Discuss with students the television program formats they enjoy when they watch stories. Select several formats, divide the class into groups according to the formats, and have each group develop a creative story or oral interpretation of literature using that format. Present the television story hour to the rest of the class or to a group of younger children.

REFERENCES

Johnson, D., & Pearson, P. D. (1984). *Teaching reading vocabulary* (2nd ed.). New York: Holt, Rinehart & Winston.

Kay, R. (1991). Commentary: Singing the praises of choral reading. *Reading Today, 8,* 12.

Fitzpatrick, K. (1994, Fall). Improving reading comprehension using critical thinking strategies. *Reading Improvement, 31,* 142–144.

Loban, W. (1976). *Language development: Kindergarten through grade twelve.* Urbana, IL: National Council of Teachers of English.

Loban, W. (1986, October). Research currents: The somewhat stingy story of research into children's language. *Language Arts, 63,* 608–616.

Purves, A., Rogers T., & Soter, A. (1990). *How porcupines make love II: Teaching a response-centered literature curriculum.* New York: Longman.

Segedy, M., & Roosevelt, C. (1986). Adapting the courtroom trial format to literature. In *Activities to promote critical thinking: Classroom practices in teaching English* (pp. 88–92). Urbana, IL: National Council of Teachers of English.

Toms-Bronowski, S. (1983). An investigation of the effectiveness of selected vocabulary teaching strategies with intermediate grade level students. *Dissertation Abstracts International, 44,* 1405A (University Microfilms No. 83–16, 328).

Ysseldyke, J., & Algozzine, B. (1995). *Special education: A practical approach for teachers* (3rd ed.). Boston: Houghton Mifflin.

CHILDREN'S LITERATURE REFERENCES

Ahlberg, Janet, and Ahlberg, Allan. *The Baby's Catalogue.* Boston: Little, Brown, 1982.

Ardley, Neil. *Music.* New York: Knopf, 1989.

Avi. *Nothing But the Truth: A Documentary Novel.* New York: Orchard, 1991.

Bauer, Marion Dane. *On My Honor.* New York: Clarion, 1986.

Carle, Eric. *My First Book of Colors.* New York: Crowell, 1974, 1985.

Cleary, Beverly. *Ramona and Her Father.* Illustrated by Alan Tiegreen. New York: Morrow, 1977.

Clifford, Nick. *The Incredible Earth.* New York: DK, 1996.

Ehlert, Lois. *Red Leaf, Yellow Leaf.* San Diego: Harcourt Brace Jovanovich, 1991.

Emberley, Rebecca. *City Sounds.* Boston: Little, Brown, 1989.

Fleming, Denise. *In the Tall, Tall Grass.* New York: Henry Holt, 1991.

Fox, Paula. *One-Eyed Cat.* New York: Bradbury, 1984.

Freedman, Russell. *Franklin Delano Roosevelt.* New York: Clarion, 1990.

Freedman, Russell, *Out of Darkness: The Story of Louis Braille.* New York: Clarion, 1997.

Freedman, Russell. *The Wright Brothers: How They Invented the Airplane.* New York: Holiday, 1991.

Fritz, Jean. *Bully for You, Teddy Roosevelt!* Illustrated by Mike Wimmer. New York: Putnam's, 1991.

Henkes, Kevin. *Lilly's Purple Plastic Purse.* New York: Greenwillow, 1996.

Hest, Amy. *The Purple Coat.* Illustrated by Amy Schwartz. New York: Macmillan, 1986.

Hirschi, Ron. *Loon Lake.* Photographs by Daniel J. Cox. New York: Dutton, 1991.

Hoban, Tana. *Circles, Triangles, and Squares.* New York: Macmillan, 1974.

Hoban, Tana. *Of Colors and Things.* New York: Greenwillow, 1989.

Hoban, Tana. *Round & Round & Round.* New York: Greenwillow, 1983.

Hoban, Tana. *Shapes, Shapes, Shapes.* New York: Greenwillow, 1986.

Howard, Ellen. *Edith Herself.* New York: Atheneum, 1987.

Jaspersohn, William. *Magazine: Behind the Scenes at* Sports Illustrated. Boston: Little, Brown, 1983.

Lauber, Patricia. *Volcano: The Eruption and Healing of Mount St. Helens.* New York: Bradbury, 1986.

Lobel, Anita. *Alison's Zinnia.* New York: Greenwillow, 1990.

Lowry, Lois. *Anastasia's Chosen Career.* Boston: Houghton Mifflin, 1987.

Matthews, Downs. *Polar Bear Cubs.* Photographs by Dan Guravich. New York: Simon & Schuster, 1989.

Morrison, Lillian. *At the Crack of the Bat.* Illustrated by Steve Cieslawski. New York: Hyperion, 1992.

Peters, Lisa Westberg. *The Sun, the Wind, and the Rain.* Illustrated by Ted Rand. New York: Henry Holt, 1988.

Pienkowski, Jan. *Haunted House.* New York: Dutton, 1979.

Pilkey, Dav. *The Paperboy.* New York: Oxford, 1996.

Rathmann, Peggy. *Ruby the Copycat.* New York: Scholastic, 1991.

Rockwell, Anne. *First Comes Spring.* New York: Crowell, 1985.

Schoenherr, John. *Bear.* New York: Philomel, 1991.

Sewall, Marcia. *People of the Breaking Day.* New York: Atheneum, 1990.

Spinelli, Jerry. *Wringer.* New York: HarperCollins, 1997.

Whitelaw, Nancy. *Theodore Roosevelt Takes Charge.,* Niles, IL: Whitman, 1992.

3

Listening Activities

Listening is probably the most frequently used communication skill. It has not been until recently, however, that listening instruction has become a major concern of elementary teachers, researchers, and methods instructors in language arts. Although research indicates that both children and adults spend a major portion of their communication time listening, elementary textbooks and teachers' manuals contain few listening activities.

The definition of *listening* is complex; many types of instructional activities can be included under the broad term. First, listening includes auditory acuity, or the ability to hear noises and sounds. Second, listening requires auditory perception: the ability to discriminate, blend, and remember sounds. Third, listening involves the ability to attend to the sounds that convey the message. Fourth, listening includes auditory comprehension, or the ability to get meaning from the listening experience. Comprehension of meaning also requires different listening abilities. These competencies may range from a factual understanding of the main idea to the ability to critically evaluate what is heard. Finally, listening includes appreciation of sounds, poetry, literature, music, drama, and media.

In a review of research on developing listening abilities, Funk and Funk (1989) provide the following guidelines:

1. Teachers and students should state the purpose for each listening experience and approach listening differently depending on the purpose.
2. Teachers and students should set the stage for listening by providing an atmosphere conducive to listening for the intended purpose.
3. Follow-up activities should be used to help achieve listening goals and encourage students to apply their new information and techniques.
4. Teachers should use instructional techniques that promote and develop positive listening habits by including many different types of listening experiences (e.g., listening to and responding to stories, poetry, and music.)

Critical analysis can be fostered by having students listen to determine a speaker's intention or bias. Students should be involved in strategies that improve listening comprehension as well as reading comprehension.

The activities in this chapter, which cover a broad definition of listening and stress auditory awareness, were developed to help children understand the importance of listening and to help them gain awareness of listening. The activities also stress the importance of understanding different purposes for listening. Improvement of listening skills would be difficult without this understanding.

A series of activities are designed to improve children's attentive listening skills. Some of these activities use a learning center format; consequently, teachers should tape-record parts of these activities so that children can learn to identify sounds and follow oral directions.

Listening comprehension activities require children to listen for the main idea, supporting details, and sequence of events. Several activities were designed to help children develop critical listening and thinking skills. Stimuli for critical listening activities include proverbs from *Poor Richard's Almanac,* fairy tales, folktales, and famous heroes from America's past and present.

This chapter concludes with activities designed to help children develop appreciative listening skills. Folktales and early radio broadcasts are used to motivate these activities. Many appreciative listening activities are also located in other chapters of this book. For example, activities involving creative drama, storytelling, and different forms of media provide children with many opportunities for developing listening skills. Because each oral activity requires an audience or listener, the activities in the oral language section also develop children's listening skills. Many of the activities in the media section also develop children's listening skills by requiring them to listen critically to television and radio commercials and other programs. Listening can be exciting if the activities are stimulating to the child. The language arts curriculum can provide children with many creative experiences.

Activity 3–1:
LISTENING FOR DIFFERENT PURPOSES—WHY AND HOW

TYPE	TERM
● CLASS	● STA
● GROUP	○ LTA
○ IND	○ LC

Purpose:
1. To realize that we listen for different purposes
2. To identify purposes for listening
3. To describe personal requirements and responsibilities for different listening experiences

Materials:
A radio for passive listening; directions or announcements for attentive listening; a paragraph for directed listening; a commercial for critical evaluative listening; a story or recording for appreciative listening.

Grade level:
All grades—examples for the different types of listening should correspond with the students' ability and interest levels. (The examples in this activity are identified according to level of difficulty. Two examples accompany each part of the activity; one example can be used with lower elementary students, and the other can be used with upper elementary students.)

Procedures:
1. While students are involved in another activity such as finishing artwork or another assignment, turn on a radio at low volume. Do not attract the students' attention to the radio. After the radio has played for a few minutes and the other assignment has been completed, ask the students if they can tell you what was on the radio broadcast. Ask them to describe the content of the radio program as specifically as possible. Discuss why some students could report what was on the radio while others could not. (Most of the students will not be able to relate very much information unless a favorite personality or subject attracts their attention.) Ask the students to describe this type of listening. When they tune out sounds for part of the time, are they able to remember a portion of what they hear? Tell the students that passive listening occurs when a person is not actively involved in the act of listening and does not have a purpose for listening. Have the students list circumstances under which they are engaged in passive listening. When is passive listening acceptable or advantageous? When is passive listening inappropriate? When could passive listening even get them into trouble?

2. Explain to students that several other kinds of listening are important and ask them if they can identify any other types of listening. Tell them that they will experience several different types of listening, describe the listening experience, and suggest purposes for each type of listening.

Examples:
Attentive Listening—Lower Elementary
   a. Give the students oral directions for drawing something without telling them the finished product. For example:

   Put a piece of paper and a pencil on your desk. Draw a circle the size of an orange in the middle of your paper. Draw a smaller circle above the first circle so the bottom of the smaller circle touches the top of the larger circle. Draw a triangle on the left-hand side of the circle; make the narrow point going away from the circle. Draw a round eye on the top circle. Draw a rectangular-shaped tail on the right-hand side of the bottom circle.

   Ask the children to tell you what they have drawn. How did they listen to the directions? Why did they need to listen carefully? What was the purpose for this kind of listening? When would they need to do this kind of listening? Why is this kind of listening important to them?

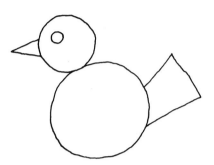

Attentive Listening—Upper Elementary

b. Tell the students to take out a piece of paper and a pencil. Give them directions for drawing a picture as follows:

Draw each item as I tell you; I will not repeat any of the directions. Put the point of your pencil on the top center of your paper and draw a circle the size of a quarter. From the bottom of the circle, draw two straight lines about one-half inch apart and one-fourth inch long. Connect the bottom of the straight lines with a horizontal line. Extend the horizontal line about one-half inch on each end. Turn this connecting line into a rectangle by drawing two one-inch lines for the sides and drawing another bottom line. Put your pencil on the bottom left-hand corner of the rectangle and draw a curved line about three inches long toward the bottom left-hand side of your paper. Put your pencil on the bottom right-hand side of the rectangle and draw a curved line about three inches long toward the bottom right-hand side of the paper. Connect the lower ends of the two curved lines with a straight line. Put your pencil in the center of the bottom straight line; draw two small half-circles on either side of the center. Now place your pencil back up on the top left-hand corner of the rectangle; draw a two-inch straight line slanted toward the bottom left corner of your paper. Put your pencil back on the rectangle; draw a second two-inch line just below the first line. Put your pencil on the top right-hand corner of the rectangle. Draw a two-inch straight line slanted toward the bottom right corner of your paper. Draw a second two-inch slanted line under the first line. Draw small circles at the open ends of each of the slanted lines. Draw a face on the top quarter-size circle.

Let the students describe their listening experience. How did they listen? Why did they have to listen carefully? Was the listening experience different than listening to the radio broadcast? Why was it different? What was their purpose for listening? When would they need to use this kind of listening? Why is this kind of listening important to the students? Have the students list on a chart the characteristics of this type of listening and when they would use it. Have the students suggest ways they could improve attentive listening.

Directed Listening—Lower Elementary

a. Read a paragraph that requires students to listen for a specific purpose, such as important details, the main idea, a sequence of events, or the like. For example:

After you listen to this paragraph, I want you to tell me where Stephanie and Steve were after school and what they saw. Stephanie and Steve, the Anderson twins, walked quietly into the kitchen. They knew they were two hours late getting home from school, and they expected that their parents would be worried and angry with them. Mom and Dad both came to the kitchen as the twins tried to make their way across the room. After their parents hugged them, the first question was, "Where have you been?" This is the answer Stephanie and Steve gave: "We left school and started to walk home our usual way. As we walked by Dexter Park, we saw that the Haunted House was ready for Halloween. We thought we would take just a few minutes to peek inside. In the first room was a coffin with a vampire inside. As we walked down the hallway, a skeleton jumped out of a closet. We started to run, but we were not sure how to get out of the house. One door led to a room covered with cobwebs and large spiders. In the next room, bats swooped down at us. Every other door we opened had white ghosts dancing toward us. One of the more friendly ghosts finally showed us the door to the outside. We hurried home as fast as we could."

Ask the students to draw a picture showing where the twins had been and what they saw. Discuss how the students listened and what they listened for. Were there any clues that helped them listen for their purpose? How could they improve this type of listening?

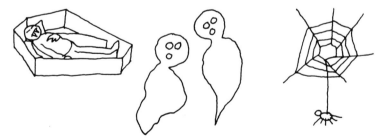

Directed Listening—Upper Elementary

b. Tell the students they will be listening to a paragraph so they can retell a sequence of events that happened in history. After they listen to the paragraph, tell them they will be expected to retell the order of events in the United States when the railroads were being built. For example:

The United States had great distances to be crossed to go from place to place. Heavy materials also needed to be moved from place to place. Many people felt that railroads could solve these problems. The first railroad built in the United States was a three-mile track in Massachusetts. Horses drew railroad cars containing the granite used to build the Bunker Hill Monument. In 1830 the Baltimore and Ohio Company began to experiment with railroads. Horses drew the first cars, but a year later the Baltimore and Ohio switched to steam locomotives. The first passenger-train service was started in South Carolina and was pulled by a locomotive called "Best Friend of Charleston." The Pacific Railroad Act, passed in 1862, was one of the most important events in railroad expansion. President Lincoln authorized the building of the transcontinental railroad that would connect the East and the West. The Central Pacific Railroad Company started laying tracks in Sacramento, California, and moved east. The Union Pacific built tracks from Omaha through the Nebraska Territory and further westward. In 1869 the two railroads met at Promontory, Utah. A golden spike was driven into the track to celebrate this great event.

Have the students identify the sequence of events that took place in the paragraph. Next, have them describe their listening experience. How did they listen? What was their purpose for listening? Were there any clues in the paragraph that helped them listen for their purpose? When would they use this type of listening? Have the students list on a chart the characteristics of this type of listening and when they would use it. Have them suggest ways they could improve directed listening.

1830		1862	1869
HORSE-DRAWN CARS ON TRACK	BEST FRIEND OF CHARLESTON	PACIFIC RAILROAD ACT	PROMONTORY, UTAH TRANS-CONTINENTAL RAILROAD

Critical Listening—Lower Elementary

a. For a critical listening experience for lower elementary students, tape-record a commercial used on a children's television show. Before you play the tape, ask the children to listen in order to identify the source of the tape and why the producer of the material wants them to listen to it. Have them listen to the tape and discuss the following: Who is trying to persuade us? What are they trying to persuade us to do? Should we believe everything we are told? Why or why not? How should we listen to this type of material? Why? How can we improve our listening when we listen to advertisements?

Critical Listening—Upper Elementary

b. Tape-record a commercial or political announcement. Prepare the students and discuss the listening experience in a similar way by using the same questions that were suggested in the activity for lower elementary students. Have the students list on a chart the characteristics of this type of listening and when they would use it. Have them suggest ways they could improve critical listening.

Appreciative Listening—Lower and Upper Elementary

Select a story to read to the students or a recording to play for them. Before reading the story or playing the recording, tell the students they will have an opportunity to share their favorite parts of the story or recording with the group after they have listened to it. After the listening experience, have them describe what they enjoyed most and why they enjoyed it. Discuss this type of listening with the group; have them list the characteristics of appreciative listening and ask them to identify when they would use it. Have students suggest ways they could improve appreciative listening.

3. Review the different types of listening, the purposes for listening, and the personal requirements and responsibilities for each type of listening. (This activity can be used as an introductory activity to instruction in listening improvement.)

Activity 3–2:
LISTENING TIMES

TYPE	TERM
● CLASS	○ STA
● GROUP	● LTA
○ IND	○ LC

Purpose:

1. To record the amount of time spent listening during the day
2. To realize the importance of listening in both school and private lives
3. To identify when we listen and what we listen to

Materials:

A form showing daily time periods allowing students to identify both time spent listening and sources of each listening experience.

Grade level:

Middle and upper elementary, middle school

Procedures:

1. Ask children if they have an idea about how much time during the day they spend listening. Write estimates on the board. Have them suggest some of the listening experiences they have at school and at home.

2. After students have provided estimates of both the amount of time they think they spend listening and what they listen to, ask them if they think they spend more or less time listening than people did sixty years ago. Discuss their answers and reasons for their responses. Tell the students that research conducted more than sixty years ago (Rankin, 1930) showed that adults spent more time listening than using any other form of communication. In fact, the study showed that 11 percent of communication time was spent in writing, 15 percent in reading, 32 percent in speaking, and 42 percent in listening. Ask the students for suggestions about how they could compare the time they or their parents spend listening with the time people spent listening sixty years ago.

3. Using student suggestions, copy a form to use for recording the time spent listening. This form might look like the following example:

WHEN DO I LISTEN? WHAT DO I LISTEN TO?
HOW LONG DO I LISTEN?

Time of Day	What I Listened To	How Long I Listened
7:00–7:30	_____	_____
7:30–8:00	_____	_____
8:00–8:30	_____	_____
8:30–9:00	_____	_____
9:00–9:30	_____	_____
9:30–10:00	_____	_____
10:00–10:30	_____	_____
10:30–11:00	_____	_____
11:00–11:30	_____	_____
11:30–12:00	_____	_____

(continue for remainder of day)

Total time spent listening = _____

4. Discuss with students how they can record their listening experiences and the amount of time they spent in each listening activity.

5. Assign the listening survey for the following day. (If possible, ask parents who wish to take part in the survey to record their listening experiences and the time they spent listening.) Ask students to return their surveys to school so the class or group can tabulate the results.

6. Tabulate the results of the survey. Total the number of hours and minutes that each student spent listening. Chart the range of hours and minutes for all of the students. Tabulate the number of students who listened for those approximate time periods. For example:

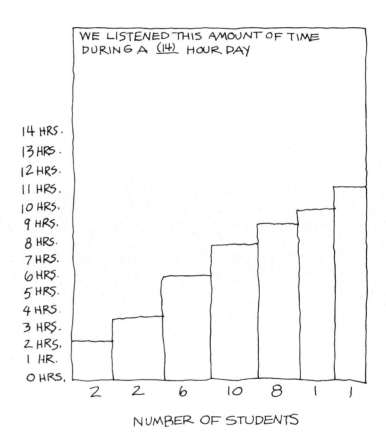

7. If parents or other adults take part in the survey, tabulate their listening times and compare the two charts.

8. Calculate an average of the amount of time students spend listening. Change the amount of time into a percentage of the waking day. Next, compare this figure with the listening estimates found sixty years ago. Do the students listen more or less?

9. Finally, have students review their listening schedules to compile a list of their listening activities. What did they listen to? Have them list their listening activities and see if they can evaluate which type of listening activity was most important in their lives. Older students can categorize their listening activities into types of listening and tabulate the amount of time they were involved in each type.

MY LISTENING ACTIVITIES

	How Often
Television programs	_____
Listening to directions	_____
Listening to a conversation	_____
Tapes/CDs	_____
School subjects	_____
Announcements and the like	_____

---

10. Comparisons can also be made among the time spent listening, speaking, reading, and writing. Percentages can be calculated for each type of activity in a day. These percentages can then be compared with the research results from sixty years ago.

PERCENTAGE OF TIME SPENT IN FORMS OF COMMUNICATION

	Sixty Years Ago (%)	*Today (%)*
Listening	42	_____
Speaking	32	_____
Reading	15	_____
Writing	11	_____

Activity 3–3:
THE LISTENING POST

TYPE	TERM
o CLASS	o STA
o GROUP	o LTA
● IND	● LC

Purpose:

1. To develop and improve auditory awareness
2. To identify sounds in the environment
3. To identify environmental locations characterized by specific sounds

Materials:

Paragraphs describing a journey and the sounds heard on that journey; paragraphs can be taped with the sounds heard replacing the identifying words (this activity is similar to a rebus story that uses pictures; instead of pictures replacing words, sounds replace words); a numbered card showing correct answers for the sounds and the location of the sound journey.

Grade level:

Lower and middle elementary, depending on the sound discrimination necessary to identify the sounds and their locations

Procedures:

1. Tape the sound journeys. Read the experiences describing the journey into the recorder; wherever a sound is specified, use a sound effect rather than the words. Pause after the sound effect so that students have an opportunity to identify the sound. Sounds may be obtained by taping actual sounds or using various sound effects recordings that contain appropriate sounds. Verbally number each sound journey on the tape. Prepare a numbered card showing the correct answers for the sound journey. (Use pictures when preparing cards for younger students.)

2. Examples of sound journeys and the corresponding self-correcting cards include the following:

   a. Sound journey number _____ .

   It is three o'clock in the afternoon, and you are entering a small, yellow, foreign sports car for your journey through sound. You put your key into the ignition and hear the roar of the [car engine]. It is a beautiful sunny day so you roll the window down to feel the warm air and hear the sounds around you. You have not gone far before you hear a [police whistle]. You have to stop your car and wait at the corner. As you wait you listen to the sounds. You hear people [talking] and [laughing]. You hear [trucks] going by, and an [air hammer] is being used to repair the street. You hear the [police whistle] again, and you can continue on your journey. You have gone a few blocks, and you must pull over to the side of the street. You hear a [fire truck siren] behind you. My, it is going fast. You continue down the street, and you know you must stop again when you hear the [railroad crossing bell]. You wait a few minutes, and you can hear the [train engine] as it rushes by. You know you have been on your sound journey for fifteen minutes because the [town clock] is chiming. You also know you are passing a school because you can hear children [yelling] on the playground. Whoops! You have been daydreaming. The light has changed, and you hear a [car horn]. The car passes you, and you can hear the [car radio] playing music. As you pass the high school, you can hear the [band playing], and if you were close enough, you could hear the [marching feet]. Your journey is now over, but you have had a chance to listen to the [sounds of the city].

Card number _____ .

Sounds, in order heard:

car engine
police whistle
talking
laughing
trucks
air hammer
police whistle
fire truck siren
railroad crossing bell
train engine
town clock
yelling
car horn
car radio
band playing
marching feet
Sounds of the city

---

b. Sound journey number _____ .

Just before the sun came up, a [cock-a-doodle-do] sound filled the air to wake me up and let me know it was time to get up and start this sound journey. I dressed quickly and ran out into the yard. As I ran across the yard, I almost stepped on a [quack]. The [quack, quack, quack] told me that I should watch where I was going. The next sound I heard was a loud [neigh] as I felt a wet nose nuzzle my arm for an apple. The [moo, moo] coming from the building told me that other animals wanted their breakfast. As I started to get the feed, a [squeak] ran from under the feed bin. The [meow] was on her feet and quickly followed the [squeak]. The [squeak] got to his hole before [meow] could get him. The [baas] were ready for their breakfast also and said so. The [bow-wow] joined the group with his song to let everyone know he was up and ready for the day.

The [moos] were given their breakfast and were preparing to be milked. The [honk], [cackle], [quack], and [gobble] were quick to get to [oink's] residence for any breakfast extras that might be left over. After all, [oink] is a messy eater.

The [cock-a-doodle-do], the [baa], the [neigh], the [meow], the [bow-wow], the [quack], the [cackle], the [gobble], the [oink], and the [moo] all settled down for a morning nap about 10:00. I was happy because I had an exciting sound journey on the [farm].

Place identifying animal names or pictures on a card corresponding with the number of this story.

c. Other sound journeys can be prepared for locations such as the airport, the zoo, the waterfront, a haunted house, an amusement park, or a train trip.

3. Students can divide into groups to prepare their own sound journeys, record them on tapes, and have other students identify the sounds and locations of the sounds.

Activity 3–4:
LISTENING FOR DIRECTIONS

TYPE	TERM
○ CLASS	○ STA
○ GROUP	○ LTA
● IND	● LC

Purpose:
1. To develop and improve attentive listening skills
2. To follow oral directions on a tape and place shapes in a described format
3. To reinforce identification of shapes (lower elementary)
4. To reinforce identification of colors (lower elementary)

Materials:
Circular, square, half-circular, triangular, rectangular, and curved shapes cut from various colors of felt; feltboard; tape containing oral directions for each activity; color-coded drawing illustrating correct placement for each activity.

Grade level:
Lower, middle, and upper elementary, depending on the difficulty level of oral instructions and terms used on the tape

Procedures:
1. Prepare a collection of different colored shapes cut from felt. This collection could include the following shapes cut from each of the basic colors: two circles; two smaller circles; two half-circles; two squares; two triangles; two rectangles; two curved shapes; two long, thin strips; and two short, thin strips.

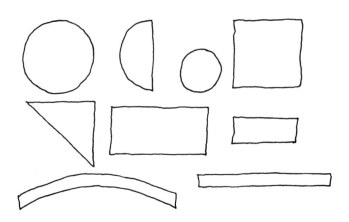

2. Tape-record the oral directions for turning the shapes into pictures. Number orally each activity on the tape. On separate cards, draw a picture of the resulting shape, color it correctly, number the card to correspond with the oral number on the

tape, and place the completed cards in a box so that students can use them for self-correcting their listening activity. Examples on the tape may range from simple to more complex directions, depending on the students' attentive listening ability. When the dialogue is read onto the tape, pause long enough for the students to carry out the direction. The following examples include both the taped directions and the corresponding cards for self-correction.

Examples:

Sailboats—Lower to Middle Elementary

a. Place two curved blue shapes on the center of the feltboard. Place them so that they both look like blue hills. Place a red half-circle on top of the left blue curved shape. Place the red half-circle so the straight side is facing the top of the feltboard. Place a green half-circle on top of the right blue curved shape. Place the green half-circle so that the straight side is facing the top of the feltboard. Place a purple triangle above the red half-circle. Place the purple triangle so that the tip of the long straight side touches the red half-circle and one point of the triangle faces the right side of the feltboard. Place an orange triangle above the green half-circle. Place the orange triangle so that the tip of the long straight side touches the green half-circle and one point of the triangle faces the right side of the feltboard. Place a large yellow circle in the right upper corner of the feltboard. Now look at your picture. What did you make? Check your listening skills by looking at card number _____ in the box.

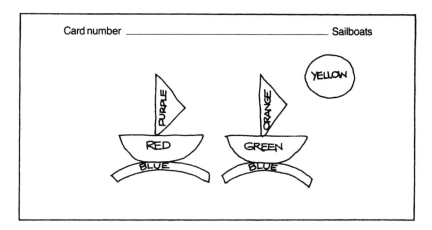

The Clown—Middle to Upper Elementary

b. Place an orange half-circle in the middle of the feltboard. Place a half-circle so that the curved part of the half-circle is toward the top of the feltboard. Now place a smaller yellow circle directly below the half-circle; the yellow circle should touch the bottom of the orange half-circle. Place an orange rectangle directly below the yellow circle; the rectangle should touch the circle. Place a long, thin, yellow strip next to the top left-hand side of the orange rectangle; angle the strip toward the bottom left-hand corner of the feltboard. Place a long, thin, black strip next to the top right-hand side of the orange rectangle and angle the strip toward the bottom right-hand corner of the feltboard. Place a red half-circle under the orange rectangle so that the curved side of the half-circle points to the left-hand side of the feltboard and the tip of the straight side touches the center of the bottom of the rectangle. Place a brown half-circle under the orange rectangle so that the curved side of the half-circle points to the right-hand side of the feltboard and the tip of the straight side touches the center of the bottom of the rectangle. Pull the bottom of the red and brown half-circles about an inch apart. Place a short yellow strip below the red half-circle; have the end of the strip pointing toward the left-hand side of the feltboard. Place a short black strip below the brown half-circle; have the end of the strip pointing toward the right-hand side of the feltboard. Look carefully at your design. What did you create? Check your listening skills by comparing your picture with card number _____ in the box.

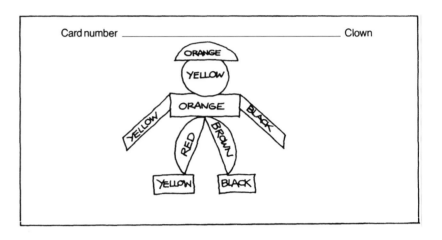

c. Many shape pictures may be described. Other suggestions include the following:

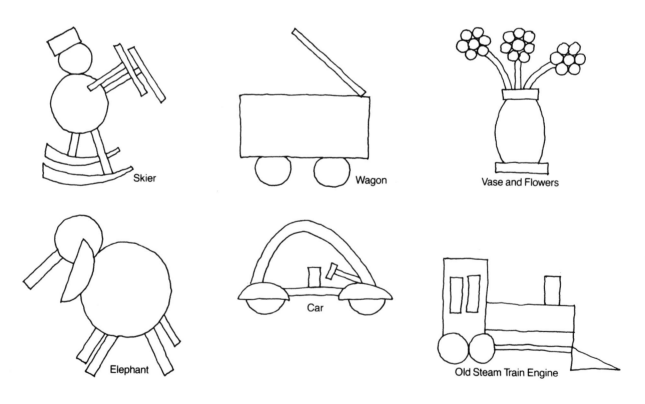

3. This activity may also be used as a group attentive listening activity by asking children to draw what they hear on the tape or what is read orally by the teacher.

4. Have children experiment with the shapes and ask them to write their own directions for other children to listen to and follow. Have them evaluate both their ability to give directions and their ability to listen to directions.

Activity 3–5:
THE CLASS CRIER

TYPE	TERM
● CLASS	● STA
● GROUP	○ LTA
○ IND	○ LC

Purpose:

1. To develop and improve attentive listening ability
2. To repeat class announcements, assignments, and special news concerning the class
3. To perform tasks required by the class announcements, assignments, and special news
4. To learn how people got the news in colonial times

Materials:

Sheet of paper with announcements or assignments for the day; a bell for special news, announcements, or assignments; pictures of a town crier.

Grade level:

Lower and middle elementary

Procedures:

1. Background information: In colonial times, there were very few newspapers; consequently, most towns had a town crier. The town crier walked through the streets calling out the news of the day. If the town crier had special news to tell, he rang a bell or banged on a drum. When the people heard the bell or the drum, they ran to the street to hear the news.
2. Show the class a picture of a town crier during colonial times. Ask the students if they know what the town crier is doing. If they do not know the job of the town crier, explain the town crier's duties and how he attracts attention.
3. Ask the students what the town crier might announce if he visited their class. Discuss suggestions with the class. Tell the students that you are going to use a "class crier" to inform them about special announcements, news, and class or group assignments.
4. Put the special announcements or assignments on a sheet of paper similar to one used by a town crier. Read the announcements or assignments to the class as if you were a colonial town crier. You may also use a bell to announce very important assignments or announcements. Ask individual members of the class to repeat the special announcements or assignments.

5. Have the students evaluate their attentive listening ability. Can they repeat announcements and assignments presented by the class crier? Can they perform the assignments announced by the class crier? Do they accomplish whatever is asked of them in the announcements? Do they believe their attentive listening is improving?

6. Students can take turns as a class crier who reads special announcements or news to the class. Develop a bulletin board of the class crier's announcements, assignments, and class news.

Activity 3-6:
THE MYSTERY OF THE KIDNAPPED CHEMIST

TYPE	TERM
o CLASS	o STA
o GROUP	o LTA
● IND	● LC

Purpose:
1. To develop and improve the ability to listen for sequential order
2. To identify the sequential order in a listening selection

Materials: Taped story of "The Mystery of the Kidnapped Chemist" (the selection can also be read orally to a group of students); the sound road map.

Grade level: Middle and upper elementary

Procedures:
1. Record the following dialogue on tape for use in the listening center or read the selection to a group of students. If the tape is used, number the activity, place complete directions on the tape, and describe the assigned follow-up activity to determine whether the students listened to the directions. Use sounds where stipulated in dialogue.

   You are going to have an opportunity to solve the case of the kidnapped chemist. The heroine in this story is a girl who invented a formula for making people invisible. Two companies want the formula; one company is honest, and the other one is not. When our heroine refuses to sell the formula to the dishonest company, its officials kidnap her, blindfold her, and put her in the backseat of a car. The kidnappers tell her that she will be taken to a secret laboratory where she will be forced to make the formula. She cannot see where the car will be taking her. She wonders how she will be able to tell the police how to find the secret laboratory; she knows she will try to escape, and she needs to know the location of that laboratory. The kidnappers have covered her eyes, but they have not covered her ears. She decides that if she listens carefully, she may be able to get enough clues to identify the route the car is traveling. She is afraid, however, that she will not be able to listen carefully enough to recognize all of the sounds and to remember in what order she hears them. The order is very important, since the sounds will form a sound road map and provide the clues for locating the secret laboratory. When you finish listening to the clues, you will mark her trip on a sound road map. Ready? The car is starting!
      The first sound she hears is a [church bell]. The sound is loud, so the car must be beside the sound. The car stops at the corner by the sound and turns toward the right. She can hear a new sound off in the distance. The car is coming closer to [zoo animal sounds]. As she rides past these sounds, she knows it is 8:00 because she can hear the [clock striking]. Many sounds are now heard in the sky. She can hear an [airplane] overhead. The road is getting bumpy, and she can hear [road construction noises]. Something big just passed the car. A pleasant sound is heard as the car travels on. She can hear [children laughing and talking] in the distance. She must be driving in the country because she can hear the sound of [frogs]. She hears a [railroad crossing bell] and thinks the car is stopping at a railroad crossing. The car moves ahead, slows, and stops. Her kidnappers tell her to get out because she has reached the secret laboratory. She

strains her hearing and thinks she hears the sound of [turkeys gobbling]. Can you help her remember her trip? Where did the car travel? Where is the secret laboratory? To show that you remember the car's movements, draw the direction the car took on the Sound Road Map in the listening center. After you have finished, listen to the tape a second time and check to see if you are correct. If you are not correct, draw in the right directions with a red pencil.

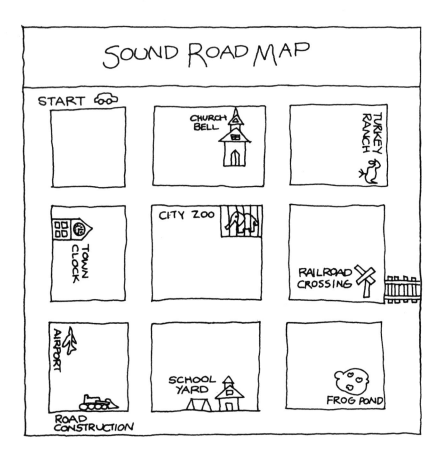

2. Other examples of sequential listening activities that may be recorded on tapes, which are also very good for use with lower elementary grades, are as follows:
   a. Select a number of interesting comic strips. Read the contents of the comic strips into a tape recorder. Cut the comic strips apart, number the correct sequential order on the back of each comic strip, and instruct the students to place each comic strip into correct sequential order after listening to the comic strip on the tape.
   b. Read sequentially developed stories, such as "Three Billy Goats Gruff," into a tape recorder. Instruct the students to use flannelboard figures to retell the story to a small group of students. Another way to assess the children's ability to place a story in correct sequence is to ask the students to draw the sequential order or to put sentences from the story into sequential order.
   c. Read sequentially ordered content-area materials onto tapes (e.g., science and social studies). Ask students to listen for signal words showing the sequence or organization of the paragraphs. For this activity, find materials that use terms such as *first, second, third, finally, to begin with, next, before, after, in conclusion,* and so forth.

Activity 3-7:
LISTENING FOR SEQUENCES

TYPE	TERM
● CLASS	● STA
● GROUP	○ LTA
● IND	○ LC

Purpose:
1. To listen attentively to identify important details
2. To place the details on a time line that shows sequences
3. To relate language arts and history

Materials:
Russell Freedman's *The Wright Brothers: How They Invented the Airplane* (1991).

Grade level:
Middle through upper elementary

Book summary:
The Wright Brothers: How They Invented the Airplane is a biography of the two brothers whose inventions and experiments revolutionized early flight experiments. The biography includes numerous photographs taken by Wilbur and Orville Wright.

Procedures:
1. Introduce the book and the time period to the students. Share and discuss the photographs that show the early experiments with gliders and airplanes. Tell the students that as you read the book to them, they will be listening to identify some of the most important details associated with Wilbur and Orville Wright and their inventions that led to the invention of the airplane.

2. Ask the students to draw a time line that begins with the years 1867-1871. On that time line they will place the important circumstances related in the book in the sequence in which they happened. Explain to the students that they should be able to support why they believe that each of the incidents is important in the lives of Wilbur and Orville Wright and their invention of the airplane. Because this is a longer book with several chapters, you may choose to read orally the first few chapters as the students listen for the information to place on the time line. You may complete the book during additional class periods, or the students may complete the book through their independent reading. The following time line was completed by fourth graders after listening to the first few chapters of the book:

1867–1871	1878	1889	1892	1899	1900	1903–1904
Wilbur's birth Orville's birth	Interest in flight begins with a toy powered by a twisted rubber band	Active in editing and publishing	Formed the Wright Cycle Company	Became interested in flight experiments Wrights' first experimental aircraft	Fly glider as unmanned kite and experiment with glider	Kitty Hawk First powered flight - 59 seconds. First flight by airplane — 1 minute, 36 seconds.

3. After listening to the book and developing the time line, ask students to respond to Amos Root's article in the January 1, 1905, *Gleanings in Bee Culture* when Root compared the Wright brothers with Christopher Columbus: "When Columbus discovered America he did not know what the outcome would be, and no one at that time knew. . . . In a like manner these two brothers have probably not even a faint glimpse of what their discovery is going to bring to the children of men" (p. 2). At this point students can do additional research and complete a time line of aviational history or research and present a report on how the achievements of the Wright brothers changed the world.

4. You may share informational books in which time lines are important. For example, read and discuss the impact of the time lines in Charles Micucci's *The Life and Times of the Apple* (1992) and *The Life and Times of the Peanut* (1997).

Activity 3–8:
LISTENING FOR DETAILS

TYPE	TERM
● CLASS	● STA
● GROUP	○ LTA
○ IND	○ LC

Purpose:
1. To develop a detailed description of an illustration
2. To listen attentively to descriptive details and to identify the correct picture
3. To relate a listening activity to geography

Materials:
Illustrations from books showing the same settings during different time periods, such as Jeannie Baker's *Window* (1991) and *Where the Forest Meets the Sea* (1988) and Ellen Levine's *The Tree That Would Not Die* (1995).

Grade level:
All grade levels, depending on the number of details developed in the descriptions

Book summaries:
Window presents detailed collage illustrations showing the same Australian setting as the setting changes over time. *Where the Forest Meets the Sea* includes prehistoric as well as possible future settings in Australia. *The Tree That Would Not Die* follows the life of the Treaty Oak in Austin, Texas, from a setting of buffalo to one of Native Americans, Spaniards, and pioneers, and finally to its contemporary setting surrounded by a city.

Procedures:
1. Divide the class into groups. Have one group compose a detailed description of one of the illustrations in *Window*. Ask another group to listen carefully, identify the appropriate illustration, and justify the decision. This activity may require several opportunities for descriptions and identifications. After the initial description, students may discuss why they could or could not identify the correct illustration. They may develop guidelines that help them provide accurate descriptions and listen for details. Older students may relate this activity to the theme of the book: People affect the environment. They may also describe the person-versus-society conflict developed in the illustrations by describing how rapidly a community changes from rural to urban and the possible consequences as the family eventually moves to another rural area.

2. Continue this activity by encouraging students to describe an illustration in *Where the Forest Meets the Sea*.

3. More detailed descriptions of the setting and listening for details including changes in areas such as transportation, clothing, people, and buildings are possible using the illustrations in *The Tree That Would Not Die*. Careful examination of the illustrations can easily accompany a theme of the changing geography of locations.

4. Students may divide into groups and create their own depictions of their town or city during different time periods. The depictions could include either photographs or drawings. Careful descriptions and listening for details will be necessary as students try to identify the correct illustrations and even the time period for the illustrations.

Activity 3–9:
LISTENING TO PREDICT OUTCOMES—PART I

	TYPE	TERM
	● CLASS	● STA
	○ GROUP	○ LTA
	○ IND	○ LC

Purpose:
1. To increase abilities and predict outcomes
2. To listen to an enjoyable story and to use details in the story to predict outcomes
3. To use repetitive language to predict outcomes
4. To take part in an oral language activity and to act out the words and actions

Materials: Michael Rosen's *We're Going on a Bear Hunt* (1989).

Grade level: Lower elementary

Book summary: *We're Going on a Bear Hunt* is a popular repetitive rhyme in which a family goes on a bear hunt. The repetitive text has them going through grass, across a river, through mud, through a forest, through a snowstorm, and finally into a cave where they meet the fearsome bear and backtrack their way home. The repetition encourages students to predict what will happen next and join in the reading. The terms used by the author to go through grass and so forth encourage acting out the vocabulary.

Procedures:
1. This is such an enjoyable book that it naturally encourages students to predict the language and join the reading. Before reading the book aloud to the students, tell them that they should join you in the reading as soon as they know what will be next. Also tell them that as you read the story to them, they will be acting out the words that describe how the family goes through the grass, the river, the mud, the forest, the snowstorm, and the cave.

2. Begin reading the book as the students listen. (They should be standing so that they can act out the vocabulary.) Notice how rapidly they join in the repetitive portion of the text:

   > We're going on a bear hunt.
   > We're going to catch a big one.
   > What a beautiful day!
   > We're not scared.

3. As you approach the first obstacle, let the students act out going through the grass: "Swishy swashy! Swishy swashy! Swishy swashy!"

4. Continue reading the text, allowing the students to join in with the language. Have them act out each of the actions as they cross the various obstacles.

5. On their return trip from the cave remind the students that they will be going through the same obstacles, but they will be proceeding backward. Encourage the students to act out each part as they proceed back to the safety of the house.

6. Students usually want to repeat this book numerous times. It does not take many repetitions before the students can predict accurately what will happen next and the language that will be used. Ask the following: "What made this book easy for you to read along with me?"

Activity 3–10:
LISTENING TO PREDICT OUTCOMES—PART II

TYPE	TERM
● CLASS	● STA
● GROUP	● LTA
● IND	○ LC

Purpose:
1. To increase abilities to predict outcomes
2. To listen to an enjoyable story and to use details in the story to predict outcomes
3. To verify predictions after listening to a book
4. To integrate language arts, social studies, and geography

Materials:
Lloyd Alexander's *The Remarkable Journey of Prince Jen* (1991).

Grade level:
Upper elementary and middle school

Book summary:
The Remarkable Journey of Prince Jen is a fantasy quest with an Asian setting. Although the book is a fantasy, Alexander integrates numerous details and beliefs from the Chinese culture. The writing style motivates predicting outcomes because each chapter concludes with comments and questions that can be used to ask students to orally hypothesize about what will happen in the next chapter or to write their own next chapter.

Procedures:
1. Introduce the setting by asking students to view and discuss the map at the beginning of the novel. As they look at the map they can predict the type of setting for the book and the genre of literature it belongs to. For example, they will find names such as the Kingdom of T'ien-Kuo and the cities of Chai-sang and Ch'an-gan. They will notice that all of these place names sound Chinese. However, they will also notice that there is a mountain called the Mountain of Sorcerers. This name should lead them to believe that the story may be a fantasy.

2. Next, introduce the book in a way that encourages students to make predictions. For example, ask the following: "Have you ever thought about the consequences of your choices? If you had two choices, what would have happened if you had done _____ instead of _____ ? Would things have been different? As you read Lloyd Alexander's *The Remarkable Journey of Prince Jen* you will learn just how important choices can be. You will also discover the importance of objects that at first seem quite usual. How would you react if you were told that you must take six gifts in homage as you travel to the legendary court of T'ien-Kuo to learn about how to govern more wisely? Why do you think you would be asked to take each of these objects: a saddle, a sword, a paint box, a bowl, a kite, and a flute? The author also uses an interesting technique at the close of each chapter to involve your responses and to have you predict outcomes. As you listen to this book, we will stop at the end of each chapter and try to answer the author's questions before we proceed to the next chapter."

3. After introducing and discussing the book, read the first chapter aloud to the students. Stop at the end of the chapter and read Alexander's statement and question: "Our hero is eager to start his journey, but Master Wu seems to be casting a dark shadow on a bright prospect. What can be the difficulty? To find out, read the next chapter" (p. 8). Ask the students to predict what they think the difficulty

is and to speculate about the conflict that will be developing in the next chapter. After they have made their predictions, read chapter 2 to verify and compare their predictions with Alexander's plot. You may continue reading this book to the class and asking students to predict outcomes, or the students may read the remainder of the book and write their own predictions or write their own chapters.

4. Choices and questions are also very important in the text. Students can respond to these choices by considering whether, if the character would have done _____ instead of _____, things would have been different. They can then speculate about these differences.

5. The book may also be related to social studies and geography. As students listen to or read the book they may identify details and beliefs that are characteristic of the Chinese culture.

6. Brian Jacques's *Pearls of Lutra: A Tale from Redwall* (1997) is another book that may be used to predict outcomes. The author provides a series of clues presented in riddles that allow the animal inhabitants of Redwall to locate each of six Tears of All Seas (pearls).

Activity 3–11:
LISTENING FOR SUPPORTIVE EVIDENCE IN LITERATURE

TYPE	TERM
● CLASS	○ STA
● GROUP	● LTA
● IND	○ LC

Purpose:

1. To increase enjoyment by listening to a story
2. To increase critical evaluation ability
3. To identify evidence that supports a position
4. To analyze variants in folktales
5. To relate language arts and social studies

Materials:

William H. Hooks's *Moss Gown* (1987); books that provide additional information, if required: Charles and Mary Lamb's *Tales from Shakespeare* (1986), E. Nesbit's *Beautiful Stories from Shakespeare* (facsimile of the 1907 edition), Joseph Jacobs's "Tattercoats" in Sutherland and Livingston's *The Scott, Foresman Anthology of Children's Literature* (1984), and various Cinderella stories such as the ones collected by the Brothers Grimm and Charles Perrault.

Grade level:

Middle elementary through middle school

Book summaries:

Moss Gown is a Cinderella variant collected in the Tidewater section of eastern North Carolina. The story has elements from Cinderella and King Lear, English elements, and elements related to the time and place of the oral storytellers. *Tales from Shakespeare* and *Beautiful Stories from Shakespeare* both contain easier and shorter versions of Shakespeare's *King Lear.* "Tattercoats" is an English version of Cinderella. Any of the Brothers Grimm or Charles Perrault versions of Cinderella can be used if required to help students review Cinderella elements.

Procedures:

1. To begin this activity remind the students that some folktales have common story types found in cultures throughout the world. These folktales are called *variants* because they have basic elements in common but frequently differ in such areas as settings, names of characters, magical objects, tasks to be completed, and obstacles to be overcome.

2. Ask students to read or listen to several of the common Cinderella stories, such as those retold by the Brothers Grimm (German) or Charles Perrault (French). Also read the English version, "Tattercoats." Ask the students to identify common elements that are found in these stories. Remind the students that the common elements should be general such as "The heroine has a lowly position in the family." Ask the students to identify and list the common elements. Student lists may be similar to the following:

   a. The heroine has a lowly position in the family.
   b. The heroine is persecuted by stepsisters or other members of the family.
   c. The heroine accomplishes difficult tasks.
   d. The heroine has an opportunity meet a person who has great worth within the culture.
   e. The heroine is kept from meeting the person of great worth because she lacks clothing to attend a function.
   f. The heroine is helped by a supernatural being.

g. The heroine is warned to return by a certain time.

h. The person of great worth is attracted to the heroine.

i. There is a test for the rightful heroine.

j. The heroine passes the test and marries the person of great worth.

Ask the students to identify how each of these common elements are developed in the German, French, and English variants.

3. After identifying and discussing these common elements, ask students what they think would happen if the people who told the tales and listened to the stories moved to a new land. Ask the following: "Would they take their oral stories with them? How do you think the stories might change over the years to reflect different settings or cultures?" Encourage the students to speculate about such areas as differences in settings, occupations, foods, and activities. Tell the students that as they listen to *Moss Gown,* another variant of the Cinderella story, they should search for (a) Cinderella elements, (b) references to time and place, and (c) evidence of the European country the early storytellers came from. (If desired, students also can search for King Lear elements in this tale. If they are not familiar with the story of King Lear they can listen to or read one of the King Lear versions written for younger audiences.)

4. Read *Moss Gown* aloud to students as they listen for and list the various elements. For example, students should identify the following Cinderella elements:

   a. The heroine, a generous young girl, has two greedy older sisters.

   b. The heroine has a helper with supernatural powers.

   c. The heroine has a gown that changes to rags at a specified time.

   d. The heroine is given the hardest kitchen work.

   e. An important person holds a dance.

   f. The heroine cannot attend the dance because she lacks a dress.

   g. A supernatural being casts a spell and provides a dress.

   h. An order is given that must be followed.

   i. The important person dances only with the heroine.

   j. The important person and the heroine are married.

5. After identifying and discussing the Cinderella elements, the students can identify and discuss the references to time and place, such as the following:

   a. a great plantation

   b. a house with eight marble columns

   c. fine fields

   d. riding and hunting in the mysterious swamp

   e. black-green cypress treetops

   f. gray Spanish moss

   g. the word used to cast a spell is a French word used in the Carolinas

   h. important person holds a frolic

6. Students should discuss how these references to time and place reflect the new environment of the original storytellers. They should also identify where they think the story takes place. Students might identify the following evidence that shows that the original storytellers had English backgrounds:

   a. The similarities to the British "Tattercoats" include servants who mistreat the girl and a man of wealthy position who loves her even though she is dressed in rags.

   b. Activities such as riding and hunting are commonly found in England.

   c. The King Lear elements reflect knowledge of the English playwright Shakespeare.

7. Students can also identify the King Lear elements in *Moss Gown* and speculate why the ending is slightly changed from Shakespeare's *King Lear.* They may discuss why they believe the ending would need to be changed to create a more Cinderella-like variant.

Activity 3–12:
LISTENING FOR MOOD

TYPE	TERM
● CLASS	● STA
● GROUP	○ LTA
○ IND	○ LC

Purpose:
1. To develop and improve critical listening and thinking skills
2. To focus attention on the author's use of language to create mood
3. To visualize mental images stimulated by listening to text
4. To verbalize responses about a book

Materials:
Any edition of Mark Twain's *Adventures of Huckleberry Finn*. The edition edited by Walter Blair and Victor Fischer (1985) contains the original text and illustrations.

Grade level:
Middle school

Book summary:
Adventures of Huckleberry Finn relates, in Huck's own words, the adventures that he and a runaway slave named Jim have as they travel on a raft down the Mississippi River to escape from slavery and "sivilization."

Procedures:
1. Before reading the following three passages from *Adventures of Huckleberry Finn,* discuss setting and mood with students. The setting of a story—its location in time and place—helps readers share what the characters see, smell, hear, and touch. Authors use settings to create moods. Through word choices and the visual pictures created by words, authors create moods that range from humorous and happy to frightening and foreboding.

2. In each passage Huck Finn experiences "lonesomeness" as he describes what he sees and hears. As you read each passage, have students close their eyes and imagine that they are Huck Finn and that they see what he sees and hear what he hears.

3. In the first passage, it is late in the evening; everyone has gone to sleep and Huck is alone in his room at the Widow Douglas's place. Direct students to close their eyes and imagine themselves alone in their rooms late at night. Tell them to think about what they see, what they hear, and how they feel.

> I went up to my room with a piece of candle and put it on the table. Then I set down in a chair by the window and tried to think of something cheerful, but it warn't no use. I felt so lonesome I most wished I was dead. The stars was shining, and the leaves rustled in the woods ever so mournful; and I heard an owl, away off, who-whooing about somebody that was dead, and a whippowill and a dog crying about somebody that was going to die; and the wind was trying to whisper something to me and I couldn't make out what it was, and so it made the cold shivers run over me. Then away out in the woods I heard that kind of a sound that a ghost makes when it wants to tell about something that's on its mind and can't make itself understood, and so can't rest easy in its grave and has to go about that way every night grieving. I got so downhearted and scared, I did wish I had some company. . . . [T]he house was all as still as

death. . . . [A]fter a long time I heard the clock away off in the town go boom—boom—boom—twelve licks—and all still again—stiller than ever. Pretty soon I heard a twig snap, down in the dark amongst the tree—something was a stirring. I set still and listened. (pp. 4–5)

4. Ask students questions such as the following: "What could you see? Could you see the darkness? What could you hear? Could you hear the twig snap and the ghostly wind whisper? How did you feel? What made you feel this way?"

5. In the next passage Huck has just escaped from Pap's cabin. Before his river journey begins, he is by himself and hiding out for a few days on Jackson's Island. When he sees a storm approach he takes shelter at the entrance of a cave. Again, have students close their eyes, but this time have them imagine that they are with Huck at the entrance of the cave during the storm.

Pretty soon it darkened up and began to thunder and lighten. . . . [I]t begun to rain, and it rained like all fury, too, and I never see the wind blow so. It was one of these regular summer storms. It would get so dark that it looked all blue-black outside, and lovely; and the rain would thrash along by so thick that the trees off a little ways looked dim and spider-webby; and here would come a blast of wind that would bend the trees down and turn up the pale underside of the leaves; and then a perfect ripper of a gust would follow along and set the branches to tossing their arms as if they was just wild; and next, when it was just about the bluest and blackest—*fst!* it was as bright as glory, and you'd have a little glimpse of treetops a-plunging about away off yonder in the storm, hundreds of yards further than you could see before; dark as sin again in a second, and now you'd hear the thunder let go with an awful crash, and then go rumbling, grumbling, tumbling down the sky towards the under side of the world, like rolling empty barrels down-stairs—where it's long stairs and they bounce a good deal, you know. "[T]his is nice," I says. "I wouldn't want to be nowhere else but here." (pp. 59–60)

6. Ask students questions such as the following: "What did you see? Could you see the lightning and the treetops blowing in the wind? What could you hear? Could you hear the thunder and the barrels rolling down the stairs? How did you feel? Frightened or comforted? What made you feel this way?"

7. In the third passage, Huck and Jim are on the raft traveling down the Mississippi River. Now have students close their eyes and think about what they see and how they feel as Huck describes the sunrise:

[The raft] slid along so quiet and smooth and lovely. . . . Not a sound, anywhere—perfectly still—just like the whole world was asleep. . . . The first thing to see, looking away over the water, was a kind of dull line—that was the woods on t'other side; you couldn't make nothing else out; then a pale place in the sky; then more paleness spreading around; then the river softened up away off, and warn't black any more, but gray . . . and you see the mist curl up off of the water, and the east reddens up, and the river. . . . [T]hen the nice breeze springs up, and comes fanning you from over there, so cool and fresh and sweet to smell on account of the woods and the flowers . . . and next you've got the full day, and everything smiling in the sun, and the songbirds just going it! . . . [W]e would watch the lonesomeness of the river, and kind of lazy along, and by and by lazy off to sleep. Wake up by and by . . . there wouldn't be nothing to hear nor nothing to see—just solid lonesomeness. . . . So we would put in the day, lazying around, listening to the stillness. . . . It's lovely to live on a raft. (pp. 156–158)

8. Ask students questions such as the following: "What did you see? Could you see the sun coming up? What did you hear? Could you imagine the stillness? How did this passage make you feel? Did you notice differences in how the three passages made you feel?"

9. Discuss the different moods created by the word *lonesomeness*. From listening to these three passages taken from the same book you can see how powerful language is and how an author uses language to create different moods.

Activity 3–13:
DEVELOPING LISTENING COMPREHENSION THROUGH ELVES

TYPE	TERM
● CLASS	● STA
● GROUP	○ LTA
○ IND	○ LC

Purpose:

1. To improve listening comprehension
2. To focus attention on the literary elements
3. To listen to predict outcomes and verify predictions
4. To visualize mental images stimulated by listening to text
5. To verbalize responses about a book

Materials:

Ann Grifalconi's *Darkness and the Butterfly* (1987), David McPhail's *The Dream Child* (1985), and Nancy Willard's *Night Story* (1981). This activity is based on Levesque's (1989) ELVES approach to developing listening comprehension.

Grade level:

Lower and middle elementary

Book summaries:

Darkness and the Butterfly is an African story about a girl who is afraid of the dark and learns to overcome her fear and even appreciate the dark. *The Dream Child* and *Night Story* are illustrated poems about children who experience adventures in their dreams.

Procedures:

1. ELVES is a five-part read-aloud strategy that progresses through the following sequence of activities: (a) *excite,* in which the discussion focuses on the listeners' experiences, the literary elements within the story, and predictions about the story; (b) *listen,* in which students listen to verify predictions and to comprehend other story elements; (c) *visualize,* in which listeners share their mental images; (d) *extend,* in which the students gain new understandings by relating previous and new knowledge; and (e) *savor,* in which students reflect on the story, verbalize their responses, and become involved with follow-up activities such as writing or readers' theater. The following example shows how the ELVES strategy may be developed with *Darkness and the Butterfly*:

   a. *Excite:* Begin the discussion by posing questions that encourage the students to relate their own experiences to various elements within the story. For example, ask students the following: "Have you ever been really afraid of the dark? How did you feel when you were afraid? How did you get over your fear? Was it important that you got over your fear? Why or why not? Pretend that you live in Africa. What could you see and hear when it is light? What could you see and hear when it is dark? Does your imagination cause you to see and hear things that might not really be there? If you were this child living in Africa, do you think you would be more afraid of what you can see in the light or what your imagination lets you see in the dark? If you were this African child, how would you get over your fear?" After students share experiences about being afraid in the dark, you can ask questions that encourage students to share additional responses and predictions about the title and the cover illustration. For example, "What do you think the author means by the title *Darkness and the Butterfly?* When you look at the front cover and the back cover, describe the feelings that you get. (If the cover has been removed from the book, ask students to look at several illustrations in the book that show both daylight and darkness.) Do you have different feelings when you look at the front cover than when you look at the back cover? Why do you have those feelings? What do you think will happen to the child on the cover? What kind of a mood do you think will be developed in the story?"

b. *Listen:* Now read the story and ask students to listen so that they can confirm or reject their earlier responses and predictions. The students might use signals in particular places in the story to show that they were right or wrong.

c. *Visualize:* You may choose especially vivid sections of the book and ask students to close their eyes and describe what they see and feel as you read or reread these parts. For example, ask students the following: "What do you see, feel, and hear in this setting: 'Have you ever been afraid of the dark? Of being alone in the night when strange things float by that seem to follow you . . . [with] eyes that glow in the darkness?' (p. 1 unnumbered)." Or, "What do you see, feel, and hear in this contrasting setting: 'She was floating up through the air like the butterfly. Flying along with the moon. High in the night sky over her village! Then she looked about her and saw that the night was not really dark at all!' (unnumbered)." You can extend this visualization portion of the activity by asking students to compare the girl in the first setting with the girl in the second setting. Ask the following: "What do you know has happened to the girl between your visualizing of the first setting and the second setting? How do you know that this change has taken place?"

d. *Extend:* Lead a discussion in which students make connections between their previous knowledge and any new insights they gain from listening and reacting to this story. For example, ask students questions such as the following: "How did the illustrator let you know that the girl was first afraid of the dark and then that she was no longer afraid of the dark? How did the author let you know that it is alright to have fears? How did the author let you know that we can overcome our own fears?" You can also extend this story into other settings. For example, "How might the story change if it took place in a city? How might the story be similar?"

e. *Savor:* Students can savor the story by describing additional thoughts and feelings about the story. They could respond to the following proverb about the butterfly and discuss how the proverb relates to the story: "Darkness pursues the butterfly." Students could develop a readers' theater production using *Darkness and the Butterfly.* You can also share and discuss additional books that have night settings, such as *The Dream Child* and *Night Story.* Both of these books create warm, happy moods as children interact with pleasant experiences in their dreams.

Activity 3–14:
POOR RICHARD

TYPE	TERM
● CLASS	● STA
● GROUP	○ LTA
○ IND	○ LC

Purpose:

1. To evaluate and interpret proverbs in Benjamin Franklin's *Poor Richard's Almanac*
2. To develop critical listening and thinking skills
3. To develop divergent thought processes and discussion skills

Materials:

Sayings from *Poor Richard's Almanac;* reference materials about Benjamin Franklin and the Revolutionary War; biographies that provide information about Benjamin Franklin's life, such as James Daugherty's *Poor Richard* (1941), Jean Fritz's *What's the Big Idea, Ben Franklin?* (1978), and Milton Meltzer's *Benjamin Franklin: The New American* (1988).

Grade level

Middle and upper elementary, middle school

Book summaries:

Poor Richard covers Franklin's life and activities. *What's the Big Idea, Ben Franklin?* is an easier biography about the inventor, ambassador, and coauthor of the Declaration of Independence. *Benjamin Franklin: The New American* is a carefully documented biography of the American statesman.

Procedures:

1. Background information: Benjamin Franklin published a yearly magazine called *Poor Richard's Almanac,* beginning in 1732. It contained weather reports, news about the tides, cooking lessons, poems, and other information for the common people. The almanac was entertaining as well as useful and was very popular. The most famous part of the almanac became the proverbs, or wise sayings, that Franklin either wrote himself or took from the writings of other wise men. He often changed the words when he chose someone else's proverbs so that his readers would understand them. Many of the proverbs stress the desirability of hard work and frugality to help a person become virtuous, wealthy, and wise.

2. Explain the background of *Poor Richard's Almanac* to the students. Discuss the time in history when Benjamin Franklin lived and wrote the almanac.

3. Read some of the proverbs from *Poor Richard's Almanac* to the students. Ask them to listen to the proverb and explain what they believe the proverb means. Ask students to share the reasons for their interpretations. Ask them if they believe the

proverb is still as worthwhile today as it was in the 1700s. Why or why not? Some of the proverbs include the following:

Eat to live, not live to eat.
Early to bed and early to rise makes a man healthy, wealthy, and wise.
When you're good to others you're good to yourself.
Content makes poor men rich; discontent makes rich men poor.
The wise man draws more from his enemies than the fool from his friends.
Keep conscience dear, then never fear.
Pardoning the bad is injuring the good.
Wealth and content are not always bedfellows.
Doing an injury puts you below your enemy; Revenging one makes you but even with him; Forgiving it sets you above him.
Words may show a man's wit, but actions show his meaning.
The sleeping fox catches no poultry. Up! Up!
Beware of little expenses; a small leak will sink a great ship.
There are lazy minds as well as lazy bodies.
Who is strong? He that can conquer his bad habits.
Lost time is never found again.
The used key is always bright.

4. Develop a class almanac of proverbs.

5. Develop a bulletin board of Poor Richard's proverbs and drawings illustrating the meaning of the proverbs.

6. Encourage students to read and discuss a biography of Benjamin Franklin. Have them give oral reports in which they relate the proverbs to some instance in Benjamin Franklin's life. Encourage the class to listen carefully and ask questions about Franklin's life and about the proverbs.

Activity 3-15:
PLAYING DETECTIVE WITH FAIRY-TALE HEROES

TYPE	TERM
○ CLASS	○ STA
○ GROUP	○ LTA
● IND	● LC

Purpose:

1. To identify the fairy-tale character represented by a descriptive paragraph
2. To identify details that support the character's identification
3. To identify details that do not support the character's identification
4. To reinforce stories heard or read

Materials:

Paragraphs describing fairy-tale characters (may be tape-recorded with answers placed on self-correcting cards or read orally by the teacher while the students analyze the answers).

Grade level:

Lower and middle elementary, depending on the characters used (activity 1 is easier than activities 2 or 3, which require students to evaluate inconsistent statements)

Procedures:

1. Prepare paragraphs describing characters from fairy tales. For example:
   a. When I was a child, my mother told me to sell our old cow. I bought some beans from a man. He said the beans were magic. I brought them home and showed them to my mother. She scolded me and sent me to bed. She was angry and threw the beans out the window. In the night, the beans sprouted and began growing. When I woke up, I saw a large beanstalk that grew up into the sky. I climbed the stalk to the top. I walked along a long road until I came to a huge house. I asked a great big tall woman for some breakfast. She warned me that her husband was a giant who loved boiled boys on toast. Who am I?

(*Answer:* Jack and the Beanstalk)

b. One day I was going to take a cake and some other goodies to my grand-mother, who was not feeling very well. My grandmother lives out in the woods so I had quite a way to go. When I walked into the woods, I met a wolf. He asked me where I was going and what I was carrying in my basket. I stopped to pick some flowers and finally reached my grandmother's house. I was surprised because grandmother's door was open, and I could walk right in. When I told my grandmother that she had big ears she said, "The better to hear you with." Believe me, I had quite an adventure that day. Who am I?

(*Answer:* Little Red Riding Hood)

Have the students identify the fairy-tale character and ask them to defend the reasons for making their identification.

2. For a critical listening activity, write paragraphs in which the majority of the sentences pertain to a familiar fairy-tale character. Include one or two sentences inconsistent with that character. Instruct the students to listen carefully to the paragraph so that they can identify the character who is speaking, the details that support the identification of the character, and the details that are not correct for that character. For example:

When I was a young girl, I was very happy until my mother, the queen, died, and my father married again. My stepmother was so jealous that she sent me out into the deep woods with a hunter, who was told to take my life. The hunter could not do this. *I roamed the woods until I found a huge castle with many rooms* (inconsistent). Inside this house, I found a table set with seven little plates and seven little beds ready for the night. I was lucky because the seven little men told me I could live with them. My stepmother was very angry when she found out I was living with the seven little men. *She mixed an evil spell and turned me into an apple* (inconsistent). The spell was finally broken and I lived happily ever after.

After the students listen to the paragraph, have them identify the character and the supporting details. Ask them to explain why these details support their choice of character. Next, have them identify the two details that are incorrect for that fairy-tale character. Have them evaluate why the two statements are incorrect.

A COTTAGE IS NOT
A CASTLE.

(*Answer:* Snow White) Incorrect details: I roamed the woods until I found a huge castle with many rooms (it was a small cottage). She mixed an evil spell and (turned me into an apple (the spell was placed on an apple—Snow White was not turned into an apple).

3. Have students develop their own paragraphs describing a fairy-tale character. Ask them to place one or two incorrect statements in the paragraph. Have them share these paragraphs with other students, who will listen for supporting details and identify incorrect statements.

Activity 3–16:
PLAYING DETECTIVE WITH FAMOUS AMERICANS

TYPE	TERM
o CLASS	o STA
o GROUP	o LTA
● IND	● LC

Purpose:

1. To identify the persons in history who might have made particular statements or described themselves
2. To select details identifying a historical figure
3. To apply previous knowledge of a historical figure to evaluate whether a viewpoint is consistent with that person
4. To identify details that are inconsistent with a person or time period
5. To reinforce learning in social studies and history

Materials:

Paragraphs written to present specific people in history, their accomplishments, viewpoints, values, or backgrounds.

Grade level:

Middle and upper elementary or middle school, depending on the historical figures used and in which grade those people are studied (activities 2 and 3 are more difficult than activity 1, because they require students to evaluate inconsistent statements)

Procedures:

1. Develop paragraphs or short stories about famous people in history; delete the name of the person in the description. You can write the dialogue in first person so that students have to listen for supporting details to identify the person. Try to illustrate both male and female heroes as well as heroes from various minority groups. Examples of paragraphs include the following:

   a. I was very proud in 1905 when I was named to the Hall of Fame for Great Americans. You may be wondering how I happened to be given this great honor. When I was a child, I spent many hours with my father in his observatory. I later went to school and studied mathematics and read a great deal about navigation. One evening while I was in my father's observatory looking through the telescope, I saw a faint and hazy object in the sky where no object had even been observed. This discovery made me famous. I was awarded Denmark's gold medal for being the first person to discover a telescopic comet. I became a professor of astronomy at Vassar and made many more astronomical discoveries. I believe that women can succeed in the sciences. Who am I?

   (*Answer:* Maria Mitchell, the first American astronomer to discover a telescopic comet)

b. When I was growing up, I lived in Boston with thirteen brothers and sisters. My father wanted me to work for him. He made candles to sell to the people of Boston. I did not want to make candles; I wanted to write articles and print my own newspaper. I worked as an apprentice in my brother James's printing shop. We did not get along very well, so after a few years, I moved to Philadelphia to look for a job in a print shop. I was fortunate, and by the time I was 22, I owned my own newspaper, *The Pennsylvania Gazette.* One of my most famous publications was an almanac that contained weather predictions, important dates to remember, and advice in the form of proverbs. I always had many ideas and enjoyed inventing things. I invented a stove that fit into a fireplace and sent heat out into a room rather than up the chimney. My most famous experiment proved that electricity and lightning are the same; in fact, I invented the lightning rod. I became involved in politics and worked for the colonies during the American Revolution. I was proud of my work. I was the only person who signed all of these papers: The Declaration of Independence, the treaty with France, the peace treaty with England, and the Constitution of the United States. Who am I?

(*Answer:* Benjamin Franklin)

c. When I was a boy, I wanted to go to school more than anything else. This was not easy, however, because I had to leave home to go to school. The local schools would not let me attend. I even had to earn my own money while I was away from home. I washed and ironed clothes, cooked, and swept floors for people so I had enough money to sleep, eat, and buy books. This was not an easy life. In 1894 I finally earned a college degree in agriculture from Iowa State College. I chose agriculture because I felt that agriculture could open the door of freedom for my people. I took a job teaching at Tuskegee University in Alabama so I could help my people learn how to prepare land to grow better crops. One morning, as I was walking to the university, I saw a strange plant growing at the edge of a field. I asked a farmer what the plant was, and he told me it was useless goobers. I found out that the plant produced peanuts. Since the peanuts would grow in soil that would not raise cotton, I decided it could not be useless. I started to experiment with peanuts and discovered more than 300 products that could be made from this very useful plant. When I died in 1943, these words were written on my gravestone: "He could have added fortune to fame, but caring for neither, he found happiness and honor in being helpful to the world." Who am I?

(*Answer:* George Washington Carver)

Have the students identify the famous person described in each paragraph. Have them identify important details, the point at which they could identify the person, and details that might be similar for more than one person in history.

2. For a more demanding critical listening activity, develop paragraphs as in the previous activity but include one or two sentences inconsistent with that person's values, accomplishments, or time in history. Instruct the students to listen carefully to the paragraph so that they can identify the person who is speaking, the details that support the identification, and the details that are not consistent with that person or time in history. For example:

When I was 17 years old, I joined a wagon train to help settlers moving west. I learned a great deal about the mountains and the western country. In 1842 I met Lieutenant John Fremont of the United States Army. He was planning an expedition to California to explore the land and report back to the government in

Washington. He had heard that I was a well-known trailblazer, and asked me to be the guide for the journey. *Fremont offered to pay me five hundred dollars a month for my services* (inconsistent with time in history). When we finally crossed the mountains and reached California, we found that the United States had declared war on Mexico. We were told to capture Monterey, San Diego, and Los Angeles for the American government. We were successful. *A dispatch was sent back on the transcontinental railroad informing the president that California had been captured* (inconsistent with time in history). I returned to California again as a guide for General Kearny. We were ambushed by the Mexican army. I reached Fort Stockton to get help by crawling through bushes, high grass, and thick brush. After that experience, I explored much of the western United States and became well known as an Indian fighter. Who am I?

(*Answer*: Kit Carson) Incorrect details: (Fremont offered to pay me five hundred dollars a month for my services. (The sum was one hundred dollars a month; five hundred dollars would have been unheard of in the 1840s.) A dispatch was sent back on the transcontinental railroad informing the president that California had been captured. (The transcontinental railroad was not completed until 1869.)

After the students listen to the paragraph, ask them to identify the person in history, list the supporting details, and tell why these details support their choice. Next, have them identify the two details in the paragraph that are inconsistent with the time of history presented in the paragraph. Have them evaluate why the two statements are incorrect.

3. Ask students to develop their own paragraphs describing famous people in history. Ask them to place one or two incorrect statements in the paragraph and share these paragraphs with other students, who will listen for supporting details and identify incorrect statements.

4. Students can write conversations between two people in history and then read them for other students to identify.

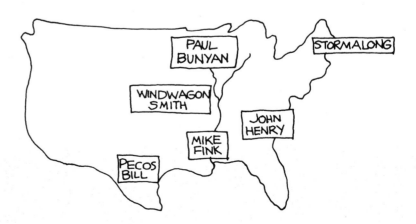

5. This type of critical listening activity can also focus on subjects other than famous Americans from history. Some other topics and suggestions for famous people might include the following:

   a. Which Tall-Tale Hero Am I?

Paul Bunyan	Davy Crockett
Pecos Bill	Mike Fink
Windwagon Smith	Captain Stormalong

   b. Which World Hero Am I?

Winston Churchill	Golda Meir
Marie Curie	Mohandas Gandhi
Dag Hammarskjöld	Sigmund Freud
Albert Schweitzer	Maria Montessori

   c. Which Famous African American Am I? (A source for identifications is *Profiles of Black Americans,* by Richard A. Boning [New York: Dexter & Westbrook, 1969].) Some possibilities include the following:

   > Patricia Roberts Harris (first African-American woman to represent the United States as an ambassador)
   > Shirley Chisholm (first African-American woman elected to Congress)
   > Ralph Bunche (worked for world peace as ambassador to the United Nations; winner of Nobel Peace Prize)
   > Bill Pickett (originated the art of steer wrestling)
   > Matthew Henson (codiscoverer of the North Pole)
   > Dr. Charles Drew (discovered blood plasma and organized Red Cross Blood Bank)
   > George Washington Carver (famous agricultural chemist who perfected many uses for the peanut)
   > Martin Luther King Jr. (symbol for the Civil Rights movement)
   > Whitney M. Young (Civil Rights leader)
   > Sammy Davis Jr. (entertainer)
   > Louis Armstrong (jazz musician)
   > Mahalia Jackson (gospel singer)
   > Wilt Chamberlin (professional basketball player)

   d. Which Living American Am I? (Choices from current or past history)
   e. Which Sports Hero Am I? (Choices from sports of interest to the students)

Activity 3–17:
RADIO'S DAYS OF OLD

TYPE	TERM
● CLASS	○ STA
● GROUP	● LTA
○ IND	○ LC

Purpose:
1. To develop appreciative listening skills
2. To develop visual imagery
3. To illustrate characters and settings described in old radio broadcasts
4. To evaluate the use of sound effects and background music on a story
5. To define the climax of a story and describe the techniques used to build excitement

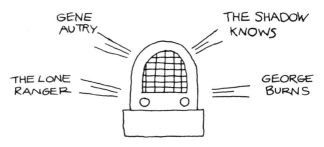

Materials:
Recordings of popular radio shows of the past; available shows include those of George Burns, Jack Benny, and Gene Autry, *The Lone Ranger, Hopalong Cassidy, Mr. Keen, Tracer of Lost Persons, The Shadow, Escape, Two Thousand Plus, My Friend Irma, Superman, The Green Hornet,* and *Sherlock Holmes's Adventures.* (Sunburst Communications, Pleasantville, NY, publishes *Tune-In,* a series of radio tapes and instructional materials for teaching listening and literature skills with radio broadcasts.)

Grade level:
Depends on broadcast selection and activities used with the selection; young children can react to theme songs on radio shows by painting to music or doing creative movement activities; activities requiring students to listen to longer segments, react to plot, or define climax are more appropriate for middle and upper elementary students. Recordings of old radio shows may be used with large groups, small groups, or individual students who wish to investigate a subject.

Procedures:
1. Ask students if they have ever heard of some of the radio broadcasts from the 1940s and 1950s. (These broadcasts are often played over educational radio stations, or students may have recordings of them.) Ask the students why they believe radio was so popular fifty years ago. Explain that they will have an opportunity to listen to some of these radio broadcasts. You may wish to suggest that after they have listened to several radio broadcasts, they will also have an opportunity to produce their own radio show, complete with sound effects and background music.
2. The listening activities depend on the contents of the radio broadcast. Be sure to listen to the recording before you use it with the students. Introduce the broadcast and prepare the students for the listening experience. The following activities lend themselves to listening to radio broadcasts.

a. Because students cannot see the characters in the story, ask them to listen to all of the clues that suggest the physical appearance of the main characters or one of the main characters. Have them draw a picture of the character and tell why they drew the character that way. Discuss with the students the clues they heard and how they interpreted these clues. (This activity does not have a right or wrong answer unless obvious clues would call for the same interpretation by all listeners.)

b. The setting for a radio show must also be imagined by each listener. Have students listen for clues about the location and time period of the story. If they do not have enough background experience with that time period, have them research the time period and illustrate the setting. They might illustrate the major setting of the story with dioramas or drawings. For a more extensive setting activity, divide the students into small groups and have them depict the setting on a roll of paper. They can place this roll setting in a box with a window opening and show it as the radio broadcast is replayed. *The Lone Ranger* stories may have several settings, such as a frontier town, an Indian village, a ranch, an old mine, an early railroad, and so forth. Students may also retell the story without using the radio broadcast.

After the students illustrate the setting, allow them to discuss whether they would like to live in such a setting.

c. After students have researched the time period, they can listen to the broadcast again and evaluate whether the broadcast is authentic for that time period. If the broadcast is a science fiction story set in the future or the distant past, would the story be written in the same way? Has scientific knowledge changed during the fifty years since the broadcast was made? How would the story be written today? If the broadcast is a comedy, what do the jokes tell us about the famous people or values of the time? Comparisons can be made with current comedians. What subjects do comedy writers use for jokes? Are there similarities between the subject matter of jokes told on television today and jokes told on radio broadcasts fifty years ago? Why may there be similarities?

d. Sound effects and music add to the radio listener's appreciation. Have the students listen to the sound effects and then allow them to discuss how the sound effects influence their appreciation of the show. Compare the sound effects of a detective show with the sound effects of a western or comedy broadcast. Could the student identify the type of program by merely listening to the sound effects? Have the students list the sound effects they hear when they listen to different types of programs.

SOUND EFFECTS

Western Programs:

Mystery Programs:

Comedy Programs:

Science Fiction Programs:

Background music also influences the listener. Have the students listen to a program's theme song or background music and discuss why that specific music was chosen. Ask them to listen to the background music and allow them to do creative movement or painting while listening. Allow them to share how the music makes them feel.

e. Radio broadcasts allow students to listen to the development of a story's climax. Have them listen to a broadcast that develops a definite climax, identify the climax, and discuss the techniques used by the actors and sound effects technicians to increase the excitement building up to the climax. Have the students act out broadcasts, demonstrating the development of an exciting climax.

f. After students have listened to old radio shows and completed a number of listening activities, encourage them to develop their own radio broadcasts, complete with sound effects and background music.

Activity 3–18:

FOOLS AND FOOLISHNESS IN FOLKTALES

TYPE	TERM
● CLASS	● STA
● GROUP	○ LTA
○ IND	○ LC

Purpose:

1. To discover that authors use literary techniques to influence the listener
2. To identify literary techniques that make the listener sympathize with, empathize with, or reject a character
3. To develop appreciation for literary techniques used in folktales
4. To respond to literary techniques used in folktales

Materials:

Examples of folktales depicting different kinds of fools; for example, "The Golden Goose" (The Brothers Grimm), "The Man, the Boy, and the Donkey" (Aesop), "The Golden Touch" (Nathaniel Hawthorne), "Simple Simon" (Mother Goose), "Jabberwocky" (Lewis Carroll), "The Blind Men and the Elephant" (John G. Saxe), "The Akond of Swat" (Edward Lear).

Grade level:

Middle and upper elementary

Procedures:

1. Background information: Many folktales have been written about fools. These fools may be cowardly, absentminded, ignorant, gullible, extremely talkative, or greedy. Simpletons, like Jack in "Jack and the Beanstalk," often win in folktales. Other fools, such as the man in "The Man, the Boy, and the Donkey," lose everything because of their foolishness. According to Francelia Butler (1977), "The literature about fools is appealing to children because fools are, above all, human—and therefore tales about fools bring them always a certain joy and delight in the human condition."

2. Discuss these different kinds of foolish characters with the students. Ask the students if they can think of some folktales that use the theme of foolishness. How do they feel about the foolish character in the story or poem? Are they sympathetic toward the character or do they dislike the character? Tell the students that you will be reading some folktales and rhymes that describe foolish characters. After they listen to the folktale or poem, they will have an opportunity to share how they feel about the character, what made them like or dislike the character, and what words the author used to make them feel that way. Some of the following selections may be used:

a. "The Golden Goose" (Brothers Grimm)—Although Dummling is considered a simpleton by his brothers, he performs a good deed for an old man and is given a golden goose. Anyone who touches the goose sticks fast. As Dummling progresses toward the city, he gains seven followers who cannot let go. Within the city is a princess who never laughs. The princess's father has proclaimed that whoever can make her laugh shall marry her. Dummling's procession is so funny that she laughs; Dummling marries her and becomes heir to the kingdom.

After the class listens to the story, have part of the class act out the story for the rest of the class. Then change roles so that all of the children have an opportunity to observe this humorous scene.

Discuss with the group members their reactions to the simpleton in the story. Were they sympathetic? Why or why not? What words did the author use to make them feel this way? What kind of picture did the author paint with words? Was it funny, sad, silly, or what? Have the group draw pictures to illustrate the foolishness in the story.

b. "The Man, the Boy, and the Donkey" (Aesop)—In this fable, the foolish person does not win. On the way to the market, the man takes advice from all of the people passing by. First he puts the boy on the donkey, and then he puts himself on the donkey; next, he and the boy ride the donkey, and, finally, the boy and the man tie the donkey's feet and carry the donkey on their shoulders. The final foolishness occurs when the donkey falls off of the bridge and drowns because his feet are tied.

After reading the fable, have the students compare the fool in this story with Dummling. Did they react in the same way to this story? Why or why not? What technique did Aesop use to get his point across to the listener? What words were used to describe the man, the boy, and the donkey? Have the students select statements that influenced the man. Have them say the following statements scornfully as if they were the people passing on the road.

"See that lazy youngster."
"Shame on that lazy lout."
"Aren't you ashamed for overloading that poor donkey?"

c. "The Golden Touch" (Nathaniel Hawthorne)—King Midas is an example of a man whose greed causes him to become a fool. King Midas values nothing but gold until he is given the golden touch. When his food, water, and child are all turned to gold, he discovers that gold is not the most important thing in the world.

This is a very good story for creative dramatics, puppetry, or storytelling. Divide the students into smaller groups and have each group plan a different creative way to present the story to the rest of the class. Have them find other folktales that depict the theme of greed and share the stories with the class.

d. Read several nonsense poems, rhymes, and limericks to the group. Let the students listen for the enjoyment of the sounds in language. These poems may also be used for choral reading (see chapter 2). Examples include "Simple Simon" (Mother Goose), "Jabberwocky" (Lewis Carroll), "The Blind Men and the Elephant" (John G. Saxe), and "The Akond of Swat" (Edward Lear).

Activity 3–19:
LISTENING FOR ENJOYMENT

TYPE	TERM
● CLASS	● STA
● GROUP	○ LTA
● IND	○ LC

Purpose:

1. To develop the realization that listening may be used to bring enjoyment and pleasure
2. To create an environment conducive to listening enjoyment
3. To bring back pleasant memories associated with listening for enjoyment

Materials:

Stories identified by children that they remember listening to for enjoyment, such as those read to them by adults when the students were young children. Examples might include Barbara Emberley's *Drummer Hoff* (1967), Beatrix Potter's *The Tale of Peter Rabbit* (1902), various Dr. Seuss books such as *The Cat in the Hat* (1957) and *The 500 Hats of Bartholomew Cubbins* (1938), and Maurice Sendak's *Where the Wild Things Are* (1963).

Grade level:

All grades

Book summaries:

The books used differ according to the students' grade level and abilities. *Drummer Hoff* is a cumulative rhyme that encourages listeners to join in with the reading. *The Tale of Peter Rabbit* is the story of the mischievous rabbit and his interactions with Mr. McGregor. *The Cat in the Hat* entertains two bored children on a rainy day. *The 500 Hats of Bartholomew Cubbins* is the story of a bewitched hat that keeps reappearing as Bartholomew tries to take off his hat before the king. *Where the Wild Things Are* is the story of a boy whose vivid imagination turns his room into a forest inhabited by wild things.

Procedures:

1. Prepare the room for listening for enjoyment. Some teachers play soft music to help prepare the setting. Ask the students what environment helped them listen to stories for enjoyment when they were younger (or now if someone reads to them for enjoyment).
2. Ask the students to describe their own experiences in which they listened for enjoyment. Ask them to list books that they remember and to discuss the feelings associated with listening to the books. Bring a collection of books into the room and read the books. Some of the books can be read to the students, while other books can be read by the students themselves.
3. Ask the students to discuss their feelings as they listen to or read the books.
4. Have older students read books to younger children. Have the younger children select the books and tell the students what about the books makes them so enjoyable.
5. You may conduct an activity similar to one completed by a group of college students who were preparing to be teachers. They read a selection of newer books and then voted for the ones that they would like to read to children for enjoyment. For very young children they chose Minfong Ho's *Hush! A Thai Lullaby* (1996), a 1997 Caldecott Honor winner with rhythmic language. For children in the primary grades they chose *My Great-Aunt Arizona* by Gloria Houston (1992), the story of a teacher who taught for many generations in the Blue Ridge Mountains.

REFERENCES

Butler, F. (1977). *Sharing literature with children.* New York: David McKay.

Funk, H., & Funk, G. (1989, May). Guidelines for developing listening skills. *The Reading Teacher, 42,* 660–663.

Levesque, J. (1989, October). ELVES: A read-aloud strategy to develop listening comprehension. *The Reading Teacher, 43,* 93–94.

Rankin, P. T. (1930, January). Listening ability: Its importance, measurement, and development. *Chicago Schools Journal, 12,* 178.

Sutherland, Z., & Livingston, M. C. (1984). *The Scott, Foresman anthology of children's literature.* Glenview, IL: Scott, Foresman.

CHILDREN'S LITERATURE REFERENCES

Alexander, Lloyd. *The Remarkable Journey of Prince Jen.* New York: Dutton, 1991.

Baker, Jeannie. *Where the Forest Meets the Sea.* New York: Greenwillow, 1988.

Baker, Jeannie. *Window.* New York: Greenwillow, 1991.

Daugherty, James. *Poor Richard.* New York: Viking, 1941.

Emberley, Barbara. *Drummer Hoff.* Illustrated by Ed Emberley. New York: Prentice-Hall, 1967.

Freedman, Russell. *The Wright Brothers: How They Invented the Airplane.* New York: Holiday, 1991.

Fritz, Jean. *What's the Big Idea, Ben Franklin?* Illustrated by Margot Tomes. New York: Coward, McCann, 1978.

Grifalconi, Ann. *Darkness and the Butterfly.* Boston: Little, Brown, 1987.

Ho, Minfong. *Hush! A Thai Lullaby.* Illustrated by Holly Meade. New York: Orchard, 1996.

Hooks, William H. *Moss Gown.* Illustrated by Donald Carrick. New York: Houghton Mifflin, 1987.

Houston, Gloria. *My Great-Aunt Arizona.* Illustrated by Susan Condie Lamb. New York: HarperCollins, 1992.

Jacques, Brian. *Pearls of Lutra: A Tale from Redwall.* New York: Philomel, 1997.

Lamb, Charles, and Lamb, Mary. *Tales from Shakespeare,* rev. ed. New York: Children's Classics, 1986.

Levine, Ellen. *The Tree That Would Not Die.* Illustrated by Ted Rand. New York: Scholastic, 1995.

McPhail, David. *The Dream Child.* New York: Dutton, 1985.

Meltzer, Milton. *Benjamin Franklin: The New American.* New York: Watts, 1988.

Micucci, Charles. *The Life and Times of the Apple.* New York: Orchard, 1992.

Micucci, Charles. *The Life and Times of the Peanut.* Boston: Houghton Mifflin, 1997.

Nesbit, E. *Beautiful Stories from Shakespeare.* New York: Weathervane, facsimile of the 1907 edition.

Potter, Beatrix. *The Tail of Peter Rabbit.* New York: Warne, 1902.

Rosen, Michael (retold by). *We're Going on a Bear Hunt*. Illustrated by Helen Oxenbury. New York: Macmillan, 1989.

San Souci, Robert D. *Young Merlin*. New York: Doubleday, 1990.

Seuss, Dr. *The Cat in the Hat*. New York: Random House, 1957.

_____. *The 500 Hats of Bartholomew Cubbins*. New York: Vanguard, 1938.

Twain, Mark. *Adventures of Huckleberry Finn*. Edited by Walter Blair and Victor Fischer. Berkeley: University of California Press, 1985.

Van Rynbach, Iris. *Everything from a Nail to a Coffin*. New York: Orchard Books, 1991.

Von Tscharner, Renata, and Fleming, Ronald Lee. *New Providence: A Changing Cityscape*. Illustrated by Denis Orloff. San Diego: Harcourt Brace Jovanovich, 1987.

Willard, Nancy. *Night Story*. Illustrated by Ilse Plume. San Diego: Harcourt Brace Jovanovich, 1981.

4

Writing Activities

Research in writing suggests that children can improve their writing by developing self-critical powers and becoming involved in the evaluation and improvement of their own writing. Therefore, teachers must provide children with many opportunities to write and should interact with their students during the writing process rather than evaluating only the final product. There is no one favored approach to teaching writing. Some educators recommend approaches that emphasize the process of writing, whereas others recommend those that emphasize the goals of writing. Kulberg (1993) emphasizes that there is a trend from descriptive, product-oriented writing to an explanatory, process-oriented approach. Applebee (1984) argues for an approach that considers both the process and the resulting products of writing:

> We must develop models of writing that more explicitly take account of topic knowledge and of interaction between the writing process and the goals of the writing event. The separation of process and product, though perhaps a needed step in the development of our research, seems now to be a major stumbling block to future progress. (p. 591)

Following a review of the findings gained from the National Writing Project, Myers and Gray (1983) state that effective teachers use writing activities that include *processing* (problem solving that involves specific stages, such as prewriting, writing, and postwriting), *modeling* (imitating written samples), and *distancing* (focusing on the relationships between writer and subject and between writer and audience). Consequently, Myers and Gray conclude that effective writing practices frequently include these elements. The writing activities developed in this chapter encourage the use of processing, modeling, and distancing.

Hillocks's (1986) comprehensive review of research on composition is one of the most frequently cited studies related to effective approaches and implications for the types of activities that should be included in the writing process. Hillocks found that the most effective mode of instruction was characterized by emphasis on (1) processes such as prewriting, composing, and revising; (2) prewriting activities that help develop the skills to be applied during the ensuing writing; (3) specific objectives for learning; (4) activities that help students learn the procedures for using those forms during the writing process; and (5) interaction with peers and feedback during the total writing process rather than primarily at the end of a composing activity. Hillocks states that the most effective instruction is characterized by specific objectives, materials and problems selected to engage the students in the processes important for that specific aspect of writing, and activities such as small-group problem-centered discussions. In this effective instruction, teachers frequently give brief introductory lessons about the principles to be studied and applied during small-group activities and then during the independent work.

The following instructional procedures that emphasize the writing process may be used with the activities in this chapter. This writing process was recommended by Proett and Gill (1986) and includes activities that they identify as "Before Students Write," "While Students Write," and "After Students Write." The before-students-write activities include content and idea building, as well as development and ordering. Content and idea building emphasize such strategies as observing, researching, experiencing, brainstorming, listing, detailing, reading, dramatizing, mapping, outlining, and watching media. Development and ordering activities include developing with details, reasons, and examples; ordering by chronology, space, importance, and logic; classifying; applying a general truth; generalizing from supporting details; and structuring by cause and effect. While students write they must be concerned with rhetorical stance and linguistic choices. Under rhetorical stance they are concerned with their chosen voice, their respective audience, their purpose for writing, and the form in which to write. Under linguistic choices, writers decide word choices, use of figurative language, sentence structure, sentence type, and syntax. After-student-write activities include revision and highlighting. Revision activities allow writers to get responses in editing groups, raise questions and expand or clarify their writing, test against a criteria, and proofread and polish their writing. Highlighting activities include publishing, reading, and other ways of sharing the written results.

Studies show that students with special needs may have particular difficulty with writing. For example, MacArthur, Graham, and Schwartz (1993) found that some students struggle with higher-level cognitive processes such as setting goals, generating appropriate content, organizing their writing, and evaluating and revising their text. Consequently, they require help in generating content, making notes, and focusing on details. Gleason (1995) emphasizes using story maps to plan elements of students' stories and providing guided practice.

The activities in this section emphasize various types of writing such as expressive, imaginative, and expository writing. In expressive writing, writers, especially young children, write as they speak. In the imaginative function, writers use language as an art medium to simultaneously inform and entertain. In the expository function, writers inform, record, report, and explain. There are no absolute divisions, however, between expressive, imaginative, and expository writing. The ideas for stimulating writing and becoming involved in the writing process are more important than the divisions.

Activity 4–1:
MYSELF AND MY FAMILY

TYPE	TERM
● CLASS	○ STA
● GROUP	● LTA
● IND	○ LC

Purpose:

1. To develop creative writing skills through artistic interpretations of the family
2. To refine oral expression by talking about something close to the family

Materials:

An accordion-pleated book with a page for each member of the family and family pets (construct an accordion-pleated book by folding large sheets of heavy drawing paper in half; connect several sheets with tape to make a book large enough to accommodate pictures of the child's family and a story about each picture).

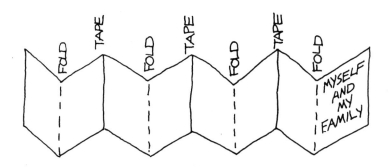

Grade level:

Kindergarten, lower elementary

Procedures:

1. Show children an accordion-pleated book with your picture on the front and the title "Myself and My Family." Read the title to the children or allow them to read it. Ask the children what they think would be inside this special book. Allow them to make suggestions; show them your book. (Young children enjoy learning more about their teachers so this activity stimulates oral discussion and questions.) Your book may contain photographs and illustrations and should include a separate page for each member of your family and a short story describing each family member. After you discuss your book, tell the children that they will have an opportunity to make their own books about themselves and their families. Allow them to suggest subjects they would like to include in their own books.

2. Help children make their accordion-pleated books. Have them illustrate their covers and print the title of the book.

3. On subsequent days, have children illustrate a page for each member of their families including pets. (Photographs may be used, if all of the children have access to pictures of their family members.) After they have drawn each picture, have students write or dictate a story about that person. Interact with the children individually as they are writing. Ask questions about the member of the family to help children develop their stories. (The length of each story will depend on the grade level of each child. Kindergarten children may dictate short labels for their pictures while second-grade children may write lengthy stories.)

4. Allow children opportunities to share their family books with the class and talk about their own families. Provide opportunities for other children to ask questions about each child's family.

Activity 4–2:
MY LOVABLE DIRTY OLD BEAR

TYPE	TERM
● CLASS	● STA
● GROUP	○ LTA
● IND	○ LC

Purpose:
1. To improve creative writing skills by writing about a favorite stuffed toy
2. To improve oral expression
3. To relate personal experiences and experiences in books

Materials:
Literature selections that include adventures with or about stuffed animals, such as Anthony Browne's *Gorilla* (1983), Jane Hissey's *Jolly Snow: An Old Bear Story* (1991), Shirley Hughes's *Dogger* (1977), A. A. Milne's *Winnie-the-Pooh* (1926, 1954), Ann Turner's *Through Moon and Stars and Night Skies* (1990), and Margery Williams's *The Velveteen Rabbit: Or How Toys Become Real* (1922, 1958). Suggest that children bring their favorite stuffed animals to school to share and to write about. Ask children who do not have an animal to draw a picture of one they would like to have.

Grade level:
Lower elementary

Book summaries:
Gorilla is the story of a young girl who has a special adventure with her toy gorilla. *Jolly Snow: An Old Bear Story* is the story of a group of stuffed animals that try to create snow and the fun they have with snow made out of materials in the house. *Dogger* is about a young boy who loses and finally retrieves his special stuffed toy. *Winnie-the-Pooh* is the classic story about all of the toy animals that live in the Hundred-Acre Wood and play with Christopher Robin. *Through Moon and Stars and Night Skies* is the story of an adopted boy who overcomes his fear of his new family, especially when he sees the teddy-bear quilt on his bed and realizes that his new family loves him. *The Velveteen Rabbit: Or How Toys Become Real* is about how a toy becomes real as a result of love.

Procedures:
1. This creative writing activity may be motivated by any of the books about beloved stuffed animals. For example, if you are using *The Velveteen Rabbit: Or How Toys Become Real,* you could show the students a stuffed toy that shows obvious signs of handling and loving. If this is your toy, you could tell the students about the many happy adventures you had with it. Ask them to think about anything that

might have happened to cause the toy to have a torn ear and so forth. Was the toy taken on many adventures? How do they know this?

2. Now introduce *The Velveteen Rabbit: Or How Toys Become Real*. Show the students the title of the book and ask them to consider possible interpretations for the title. Ask the following: "What do you think the author means when she writes, 'Or How Toys Become Real'?" Discuss the various possibilities with the students.

3. Read the book to students and encourage them to respond to the characters and the plot. Then ask them to consider again what the author meant when she wrote "Or How Toys Become Real." Discuss the various activities the boy engaged in with his stuffed toy and how love made the toy real.

4. Allow the students to show and talk about their stuffed toys or pictures of their stuffed toys. Suggest that your stuffed toy would like to share adventures with their toys. Have the students write or dictate adventures they have had with their stuffed animals or an adventure that your stuffed animal had with their stuffed animals. Young children may enjoy drawing a large picture of their toy and then writing or dictating a story inside the picture. Have the students share their

stories. These stories might then be put together to form "The Toy Adventure Book" or "The Bearish Adventure Book."

5. Encourage students to read or listen to the various books about stuffed toys. Allow them to respond orally to the stories.

6. Additional activities may accompany any of these books. For example, after reading *Through Moon and Stars and Night Skies* the students could draw their own quilts with favorite stuffed animals depicted on them. They could then write stories about the quilts.

7. After reading either *Jolly Snow: An Old Bear Story* or *Winnie-the-Pooh,* they could pretend that their stuffed animals have lives of their own and write a story about their adventures.

Activity 4–3:
IMAGINE YOU ARE A . . .

TYPE	TERM
● CLASS	● STA
● GROUP	○ LTA
● IND	○ LC

Purpose:

1. To develop oral expression and creative writing skills through a teacher-introduced experience
2. To explore knowledge of various animals
3. To write a creative story using one's imagination

Materials:

Books that invite children to use their imaginations by pretending to be various animals; Karen Wallace's *Imagine You Are a Crocodile* (1997) is a good choice for younger children.

Grade level:

Lower elementary

Procedures:

1. Present the title *Imagine You Are a Crocodile* and ask children to think about the title and to consider what the book might say.
2. After they have shared their ideas, read the book and ask the children to compare the author's text and artist's illustrations with what they thought would be in the text.
3. Then ask children to imagine they are that crocodile. How would they catch food? How would they protect their babies from enemies? How would the world look if they were in a swamp with only their eyes above the water? What other animals and plants would they see?
4. Have students write their own stories in which they imagine that they are a crocodile living in a swamp.
5. Children in the primary grades may write additional "Imagine You Are a . . ." stories. Books that could provide background information or motivation for younger readers include Sneed B. Collard's *Animal Dads* (1997), Brenda Z. Guiberson's *Into the Sea* (1996), Sandra Markle's *Creepy, Crawly Baby Bugs* (1996), Joanna Cole's *My Puppy Is Born* (1991), and Jean Craighead George's *Look to the North: A Wolf Pup Diary* (1997).

Activity 4-4:
HATS CHANGE MY IDENTITY

TYPE	TERM
● CLASS	● STA
● GROUP	○ LTA
● IND	○ LC

Purpose:

1. To refine oral expression and creative writing skills by writing about a character who wears a specific kind of hat
2. To pantomime the actions of a character who might wear a specific kind of hat

Materials:

A collection of many different hats; ask children to bring a variety of hats or begin a collection of cowboy hats, firefighters' hats, motorcycle helmets, nurses' caps, safari hats, police officers' hats, forest rangers' hats, bakers' hats, football helmets, baseball caps, swimmers' caps, army helmets, trappers' hats, northeaster rain hats, straw hats, babies' bonnets, ladies' hats, ladies' large flowered hats, derbies, top hats, yachtmen's caps, and hard hats.

Grade level:

Lower and middle elementary

Procedures:

1. Provide a collection of different hats that suggest various occupations, characters, adventures, and actions.
2. Put on a hat. Ask students to suggest who might wear a hat like the one you are wearing. What would the person look like? What would he or she do when wearing that hat? Suggest to the students that the hat caused the person to have a special adventure. Have them suggest adventures that might be appropriate.
3. Tell the students that they will have an opportunity to put on a special hat, change their identities, and have an adventure. Discuss the various hats. Allow students to choose a hat or mark hats with numbers and have students draw a number to determine their hat selection. Ask the students to put on their hats, think about their new identities, close their eyes, and imagine themselves as the person wearing the hat. Have them write a story about an adventure they might have while wearing the hat. Interact with the students as they write their stories individually.
4. Have students share their stories orally with the class or with a group of children.
5. Play a pantomime game in which students act out the occupations of people who might wear the various hats. Have other members of the group identify the occupation and the hat that would be worn by the pantomimed character.

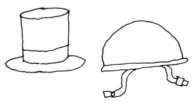

Activity 4–5:
MY FIRST HUNDRED YEARS

TYPE	TERM
● CLASS	● STA
● GROUP	○ LTA
● IND	○ LC

Purpose:

1. To refine creative writing skills by writing about an old doll, old toy, or picture of an old doll or toy
2. To participate in a discussion about the experiences and adventures of a toy and its owner

Materials:

An old or antique doll that has obviously been played with, an old toy soldier, or other toy or a picture of an antique toy that looks as if it has been used by children. This activity could be used to motivate the reading of Rachel Field's *Hitty: Her First Hundred Years* (1929, 1957) or Holling Clancy Holling's *Paddle to the Sea* (1941).

Grade level:

Lower and middle elementary

Book summaries:

Hitty: Her First Hundred Years develops the memoirs of a doll who began her life in Maine and had many adventures, including sailing on a whaler. *Paddle to the Sea* is the story of a "Paddle Person" and his small canoe, which was carved by a Native American boy and placed into Lake Superior. On the bottom of the canoe is carved "Please put me back in the water. I am Paddle to the Sea." The story and illustrations follow Paddle to the Sea as he goes from Lake Superior to the Grand Banks off the coast of Newfoundland.

Procedures:

1. Show the toy to the students. Ask them if the toy looks like one they could buy in a toy store today. What is different about this toy? How do they know the toy is old? Who do they think might have owned this toy? Did the girl or boy love the toy?

    Continue a discussion about the historic time during which this toy was popular and ask the students to speculate about adventures the doll or toy may have had with one or more owners. For example, did the toy go west on a covered wagon? Did the toy go down the Mississippi on a riverboat?

2. Ask the children to write a story about the adventures of the toy and its owner or owners. Interact with the children as they write their stories.

3. Allow students to share their adventure stories with the class or with a small group.

4. Another time you might introduce an old toy by telling where you found or bought the toy; then let children speculate about the child who left, owned, or lost the toy. For example:

    I have been trying to solve a mystery about this old doll and the girl who owned and played with her. Maybe if you hear about how I got the doll, you can help me with this mystery.
    There once was a big, old, deserted house on a farm in Iowa. A man who builds houses saw the farm and decided he wanted to tear down the old house and build a new house on the same spot. It was a beautiful site for a house. There

were gnarled apple trees in the backyard and a huge, green, grassy space covered with wild flowers in front.

This builder decided to check the house to make sure there was nothing in it before he sent for the wrecking crew to tear it down. As he was going through the old house, he came to a second-floor bedroom that looked as if it had belonged to a child. The walls were covered with faded wallpaper with pink roses, and a child's drawings could be seen on the walls. The room had a large closet that probably held the child's clothes and other possessions. The builder opened the closet door to make sure nothing was inside. Something attracted his attention when he looked up at a high shelf. He put his hand up on the shelf and found this old doll tucked away there.

Will you help me solve this mystery? Who do you think left this doll? Why do you think it was left? The doll looks as if it was played with a great deal. What adventures do you think the girl and her doll had? How do you think the girl felt when she discovered she did not have her doll? How do you think the doll felt when it was left behind?

5. This writing activity may be used to motivate reading or listening to *Hitty: Her First Hundred Years* or *Paddle to the Sea.* Both of these award-winning books follow the adventures of toys or miniatures as they face the unknown. Explain to students that the authors have written stories about possible adventures of old toys. Tell the students that professional authors may be motivated about the "what-ifs" associated with toys that have lived long lives or are placed in settings in which they are on their own. Read and discuss each of the books. Allow students to respond to the plots and compare the types of adventures developed by the authors with those developed by the students. Before reading *Paddle to the Sea,* the students will benefit from looking at maps that show the Great Lakes and the St. Lawrence River. They should realize just what type of challenge Paddle to the Sea faced.

Activity 4–6:
THE WONDERFUL MIRACLE

	TYPE		TERM
●	CLASS	●	STA
●	GROUP	○	LTA
●	IND	○	LC

Purpose:

1. To develop imaginative oral and written expression by encountering a new material for the first time
2. To investigate and answer sensory questions about a mysterious substance
3. To write a creative advertisement for a product using the substance
4. To write a creative story about the miracle substance

Materials:

Polyox water-soluble resin—a safe powder concentrate that mixes with warm water (and food coloring, if you want a colored material) to create a substance with unusual properties—it forms long, sticky strings when a finger is stuck into and pulled out of it, and it reduces friction (Polyox water-soluble resin is used by firefighters to deliver water at a faster rate and is added to paints and toothpaste); writing materials.

Grade level:

All grades—young students can experiment with this substance and dictate a chart story; older children can try more detailed experiments and write individual stories or advertisements about products they would develop from the substance.

Procedures:

1. Tell the students they are famous magicians, inventors, or scientists. Tell them they have just created a new, magical substance but are not sure what the substance will do or how they can use it. Show them the magic white powder. Ask them what they think it is. What does it look like? What does it feel like? What does it smell like? How do they think it could be used? Allow children to brainstorm ideas.
2. Suggest to the student magicians that they imagine something quite different might happen to the substance if water were added to the powder. Have them make suggestions about what they think might happen when water is added. Ask them to watch carefully as water is added to the magic powder. Allow them to experience and experiment with the magic substance. Give each magician a small amount of the substance on plastic wrap to experiment with individually. Have the students describe the experience and suggest its properties. How does it feel? How does it look? What will dissolve in it? How strong is it? How fast will it move? What can it do? What happens when I put my finger into it?
3. Allow the magicians to gather into small brainstorming groups. Have each group suggest as many magical uses as it can for this substance. Ask the students to select their best idea and write an advertisement to introduce and sell their new substance. Have them present their advertisement to the rest of the class. Allow the other groups to ask questions about the new use or product.
4. Suggest that students write individual stories about what would happen if they were real magicians and created a miracle substance. What would their miracle look like? What special things could it do? How would they use their miracle?
5. Develop a bulletin board of miracle substance posters and creative stories.

Mighty Miracles
by
Mastro
the Magician

Activity 4-7:

WOW! I JUST WON ONE HUNDRED DOLLARS

TYPE	TERM
● CLASS	● STA
● GROUP	○ LTA
● IND	○ LC

Purpose:

1. To develop oral expression and creative writing skills through a teacher-introduced experience
2. To write a creative story stimulated by anticipated purchases in a catalog

Materials:

A copy of a one-hundred-dollar check made out to each student (the amount is variable depending on age and expectations of the children)—this activity could also be introduced in game-show format, with each child selecting a check for a different amount); variety of catalogs, including Christmas, department store, large mail order, and specialty catalogs; writing materials.

Grade level:

All grades—the assignment can use toy catalogs for younger children and catalogs with clothing, sports equipment, or hobby items for older students

Procedures:

1. Show the children a check made out to you. Ask them how they would feel if they received such a check. Ask them if they have ever seen television shows or read stories about people winning money or prizes. Ask the students how they would feel if they won money or prizes. Ask them what they would like to win. Give each student a copy of a check for the desired amount made out in the name of the student. Tell the students that they are going to pretend they have just won a contest. The contest prize is a check that they must turn in for the merchandise of their choice.

2. Provide a variety of catalogs. (The type of catalog depends on the children's ages and interests.) Tell the children that the rules of the contest state that they must select items from a catalog that add up to the amount of their checks. Tell them they can select anything they choose. Discuss the types of items available in each catalog.

3. Ask the students to make their selections and write a story about why they chose their merchandise. Have them include a description of themselves using their winnings.

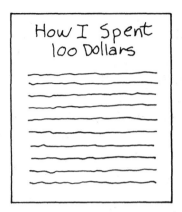

4. Catalogs can be used for many other writing activities; for example:
   a. Catalogs of camping equipment—Ask the students to select materials they would need to go on a camping vacation with their families and have them write a story about their trip. Tell them to include information about how they used the camping equipment they chose from the catalog.
   b. Catalogs of household furniture, draperies, art objects, and so forth—Ask students to think about a room in their house they would like to decorate. This room might be their bedroom, family room, or the like. If they could decorate this room any way they desired, what would they include? After they have selected items from the catalogs and placed the cutout items on a sheet of paper representing the room, ask them to write a story describing the new room.

   c. Catalogs of clothing—Have the children bring a photograph of themselves to class; then have them select a complete new outfit, cut out the items, and place them on the photograph. Ask the children to think about what they would like to do while wearing their new clothes. Have them write a story telling why they chose their clothes and what they would do while wearing them.
   d. Tell the children to choose an item out of a specialty catalog and describe the person to whom they would give the item.
   e. Choose a famous person in history or a well-known current celebrity. From a catalog, have students choose one gift they think would be especially appropriate for that person. Have them write a story explaining why they chose the gift for that person.

Activity 4–8:
CREATING A MYSTERY IN YOUR CLASSROOM

TYPE	TERM
● CLASS	● STA
● GROUP	○ LTA
● IND	○ LC

Purpose:

1. To promote problem-solving and logical thinking skills
2. To foster creative writing and creative thinking
3. To develop oral language and writing skills

Materials:

Construction paper; a box with a lock or a covered basket; other materials for clues that relate to the mystery you will be creating in your classroom

Grade level:

Middle elementary

Procedures:

1. Leave clues in your classroom. Ask students to pretend they are detectives who have been brought in to help you solve the mystery. For example, you might cut shoe prints out of construction paper. Position them and tape them to the floor in a pattern coming from either the front or back door of the school into your classroom. They might lead into the school, into your classroom, circle your desk, and continue through the window. A padlocked box or a covered basket could be left on your desk.

   The mystery you set up could coincide with a class field trip. For example, the box might contain an invitation for the class to take a field trip to the symphony, a ballet, a national park, a museum, or an aquarium. The clues around the classroom could be related to this field trip. If the class is going to the ballet, you might use a pair of ballet slippers and some sand or chalk (the footprints could be chalk prints from a ballerina's slippers). If the class is going to the symphony, you might have a violin, a bow, musical notes made out of construction paper, and a score for classical music. If the class will be visiting a national park, you might use a pair of binoculars, insect repellent, sunscreen, and a naturalist's hat. One of the clues might be a note with a double meaning in order to create a feeling of suspense. For example, the note might say, "I have been planning this for a long time. Catch you soon."

2. Discuss the clues. What could they mean? Why would they have been left in the classroom? What do the clues have in common? Who might have left the clues? You might write the clues and what they have in common on the chalkboard.

3. Have students write their own mysteries using the clues that were found in the classroom. Encourage them to pretend that they are detectives and it is their job to solve the mystery. To solve the mystery, they must create an imaginative story and be as creative as possible as long as the clues are introduced as details in the story. Ask students to think about the person who left the footprints and the clues. Why were the clues left in the classroom?

4. Have students share their stories orally with the class or with small groups of students.

5. After all of the students have read their stories, reveal the contents of the box. The contents might be an invitation, tickets, or a letter addressed to the class announcing a special field trip.

6. You could expand the activity to include a discussion of books that are within the mystery genre. Include books and stories in which clues are important to the story and observation plays an important role. How do the characters use the clues to solve the mystery? In Joan Lowery Nixon's *Whispers from the Dead* (1980) the ghost of a murdered character helps solve a mystery and prevent a second murder. Younger children will enjoy reading Donald J. Sobol's "Encyclopedia Brown" series. In each book, the ten-year-old Leroy Brown helps his father solve crimes by figuring out clues. Books for older children might include Virginia Hamilton's *House of Dies Drear* (1968), Robert Newman's *The Case of the Baker Street Irregular* (1978) and *The Case of the Vanishing Corpse* (1980), Ellen Raskin's *The Westing Game* (1978), and Robert Westall's *Yaxley's Cat* (1992). Older students may also want to read the short stories by Edgar Allan Poe, short stories and novels by Agatha Christie, and stories about the detective Sherlock Holmes.

Activity 4–9:
CREATING A HISTORY OF YOUR TOWN

TYPE	TERM
● CLASS	○ STA
● GROUP	● LTA
○ IND	○ LC

Purpose:

1. To research, write and publish a history of your town
2. To learn note-taking, interviewing, and research skills
3. To organize events chronologically
4. To work cooperatively

Materials:

Source materials from newspapers, archives, and interviews pertaining to the history of your town.

Grade level:

Middle and upper elementary, middle school

Procedures:

1. Discuss the overall project with students. Remind them that their goal is to research, write, and publish the history of their town using as many different resources as possible to make the history complete and interesting. Discuss various research questions. How will the history of their town be organized? Will it read as a chronological history with personal anecdotes interspersed throughout? Will there be different chapters? Will photographs or drawings be used?

   Overall questions might include the following: What is your town most famous for? What is your town's population? What was your town like one hundred years ago? What is it like today? What is something that very few people might know about your town? What do you like most about your town? What do you think is most interesting about your town? What do you think is least interesting about your town? What is the primary industry in your town? Has this always been true? Who have been some of the most famous people to come out of your community? Starting with the earliest settlers, describe your town and how it has changed over different time periods.

2. Discuss with students the various research techniques they might use to collect information about their town. Will they interview people? Who should they interview? Will they visit library archives? Are there organizations that keep scrapbooks about their town? Are there individuals with interesting stories or with old photo albums? What might students find in newspaper accounts and library archives? What details would personal interviews add to the history of their town that they might not find in archives?

3. Divide the class into different interest groups. Each group will be responsible for conducting, presenting, and organizing research for a specific area in the history of their town. This information will be included in the final class publication. Interest group topics might include the history of your school, churches, various industries, agriculture, parks, sports, libraries, and other schools in the community.

4. Once students have divided into interest groups, have the groups discuss how members will conduct research. What research questions apply to their specific interest group? What kinds of questions are they trying to answer? How will they find answers to their research questions? Who will they interview? For example, students might interview the mayor, city council members, librarians, historians,

the oldest citizen, neighbors, a park planner, the chief of police, and other members of the community. They could also search the archives of libraries, historical societies, city hall, churches, schools, and newspaper offices. Will students work in pairs or alone? Will each member have a different assignment? Remind students of the research techniques they will use. How will each member of the group conduct research that will contribute to the group's project?

5. Give students an opportunity to share their findings within their groups and then with the rest of the class. Using the writing process, have students write, edit, and complete their histories.

6. Have students discuss how their town history publication will be distributed to members of the community. Will it be given away or will it be sold to pay for publishing costs? Will copies be distributed to the school library, city hall, the public library, teachers, parents, and other students? Will the publication be sold during an open house or parents' day? If the publication will be sold, you might discuss how any profits will be spent. Will the class buy new books for the library or new software for your school computers? You could also use any profits to reward your class with a field trip or class party.

Activity 4–10:
SHOES TAKE US . . .

TYPE	TERM
● CLASS	● STA
● GROUP	● LTA
● IND	○ LC

Purpose:
1. To refine oral expression and creative writing skills
2. To expand the imagination
3. To develop creative thinking skills
4. To conduct research and develop research skills

Materials:
Books about shoes such as Charlotte Yue's *Shoes: Their History in Words and Pictures* (1997) and Laurie Lawlor's *Where Will This Shoe Take You?: A Walk through the History of Footwear* (1996); stories in which shoes are central to the plot such as *The Wizard of Oz*, Cinderella, and "The Elves and the Shoemaker"; pictures of shoes or actual shoes that suggest different time periods and different occupations or hobbies. For example, you might include large shoes, small shoes, baby shoes, men's shoes, women's shoes, basketball shoes, baseball shoes, tennis shoes, golf shoes, ballet slippers, tap shoes, hiking boots, riding boots, Victorian shoes, Roman sandals, clogs, snowshoes, ice skates, cowboy boots, in-line skates, moccasins, flippers, clown shoes, elf shoes, and spy shoes with gadgets.

Grade level:
All grades

Book summaries:
Shoes: Their History in Words and Pictures provides a history of shoes and their lore and styles. The black-and-white drawings show how shoes are made and how fashions have changed throughout history. *Where Will This Shoe Take You? A Walk through the History of Footwear* emphasizes the role of shoes in different societies and cultures. It also features various historical figures and their shoes.

Procedures:
1. Using *Shoes: Their History in Words and Pictures* and *Where Will This Shoe Take You?: A Walk through the History of Footwear*, discuss the role of shoes. Are all shoes the same? Discuss the title *Where Will This Shoe Take You?: A Walk through the History of Footwear*. What special skills would one need when wearing different shoes?

   Have students close their eyes and imagine what kinds of shoes are in their own closets. Have them discuss the purposes of different types of shoes. Think of stories in which shoes play an important role, such as *The Wizard of Oz*, Cinderella, or "The Elves and the Shoemaker." Discuss the role of the shoes in the story. How would the story change if the characters wore a different type of shoe? What if Cinderella had worn tennis shoes? Would she have lost a shoe on the stairs as she was leaving the ball? What if Dorothy had worn snowshoes or moccasins? What do the shoes symbolize in each story?

2. Provide a collection of pictures of shoes or actual shoes that suggest different time periods, lifestyles, occupations, or hobbies. Discuss the various shoes. Allow students to choose a shoe or mark shoes with numbers and have students draw a number to determine their shoe selection. What do they think the original owner's life was like? In what time period would they have lived? Have students close their eyes and imagine themselves as the person wearing the shoe. Ask them to think about their new lifestyle, occupation, or hobby.

3. Have students write a story of the adventures they might have while wearing this shoe. Perhaps one shoe offers the possibility of transport, such as Dorothy's ruby slippers, or the ability to change appearance, such as Cinderella's glass slippers. Other shoes might provide the opportunity to become the fastest runner or the highest jumper. Have students write the shoe's history and adventures. What makes this shoe special? Have them write one story from the shoe's perspective and another story from their own perspective as they have an adventure wearing the shoe. For example, one story could be from the perspective of a clown as he makes his debut in a circus. Another story could be from the perspective of the clown's shoe. What is the life story of the shoe? Has it been worn by other clowns? What does the shoe see? What are its activities? Who are its friends? How does it feel knowing that it is being worn by a clown who has never performed in front of people? Can the shoe's previous experience help the clown get through his first performance?

4. Have students share their stories orally with the class or with small groups of students.

5. After reading either *Shoes: Their History in Words and Pictures* or *Where Will This Shoe Take You?: A Walk through the History of Footwear,* older students could conduct research into the history of shoes. Each student could research the history of one specific type of shoe.

6. Have older students conduct research into a famous person who would have worn the shoe. For example, Ellen Levine's *Anna Pavlova: Genius of the Dance* (1995) is a biography that paints a vivid picture of the life of a ballet dancer in Russia during the late 1800s and early 1900s. Sue Macy's *Winning Ways: A Photohistory of American Women in Sports* (1996) provides information about specific sports heroines as the author presents a history of women's sports in America. Matt Christopher's *In the Huddle with . . . Steve Young* (1996) is a biography of the quarterback of the San Francisco 49ers. Kathleen Krull's *Wilma Unlimited: How Wilma Rudolph Became the World's Fastest Woman* (1996) provides younger readers with a biography of the African-American runner who overcame polio while growing up in the segregated South to become the first woman ever to win three gold medals in a single Olympics.

7. Develop a bulletin board on the history of shoes. Under the picture of each type of shoe, display its description and history.

Activity 4–11:
DEVELOPING IMAGERY WITH SIMILES

TYPE	TERM
● CLASS	● STA
● GROUP	● LTA
● IND	○ LC

Purpose:

1. To identify and define *simile*
2. To develop imagery through creation of similes using common words and experiences in uncommon ways

Materials:

Examples of common and uncommon similes; literature selections that contain similes such as Bill Brittain's *The Wish Giver* (1983) and Sid Fleischman's *The Midnight Horse* (1990).

Grade level:

Middle and upper elementary or middle school, depending on the degree of simplicity or sophistication of the similes

Book summaries:

The Wish Giver includes a series of stories in which people are given wishes that come true in unexpected ways. The author uses numerous similes to develop setting and characterization in this fantasy. *The Midnight Horse* is historical fiction set in New Hampshire during the late 1800s. Numerous similes are used to describe the settings and the characters. The characters include an orphan boy, a thief, an innkeeper, and a miserly great-uncle.

Procedures:

1. Explain to students that writers often paint a word picture for the reader by using an object or concept in a way that makes the reader "see" the words in a new way. Ask students to close their eyes and visualize the following examples:

   The surface of the lake was as smooth as a large pane of glass.
   When he opened his present, he was as happy as a kid eating a chocolate doughnut.
   The inside of the cave was as cool as a winter morning after a snowfall.

2. After you read each simile (expressed comparison), ask the students to describe what they "saw" in their minds. Ask them to explain what device was used in each sentence. Lead them to the realization that a *simile* is used to suggest that one thing resembles another. Similes use words such as *like* and *as* to express comparisons. Ask them why they think authors use similes.

3. Suggest that some common similes are often overused and ask the students to suggest some of them. Such a list might contain the following examples: as cool as a cucumber, as light as a feather, as blind as a bat, as pretty as a picture, as quick as a wink, as fresh as a daisy, as playful as a kitten, as happy as a lark, as hard as a rock, as quiet as a mouse, as sharp as a tack, and as smooth as silk.

4. Tell students that they will have an opportunity to paint their own word pictures by using imaginative and original comparisons. Allow students to experience the environment and to look, see, feel, smell, hear, and talk about what they experience. Then have them write their own creative similes. This activity can be used in many learning situations. For example, students might go into a meadow

in early spring; experience the wildflowers, the new leaves, ferns, and cloud formations; and then write similes for the following:

As soft as _____; as pretty as _____; as light as _____; as green as _____; as loud as _____; as quiet as _____; as quick as _____; as slow as _____.

Another time, they might experience a harsher environment in a downtown city or factory area. If students cannot visit such an area in person, they could experience the environment through a film and then write similes for the following:

As loud as _____; as harsh as _____; as strong as _____; as heavy as _____; as slow as _____; as hard as _____.

Personal feelings can be expanded by developing similes such as the following:

As nervous as _____; as excited as _____; as frightened as _____; as tired as _____; as lonely as _____; as relaxed as _____.

5. Before introducing a book in which the author uses numerous similes, lead a discussion in which the students predict the types of similes that might be found in certain books. For example, books that have rural settings might develop comparisons that use many rural images. Likewise, books set in various historical settings would have comparisons that relate to that time in history. Ask the students to provide similes that they believe would be appropriate for stories set in rural areas, cities, or jungles. Likewise, ask them to identify similes that might describe characters from different time periods in history. Remind the students that these similes should relate to the time period if they are to create the best images of that time.

6. Introduce *The Wish Giver* in such a way that students will be interested in the story and in searching for interesting similes that describe the setting or the characters. You might say: "Pretend that you are living a long time ago in a rural New England community in which people believe in magic. Pretend that you are given a special card by a little man named Thaddeus Blinn. He tells you that you can have one wish if you press the dot on the card and wish for whatever you want. But he also tells you to be very careful of that wish, because you will get what you ask for. As we read this book we will be looking for ways that the author describes the characters so that we can visualize them. How would you use similes to describe the characters of Thaddeus Blinn, the man who seems to be able to give magical wishes; Polly Kemp, a girl whose sarcastic language prevents her from being liked; Rowena Jervis, a girl who has a crush on Henry Piper; and Adam Fiske, a boy who detests carrying water from the creek to the farm? As we read this book we will search for similes that reveal the characters and allow us to see those characters."

7. As *The Wish Giver* is read, encourage the students to identify and discuss particularly vivid similes. Examples of these similes might include the following:

> Descriptions of an angry Thaddeus Blinn: " 'Oh, the shame that my talents should be taken so lightly.' The words tumbled out of Thaddeus Blinn's mouth like wasps from a burning nest" (p. 13). Later, "He snapped the tent flaps tight shut like a magician doing a disappearing act" (p. 15).
>
> Descriptions of the twins: The twins, who knew the mountains and woods and streams around Coven Tree, were "as shy as wild foxes most of the time" (p. 21).

Polly's language that makes people not like her: Polly said Mrs. Peabody's cookies "tasted like biting into a sofa pillow." She calls the girls "frilly little skunkweeds" (p. 25). Later, after Polly receives her wish, they tried to irritate her so she would start "jug-a-ruming," but their words did not affect Polly; "It was like water rolling off a duck's back" (p. 63).

8. Encourage students to identify and share additional similes that they believe are particularly vivid and appropriate for the story.

9. A similar type of activity may be used with *The Midnight Horse.* Encourage students to find and discuss similes that are particularly vivid in describing the various characters. They may identify and discuss similes that reveal the nature of the characters. For example, students can search for similes that reveal which characters are good and which are bad and discuss the appropriateness of those similes for developing characterization. Examples of these similes might include the following:

> Descriptions of Touch, the orphan: "Touch was skinny and bareheaded, with hair as curly as wood shavings" (p. 1). "He chose to bring himself up, free as a sail to catch any chance wind that came along" (p. 29).
>
> Descriptions of Otis Cratt, the thief: This long-armed man had his face wrapped with a muffler so that he looked "like a loosely wrapped mummy" (p. 3). When Otis saw the blacksmith's billfold, his eyes were "drawn to it like a compass needle to true north." His arm started to weave "like a snake stalking its prey" (p. 4).
>
> Descriptions of Judge Henry Wigglesforth, Touch's greedy great-uncle: Touch refers to his great-uncle: "My great-uncle is tighter'n a wet shirt" (p. 32). The judge stood in front of the fireplace "warming his hands as if stealing all the heat he could, free of charge" (p. 32). The blacksmith refers to the judge: "Lad, he'll stick to you like a fishhook until he's swindled you legal out of what's coming to you" (p. 39).

10. Have students make simile books including their own similes and similes found in literature.

11. Students may extend their understanding of similes by writing stories about specific settings and using appropriate similes. They may also write characterizations that develop the characters through appropriate similes.

Activity 4–12:
ILLUSTRATIONS INCREASE UNDERSTANDING OF SIMILES

TYPE	TERM
● CLASS	● STA
● GROUP	○ LTA
● IND	○ LC

Purpose:
1. To describe how the illustrator's choice of pictures can help the author and illustrator improve the reader's understanding of similes
2. To evaluate the appropriateness or inappropriateness of the comparisons
3. To write and illustrate a book that increases the reader's understanding of similes

Materials:
Picture storybooks that illustrate similes, such as *Jafta* and *Jafta's Mother* by Hugh Lewin (1983).

Grade level:
The picture books may be read and discussed in lower-grade-level classrooms. Upper-grade-level teachers may consider the appropriateness or the inappropriateness of the comparisons and may describe whether the illustrations increase the reader's understanding of similes.

Book summaries:
The illustrations in *Jafta* depict similes as they each illustrate one of Jafta's feelings. For example, the text states, " 'When I'm happy,' said Jafta, 'I purr like a lioncub.' " The illustration then shows a happy boy hugging an equally happy lioncub. The illustrations show animals that are native to South Africa. The illustrations and text in *Jafta's Mother* use numerous similes to depict the mother's various moods and characteristics. The author, Hugh Lewin, was born in South Africa, where he served a seven-year prison sentence because of his opposition to apartheid. He wrote the books because he wanted to introduce his children to South Africa.

Procedures:
1. Read *Jafta* aloud and show the illustrations to the students.
2. Lead a discussion in which the students describe the comparisons made by the author, identify the characteristics of similes, and explain how the illustrations help the reader visualize the comparisons. Examples of similes in *Jafta* include the following:

   When Jafta is happy he purrs like a lioncub, skips like a spider, laughs like a hyena, jumps like an impala, dances like a zebra, and nuzzles like a rabbit. When Jafta is cross he stamps like an elephant and grumbles like a warthog. Jafta wants to be as fast as a cheetah, as quick as an ostrich, as long as a snake, and as tall as a giraffe.

3. Lead a discussion in which the class identifies animal actions or characteristics that students could use to describe their own characteristics.
4. Ask the students to define *simile* in their own words.
5. Share *Jafta's Mother* with the class. Ask the students to identify the similes used by the author and the characteristics developed by the illustrator. Have them discuss the appropriateness or inappropriateness of the textual comparisons and illustrations.
6. Have the students write and illustrate a story about themselves or about someone they know. Encourage them to use and illustrate similes.
7. Share the stories with an audience.

Activity 4-13:

OBSERVE AND WRITE DESCRIPTIONS
OF OBJECTS

TYPE	TERM
● CLASS	● STA
● GROUP	○ LTA
● IND	○ LC

Purpose:

1. To develop observational and analytical abilities
2. To identify specific details that allow students to separate two objects that are similar in color, shape, and size
3. To write specific descriptions that allow other students to select the correct objects
4. Within peer groups, to critically evaluate the descriptions and to rewrite them so that they include clear, specific details

Materials:

Numerous rocks or seashells that are similar in color, shape, and size but have specific characteristics that separate them from the other objects in the group. This activity is based on Hillocks's (1986) research on composition.

Grade level:

All grades—at the lower levels, the objects may have only one similarity, such as color or size. Objects for older students may have greater similarities so that students must observe small details.

Procedures:

1. Begin the activity by placing two shells or stones that are similar in color, shape, and size in front of the students. Challenge the students to identify ways that they could describe each of the shells or stones so that someone looking at them would be able to pick the correct object.
2. Divide the students into small groups. Then ask them to choose one of the shells or stones and brainstorm a list of details that could be used to specifically identify their shell or stone.
3. After they have brainstormed their list, ask the students to write a brief description that presents the details that characterize their object and make it different from the other objects. This description should be a group project.
4. After completing this group activity, the groups exchange the compositions with another group. Ask the second group to read the composition, identify the appropriate object described in the composition, and discuss the effectiveness of the details and descriptors.
5. Bring the groups together and discuss the effectiveness of each composition. As a group, students may rewrite their best descriptions of one of the objects and discuss the importance of specific details, defending their choices.
6. After students have completed this group activity, provide a larger number of stones or shells (one for each student). Ask each student to select an object and describe the object in such specific detail that a classmate reading the description could pick out the object from among all of the other similar objects.

7. After this individual writing is completed, have the students read and discuss the brief compositions within peer groups. Ask the peer groups to identify the object being described and critique the effectiveness of the descriptions. Allow all students to benefit from any suggestions and to revise their descriptions so that they provide the best specific description of the object.

8. You may choose to develop a display in which the objects and descriptions are shown together. Encourage all of the students to read each of the descriptions and to focus on the qualities that make the descriptions specific for the objects.

Activity 4–14:

OBSERVE AND WRITE DESCRIPTIONS OF SETTINGS

TYPE	TERM
● CLASS	● STA
● GROUP	○ LTA
● IND	○ LC

Purpose:

1. To develop observational and analytical skills
2. To identify and respond to the details or moods in pictures or illustrations and to write descriptions that accompany the pictures or illustrations

Materials:

A selection of illustrations from magazines or books that depict various details, moods, characterizations, or settings. For example, books that are good for observing and describing details include wordless books such as Mitsumasa Anno's *Anno's U.S.A.* (1983) and David Wiesner's *Free Fall* (1988) and *Tuesday* (1991). Books that are good for observing and describing moods include Eve Merriam's *Halloween ABC* (1987) (frightening mood) and Cynthia Rylant's *When I Was Young in the Mountains* (1982) (warm, happy mood). Books that are good for observing and describing characterizations include Mavis Jukes's *Like Jake and Me* (1984) and Arthur Yorinks's *Hey, Al* (1986). Books that are good for observing and describing various settings include Edith Baer's *This Is the Way We Go to School: A Book about Children around the World* (1990) and Susan Campbell Bartoletti's *Growing Up in Coal Country* (1996).

Grade level:

All grades—the grade level depends on the complexity of the pictures or illustrations

Book summaries:

Anno's U.S.A. follows a traveler across the United States; different time periods are shown. *Free Fall* describes a boy's dream. *Tuesday* develops a rural setting in which frogs fly on Tuesday night. *Halloween ABC* is a specialized alphabet book that categorizes Halloween poems according to the letters of the alphabet. *When I Was Young in the Mountains* presents a nostalgic view of growing up in the eastern mountains of the United States. *Like Jake and Me* develops the characters of a boy and his stepfather as they learn to know each other. *Hey, Al* is a fantasy story in which a man must choose between living in luxury on an island and living in the city. *This Is the Way We Go to School: A Book about Children around the World* presents various geographical locations and encourages readers to identify those locations. *Growing Up in Coal Country* presents a photographic essay of children in Pennsylvania about one hundred years ago.

Procedures:

1. In a group, share one of the pictures or illustrations. Lead a discussion in which the students look at the picture or illustration and observe as many details about the picture as possible. The nature of this discussion differs depending on whether the students are focusing on general details, moods, characterizations, or various geographical settings.
2. Divide the students into smaller groups and ask them to write a descriptive paragraph about the illustration. Share and discuss the paragraphs with the whole group. Ask students to provide suggestions for making the paragraphs more descriptive.

3. This activity may be extended as students select additional pictures and illustrations, individually write descriptions, share the descriptions in peer editing groups, and make revisions in their descriptions.

4. Students enjoy reversing this activity and drawing the illustrations that are depicted in the paragraphs. Interesting comparisons may be made between the student illustrations and those provided in the photographs or books.

Activity 4–15:
IMAGINATIVE WRITING MOTIVATED BY BOOK CHARACTERS

TYPE	TERM
● CLASS	● STA
● GROUP	○ LTA
● IND	○ LC

Purpose:
1. To expand the imagination
2. To empathize with a book character and to create a new experience for that character
3. To write a creative story in which a figure from literature comes to life

Materials: Any book characters that are familiar to the students are appropriate for this activity. Younger students may be motivated by reading Else Holmelund Minarik's *The Little Girl and the Dragon* (1991); all students enjoy looking at the illustrations in David Wiesner's *Free Fall* (1988). Videotape of the 1984 film *The Neverending Story* (Peterson, 1986).

Grade level: All grades—this activity is influenced by students' choices of characters from books

Book summaries: *The Little Girl and the Dragon* is a story in which a girl has an adventure when the dragon in her book comes to life and she must control him. *Free Fall* shows various books and characters that might have influenced the boy's adventurous dream.

Procedures:
1. Begin this activity by asking the students to identify favorite fantasy or realistic characters from books. Ask them to describe some of these characters and the types of adventures preferred by the characters. For example, if one of their chosen characters is the wooden puppet in *Pinocchio,* how would they describe his character, his personality, his friends, his likes and dislikes, and his preferred actions? After they have brainstormed their responses, ask students to consider what would happen if, as they are reading the book, the character comes out of the pages and becomes real, or if the character pulls them into the story. Allow the students to explore and expand on their various responses.

2. You may choose to share a book such as *The Little Girl and the Dragon,* in which a dragon from a book comes to life and swallows a girl's toys. She solves her problem by finding a way to get him to return to the book. After students discuss the book, they can choose a figure from a fictional book and pretend that it comes to life. What would happen? What might the figure do for good or for bad? What adventures would the figure create for the students? How would they control the figure? Ask the students to write their own creative adventures and share them with the group.

3. Books such as *Free Fall* may be used to motivate students to write stories in which book characters, story plots, and objects in a room influence dreams and create new adventures for the dreamers. Introduce the book and ask the students to respond to the dream sequence. Do they notice any influences of literary characters, types of books that the boy might have been reading, or objects that are found in his room? Ask the students to identify their own reading and objects in their rooms that might influence their dreams. Have them create their own dream

sequences that might be motivated by these experiences. Ask the students to illustrate their stories and share the stories with their group.

4. For upper elementary and middle school students, as a special treat, you may wish to show a videotape of the film *The Neverending Story* (based on the book of the same title by Michael Ende), in which the book a boy is reading magically draws him into the story to save the other characters. Ask students to imagine what they would do if they suddenly found themselves a character in one of their favorite stories. Have them share their responses with the class.

Activity 4–16:
WRITING BIOGRAPHICAL SKETCHES ABOUT POETS

TYPE	TERM
● CLASS	● STA
● GROUP	● LTA
● IND	○ LC

Purpose:

1. To read a selection of poems by one poet and to write a biography of the poet using the poetry to support the biography

2. To select clues from poetry that reveal the poet's possible past experiences, likes and dislikes, various moods, choices in style, childhood background including family and friends, and so forth

3. To use quotes from poems to support statements

4. To respond to poetry and to include the response when describing the various moods of the poet

5. To write a poem that reflects the information gained about the poet

Materials:

Collect a selection of poems written by various poets. For example, the following poets have written numerous poetry books for children: Arnold Adoff, N. M. Bodecker, Lewis Carroll, John Ciardi, William Cole, Aileen Fisher, Eloise Greenfield, Langston Hughes, X. J. Kennedy, Edward Lear, Myra Cohn Livingston, David McCord, Eve Merriam, A. A. Milne, Jack Prelutsky, Shel Silverstein, Nancy Willard, and Valerie Worth.

Grade level:

All grades—the grade level depends on the poems selected and the versions chosen

Procedures:

1. Before sharing poems written by a published poet, ask students to think about their own poetry writing. Ask questions such as the following: "What influences your own writing? When do you write poetry? What experiences motivate you to write poetry? What experiences are reflected in the poems you write? Would readers of your poetry by aware of these experiences? How and why?" After they have shared these personal experiences, ask students to consider what might motivate a poet to write a poem. If they read enough poetry by the same poet, could they discover information about the poet?

2. Explain to the students that they will be reading numerous poems by the same poet. As they read these poems they will search for clues that can be used to describe the personal life and experiences of the poet. They will find quotes from the poems that support their ideas about the poet and information such as the poet's past experiences, likes and dislikes, moods when writing the poems, choices of style, and childhood background including information about family and friends. After they have discovered enough clues, students will write a biography that describes the life of the poet.

3. Remind the students that a biographer uses research to discover the background of a biographical character. The students' research will be the poetry of the poet as well as the clues and quotes they find within the poetry. As a group activity, choose one of the poets, read the poetry, and search for clues that could provide background information about the person. Ask the students to identify these clues, to tell what they think the clues imply about the poet, and to defend their reasoning. For example, if the first choice for this activity is the poetry of Shel

Silverstein found in his collection *Where the Sidewalk Ends* (1974), the students might find clues such as the following: the first poem, "Invitation," invites dreamers and pretenders to come in and enjoy the poems; the subjects of many of his poems are magic and adventure; "Ickle Me, Pickle Me, Tickle Me Too" shows fun with words and a sense of humor; "The Loser" shows that Silverstein had a mother who frequently complained that he would lose his head if it wasn't fastened on; "For Sale" reveals that he had a sister, but they did not always get along; "Sick" shows that he tried to get out of going to school; and many of the poems reveal that he was a mischievous boy who frequently got into trouble.

4. Divide the students into groups and ask each group to write a brief biography of the poet. They should support any conclusions they make about the poet with quotes from the poetry. When the groups are finished, have them share their biographies with the class. Lead a discussion in which students respond to the strengths and weaknesses of each biography supported by information found in the biography. The groups may rewrite their biographies to reflect the contributions of the group.

5. After the groups have finished one biography, ask each student to select his or her own poet, to read numerous poems written by that poet, and to write a biography of the poet that is supported by quotes from the poetry. Ask the students to share their biographies in their peer editing groups and to respond to suggestions made by the groups.

Activity 4-17:
KNOWING MY AUDIENCES AND MY PURPOSE

TYPE	TERM
● CLASS	● STA
● GROUP	○ LTA
○ IND	○ LC

Purpose:
1. To understand how knowledge of audience and purpose influences writing
2. To understand different purposes for writing
3. To understand that to communicate effectively through writing, a writer needs to consider the reader or audience
4. To understand that a writer needs to know her audience and purpose for writing before evaluating the writing's effectiveness
5. To understand the audience and purpose during the writing process

Materials:
Examples of student-produced materials written for several different purposes and audiences.

Grade level:
All grades—the grade level depends on the degree of difficulty of the written examples

Procedures:
1. Ask students if they always write for the same reason. Have them suggest the purpose they have for writing. A list such as the following might emerge:

WHY DO WE WRITE?

1. We write true stories to describe experiences in class.
2. We write letters to our friends and relatives to tell them what we are doing and to ask about what they are doing.
3. We write invitations to ask people to come to our class.
4. We write puppet shows to entertain our class and ourselves.
5. We write in our diaries to remind us about what we are doing and thinking.
6. We write stories for our class newspaper.
7. We write book reports to tell about books we read.
8. We write charts to describe how we do something.
9. We write about science experiments to explain what happens.
10. We write poetry and stories to entertain ourselves, our class, and our parents.

---

2. Ask the students if the same audience reads each of these types of writing. Discuss the intended audience for each writing purpose listed. Discuss differences in the audiences and how they might affect the content of the writing.
3. Read several examples of student writings to the group or place the writings on transparencies. Ask the students to listen carefully to each example to identify the purpose for writing and the intended audience. Selections can include comic strips, letters to parents, letters to friends, letters to companies asking for information, creative stories, creative poetry, book reports, daily schedules, science experiment charts, and so forth.

4. Read several examples of professional writing. Ask the students to listen carefully and identify the author's purpose for writing and the intended audience. Examples can include children's literature selections, magazine articles, news articles, comic strips, recipes, newspaper feature articles, editorials, and the like.

5. Ask students if they think it is helpful to know the intended purpose and audience before they write. Draw conclusions about how understanding the purpose and audience for writing can make one's writing more effective.

Activity 4–18:
WRITING LETTERS

	TYPE	TERM
	● CLASS	● STA
	● GROUP	○ LTA
	○ IND	○ LC

Purpose:

1. To understand that personal letters have a different purpose and audience than business letters
2. To identify the purpose and audience for a personal letter and contrast it with the purpose and audience for a business letter
3. To write a personal letter to a friend or relative
4. To request information in a business letter addressed to a stranger
5. To relate literature to letter writing and to motivate letter writing using literature

Materials:

Examples of personal and business letters; letter-writing forms (see activity 5–13); literature in which letters are part of the text. For example, Judith Caseley's *Dear Annie* (1991), Janet and Allen Ahlberg's *The Jolly Postman* (1986), Simon James's *Dear Mr. Blueberry* (1991), and Vera B. Williams and Jennifer Williams's *Stringbean's Trip to the Shining Sea* (1988) are appropriate for younger students; Beverly Cleary's *Dear Mr. Henshaw* (1983) is more appropriate for older students.

Grade level:

All grades—writing personal letters is an appropriate activity for all children, and older children may also write business letters

Book summaries:

Dear Annie is based on a series of letters written by Annie and Annie's grandfather. The letters span a number of years between Annie's birth and her years in the early elementary grades. *Dear Mr. Blueberry* is the correspondence between a child and her teacher. The child is convinced that a whale lives in her pond. Mr. Blueberry's letters provide factual information about whales and suggest that a whale could not live in the small pond. In *The Jolly Postman,* the postman delivers letters to fairy-tale characters. *Stringbean's Trip to the Shining Sea* is a series of postcards and snapshots sent home by a boy as he travels across the United States. The plot in *Dear Mr. Henshaw* develops as ten-year-old Leigh Botts writes letters to his favorite author.

Procedures:

1. The purpose of this activity is to write a letter to a friend or relative. Begin by showing the children an envelope with a personal letter enclosed. Ask them if they like to receive letters written just to them. If this letter was addressed to them, who would they wish the sender to be? What would they like to read in the letter? Who would be the audience for the letter? What would be the purpose of the letter?
2. Read examples of two letters; one should be an interesting personal letter to someone the writer knows and the other should be a business letter requesting information from someone the writer does not know. Ask the students to listen to each letter and identify the purpose and audience for each; for example:

July 23,

Dear Sally,

This is the most exciting time I have ever had at camp. Do you remember that I wanted to ride horseback every day? You just wouldn't believe the beautiful horse they gave me. His name is Cinnamon. He is brown and has a black mane and tail. He is real spicy, too. I feel just great when we run across the meadows. I'd like to ride on forever, or at least till I get hungry again.

Speaking of food—do you remember what happened last year when we found a worm in the salad? You wouldn't believe what I found in my chili burger yesterday! A real grasshopper was sitting there staring at me! I screamed, and everyone stopped talking. Our table decided to protest this new food. The camp cooks say it will never happen again. They gave me an extra brownie. I think it was to keep me quiet so I wouldn't complain any more.

Say hello to everyone for me. Don't have that slumber party you talked about until I get home. I'll talk to you about it when I see you next week.

Your best friend,

Jean

---

13 Rosewood Circle
Turnersville, NJ 08012
October 14,

Alaska State Division of Tourism
Pouch E-907
Juneau, Alaska 99811

Dear Sirs:

The fourth-grade class at Jefferson Elementary School is studying festivals in Alaska. Several free brochures for festivals are listed in the State of Alaska Visitor Guide. We would like to order the following brochures:
    L-001 Alaska Festival of Music
    L-002 Anchorage Fur Rendezvous
    L-003 Iceworm Festival
    L-004 Muskeg Stomp
    L-005 Equinox Marathon
    L-012 Cry of the Wild Ram
    L-024 Alaska State Sled Dog Championship
    Thank you for sending us the brochures.

Sincerely,

Jerry Johnson
Fourth-grade class
Jefferson Elementary School

3. Contrast the differences between the purposes and audiences for a personal letter and a business letter. The children may come up with the following points:

Purposes and Audiences for Personal and Business Letters

	Purpose	Audience
Personal Letter	1. To exchange interesting personal information	1. Friend 2. Relative
Business Letter	1. To request information	1. Business person who does not know me
	2. To give information about a business or product	2. Government official who does not know me
	3. To influence a policy maker	

4. Discuss the contents of the personal and business letters. What is the subject matter of each? Are there any special requirements for each letter? Suggest that the personal letter is an informal, friendly exchange between two people who know each other well. It is like having a conversation. The business letter is more formally written. The letter usually requests or gives information to a busy company or business establishment that does not know the writer. The request for information needs to be clearly stated so that the correct information or product will be received.

5. Have the students write a personal letter to a friend or relative, helping the students during the writing process. Have the students mail the letters.

6. Provide a purpose for composing a business letter such as the request for information from the Alaskan travel bureau. Ask students to write and mail the letters.

7. Introduce the books based on letter writing to the students. Ask them to notice how each author writes his or her story around a series of letters or postcards. Encourage students to notice that *Dear Annie* is based on personal letters between a grandfather and his granddaughter. The content of the letters is based on everyday experiences that interest both of the writers. In contrast, *Dear Mr. Blueberry* includes factual information about whales provided by the girl's teacher. Both of these books include exchanges between two people, although the purposes for the letters are quite different. *The Jolly Postman* offers opportunities to relate folklore to letter writing. *Stringbean's Trip to the Shining Sea,* however, focuses on postcards, photographs, and travel experiences that allow the sender to provide information to his family at home. There are no exchanges of ideas, but the postcards are written to a family audience. *Dear Mr. Henshaw* is a much longer and more complex book. Now the author uses letters written by a ten-year-old boy to his favorite author to reveal information about the boy and changes that occur to him during the plot of the story. Ask the students to discuss the purposes for the letters in each of these books.

8. Use these books to motivate students to write their own stories based on letters or postcards. These stories may be based on exchanges of letters between friends or family members, exchanges of letters to gain information, or postcards that might be sent if the students were on a vacation. Or, students can use Beverly Cleary's idea in *Dear Mr. Henshaw* and write letters to a favorite author.

Activity 4–19:
WRITING INVITATIONS

TYPE	TERM
● CLASS	● STA
● GROUP	○ LTA
○ IND	○ LC

Purpose:
1. To understand that invitation writing has a specific purpose and audience
2. To identify the purpose and audience for an invitation
3. To write an invitation that includes information about what, who, why, when, and where

Materials:
Writing materials for invitations.

Grade level:
All grades—the invitations can be dictated by young children and individually written by older children

Procedures:
1. This invitation-writing activity should accompany a classroom activity that stimulates the need to write a real invitation. For example, the following classroom projects might generate invitations:

Project	*Invited Audience*
a. Puppet show	Parents or another class
b. Class art exhibit	Parents or another class
c. Choral reading program	Parents or another class
d. Guest speaker for a science unit, safety unit, health unit, or the like	Scientist, police officer, firefighter, doctor, or the like
e. Band concert	Parents or community (could be a newspaper announcement)
f. Guest speakers during a study of occupations	Engineer, doctor, nurse, dentist, teacher, accountant, mechanic, or the like
g. Open house	Parents or community
h. Athletic events	Another school

2. Discuss the purposes for writing the invitation and the person or persons who will be invited. Suggest that the students pretend to be that person or group. What would they need to know? Contrast any differences between invitations written to schoolmates, parents, all members of the community, and guest speakers whom the students do not know. What characteristics of each audience might influence the way the invitation is written? Compile a list of student suggestions for invitations; for example:

OUR INVITATION SHOULD CONSIDER

1. What are we inviting our guest or guests to attend?
2. Who are we inviting to our class or school?
   Do we know each person we are inviting?
   How old are our invited guests? This will influence the words we use.

3. Why are we inviting our guest or guests?
   Do we want them to be entertained?
   Do we want them to tell us something? If so, what do we want to know? Do we want them to participate in an activity? If so, do they need to come prepared for something?
   Do we want them to see what we are doing and be proud of our school?
4. When do we want our guests to come?
   How long do we want our guests to stay?
5. Where do we want our guests to come?
   Did we give our guests all of the information they will need to find our school, room, gymnasium, or athletic field?
   If our guests do not know our school, did we include an address, directions, and a telephone number if they need more information?

3. Have each student write or dictate an invitation or have the class dictate a group invitation. Interact with the students during the writing process. When necessary, help the students so that their invitation will be clear to the intended audience.

4. Have the students evaluate their invitations. If they were the intended audience, would they have all of the important information after reading the invitations? Are their invitations clear to the audience at which they are aimed? Were the invitations attractive? Would students want to receive the invitations?

5. Have the students send or deliver the invitations to the appropriate audience.

Activity 4-20:
WRITING A NEWS STORY

TYPE	TERM
● CLASS	● STA
● GROUP	○ LTA
○ IND	○ LC

Purpose:
1. To understand that news writing has a specific purpose and audience
2. To identify the purpose and audience for news writing
3. To write a clear, informative, and accurate news story

Materials:
Examples of news stories from school newspapers, city newspapers, and news magazines; writing materials.

Grade level:
Middle and upper elementary, middle school

Procedures:
1. Ask students to bring examples of interesting news stories to school. Provide other examples of news stories from school or class newspapers, city newspapers, and news magazines. As students share their examples, ask them to listen carefully so that they can define the purpose of the kind of information included in, and the intended audience for, each article. Construct a chart of the information students discovered similar to the following:

NEWS STORIES INFORM ABOUT EVENTS

Types of News Articles	Purpose	Information	Audience
1. Sports report of the sixth-grade basketball game—school paper	To tell details of the game	Score; who played; where, when, and how the game was played	Elementary school children, parents, teachers
2. News report of tornado's destruction	To report details of tornado	Where the tornado struck; when it hit; who was hurt; the extent of the damage; how people reacted	All people who read the city paper

2. Have the students discuss the purposes, types of information included, the requirements for news writing, and the intended audience.
3. Ask students to brainstorm ideas for news items that might make up the front page of a classroom newspaper (e.g., a baseball game at recess, an art exhibit in the gym, a guest speaker, the results of a science experiment, a report on a field

trip to the zoo, a fire station, a television station, a museum, a dairy, a class spelling contest, a puppet show presentation, a mock trial, or a report of a film seen in class.

4. Ask students to write news articles for the "Classroom Gazette." Interact with the students while they write to help them improve their ability to produce accurate and clear news stories. Discuss the need for editing and proofreading in newspaper stories. After students have edited and proofread their news stories, duplicate the news stories for a classroom paper.

Activity 4–21:
EVALUATING AND COMPARING SOURCES

TYPE	TERM
● CLASS	● STA
● GROUP	● LTA
● IND	○ LC

Purpose:
1. To develop critical evaluation skills
2. To compare and evaluate sources of information
3. To conduct research
4. To integrate history into the curriculum

Materials:
Jim Murphy's *The Great Fire* (1995) and Pam Belluck's "Barn Door Reopened on Fire after Legend Has Escaped." Adult sources about the Chicago fire include Karen Sawislak's *Smoldering City: Chicago and the Great Fire* (1995). Carl Smith's *Urban Disorder and the Shape of Belief* (1995) places the Chicago fire within the context of American popular culture and Mel Waskin's *Mrs. O'Leary's Comet! Cosmic Causes of the Great Chicago Fire* (1985) speculates that the fire may have been caused by pieces of a comet hitting Chicago.

Grade level:
Middle and upper elementary

Book summaries:
In *The Great Fire,* Murphy uses photographs and personal accounts to present the history of the growth and development of the city before the fire, the destruction and deaths caused by the fire, and the beginnings of regrowth that the city experienced after the fire. In the article "Barn Door Reopened on Fire after Legend Has Escaped," Pam Belluck presents an insurance lawyer's recent findings that the fire may actually have been caused by Mrs. O'Leary's neighbor, Daniel "Peg Leg" Sullivan.

Procedures:
1. To motivate interest in a study of the history of the Chicago fire, discuss the various causes and destructive possibilities of fire. Locate the city of Chicago on a map of the United States. Show a photograph of present-day Chicago. Compare and contrast it with photographs of the Chicago of 1871, before the fire.
2. Have students read *The Great Fire*. Divide the class into seven groups, making each responsible for one of the following seven chapters: "A City Ready to Burn," "Everything Went Wrong," "The Dogs of Hell Were Upon the Housetops," "A Surging Ocean of Flames," "Chicago Is in Flames," "The Ghost of Chicago," and "Myth and Reality." Have each group discuss and summarize its chapter and then report its findings to the rest of the class.
3. Read "Barn Door Reopened on Fire after Legend Has Escaped" aloud to the class.
4. Ask students to compare and contrast the information presented in Jim Murphy's book and in Pam Belluck's article. What point of view does each publication take? How is the information presented? Do the authors separate fact and theory? What techniques do the authors use to make you visualize the fire and the circumstances surrounding the fire?
5. Have students summarize the strengths and weaknesses of each point of view. How do illustrations add to the authenticity of the publications? What is it about the fire that keeps people interested in it?

6. Discuss the lore and legend surrounding the fire. Introduce and discuss the popular folk song about the fire:

> One dark night when we were all in bed
> Old Lady Leary lit the lantern in the shed
> When the cow kicked it over she winked her eye and said,
> "It'll be a hot time in the old town tonight."

Which story does this song support? What details are emphasized? Which facts are overlooked?

7. For a related activity, have students investigate other great fires such as the Yellowstone fire. Discussion could relate to a science activity and center around the fire's role in the destruction and regeneration of nature.

Activity 4–22:

THE CONTROLLING IDEA IN A PARAGRAPH

TYPE	TERM
● CLASS	● STA
● GROUP	○ LTA
○ IND	○ LC

Purpose:
1. To identify the controlling idea in a paragraph
2. To write paragraphs with the controlling idea appearing in different positions in the paragraph

Materials:
Examples of paragraphs written in the following formats:

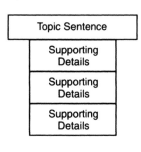 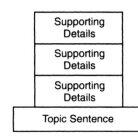 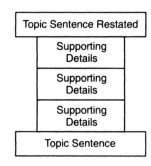

Grade level:
Middle elementary

Procedures:
1. Discuss the fact that topic sentences or the main idea of a paragraph may be found in different positions in the paragraph.
2. Show examples and discuss these paragraph forms. (Use the same topic and supporting details but write the information in three different paragraph forms.) For example, all of the following paragraph forms contain the main idea "Spring is my favorite season of the year":

Spring is my favorite season of the year.

In spring, the wild flowers make the meadows bright with color.

The days in spring become longer so I can play outside.

Best of all, baseball season starts in the spring so I can play my favorite sport.

In spring, the wild flowers make the meadows bright with color. The days in spring become longer so I can play outside. Best of all, baseball season starts in the spring so I can play my favorite sport.

Spring is my favorite season of the year.

```
┌─────────────────────────────────────────┐
│   Spring is my favorite season of the year. │
├────┬─────────────────────────────────┬───┤
│    │ In spring, the wild flowers     │   │
│    │ make the meadows bright         │   │
│    │ with color.                     │   │
│    │ The days in spring              │   │
│    │ become longer so I can          │   │
│    │ play outside.                   │   │
│    │ Best of all, baseball season    │   │
│    │ starts in the spring so         │   │
│    │ I can play my favorite sport.   │   │
├────┴─────────────────────────────────┴───┤
│  I think spring is the greatest time of the year. │
└─────────────────────────────────────────┘
```

3. Have the students turn the topic sentence into a question: Why is spring my favorite season of the year? Ask them if each of the supporting details answers the topic-sentence question.

4. Next, have the students choose a topic sentence and write their own paragraphs illustrating each of the paragraph forms. This activity can be done by first dividing the students into groups and having them write group-suggested paragraphs and later asking them to develop paragraphs individually.

Activity 4–23:
ORGANIZATION USING CHRONOLOGICAL ORDER

TYPE	TERM
● CLASS	○ STA
● GROUP	● LTA
○ IND	○ LC

Purpose:
1. To identify the chronological organization of a paragraph and a longer selection
2. To write a paragraph and a longer selection using chronological organization

Materials:
Examples of paragraphs written in chronological order; examples of multiparagraph selections showing chronological organization (e.g., descriptions of historical events, class trips, and experiments).

Grade level:
Middle and upper elementary, middle school

Procedures:
1. Display and discuss several paragraphs written in chronological order. Read the paragraphs with the children and let them figure out the organization of the paragraph; for example:

MAKING DECORATIVE CANDLES

You can make very pretty candles if you have paraffin wax, coloring, a can, and string. First, you melt the paraffin wax in the top of a double boiler. After the wax has melted, you may add wax coloring, if you wish. Tie a string or candlewick around a pencil. Place the pencil over the top of an empty orange juice can, making sure that the string hangs in the middle of the can. Pour the hot wax into the can. Let the wax cool and harden. Finally, remove the candle from the can and cut the string to remove the pencil.

Lead the class into the discovery that the paragraph is organized according to the order of events. You could draw the order of this paragraph in the following manner:

Chronological Order	*Steps in Making Candles*
first	↓ melt paraffin
to	↓ add wax coloring
↓ last	↓ place string tied to pencil on can
	↓ pour wax into can
	↓ let wax harden
	↓ remove candle from can

Ask the students to suggest other topics that could be written about in chronological order.

2. Provide a variety of one-paragraph and multiparagraph selections using chronological order. Ask children what types of subjects use this order.

3. Present a variety of experiences to the children such as performing an experiment, going on a field trip, describing the steps in playing a game, making a recipe, or researching historical events. Have the students write chronologically ordered one-paragraph and multiparagraph reports, depending on the subject matter.

Activity 4–24:

ORGANIZATION USING QUESTIONS AND ANSWERS

	TYPE		TERM
●	CLASS	○	STA
●	GROUP	●	LTA
○	IND	○	LC

Purpose:

1. To identify the organizational pattern of a paragraph or multiparagraph selection that uses a question-and-answer format
2. To brainstorm ideas for questions to answer
3. To write a paragraph or multiparagraph article that uses a question-and-answer format

Materials:

Examples of paragraphs written in a question-and-answer format (science and social studies materials frequently use this format, or a literature selection may ask a question about a character and then describe the character).

Grade level:

All grades

Procedures:

1. Show and discuss several paragraphs written in question-and-answer form. Read the paragraphs with the children and help them discover the organization. For example, an early elementary question-and-answer paragraph might be developed this way:

I PLAY WITH MY BEST FRIEND

What do I like to do with my best friend? Penny and I play every day after school. We like to take our skateboards over to the park. We race on the sidewalk and try to do tricks on the skateboard. When we get tired of the skateboards, we play on the swings. My friend and I like to fly high in the air.

Help the students discover the question-and-answer format of the paragraph. Ask the following: "Does each sentence in the paragraph answer the question at the beginning of the paragraph?" You could draw the order of this paragraph in the following way:

Question   ***What do I like to do with my best friend?***
  ↓ Answer | Play after school
                                     | Skateboard in the park
                                 ↓ Play on the swings

A longer, multiparagraph composition can follow the same format, with each paragraph asking and answering a question about the main topic; for example:

Santa Claus Around the World

Question   *Who was the original Saint Nicholas?*
  ↓Answer   │Discuss bishop of Myra, in Asia
                                 ↓Minor, 4th century A.D.
Question   *Who brings Christmas presents in the*
                                 Netherlands and Belgium?
  │
  ↓ Answer   │Discuss Sinter Klaas and his assistant,
                                 ↓Black Peter
Question   *Who brings Christmas presents in*
  │   *Great Britain?*
  ↓ Answer   ↓ Discuss Father Christmas
Question   *Who brings Christmas presents in France?*
  ↓ Answer   ↓ Discuss Père Noël
Question   *Who brings Christmas presents in the*
  │   *United States?*
  ↓ Answer   ↓ Discuss Santa Claus

2. Provide a variety of one-paragraph or multiparagraph selections using a question-and-answer format. Have students find different types of materials that use this format. Ask them to include selections from their textbooks.

3. Allow children to write their own questions and answers in paragraph or multi-paragraph form. Have students list, in a brainstorming activity, a number of questions they might like to investigate; for example:

QUESTIONS WE COULD INVESTIGATE

1. How do they celebrate Christmas in Mexico? (Russia, England, Norway, and so forth)?
2. What kind of training does an astronaut have?
3. What happens to a letter when it gets to our post office?
4. Why is a fir tree a symbol for Christmas?
5. Why does a plant need light to grow?
6. How does a cloud form into a rainstorm?
7. Why do your eyes blink?
8. How does a windmill pump water without using electricity?
9. Why does a microwave oven cook food more rapidly than a regular electric or gas oven?
10. What qualifications does the president of the United States need to have?
11. Why do I like Fridays?
12. What do we like to do on weekends?
13. What do we like to do at the zoo?

Activity 4–25:

ORGANIZATION USING SPATIAL CONCEPTS OR PHYSICAL DETAILS

TYPE	TERM
● CLASS	○ STA
● GROUP	● LTA
○ IND	○ LC

Purpose:

1. To identify the organizational pattern of a paragraph or multiparagraph selection that uses a spatial concept of direction or physical detail
2. To write a paragraph and a longer selection using a spatial concept of direction or physical detail

Materials:

Examples of paragraphs that describe spatial order (materials that describe happenings in one location, then in another location; stories or reports that proceed from inside to outside; paragraphs that take the reader on a visual trip from right to left or top to bottom).

Grade level:

Middle and upper elementary, middle school

Procedures:

1. Show and discuss several paragraphs that describe spatial order. Read the paragraphs with the children and help them discover the organization; for example:

A VISIT TO A MOAT AND BAILEY CASTLE

Today Sue and Brad Martin went to visit a very old, dilapidated castle that had once defended a village. They were very excited as they got out of the car and looked toward the castle. They saw the moat and the drawbridge that would take them into the castle compound. Their eyes followed the worn path up to the castle. The castle appeared to be built of thick stone walls with slit windows that allowed the guards to watch the countryside. Sue and Brad had studied such castles. They knew that if they could look into the lower windows, they would see rooms used for storage. The middle windows would probably look into eating rooms, and the upper windows would look into sleeping rooms. When their eyes reached the top of the tower, they imagined they saw several guards pointing excitedly into the distance. Sue and Brad could not wait to start their exploration of the castle.

Lead the class into the discovery that the paragraph is organized according to direction. The paragraph illustrates a visual trip from the moat to the drawbridge and up to the top of the castle tower. You could diagram the order of this paragraph in the following way:

Bottom	*Looking at the castle*
↓ Top	↓ moat and drawbridge
	↓ worn path to castle
	↓ lower rooms
	↓ middle rooms
	↓ upper rooms
	↓ tower

A longer story describing Sue and Brad's adventure exploring the castle could be written using the same bottom-to-top format. Each paragraph could describe what they see in each level of the castle.

Authors of literature selections often use a directional format to describe a character. The following example of such a descriptive paragraph can be used with older elementary children:

THE OLD MAN IN THE PARK

While walking through the park, we saw an old man sitting on a bench. His shoes were new and shiny black. The shiny black of his shoes contrasted with his milky white ankles that were bare of stockings. His pants were cuffed, baggy, and torn. His shirt was made of faded flannel, a pocket was missing, and his sleeves were rolled over the elbows. The arms extending from the sleeves were gray, but his hands were calloused from hard work. On his wrinkled face was an expression of contentment and satisfaction because today he had found a new pair of shiny black shoes.

---

2. Provide a variety of one-paragraph and multiparagraph stories or reports using directional organization. Ask children to suggest subjects that might use this type of organization.

3. Have children propose topics and write their own paragraphs, using directional organization.

Activity 4–26:

ORGANIZATION USING A PROBLEM, CAUSE, AND SOLUTION FORMAT

TYPE	TERM
● CLASS	○ STA
● GROUP	● LTA
○ IND	○ LC

Purpose:
1. To identify the organizational pattern of a paragraph or multiparagraph selection using a problem, cause, and solution of problem format
2. To brainstorm ideas for problem investigations
3. To write a paragraph or multiparagraph selecting using a problem, cause, and solution of problem format

Materials: Examples of paragraphs or multiparagraph selections using this format (from social studies or science writing).

Grade level: Middle and upper elementary, middle school

Procedures:
1. Show and discuss several paragraphs written in a problem, cause, and solution of problem format. Read the paragraphs with the children and help them discover the type of organization. For example, the problem of an argument on the playground might be written about in the following way:

THE BASKETBALL AND MARBLE FEUD

Every day this week, our third-grade class has had an argument at the beginning of recess. Some of the students want to use the blacktop on the school yard to play basketball. Other students want to play marbles on that same space. Both groups get in each other's way and shout at each other. We are trying to solve this problem. We could take turns. The basketball players could use the blacktop during morning recess; the marble players could use the blacktop during afternoon recess. We are also looking for other good places to play marbles. If we find a good spot, we will all be happy during both recesses.

Help students discover the organization of the paragraph. You could draw the order of this paragraph in the following way:

Problem
   ↓ Cause of problem

       ↓ Possible solutions
        to problem

An argument at recess
   ↓ Some students want to play
      basketball and some want to
      play marbles in the same space

   ↓ Taking turns on the blacktop
     Another place to play marbles

2. Provide a variety of one-paragraph or multiparagraph selections using this form. Encourage students to think of materials that are organized in this format including social studies texts and newspaper articles.

3. Provide opportunities for students to write their own paragraphs or longer articles. Brainstorm with the class and list a number of problems the students could investigate. Some problems might be closely related to the school and community and would require investigation by observation and interviewing. Other problems may be related to content subjects or national concerns and require library research. (The subject matter also depends on the students' grade level.)

PROBLEMS WE COULD INVESTIGATE

The taste and appearance of the spinach served in the school cafeteria
Discovering that your bicycle is missing
The pollution of the river near our school
A forest fire in our state park
The electricity was off for four hours this morning
A small percentage of people voted in the last election

Activity 4–27:
SEQUENCE FOR WRITING ABOUT LITERATURE

TYPE	TERM
● CLASS	○ STA
● GROUP	● LTA
● IND	○ LC

Purpose:
1. To learn how to write about literature
2. To collect data to support a claim and to generate evidence
3. To learn to use quotations as supporting evidence for conclusions
4. To develop higher thought processes
5. To analyze, through writing, an author's ability to develop believable characterizations in biographies

Materials:
Biographies such as Jean Fritz's *The Great Little Madison* (1989) that provide numerous supporting details and credible quotations; illustrated books that provide background information about the time periods of the biographies, such as Alice Provensen's *The Buck Stops Here: The Presidents of the United States* (1990).

Grade level:
Middle elementary through middle school, depending on the complexity of the writing task and the amount of detail used as supporting evidence

Book summaries:
The Great Little Madison is a biography about the fourth president of the United States. The biography traces Madison's life from being a sickly child to becoming a powerful leader. *The Buck Stops Here: The Presidents of the United States* is a highly illustrated information book that presents the major happenings associated with various presidents.

Procedures:
1. This activity is designed to instruct students in the use of Kahn, Walter, and Johannessen's (1984) sequence for writing about literature. This sequence may be used with many different genres of literature. The sequence has the following elements:
   a. First, establish a focus or reason for reading and analyzing. This focus includes elaborating reasoning for an audience, preliminary thinking about a subject, and identifying and defending views when challenged.
   b. Second, extract evidence or collect data to support a claim. This phase requires collecting and evaluating evidence to determine whether it is specific enough, generating good evidence, and helping students to search for and learn to use specific quotations and details from a literary work as supporting evidence for their conclusions.
   c. Third, link the data and the claim with warrants. This phase requires helping students to explain how each piece of evidence supports the conclusion.
   d. Fourth, plan and compose for a new but related paper about the same subject. This phase requires helping students to argue their viewpoints and applying skills practiced in the previous activities in a new situation.
2. To help students establish a focus or reason for reading and analyzing *The Great Little Madison,* introduce the book by providing some information about the author as well as the time period. For example, information about the author might include the following:

The author, Jean Fritz, is a well-known biography writer. She believes that well-written biographies allow readers to explore human behavior and to come to grips with how characters relate to their times. She believes that biographies should provide clues for life and be truthful accounts of the personages. Consequently, the characters need to be well developed and should allow readers to understand that the characters have many sides, both good and bad. We are going to read and analyze Fritz's ability to create believable and truthful characters in one of her biographies, *The Great Little Madison*. As you read and analyze this book you will also be deciding if you think that the awards given to this book are justified. For example, the book was the 1990 winner of the Boston Globe–Horn Book Nonfiction Award and the winner of the Orbis Pictus Award.

Information about the time period is also helpful. It is beneficial if students understand Madison's time period, 1751–1836, and the role he played in both the Continental Congress and as the fourth president of the United States. Share maps with the students to show them the locations of the original colonies. Also share illustrations that depict the historical setting of the United States during Madison's lifetime. The highly illustrated *The Buck Stops Here: The Presidents of the United States* may be used to introduce students to the accomplishments of the previous presidents and to the contributions of the fourth president, James Madison. Spend as much time as necessary to acquaint the students with this important period in history.

After introducing the book and the time period, ask students the following: "How could the author make James Madison into a believable character, a person whom you understand? How can an author make you understand the many sides of a character?" Allow students to identify what makes a character believable for them and what an author might do to create such a character. After the students have presented their opinions, tell them that they are going to read *The Great Little Madison,* draw conclusions about Madison's character as presented in the text, provide evidence that supports those conclusions, and decide whether Madison, for them, is a believable character. They will also support why Fritz did or did not create a believable character. To justify their positions, however, students will need to elaborate on their conclusions about characterization and their reasons for deciding whether Madison is a believable character and identify ways that Fritz used to make him believable. If they decide that Madison is not a believable character, they must also justify their beliefs. Remind the students that to identify and defend their views they will need to use evidence from the book or other sources. This evidence frequently is developed in the form of quotes.

Explain to the students that they will be approaching this task in two parts. During the first part of the task, they will read, discuss, and analyze the first chapter in groups and present their evidence and reasoning to the whole class. During the second part, they will individually read the remainder of the book; define any additional information about Madison's character; and support or reject their original beliefs about Madison's character, the believability of Madison's character, and the author's ability to create such a character. These individual papers will be shared and discussed with the class. (If desired, these papers may be used to form a debate as students decide on Madison's character and defend the believability of the Madison character.)

3. Tell the students that they will read, or listen to, the first chapter of *The Great Little Madison* as they identify as much information as possible about James Madison, make conclusions about Madison's character, and explore how Jean Fritz develops believable characterization. As they analyze James Madison's characterization, they will collect and evaluate evidence to analyze the effectiveness of the

technique used by Fritz. They will also find specific quotations and details from the biography that support their conclusions.

Begin this task by doing one or two examples together as a group. For example, ask the students to listen carefully and identify an example of characterization that they can support with evidence. (Many of these characterizations will be implied in the text.) Students usually identify the information about characterization presented on the first page: "James Madison was a small, pale, sickly boy with a weak voice. If he tried to shout, the shout shriveled up in his throat, but of course he was still young. His voice might grow as he did. Or he might never need a big voice" (p. 7). Ask students to identify what this passage tells them about Madison's physical characteristics, what evidence supports this characterization, and how effective a technique it is for allowing them to "see" and understand Madison.

Continue by doing another example together. Students usually identify characterization implied by the text on pages 7 and 8: "At nine he was reading, and although he had always asked questions of his own (Where do the redbirds fly in winter?), he was discovering in his father's library questions he would never have thought of asking. His father had eighty-five books and by the time he was eleven, James had read them all. They had titles like *The Duty of Man, The Employment of the Microscope.* There was one on cold bathing; one on children's diseases. He may have been especially interested in the diseases for he was sick a great deal. . . . In any case, sickness didn't often keep him from reading. Nothing ever would" (p. 8).

Ask the students to identify what this information tells them about Madison's character. For example, they may state that they think that Madison was an excellent and avid reader who was also sick a great deal. If they have background information about the time period, they may tell you that Madison was a member of a wealthy and highly educated family. They may also tell you that Madison had great curiosity and asked many questions that could be answered by reading. They may also draw some conclusions about Madison's interests in reading such as books on politics, science, and children's diseases.

Then ask the students to support their conclusions about Madison's character with evidence from the text or even background information from other sources. Ask them to identify the quotes that support their conclusions and to defend why their quotes provide supporting evidence for their conclusions. Ask them to discuss the techniques that Fritz uses to develop these characterizations and to provide some evaluation about the effectiveness of these techniques. Also encourage the students to realize how successive evidence builds to support or reject various conclusions. For example, several details in this second quote reinforce the fact that Madison was a sickly child.

After students have identified and discussed several examples, divide the class into groups. Have each group read the first chapter, identify instances of characterizations, collect evidence to support their characterizations, and discuss why these quotes and other evidence do or do not support specific conclusions about the character. Ask each group to compose a group statement about Madison's characterization as developed in the first chapter. They should select their best evidence and defend that evidence as it relates to Madison's character. If necessary, help the students explain how and why each piece of evidence supports the conclusion. Ask them to develop a group statement about the effectiveness of Fritz's techniques to develop characterization. Have each group present its statements and arguments to the rest of the groups. Allow students to discuss their various positions and to defend why their evidence supports their conclusions.

4. After students have completed this first activity, allow them to individually finish the book. They should continue to draw conclusions about Madison's character, provide evidence that supports those conclusions, and evaluate the effectiveness

of Fritz to create a believable character. Provide as much individual guidance as necessary. You may encourage students to share their work in peer editing groups and to receive reactions from their peers as part of the revision process. When completed, allow the students to share and discuss their papers on Madison's characterization.

5. This sequence may be used with any genre of literature. For example, students could identify themes in literature, provide evidence for those themes, and defend why their quotes and other evidence support those themes.

Activity 4–28:

COMPOSITION: POSITIVE VERSUS NEGATIVE VALUES OF LIVING FOREVER

TYPE	TERM
● CLASS	● STA
● GROUP	○ LTA
● IND	○ LC

Purpose:
1. To identify and defend a position through writing
2. To develop a carefully detailed argument
3. To develop higher cognitive skills
4. To analyze point of view in a book and to relate the point of view to a position
5. To work together to develop a position

Materials: Natalie Babbitt's *Tuck Everlasting* (1975).

Grade level: Upper elementary and middle school

Book summary: *Tuck Everlasting* is a fantasy set in rural America during an earlier time period. As Winnie interacts with the Tuck family, she discovers the real consequences of living forever. She also must make a decision. Should she join the Tucks in their everlasting life?

Procedures:
1. This activity is designed to help students identify a position and defend the position with evidence from the text as well as personal knowledge.

2. Introduce the book so that the students are interested in the topic and motivated to do the activity. For example, ask the following: "Have you ever had the desire to live forever? Try to imagine that you can live forever. What would your life be like? How would people respond to you? How would this ability change the way you live right now? Now try to imagine that you have a choice. Right now you cannot live forever, but you have found people who can. You have also discovered their secret. What would you do? Would you choose your life the way it is now? Or, would you choose to do whatever is necessary to have everlasting life? This is the problem facing ten-year-old Winnie Foster when she meets the Tuck family in *Tuck Everlasting*. As you read (or listen to) the book try to imagine what is would be like to be part of the Tuck family. As you interact with the characters try to decide if, for them, eternal life is a blessing or a curse. As you read about the interaction between the Tucks and Winnie, imagine that you are Winnie Foster. What advice would you give her as she discovers the Tuck family secret? What advice would you give her as she makes the most important decision in her life? At the end of the book, do you believe that she made the correct decision? Why or why not?"

3. Point of view is very important in this book. Discuss these different points of view so that students will realize that point of view could make a big difference as they try to answer the question about the positive and negative values of living forever. Several points of view are developed in the book: that of the Tuck family as they face and often hide from the consequences of their everlasting life, that of ten-year-old Winnie as she faces her own inner conflicts and makes her decision about joining the Tucks in everlasting life, and that of the stranger who follows

Winnie and wants to market the spring water and gain a fortune. There is also the implied point of view of various people in the book who do not know that the Tuck family lives forever.

4. As the students read or listen to the book, ask them to try to identify the positive and negative values of living forever. After they complete the book, ask them to write a paragraph in which they choose to write about and defend either the positive or negative values of living forever, students may also write a paper in which they contrast the positive and negative values of living forever. Another option for the paper would be to choose a point of view of one of the characters in the book and to write a response from that point of view. After they have completed their papers, divide the students into peer groups and ask them to share their papers with the peer groups. At this point they can edit their papers following the interactions with the peer group or they can write a group paper that incorporates the best features of the individual papers.

Activity 4–29:

COMPOSITION: ARE *LIKE* AND
EQUAL THE SAME THING?

TYPE	TERM
● CLASS	● STA
● GROUP	● LTA
● IND	○ LC

Purpose:

1. To identify and defend a position through writing
2. To develop a carefully detailed argument
3. To develop higher cognitive skills
4. To work together to develop a position

Materials:

Madeleine L'Englè's *A Wrinkle in Time* (1962).

Grade level:

Upper elementary and middle school

Book summary:

A Wrinkle in Time is a science fiction novel set on both Earth and distant planets. The power of love allows Meg to rescue her father from the evil influence of It.

Procedures:

1. This activity is designed to help students take, defend, and support a position through writing. Explain to the students that *A Wrinkle in Time* includes a debate between one of the main characters and a powerful being from another planet. Tell the students that after reading this book they will choose a position and write a paragraph about why they chose that position.

2. Before reading the book write the words *like* and *equal* on the board. Encourage the students to brainstorm meanings of the two words. Ask the following: "Do you think *like* and *equal* are the same thing? Why or why not?"

3. Introduce the book in such a way that it stimulates interest and motivates the students to participate in the activity. You might ask the following: "Have you ever wanted to have an adventure that took you to strange and different planets? What do you think you would find there? Are the inhabitants like those on earth, or do you think they would be very different? What would happen if you discovered a very evil being on one of these planets? Would you be able to rescue a family member from that evil being? What power do you think you have that would help you make such a rescue? This is the exciting adventure that happens to Meg and Charles Wallace Murry in *A Wrinkle in Time*. Throughout this book you will follow the children as they travel in the fifth dimension to a far-distant planet, where their father has been imprisoned by the evil power It. As you read the interactions between Meg and It, be sure to follow the argument and try to identify how you would respond to the questions 'Are *like* and *equal* the same thing?' and 'Will people be happier if they are all alike?' "

4. As students read or listen to the book ask them to think about the following questions: "Are *like* and *equal* the same thing?" and "Will people be happier if they are all alike?" Ask the students to pretend that they have an opportunity to respond during this discussion between Meg and It. How would they respond to these questions?

5. After completing the book, ask the students to write a paragraph in which they answer the following questions: "Are *like* and *equal* the same thing?" and "Will

people be happier if they are all alike?" They should defend their answers with evidence from the book and from other sources including their own experiences.

6. After the compositions are completed, divide the class into peer groups and encourage the students to read their paragraphs to the peer groups. They may either react to each other's papers and write improved individual papers or a group paper that includes the best points from the individual papers and the student's discussions. Share these papers with the whole class.

7. If preferred, this activity may be developed as an oral debate topic in which the students are divided according to the positions. "*Like* and *equal* are the same thing" or "*Like* and *equal* are very different." Likewise, they may debate the positions "People will be happier if they are all alike" or "People will not be happier if they are all alike."

8. Another contrasting topic developed in this book is the power of love versus the power of evil. Students can develop compositions or debate which power they believe is the greatest.

Activity 4–30:

COMPOSITION: WHICH CHARACTER GAINED THE GREATEST UNDERSTANDING?

TYPE	TERM
● CLASS	● STA
● GROUP	○ LTA
● IND	○ LC

Purpose:

1. To identify and defend a position through writing
2. To develop a carefully detailed argument
3. To develop higher cognitive skills
4. To work together in a group

Materials: Sid Fleischman's *The Whipping Boy* (1986).

Grade level: Middle and upper elementary

Book summary: *The Whipping Boy* is set in an earlier time period, a time in which an heir to the throne cannot be whipped for bad behavior. In this story, the prince has a whipping boy, a poor orphan, who is frequently spanked but also learns to read and write because he must be with the prince during his lessons. In a plot twist the prince and his whipping boy are kidnapped and held for ransom. The outlaws believe that the whipping boy is the prince, because he can read and write.

Procedures:

1. This activity is designed to help students take and defend a position about which of the characters in the book, the prince or the whipping boy, gained the greatest understanding from his experiences. As long as students defend their answers, there is no correct answer.

2. Introduce the book in a way that will interest and motivate the students. For example, ask students the following: "What would your life be like if every time you got into trouble someone else was punished for your actions? What kind of a person would you be if you did not have to pay for your own actions? Would you like the person who received your punishment? Would you try to prevent the person from being punished, or would you behave so that the person received harsh punishment? If you were the person who received the punishment, would you like the person whose punishment you received? This is the problem faced by the characters in *The Whipping Boy.* The story takes place a long time ago when royalty could not be whipped for their actions. Consequently, if you were a prince you would always have someone nearby to receive your rightful punishment. As you read (or listen to) this story, imagine that you are Jemmy, the whipping boy for the arrogant and spiteful 'Prince Brat.' Try to imagine what it would be like if Prince Brat forces you to run away with him and you are both captured by outlaws who want to hold you for ransom. Follow the changes in both the prince and his whipping boy as they take charge of their situation and learn to better understand each other. How would you feel at the end of the story? Which character gained the greatest understanding, the prince or Jemmy?"

3. Ask students to trace the changes in the story as the characters go from individuals who hate each other to friends. Both Jemmy and the prince learn about themselves and each other as they solve their problems. Ask the students to consider

what happened to each character as a consequence of the story. Ask students the following: "How did each character change? Which character do you believe gained the greatest understanding by the end of the story? Why do you believe that the character gained the greatest understanding? How would that understanding change the character's life?"

4. After reading or listening to the book, ask students to choose the character whom they believe gained the greatest understanding and to write a paragraph about why they chose either the prince or Jemmy. Make sure that students defend their answers with evidence from the book.

5. After completing their paragraphs, divide the students into groups according to those who chose the prince and those who chose Jemmy. Ask the students to read their paragraphs in their peer groups. Ask one of the students to record the arguments and the evidence that various students used to develop their points. Allow the students to write a group composition in which they incorporate their best ideas. After the group compositions are completed, ask the students to share their compositions with the entire class. Discuss how each group used evidence to develop the position.

6. If preferred, this activity may be developed as a debate in which students choose either side: "The Prince Gained the Greatest Understanding by the End of the Story" or "Jemmy Gained the Greatest Understanding by the End of the Story." Just as in the writing activity, encourage the students to defend their positions with evidence from the book.

7. Students may choose additional books in which two characters are in conflict and develop position papers around those characters.

Activity 4–31:

COMPOSITION: WHAT IS COURAGE?

TYPE	TERM
● CLASS	● STA
● GROUP	● LTA
● IND	○ LC

Purpose:
1. To identify and defend a position through writing
2. To develop a carefully detailed argument
3. To develop higher cognitive skills
4. To work together to develop a position

Materials:
Maia Wojciechowska's *Shadow of a Bull* (1964) and Mary Downing Hahn's *Stepping on the Cracks* (1991).

Grade level:
Upper elementary and middle school

Book summaries:
Shadow of a Bull is set in Spain. The book develops a person-against-self conflict as a boy struggles with his own feelings when the men of the village begin training him to become a bullfighter like his father. The boy prefers to be a doctor but does not know if he has the courage to go against the wishes of the townspeople. *Stepping on the Cracks* is set in the United States during World War II. The characters in the book must decide whether they will help an army deserter.

Procedures:
1. This activity is designed to help students define, for themselves and the class, the elements of courage. After reading a book and debating the subject, students write a paper that documents what they believe courage is. They will share their ideas and write a group paper that characterizes courage. Begin the activity by brainstorming with students to answer the following questions: "What is courage? When do we know that a person has courage? What are the characteristics we would look for?" Write the list of attributes related to courage on the board.

2. Tell students that they will be reading or listening to a book about a boy who has a special problem. As they read the book, they will be deciding the following: "What is *courage*? Does this boy demonstrate courage?" Introduce the book so that students are interested in the subject. For example, you might say:

   Imagine that you live in Spain. Your father was a famous and fearless bullfighter, and the whole town expects you to be just like your father. What would you do if you did not want to be a bullfighter? How would you feel if you were afraid of bulls and if you thought that you were a coward? How would you work it out if you had a dream for a career that was quite different from that of your father? How would you convince people that it was all right for you to follow your own dream? This is the problem that you will read about in *Shadow of a Bull*. As you read this book, place yourself in Manolo's position. You have your own preferences, but everyone believes that you will follow in your dead father's footsteps. Try to imagine Manolo's inner conflicts as he learns to be true to himself. What do you think Manolo learns about himself? What do you think the people in his town discover about Manolo? When you finish this book, try to decide what courage is. Do you believe that Manolo is courageous? Why or why not?

3. As the students read or listen to the book ask them to be thinking about the question "What is *courage*?" For example, is it courageous or cowardly to admit fear of the bull? Is it more courageous to face the bull in the bullring or to face the crowd and tell them that you prefer being a doctor? After students have finished the book, ask them to write a paragraph on the theme "What is courage?" They should decide whether they believe that Manolo is courageous or cowardly and document their answers by providing support from the text.

4. After students have finished their paragraphs, divide them into writing groups and ask them to share their paragraphs with their peer groups. Ask someone in each group to list the various definitions of *courage* as well as the pros and cons of Manolo's actions that make him either courageous or cowardly. After the group members have shared and recorded all of their thoughts, ask them to write a joint paragraph that develops the beliefs of the majority of students. Make sure that they carefully develop their arguments with evidence from the book. After these group papers are completed, share each of the group papers with the whole class.

5. You may use *Stepping on the Cracks* to motivate a similar activity. Now students must again define *courage* and answer the question "Is Stuart courageous?"

6. Students may extend this activity into an oral debate as they discuss the various definitions of and attributes related to courage. Again, they should support their arguments with details and evidence.

7. Another extension activity can develop as students identify other real-life or literary characters whom the students believe demonstrate the characteristics of courage and meet their definitions of "What is *courage*?"

Activity 4–32:
WRITING AN AUTOBIOGRAPHY

TYPE	TERM
● CLASS	● STA
● GROUP	● LTA
● IND	○ LC

Purpose:
1. To develop and improve creative and factual writing skills
2. To introduce the concept of autobiography as a genre of literature
3. To increase self-awareness and self-understanding through a writing activity
4. To verbalize and share real and hypothetical experiences

Materials:
Bill Peet: An Autobiography (1989).

Grade level:
All grades

Book summaries:
Bill Peet: An Autobiography uses words and illustrations to trace Bill Peet's life from his early boyhood in Indiana through his esteemed career as an artist for Disney Studios, where he was the top writer-illustrator for such films as *Fantasia, Cinderella, Peter Pan,* and *One Hundred and One Dalmatians.*

Procedures:
1. Introduce and define the concept of *autobiography.* Tell students that it is an account of a person's life written by that person. It is usually written in the first person and provides a record of how a person thinks and feels as he or she experiences life. Give examples of information that people often include in autobiographies and mention what you might include in your own autobiography. Also give examples of what a public figure such as the president of the United States, an author, or a sports figure might include in his or her autobiography.

2. Have students read or listen to *Bill Peet: An Autobiography.*

3. Ask students what they discovered about Bill Peet, his experiences, and his life.

4. Have students write their own autobiographies up to the present. Tell them to include information about where they were born and about their family members, friends, pets, memorable trips, hobbies, and likes and dislikes.

5. Once they have finished their factual autobiographies have students write futuristic, creative autobiographies. Tell students to pretend that they are ninety years old, they are well-known in whatever field they have chosen, and they have been asked to write an autobiography telling about their experiences and accomplishments. Tell students to brainstorm and visualize what they would like to have accomplished by the time they are ninety.

6. Have students write their futuristic autobiographies. Give examples of your own goals to stimulate their creativity.

7. Once students have written their futuristic autobiographies, attach their factual autobiographies to the front. Have students share their completed factual and creative autobiographies with the class.

8. Encourage students to keep journals of their daily activities. Also encourage them to keep journals of their goals and what they would like to accomplish as they grow older.

REFERENCES

Applebee, A. N. (1984, Winter). Writing and reasoning. *Review of Educational Research, 54,* 577–596.

Gleason, M. (1995). Using direct instruction to integrate reading and writing for students with learning disabilities. *Reading and Writing Quarterly: Overcoming Learning Disabilities, 11,* 91–108.

Hillocks, G., Jr. (1986). *Research on written composition: New directions for teaching.* Urbana, IL: National Conference on Research in English.

Kahn, E., Walter, C., & Johannessen, L. (1984). *Writing about literature.* Urbana, IL: National Council of Teachers of English.

MacArthur, C., Graham, S., & Schwartz, S. (1993). Integrating strategy instruction and word processing into a process approach to writing. *School Psychology Review, 22,* 671–681.

McCormack, A. J. (1979, January). Science, wonderblob, and the idea machines. *Instructor,* 111–112, 114, 116.

Myers, M., & Gray, J. (1983). *Theory and practice in the teaching of composition: Processing, distancing, and modeling.* Urbana, IL: National Council of Teachers of English.

Peterson, W. (Director). (1986). *The neverending story* [Videotape]. Los Angeles: Warner Home Video (original film released 1984).

Proett, J., & Gill, K. (1986). *The writing process in action: A handbook for teachers.* Urbana, IL: National Council of Teachers of English.

ADULT SOURCES ABOUT THE CHICAGO FIRE

Belluck, Pam. "Barn Door Reopened on Fire after Legend Has Escaped." *New York Times,* August 17, 1997, sec. 1, p. 10.

Sawislak, Karen. *Smoldering City: Chicago and the Great Fire.* Chicago: University of Chicago Press, 1995.

Smith, Carl. *Urban Disorder and the Shape of Belief.* Chicago: University of Chicago Press, 1995.

Waskin, Mel. *Mrs. O'Leary's Comet! Cosmic Causes of the Great Chicago Fire.* 1985.

CHILDREN'S LITERATURE REFERENCES

Ahlberg, Janet, and Ahlberg, Allen. *The Jolly Postman.* Boston: Little, Brown, 1986.

Anno, Mitsumasa. *Anno's U.S.A.* New York: Philomel, 1983.

Babbitt, Natalie. *Tuck Everlasting.* New York: Farrar, Straus & Giroux, 1975.

Baer, Edith. *This Is the Way We Go to School: A Book about Children around the World.* Illustrated by Steve Bjorkman. New York: Scholastic, 1990.

Bartoletti, Susan Campbell. *Growing Up in Coal Country.* Boston: Houghton Mifflin, 1996.

Brittain, Bill. *The Wish Giver.* Illustrated by Andrew Glass. New York: Harper & Row, 1983.

Browne, Anthony. *Gorilla.* New York: Watts, 1983.

Caseley, Judith. *Dear Annie.* New York: Greenwillow, 1991.

Christopher, Matt. *In the Huddle with . . . Steve Young.* Boston: Little, Brown, 1996.

Cleary, Beverly. *Dear Mr. Henshaw.* Illustrated by Paul O. Zelinsky. New York: Morrow, 1983.

Cole, Joanna. *My Puppy Is Born.* New York: Morrow, 1991.

Collard, Sneed B. *Animal Dads.* Illustrated by Steve Jenkins. Boston: Houghton Mifflin, 1997.

Field, Rachel. *Hitty: Her First Hundred Years.* Illustrated by Dorothy P. Lathrop. New York: Macmillan, 1929, 1957.

Fleischman, Sid. *The Midnight Horse.* Illustrated by Peter Sis. New York: Greenwillow, 1990.

Fleischman, Sid. *The Whipping Boy.* New York: Greenwillow, 1986.

Fritz, Jean. *The Great Little Madison.* New York: Putnam, 1989.

George, Jean Craighead. *Look to the North: A Wolf Pup Diary.* Illustrated by Lucia Washburn. New York: HarperCollins, 1997.

Guiberson, Brenda Z. *Into the Sea.* Illustrated by Alix Berenzy. San Diego: Holt, 1996.

Hahn, Mary Downing. *Stepping on the Cracks.* New York: Clarion, 1991.

Hamilton, Virginia. *House of Dies Drear.* New York: Macmillan, 1968.

Hissey, Jane. *Jolly Snow: An Old Bear Story.* New York: Philomel, 1991.

Holling, Holling Clancy. *Paddle to the Sea.* Boston: Houghton Mifflin, 1941.

Hughes, Shirley. *Dogger.* London: Bodley Head, 1977.

James, Simon. *Dear Mr. Blueberry.* New York: Macmillan, 1991.

Jukes, Mavis. *Like Jake and Me.* Illustrated by Lloyd Bloom, New York: Alfred Knopf, 1984.

Krull, Kathleen. *Wilma Unlimited: How Wilma Rudolph Became the World's Fastest Woman.* Illustrated by David Diaz. San Diego: Harcourt, 1996.

Kulberg, Janet. (1993). "What School Psychologists Need to Know About Writing Disabilities." *School Psychology Review, 22,* 682–84.

Lawlor, Laurie. *Where Will This Shoe Take You?: A Walk through the History of Footwear.* New York: Walker, 1996.

L'Engle, Madeleine. *A Wrinkle in Time.* New York: Farrar, Straus & Giroux, 1962.

Levine, Ellen. *Anna Pavlova: Genius of the Dance.* New York: Scholastic, 1995.

Lewin, Hugh. *Jafta.* Illustrated by Lisa Kopper. Minneapolis: Carolrhoda, 1983.

Lewin, Hugh. *Jafta's Mother.* Illustrated by Lisa Kopper. Minneapolis: Carolrhoda, 1983.

Livingston, Myra Cohn. *Space Songs.* Illustrated by Leonard Everett Fisher. New York: Holiday, 1988.

Macy, Sue. *Winning Ways: A Photohistory of American Women in Sports.* New York: Scholastic, 1996.

Markle, Sandra. *Creepy, Crawly Baby Bugs.* New York: Walker, 1996.

Merriam, Eve. *Halloween ABC.* Illustrated by Lane Smith. New York: Macmillan, 1987.

Milne, A. A. *Winnie-the-Pooh.* Illustrated by Ernest H. Shepard. New York: Dutton, 1926, 1954.

Minarik, Else Holmelund. *The Little Girl and the Dragon.* Illustrated by Martine Gourbault, New York: Greenwillow, 1991.

Murphy, Jim. *The Great Fire.* New York: Scholastic, 1995.

Newman, Robert. *The Case of the Baker Street Irregular.* New York: Atheneum, 1978.

Newman, Robert. *The Case of the Vanishing Corpse.* New York: Atheneum, 1980.

Nixon, Joan Lowery. *Whispers from the Dead.* New York: Delacorte, 1980.

Peet, Bill. *Bill Peet: An Autobiography.* Illustrated by Bill Peet. Boston: Houghton Mifflin, 1989.

Provensen, Alice. *The Buck Stops Here: The Presidents of the United States.* New York: Harper & Row, 1990.

Raskin, Ellen. *The Westing Game.* New York: Dutton, 1978.

Rylant, Cynthia. *When I Was Young in the Mountains.* Illustrated by Diane Goode. New York: Dutton, 1982.

Silverstein, Shel. *Where the Sidewalk Ends.* New York: Harper & Row, 1974.

Turner, Ann. *Through Moon and Stars and Night Skies.* Illustrated by James Graham Hale. New York: HarperCollins, 1990.

Wallace, Karen. *Imagine You Are a Crocodile.* Illustrated by Mike Bostock. San Diego: Holt, 1997.

Westall, Robert. *Yaxley's Cat.* New York: Scholastic, 1992.

Wiesner, David. *Free Fall.* New York: Lothrop, Lee & Shepard, 1988.

Wiesner, David. *Tuesday.* New York: Clarion, 1991.

Williams, Margery. *The Velveteen Rabbit: Or How Toys Become Real.* New York: Doubleday, 1922, 1958.

Williams, Vera B., and Williams, Jennifer. *Stringbean's Trip to the Shining Sea.* New York: Greenwillow, 1988.

Wojciechowska, Maia. *Shadow of a Bull.* New York: Atheneum, 1964.

Yorinks, Arthur. *Hey, Al.* Illustrated by Richard Egielski. New York: Farrar, Straus & Giroux, 1986.

Yue, Charlotte. *Shoes: Their History in Words and Pictures.* Illustrated by David Yue. Boston: Houghton Mifflin, 1997.

5

Activities for the Mechanics of Language

Without an understanding of sentence structure, it would be difficult for anyone to develop either written or oral sentences that make sense to a listener or reader. Modern grammarians advocate teaching grammar in such a way that children will understand their language. Instruction should lead children into an exploration of language and help them discover how it works. Combining, expanding, transforming, and exploring sentence patterns are activities that allow children to understand language (Norton, 1997).

Unlike grammar, usage deals with attitudes and language standards of a group rather than with the way words are structured to convey meaning. Different levels of usage are appropriate for different audiences and purposes. Modern usage instruction stresses the appropriateness of both audience and purpose; instruction is flexible and should increase the number of levels of usage available to the child. Many of the oral language activities (chapter 2) provide children with opportunities to expand and experiment with their levels of usage.

Language standards have changed a great deal over the last few hundred years and are still changing today. The first four activities in this chapter may be used to introduce children to the concept that spelling, graphic representations, and accepted usage change with time. Progressing from excerpts from Shakespeare's *Comedie of Errors* to examples of modern citizen's band (CB) radio slang dramatically demonstrates this change in language. A study of the development of English and the major influences for change in the language is a logical extension of this activity.

Writing demands more from the student than oral language. The ability to spell words correctly helps children communicate with their intended audience. Spelling is especially difficult for some students who may be inattentive and easily distracted during academic activities (Harris, Graham, Reid, McElroy, & Hamby, 1994). These researchers suggest that students be encouraged to self-monitor their spelling performance. Posting of successful student performance has also proven to be helpful with improving spelling (Struthers, Bartlamay, Bell, & McLaughlin, 1994). The spelling activities in this section reinforce spelling through motivational activities. Punctuation and capitalization are also important in helping writers to convey meaning to the reader. This section concludes with ideas for a personal learning center to reinforce these aspects of writing mechanics.

Activity 5-1:
THE COMEDIE OF ERRORS

TYPE	TERM
● CLASS	● STA
● GROUP	○ LTA
○ IND	○ LC

Purpose:

1. To understand the dynamic quality of language
2. To realize that spelling, graphic representation, and accepted usage change with time

Materials:

Sentences written in archaic English; one source is Charlton Hinman's *The First Folio of Shakespeare* (1968).

Grade level:

Upper elementary, middle school

Procedures:

1. Ask students if they think our language has always been written and spoken as it is today. Show them an example of Elizabethan English copied from *The First Folio of Shakespeare.*

   line 91, p. 103

The Comedie of Errors

At length the fonne gazing vpon the earth,
Difperft thofe vapours that offended vs,
And by the benefit of his wifhed light
The feas waxt calme, and we difcouered
Two fhippes from farre, making amaine to vs :
Of *Corinth* that, of *Epidarm* this,
But ere they came, oh let me fay no more,
Gather the fequell by that went before.

From THE NORTON FACSIMILE, THE FIRST FOLIO OF SHAKESPEARE, prepared by Charlton Hinman, by permission of W. W. Norton & Co., Inc. Copyright © 1968 by W. W. Norton & Company, Inc.

2. Ask the students to look at the copy and try to read it. Ask them whether it is written in English. Read the sentences with the students. Ask the students if they understood the language and if they could read the words. Encourage them to discuss the meaning of the words and the differences in acceptable usage, spelling, and letter formations.

3. Have students search for other spelling and usage differences. Compile a list of sentences written in archaic English. Have the students suggest comparable current spellings and how they would express the sentences today. For example:

	Elizabethan English	Current English
p. 105 line 280	Good Sifter let vs dine, and neuer fret;	
p. 105 line 271	I greatly feare my monie is not fafe.	
p. 105 line 339	'Tis dinner time, quoth I: my gold, quoth he:	
p. 106 line 476	Why, but theres manie a man hath more haire then wit.	
p. 108 line 727	It would make a man mad as a Bucke to be fo bought and fold. ·	
p. 108 line 673	O villaine, thou haft ftolne both mine office and my name	

NOTE: Page references are from Hinman's THE FIRST FOLIO OF SHAKESPEARE.

4. Allow the students to suggest why they think language changes. Do they think the language they speak and write today is changing? (The following activity on CB slang is a good comparative activity. Students can see some drastic changes in usage over a relatively short period in history.)

Activity 5–2:

CB SLANG

	TYPE	TERM
	● CLASS	● STA
	● GROUP	○ LTA
	○ IND	○ LC

Purpose:
1. To understand the changing quality of language
2. To realize the need for an understandable vocabulary when speaking to or writing for an unknown audience who may not understand slang

Materials: Paragraph written in CB slang; references that define CB slang in terms of standard English.

Grade level: Upper elementary, middle school

Procedures:
1. Instruct students to listen to the following paragraph. Ask them to listen carefully and pretend that they are visiting the United States for the first time. They can all speak and understand "textbook English." After they listen to the paragraph, they will be asked to draw a picture illustrating their understanding of the paragraph.

CB SLANG

Breaker one nine. Let's modulate for a while. My twenty is hill town. A plain blue wrapper just blew by so brush your teeth and comb your hair; his picture taker's out. Better hang on the double nickel so you don't get any green stamps. There's a blinkin winkin over my shoulder that's buying the orchard. Good trucking, stack them eights, and the good numbers to you.

---

2. Have the students draw a picture illustrating the meaning of the paragraph. Discuss the finished pictures and talk about the various interpretations. Ask the students if they think their pictures indicate what the writer of the paragraph really meant to communicate. Have students describe the intended audience for this communication. Discuss the importance of knowing your audience before you can communicate effectively through speaking or writing.

3. What does the paragraph actually mean? Direct the class to investigate CB slang and to rewrite the paragraph with a vocabulary recognizable to a foreign visitor who speaks textbook English.

STANDARD ENGLISH INTERPRETATION

I would like to break in on your conversation and talk to you for a few minutes. My location is San Francisco, California. A blue, unmarked police car just drove past me. He has his radar working, so I would advise you to slow down to 55 miles per hour to avoid any speeding tickets. There is a school bus behind me that has had an accident. I want you to drive safely, best regards to you, and goodbye.

---

4. Have students compare the clarity of the two paragraphs and the appropriate audience for each one.

5. Have students compile a chart showing CB slang expressions and their equivalent terminology in standard English.

CB Slang	Standard English Meaning
Advertising	Police car with warning lights flashing
Baby bear	Rookie police officer
Baloneys	Tires
Bear bait	Speeder
Big ten-four	I approve of what I hear
Blinkin winkin	School bus
Blowing your doors in	Passing a car or truck
Brush your teeth and comb your hair	Reduce your speed
Buying an orchard	Traffic accident
Ears	Citizen's band radio
How you be?	How are you?
Modulate	Talk
Motion lotion	Gasoline
Negative copy	I am unable to understand you
Peanut butter in ears	You are not listening to your CB set
Plain blue wrapper	Unmarked blue police car
Pumpkin	Flat tire
Singing waffles	Radial tires
Tar	Coffee
Wall to wall and treetop tall	I am getting very good audio reception

Activity 5–3:

THE BEGINNING OF THE ENGLISH LANGUAGE

TYPE	TERM
● CLASS	○ STA
● GROUP	● LTA
○ IND	○ LC

Purpose:
1. To investigate the development of the English language in England
2. To investigate major influences that have caused changes in the English language

Materials:
Map showing England and the countries of the continent that influenced English language; references on language development, such as George H. McKnight's *The Evolution of the English Language, From Chaucer to the Twentieth Century* (1956); Bruce Finnie's *The Stages of English* (1972); and Robert McCrum, William Cran, and Robert MacNeil's *The Story of English* (1986).

Grade level:
Upper elementary, middle school

Procedures:
1. Explain that the English we speak today is the result of a long series of historical events and many different influences. The language of Shakespeare (see activity 5–1, "The Comedie of Errors") is not the same language we speak today, although we can understand most of it. The English we speak has its origins in England, the country in which Shakespeare wrote his plays. When people who spoke a different language either invaded or moved into the country, many words were added to the English language. (Ask students to suggest some words they may know because people who speak a different language live in their community.)

2. Show a map of England and continental Europe. Have the students locate the areas that have influenced the English language. Compile a list of words that have been added to the English language because of influence from other countries. (Many upper elementary and middle school students begin studying European history. A study of language development can stimulate the study of history.)

ROMAN INFLUENCE

Roman traders brought new words:

wine	cheese	kettle	cup
Lancaster	Winchester	(names of cities)	

Roman missionaries brought new words:

temple	synod	abbot
organ	hymn	candle

DANISH INFLUENCE

In the late 700s, Denmark invaded England and added many new words to the language:

house   mother   father

Words that have the /sk/ sound are Scandinavian:

skin   sky   skill   scrape   scrub
bask   whisk

Plural forms of pronouns:

they   their   them

Adverb prepositions combining *take:*

take up   take in
take out   take down

More than 1,400 English towns have Danish names; *-by* added to the name is the Danish word for town and *-thorp* means village:

Rugby   Grinsby
Althorp   Linthorpe

FRENCH INFLUENCE

Normans ruled England.

Foods:

biscuit   jelly   cream
veal   beef   bacon

Government terms:

parliament   government   tax

Religious words:

religion   parson   sermon
baptism   incense   crucifix

Household words:

parlor   blanket   curtain
chair   lamp

Color words:

vermilion   scarlet   blue

Recreational words:

leisure   music   conversation
chess   dance

Educational words:

logic   study   grammar
noun   surgeon   anatomy

3. Discuss the meanings of the various words and their uses in modern English. Create a bulletin board showing the origins of modern English words. Place appropriate words on charts next to the countries from which they came.

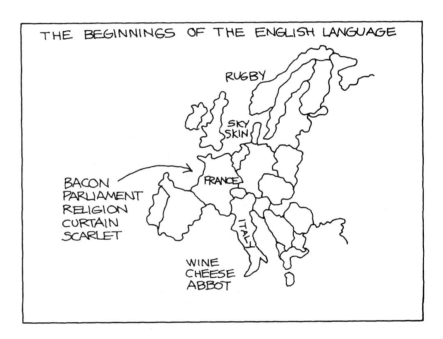

THE BEGINNINGS OF THE ENGLISH LANGUAGE

Activity 5–4:

THE ENGLISH LANGUAGE IN THE UNITED STATES

TYPE	TERM
● CLASS	○ STA
● GROUP	● LTA
○ IND	○ LC

Purpose:

1. To investigate the development of the English language in the United States
2. To investigate the major influences for change in the English language in the United States
3. To understand that the English language is constantly changing

Materials:

Tapes of English speakers from England and the United States; references such as dictionaries that describe the history of American English (e.g., Mitford Mathews's *Dictionary of Americanisms on Historical Principles* (1951); maps of the United States and Europe.

Grade level:

Upper elementary, middle school

Procedures:

1. Ask students if they believe that a person speaking English in England and a person speaking English in the United States would sound alike or if all of their words would mean the same thing. This would be a good opportunity to play a tape of a speaker from England or to have a visitor from England talk to the students. Have the students listen for words that are used differently than in the United States and for differences in dialect.

   The following story was written by Jacki Thomas, a graduate student from Bristol, England. She is illustrating some differences between English and American usage:

   Lavinia Prendergast was awoken one day by a telephone call. It was her mother-in-law phoning to ask if she could come to stay with her and her husband for a fortnight. "Gosh!" she thought when she put the phone down, "this flat is a mess, I'd better start tidying up!"

   But first she weighed herself on the scales—"Oh, that's good, still only 9 stone 3," she said with relief. Then she started rushing around to get the flat cleaned up.

   She thought she would do the curtains while she was doing the washing, but she couldn't get the tap to the washing machine on, so she started washing up . . . no washing-up liquid left! So she had to get dressed to nip down to the corner shop, and she threw her dressing gown on the bed. "It's gonna be one of those days!" she exclaimed. Even as she said it, she noticed the moths had got to the jumper her mother-in-law had knitted for her last Christmas, and she knew she'd lost the spare darning wool she had sent with it.

   Lavinia put the baby in the pram and put her purse in her handbag, when the phone went again. It was her friend, asking if she could come round for a chat and a cup of tea, but Lavinia thought she'd be too busy to stop for elevenses today.

She wasn't long getting the washing-up liquid and started washing the dishes as soon as she got back—she dried up the cutlery and crockery but left the frying pan and saucepans to drain. She washed out a few smalls and hung them out on the line with her new plastic pegs. She vacuumed the carpets, tidied up the living room, mopped the floors in the toilet and kitchen, then laid the table for lunch.

She just had time to get a couple of biscuits and get a glass of milk out of the fridge and was going to turn on the telly when she heard a car-door slam outside the flat; she looked out and recognized her mother-in-law's estate car—she was just getting her case out of the boot.

fortnight	two weeks
flat	apartment
curtains	drapes
do the washing	do laundry
washing-up liquid	detergent
nip	hurry
corner shop	small all-purpose store
dressing gown	housecoat
jumper	pullover sweater
darning wool	repair yarn
pram	baby buggy where baby lies down
purse	billfold, wallet
handbag	purse
come round	come over
elevenses	cup of tea, or coffee and cookies
cutlery	silverware
crockery	dishes
smalls	underwear
pegs	clothespins
9 stone 3	141 pounds
tap	faucet
boot	trunk
estate car	station wagon
biscuits	cookies

2. Discuss the following: "We have learned that the English language was greatly influenced by people from other European countries when these people invaded England, came to live in England, or traded with the English." Since the English language spoken in England is somewhat different from the English language spoken in the United States, ask the students to suggest possible situations that might have influenced and changed the English language spoken in the United States.

3. Allow students to form groups to investigate a specific period of history and its influence on our language. Historically accurate fiction offers many examples of speech that is authentic for both time and place. Historical dictionaries are also useful. Some suggested study groupings include the following:

SKILLET

SPIDER

The colonists brought English to America

Pioneer America added colorful language (e.g., to go on the warpath, to take to the woods)

European immigrants brought their language to America (e.g., a frying pan is called a *skillet* by some and a *spider* by others; a pail and faucet may be called a *bucket and spigot*)

Technology and new inventions add to language (e.g., television is new to this century; acronyms, such as *radar,* are created from the first letters of words: *radio detecting and ranging*)

Slang expressions add color to language and change meanings of common words (e.g., a term such as *turkey* does not necessarily refer to the bird served for Thanksgiving dinner)

Have the research groups present their findings aloud to the class, using the speech patterns of the period. Suggest creative methods for sharing the language of the periods such as an original play or a scene from authentic literature.

4. One way to study the influence of a nationality or a period in history on the United States is to investigate cities, towns, and areas that have names signifying foreign, Native American, or historical influence. Have students locate names in the area, state, or nation that demonstrate the influence of a group or period in history. Among many other locations, Native American place names show up in Menomonie and Winnebago, Wisconsin; Cheyenne and Ten Sleep, Wyoming; Ketchikan, Alaska; and Pontiac, Michigan. Spanish influence appears in El Cajon and Escondido, California, and La Junta, Colorado. German influence is felt in New Braunfels, Texas, and French influence in New Orleans and Lafayette, Louisiana, and Ste. Anne de Beaupre, Quebec.

Activity 5-5:
BUILDING SENTENCE PATTERNS

TYPE	TERM
● CLASS	● STA
● GROUP	○ LTA
● IND	○ LC

Purpose:
1. To develop an understanding of sentence form
2. To identify words and types of words that fit a specific pattern in a sentence

Materials:
Examples of model sentences.

Grade level:
Lower elementary (sentences may be read aloud to children who cannot read)

Procedures:
1. Show students sentences using a cloze technique. Have students suggest words that might fit the position. In each case, talk about the types of appropriate words. For example:

Julie _____.

    ran   jumped   laughed
    hopped   sang   skipped

The _____ jumped.

    girl   boy   cat   cricket   dog
    rabbit lion   man   woman

The _____ clown laughed.

    funny   clumsy   small   fat   skinny
    tall   tiny   silly   red

Suzie walked _____ down the street.

    slowly   rapidly   hurriedly
    clumsily   happily   quietly

2. These sentences can be finished with a pantomime activity; for example, a child chooses an action word to complete a sentence and pantomimes the action so that the rest of the group can identify the action and complete the sentence.

Activity 5–6:
SENTENCE EXPANSION

TYPE	TERM
● CLASS	● STA
● GROUP	○ LTA
● IND	○ LC

Purpose:
1. To expand noun and verb phrases
2. To write expanded sentences
3. To evaluate nonexpanded and expanded sentences

Materials:
Examples of expanded and nonexpanded sentences to evaluate; examples of simple sentences with the construction noun phrase plus verb phrase to use for expansion activities.

Grade level:
Middle elementary

Procedures:
1. Have students listen to one nonexpanded and one expanded sentence. Ask them to draw a picture illustrating each sentence:

   The flower bloomed.
   The dainty alpine flower bloomed next to an icy mountain stream.

   After they draw their pictures, ask students to describe the differences between the two sentences. Which sentence was more interesting? Which sentence gave more information? Show the students examples of other nonexpanded and expanded sentences. Discuss the differences in each pair. For example:

   The crowd cheered.
   The football crowd cheered wildly this afternoon.

   My brother skates.
   My younger brother skates on the champion hockey team.

   Everyone walked.
   Everyone at the picnic walked along the beach.

   Sebastian laughed.
   My uncle Sebastian laughed at all of the clown's jokes.

2. Present some nonexpanded sentences to the students. Have them orally expand them in as many ways as they can. Discuss the type of information given in each expansion; for example:

   The boy ran.
   The hunter started.
   The bell rang.
   Jacqueline returned.
   Pepper smarts.

3. Help the children use expanded sentences during their writing experience.

Activity 5–7:
SENTENCE COMBINING WITH EASY-TO-READ BOOKS

TYPE	TERM
● CLASS	● STA
● GROUP	○ LTA
● IND	○ LC

Purpose:

1. To increase syntactic control
2. To make sentence construction more automatic
3. To explore, discuss, and evaluate various stylistic options

Materials:

Sentence-combining guidelines and introductory activities, such as those provided by William Strong (1986); easy-to-read books that provide sources for sentence combining such as Joanna Cole and Stephanie Calmenson's *Ready . . . Set . . . Read!: The Beginning Reader's Treasury* (1990) and Jean Van Leeuwen's *Oliver, Amanda, and Grandmother Pig* (1987) and *Oliver Pig at School* (1990).

Grade level:

Middle and upper elementary

Book summaries:

Ready . . . Set . . . Read!: The Beginning Reader's Treasury is an anthology of numerous easy-to-read stories and poems. *Oliver, Amanda, and Grandmother Pig* includes five short stories about experiences when Grandmother Pig comes for a visit. *Oliver Pig at School* includes four short stories about Oliver's experiences at school. All of these books have short sentences and controlled vocabularies.

Procedures:

1. Read Strong's guidelines for developing sentence-combining activities and complete a few of these activities with the students.
2. After students have completed several sentence-combining activities, tell them that they will have an opportunity to rewrite easy-to-read books so that they are more appropriate for older readers. Explain to the students that easy-to-read books are designed to be read by beginning readers. Consequently, the books have shorter sentences and easier vocabularies.
3. Introduce one of the books to the students. Read a selection and ask the students if they notice the shorter sentences and easier vocabularies. Following this reading, ask the students if they think that they could use sentence-combining techniques to change the complexity of the sentences. As a group, explore various ways that sentences from one of the stories might be combined. For example, in the "Helping" story in *Oliver, Amanda, and Grandmother Pig,* how would they combine the first page of the story?

   Amanda woke up early.
   Everyone else was sleeping.
   She went to the kitchen
   and Grandmother was there. (p. 17)

4. When this activity was completed with fourth-grade students, they identified and discussed the following ways of combining the sentences:

   Although it was early in the morning and everyone else was asleep, Amanda woke up and went to the kitchen and saw her grandmother.

   Even though everyone else was asleep, Amanda woke up early, went to the kitchen, and there was Grandmother.

5. After completing and discussing the results of several sentence-combining activities as a group, provide individual students or small groups with easy-to-read books. Encourage the students to use sentence-combining strategies to increase the syntactic complexities of the stories. After they have completed the stories, ask them to share the stories with the class. Discuss with the class the various ways of using sentence combining.

Activity 5–8:
PLAY SENTENCE DETECTIVE

TYPE	TERM
○ CLASS	● STA
● GROUP	○ LTA
● IND	○ LC

Purpose:
1. To study word forms (morphology) and identify words signifying plurality—plural noun forms, verb forms, and numbers
2. To become aware that a sentence contains several clues to plurality

Materials:
Lists of sentences containing several clues to plurality; literature sources that encourage students to search for clues to plurality.

Grade level:
Middle and upper elementary

Procedures:
1. Suggest that writers and speakers use several clues to inform a reader or listener that a sentence is plural. Ask the students to tell you any clues they use when they mean more than one.
2. Tell the students they will be playing sentence detectives and will have an opportunity to find as many clues as they can that signify plurality of a sentence. (This activity may be played as a game by dividing the students into small groups and having each group identify as many clues as possible.)
3. Present sentences to the students. After each sentence, ask them to identify the clues that led them to the subject's plurality or singularity. For example:
   a. The three squirrels were running from limb to limb.
   b. Glen saw a new red station wagon.
   c. The Siamese cats were Mrs. Hatfield's best friends.
   d. Some of the pencils were broken.
   e. The bird is sitting on a picket on the fence.
4. Ask students to select library books and search for sentences and paragraphs that provide clues to the subject's plurality or singularity. Have the students share these examples with the class.

Activity 5–9:
PAST, PRESENT, FUTURE

TYPE	TERM
○ CLASS	● STA
● GROUP	○ LTA
○ IND	○ LC

Purpose:

1. To reinforce understanding of past, present, and future tenses of verbs
2. To write a paragraph in past tense, in present tense, and in future tense
3. To strengthen writing skills by using a personal subject

Materials:

Three paragraphs about a person, object, or animal with one in past tense, one in present tense, and one in future tense; paragraphs from literature or newspapers.

Grade level:

Upper elementary

Procedures:

1. Discuss the fact that both authors and speakers use signals to let a reader or listener know when something takes place. Place paragraphs on transparencies or duplicate them. Ask students to listen carefully while you read three paragraphs.

    (Present) The large oak tree in our backyard is an apartment house for many animals. Many different kinds of bugs live in the lowest apartments of the tree trunk. We can see a spider decorating her apartment with a beautiful web. Above the spider, a frisky gray squirrel is filling his cupboard with nuts. Two robins are hovering around their nest. As we look closer, we see that they are the proud parents of five babies. This apartment house must be a happy place to live.

    (Past) The apartment in our backyard was not always so big and fully occupied as it is today. Many years ago, a squirrel buried an acorn on the open lawn. The warm rains came, and a sprout grew out of the acorn and up through the ground. Little by little, it grew bigger and bigger. We placed a stake next to the young tree so it would not be cut by the mower. We watched the leaves turn red during many falls. Each spring, more branches and leaves grew on the tree. We hoped it would grow big enough for a bird to build a nest in the branches.

    (Future) In three months, we will lose the apartment in our backyard. We are going to add a new room to our house. To build the room, we will need to cut down the tree or cut a hole in the roof. We will use the lumber from the tree to make paneling for the new room. We will not forget this special oak tree.

2. Ask the students if all three paragraphs take place within the same time period. Ask them to identify the times. How do they know the first paragraph is right now, or in the present tense? Have them identify the verbs that signal the time as right now. How do they know the second paragraph happened in the past? Have them identify the verbs or other words that signal the past. How do they know the final paragraph will happen in the future? Have them identify the verbs and other words that signal events that will happen in the future.

3. Suggest to the students that we can also write about ourselves in the past, present, and future tenses. Have them suggest topics they can write about in each tense. Ask students to write paragraphs about themselves illustrating each tense. Interact with the students as they write their paragraphs and provide assistance as needed.

4. To reinforce the students' understanding of how to use the future tense, have them write predictions about the future.

Activity 5–10:
TIC-TAC-TOE

TYPE	TERM
o CLASS	● STA
● GROUP	o LTA
o IND	o LC

Purpose:
1. To strengthen spelling skills
2. To write spelling words during an enjoyable game activity

Materials:
Lists of spelling words; tic-tac-toe game boards drawn on cardboard or on the chalkboard.

Grade level:
All grades

Procedures:
1. Several procedures may be used for spelling reinforcement with a tic-tac-toe format. Some possibilities include the following:

   a. Divide the spelling group into two teams. Pronounce a spelling word for the first person on one team. Have the person write the word. If she writes the word correctly, the team member places an *x* or an *o* on the tic-tac-toe board. Next, pronounce a word for the first person on the opposing team. Continue pronouncing words to members of each team until a team has won horizontally, diagonally, or vertically.

   b. Divide the spelling group into two teams. Pronounce the spelling word for the first team. Have each person on the team write the word. If all team members write the word correctly, the team places an *x* or *o* on the tic-tac-toe board. (This approach allows every team member to participate in the spelling activity. However, team members should be matched according to spelling ability.)

   c. Divide the spelling group into two teams or divide the spelling groups into two individual players per game. Place spelling words on individual cards. Shuffle the spelling word cards and place them face down on a tic-tac-toe board. The first team chooses a square, the caller pronounces the word, and the first team member or the whole team writes the word. If the word is spelled correctly, the team places its *x* or *o* on the appropriate square. If the team cannot spell the word correctly, the second team or individual can try to spell the word. Continue playing until a team or individual wins the game.

Activity 5–11:
RIDE THE AMTRAK LINE

TYPE	TERM
○ CLASS	● STA
● GROUP	○ LTA
○ IND	○ LC

Purpose:

1. To reinforce spelling skills
2. To write spelling words during a motivating activity

Materials:

Game board showing a railroad track (may depict specific areas of the country or can be general in nature—if a specific area is depicted, students can draw a game board as a social studies assignment after studying a map of the area).

Grade level:

All grades

Procedures:

1. Create a game board depicting an Amtrak or other railroad line.

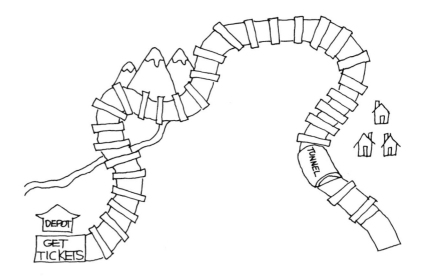

2. Write spelling word cards that list a word to be spelled, use the word in a sentence, and give directions for the speller if he spells the word correctly. For example:

ATHLETE

An *athlete* is a person trained in physical strength and skill. Move ahead three spaces.

THUNDER

Thunder is a loud noise that follows a flash of lightning. Move ahead two spaces.

You passed your spelling test. Move ahead three free spaces.

You missed too many words on your spelling test. Move back two spaces.

3. Create railroad-related game-board markers for individual players. Markers might include an engine, caboose, passenger car, freight car, conductor's cap, engineer's cap, or train ticket.

4. This game can be played by two or more players. Shuffle the cards and place them face down in a pile. Have the first player select a card and ask the second player to read the card to the first player. If the first player spells the word correctly, the player moves ahead the number of spaces indicated on the card. If the player misses the word, the player does not move ahead on the game board. The second player selects a card, and the next player reads the card to the second player. Continue until one passenger reaches the end of the line.

Activity 5–12:
RELATING MEANING AND SPELLING

TYPE	TERM
○ CLASS	● STA
● GROUP	○ LTA
○ IND	○ LC

Purpose: To identify the relationship between spelling and meaning

Materials: Lists of word pairs that demonstrate the relationship between spelling and meaning.

Grade level: Middle and upper elementary, middle school

Procedures:

1. Background—Carol Chomsky's (1970) work suggests that many spellings relate to semantic function in the language rather than to phonetic representation. Lexical spellings thus represent meaning and lead speller and reader directly to a word's meaning. This research suggests that instruction should emphasize regularities in meaning between related words. This instructional approach may be used for spelling, vocabulary development, and reading.

2. Discuss with students the fact that many words give clues to spelling. If we understand the meanings of two similar words, we can improve spelling ability. Ask students to pronounce and identify the relationship between *nature* and *natural*. Even though the two words are pronounced differently, there is a close relationship in meaning. Ask students to use the two words in sentences and have them compare the meanings so that they can identify the similarities in spelling. Study other words the same way:

major	majority	
culture	cultural	
gymnasium	gymnastics	
library	librarian	
photograph	photography	
microscope	microscopic	
govern	governor	government
history	historical	historian

3. Ask students to become word detectives and have them look for their own examples of word families that share similar meanings and spellings.

4. Have students develop booklets of spelling word pairs or families that show a relationship between meaning and spelling. Have them use their words in sentences and ask them to share their word detective books with other members of the class.

```
┌─────────────────────────────────┐
│      MY WORD DETECTIVE          │
│            BOOK                 │
│                                 │
│   SPELLING SHOWS MEANING        │
│                                 │
│   PHOTOGRAPH       ( )          │
│   PHOTOGRAPHER  ( )             │
│   PHOTOGRAPHY      ( )          │
│                                 │
└─────────────────────────────────┘
```

Activity 5–13:

PERSONAL LEARNING CENTERS FOR WRITING

TYPE	TERM
● CLASS	○ STA
○ GROUP	○ LTA
○ IND	● LC

Purpose:

1. To develop a useful personal learning center for spelling, handwriting, punctuation, capitalization, and letter writing
2. To reinforce spelling, handwriting, punctuation, capitalization, and letter-writing skills

Materials:

Cardboard box (about the size of a desktop) for each child; lists of spelling words; manuscript or cursive writing forms; punctuation chart; capitalization chart; letter-writing forms.

Grade level:

All grades

Procedures:

1. Provide directions so that each student can make his or her personal learning center. Cut the bottom, top, and front out of a cardboard box, leaving the left side,

2. Tape large pockets onto the inside of the left, back, and right sides of the cardboard frame. (Construction paper or used file folders can be taped on three sides to form these pockets.)

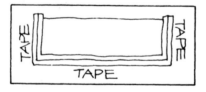

3. Next, discuss the kinds of information that would be helpful to the students when they write a story, a content area assignment, or a letter. (This information can change and should be designed according to the needs of the individual children.) The following is suggestive of the types of information many students find valuable:

   a. Alphabetical lists of basic spelling words. Words from the spelling series used by the school and Dolch or Thorndike lists of utilitarian words can be compiled and placed in a pocket marked "spelling." This basic list can be supplemented with words each child uses frequently in writing.

b. Alphabetical lists of words the child frequently misspells. Older students may find it helpful to include a list of words often confused in writing; for example:

WORDS OFTEN CONFUSED IN WRITING

affect	to influence
effect	outcome
capital	city where government is located; a capital letter *(A)*
capitol	building where the legislature meets
desert	dry, barren region
dessert	a sweet served at the end of a meal
hear	to listen to
here	in this place
lose	to misplace
loose	not fastened
principal	something of importance; the administrator of a school
principle	a truth or belief
stationary	unmoving
stationery	paper used for writing letters
there	in that place
their	belonging to them
they're	contraction of *they are*
to	in the direction of
too	also
two	the number 2
weather	condition of the atmosphere
whether	choice or alternative

---

c. A copy of the appropriate manuscript or cursive alphabet. Lower elementary students usually use a manuscript style of writing, whereas middle and upper elementary students usually use cursive writing.

d. A punctuation chart. The items included again depend on the student's needs. Such a chart might include the following information:

PUNCTUATION CHART

Punctuation:	*Example:*
Period.	
1. Use periods at the ends of sentences	This is Monday morning.
2. Use periods after abbreviations.	U.S.A., Fri., Aug., Mr.
3. Use periods after numbers in a list.	1. Seeds 2. Soil
Question Mark ?	
1. Use a question mark after a sentence that asks a question.	When are you going to the movie?

Exclamation Mark!

1. Use an exclamation mark after a statement of excitement.

Great! We will win!

Comma,

1. Use a comma to separate a series of three or more items.

We had hot dogs, corn, milk, and cake for lunch.

2. Use a comma between the name of a city and state.

We visited San Francisco, California.

3. Use a comma between the month and the year.

Our Independence Day was July 4, 1776.

4. Use a comma after the salutation of a letter.

Dear Mom,

5. Use a comma after the closing of a letter.

Sincerely,

6. Use a comma before a coordinating conjunction that separates two independent clauses.

She wanted to buy a new coat, but she could not find one she liked.

Apostrophe'

1. Use an apostrophe to show possession of a singular noun.

This is Toby's bicycle.

2. Use an apostrophe to show possession of a plural noun.

We saw the boys' basketball team play this afternoon.

3. Use an apostrophe to show that letters have been left out in a contraction.

You're, can't, isn't, I'll

e. A sample of the form and punctuation for a letter. For example:

Street Address

City, State, Zip

Month, Date, Year

Greeting,

Message

_____

_____

_____

_____

Closing,

Signature

f. Guidelines for capitalization. For example:

USE CAPITAL LETTERS

1. Sentences begin with capital letters.

    The dog was lost for one week.

2. Names begin with capital letters.

    George Washington

3. Names of cities, states, countries, and rivers begin with capital letters.

    Seattle, New Jersey, Canada, Mississippi

4. Names of days, months, and holidays begin with capital letters.

    Monday, January, Memorial Day

5. Titles of books begin with capital letters.

    Across Five Aprils

6. Titles such as Miss and Mr. begin with capital letters.

    Miss, Mr., Mrs., Ms., Dr.

7. The greeting of a letter begins with a capital letter.

    Dear Jackie,

8. The closing of a letter begins with a capital letter.

    Your friend,
    Sincerely,

---

4. Any other useful equipment can be included in the personal learning center such as the child's personal writing folder, proofreading suggestions, or a dictionary and reference guide.

5. When the personal writing center is complete, the students can fold it flat for easy storage. They can use the center whenever they need it.

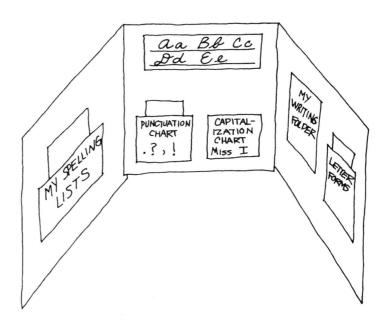

Activity 5–14:

VOCABULARY EXPANSION THROUGH SEMANTIC MAPPING

TYPE	TERM
● CLASS	● STA
● GROUP	○ LTA
○ IND	○ LC

Purpose:

1. To expand vocabulary development
2. To brainstorm ideas and develop a semantic map of synonyms
3. To brainstorm ideas and develop a semantic map of antonyms
4. To identify synonyms and antonyms as specific parts of speech: verbs, adverbs, adjectives, and nouns
5. To use specific synonyms and antonyms in sentences
6. To strengthen dictionary and thesaurus skills

Materials:

Chalkboard; dictionary; thesaurus.

Grade level:

Middle and upper grades; a vocabulary semantic map may be developed with younger children if the vocabulary and concepts are at a lower level.

Procedures:

1. Introduce the word *right* to your students. Ask them to identify several words that mean approximately the same as *right*. (Remind them that words that have similar meanings are called *synonyms*.) List the words on the chalkboard and ask the students to use the words in sentences. Write the sentences on the chalkboard. Ask the students if each of the words is used in the same way within the sentence. Are the words from the same part of speech?

2. Have the students identify the various parts of speech that are found in the sentences. If they have not identified verbs, adjectives, adverbs, and nouns, provide them with sentences that use words meaning *right* as each part of speech. Draw a semantic map of *right* on the chalkboard:

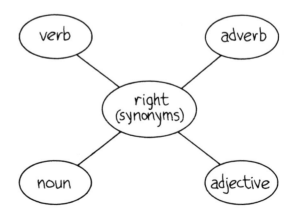

3. Lead the students in a brainstorming activity in which they identify words that have a similar meaning as *right*. Ask the students to use the word in a sentence and identify where the word should be placed on the semantic map. Students should verify questionable placement of words on the semantic map by using a dictionary or a thesaurus. A group of fourth and fifth graders developed the following semantic map:

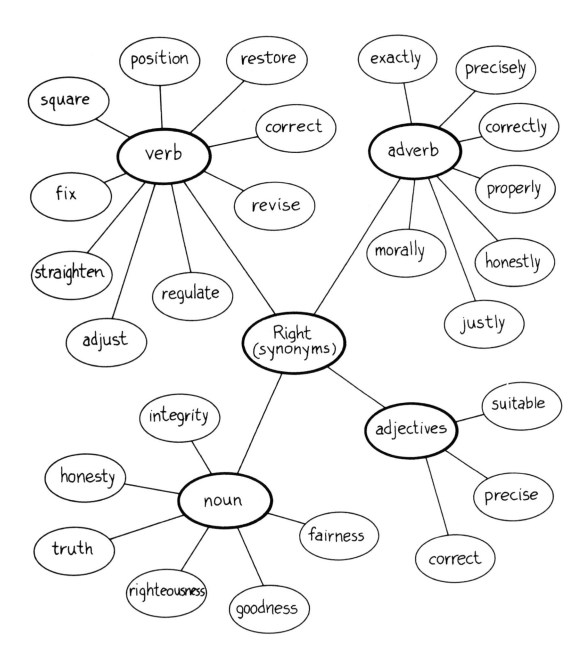

4. Lead a brainstorming activity in which students identify words that mean the opposite of *right*. (Remind students that words that mean the opposite of other words are called *antonyms*.) Draw another semantic map using the placement of these antonyms to show that the words are verbs, adverbs, adjectives, or nouns. The following semantic map resulted from this activity:

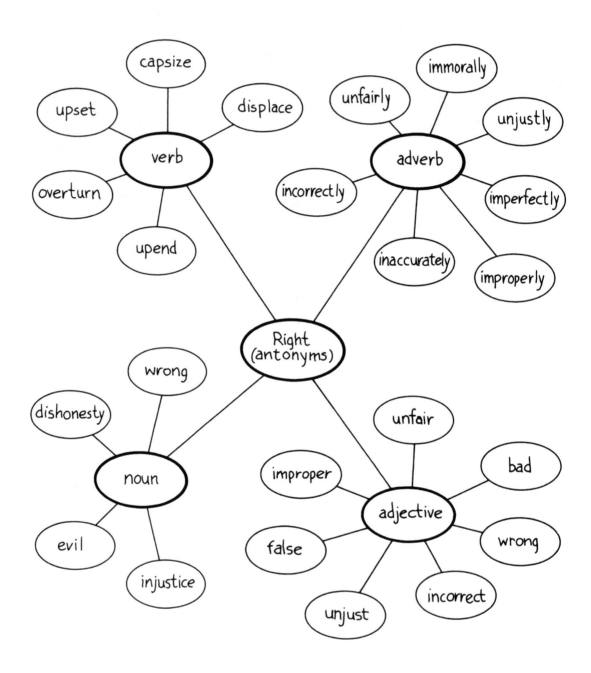

Activity 5–15:

COHESIVE DEVICES: PERSONAL PRONOUNS

TYPE	TERM
o CLASS	● STA
● GROUP	o LTA
● IND	o LC

Purpose:

1. To develop an understanding of cohesive devices
2. To teach students to comprehend personal pronouns and to apply this knowledge when reading or listening to picture storybooks
3. To use personal pronouns in students' writing

Materials:

Eve Bunting's *The Man Who Could Call Down Owls* (1984) and *The Mother's Day Mice* (1986), Mary Calhoun's *High-Wire Henry* (1991), Susan Cooper's *Matthew's Dragon* (1991), Rachel Isadora's *At the Crossroads* (1991), and Beatrix Potter's *The Tale of Mrs. Tiggy-Winkle* (1905).

Grade level:

Lower and middle elementary

Book summaries:

The Man Who Could Call Down Owls is the story about a man who has a special relationship with owls. *The Mother's Day Mice* is the story of mice who search the woods for perfect gifts. Overcoming jealousy between a cat and a new puppy is the subject of *High-Wire Henry*. *Matthew's Dragon* is a fantasy picture book in which a dragon comes to life. *At the Crossroads* is the story of a group of South African children who welcome their fathers after the fathers have been away working in the mines. *The Tale of Mrs. Tiggy-Winkle* is one of Ms. Potter's famous books about small animals living in the Lake District in England.

Procedures:

1. The sequence in this lesson is based on research by Baumann and Stevenson (1986). They recommend the following four-step procedure:

   a. Introduce the lesson by telling the students what skill related to cohesive devices you will teach, by providing an example of the cohesive device, and by explaining why the acquisition of that skill is important.

   b. Provide direct instruction in which you model, show, demonstrate, and lead the instruction in the skill.

   c. Provide students with guided application of the skill, but use materials not used during previous instruction.

   d. Provide independent practice, in which the students apply the skill in their comprehension of text. Trade books and other primary sources as well as content-area texts are effective materials for this activity and increase the transfer of the skill to additional contexts. Trade books also allow students to practice their skills within passage-length texts rather than isolated sentences that do not consider prior information.

2. Provide an introduction to the cohesive device of personal pronouns. For example: "When people write they often use words that stand for other words. These words allow writers to repeat an idea without repeating the same words. Look at the following sentences written on the board and read the sentences with me:

   Jerry likes to visit the zoo. He likes to look at the elephants and the tigers.

In the first sentence, find the word *Jerry*. In the second sentence, find the word *he*. This is an example of a sentence in which one word replaces another word. *He* means the same thing as *Jerry*. Words such as *he* are called *pronouns*. Check to see if we are right in our identification of the meaning of the word by reading both sentences but replacing *he* with *Jerry* in the second sentence. Now read these sentences with me:

Jerry likes to visit the zoo. Jerry likes to look at the elephants and the tigers.

Notice that the two sentences still mean the same thing. If we replace *he* with a different boy's name, the second sentence has a different meaning. These sentences are examples of what we will learn about today. We will learn that words such as *we, her, you, they, their,* and *it* stand for other words. This is important because it helps you understand what writers are trying to tell you. It is also important so that you can use this skill in your own writing."

3. For the teacher-directed instruction, write several sentences on the board that include the pronouns to be emphasized. Create these sentences according to the reading and interest levels of your students. For example:
   a. Cinderella lived with her stepmother and her stepsisters. She sat in the cinders in the kitchen, and that is how she got her name.
   b. The prince wanted to marry one of the girls in the kingdom. He gave a ball to meet the girls.
   c. The stepsisters and the stepmother dressed in their best clothes. They went to the ball.
   d. Cinderella was unhappy because she wanted to go to the ball. She was granted a wish by her fairy godmother.
   e. A magical carriage took her to the ball. It turned back into a pumpkin at midnight.

You may then say to students: "Read the first group of sentences with me *(a)*. Look for the words used in place of *Cinderella*. Notice that the words are underlined. Now listen as I tell you how I figured out the meanings of the words. First, I noticed that *her* was used twice in the first sentence. I thought about whose stepmother and whose stepsisters the sentence meant. I replaced both of the *her*s with *Cinderella* and the sentence made sense. Then I noticed *she* was used twice in the next sentence. I thought about the first sentence and I asked myself if *she* and *her* referred to *Cinderella,* the *stepmother,* or the *stepsisters*. I knew that *she* could not mean the *stepsisters* because the word would have to be *they*. I used the meaning of the first sentence to help me identify that *she* meant *Cinderella*. I knew from the story about Cinderella that Cinderella was given her name because she sat in the cinders and ashes in the kitchen fireplace. Now, let's read the second sentence together and replace *she* and *her* with *Cinderella*. Does the sentence have the correct meaning? Also, notice how much better the sentences sound when *she* and *her* replace *Cinderella*. These sentences also show that we often need to read the sentences before or after a pronoun to understand what the author means.

"Now look at the second group of sentences *(b)*. Read the sentences with me. I want you to think through the meaning of the sentences. What word is substituted? (He) Good. Who gave the ball? (The prince) Good. How do you know that *he* refers to the *prince*?" (Students provide evidence and reasoning.) Continue with a teacher-led discussion for the remainder of the sentences in items *c* through *e*. Add additional sentences if the students do not master this portion of the lesson.

Tell the students that they are now going to read some examples of these pronouns used by authors of books. Place examples of paragraphs on transparencies and ask the students to look at the paragraphs. For example, the following is from Beatrix Potter's *The Tale of Mrs. Tiggy-Winkle:*

> Once upon a time there was a little girl called Lucie, who lived at a farm called Little-town. She was a good little girl—only she was always losing her pocket-handkerchiefs!
>
> One day little Lucie came into the farm-yard crying—oh, she did cry so! "I've lost my pocket-handkin! Three handkins and a pinny! Have you seen them, Tabby Kitten?"
>
> The Kitten went on washing her white paws; so Lucie asked a speckled hen—
>
> "Sally Henny-penny, have you found three pocket-handkins?"
>
> But the speckled hen ran into a barn, clucking—"I go barefoot, barefoot, barefoot!" (pp. 9–10)

Lead a discussion with the students in which they identify the pronouns and the character that the pronoun stands for. Have them notice that they have to read carefully because *I* does not always mean the girl and *you* does not mean the same animal. Discuss how the use of pronouns improves the beauty of the text.

4. For the teacher-guided application identify additional paragraphs taken from literature. Underline the words that you want the students to identify. Ask them to read the paragraphs, think about the meanings for the pronouns, and write the correct meaning over each underlined word. Do the first sentence together to make sure that the students understand what to do. Then ask the students to do the rest of the sentences by themselves. Tell them to read the whole selection to make sure that their choices make sense and are accurate. When the students are finished, have them read the paragraphs together and discuss their answers. The following example comes from Susan Cooper's *Matthew's Dragon:*

> Matthew's mother was sitting on his bed, reading him a bedtime story. She had just turned the last page.
>
> "And so the dragon flew back to his castle, and pulled up the drawbridge, and went to sleep," she read.
>
> She held up the picture of the sleeping dragon to show Matthew, and closed the book.
>
> "Just one more," said Matthew hopefully. All his favorite stories were about dragons.
>
> His mother said firmly, "Tomorrow." She put the book on the bedside table and tucked him in. "Good night, Matt. Sleep tight."
>
> Matthew sighed. "Night." He snuggled down, as his mother kissed the top of his head and turned out the lamp. The door closed behind her. In the dark room, Matthew shut his eyes—and the he opened them again. He gasped. (p. 1 unnumbered)

After students complete this activity independently, conduct a guided discussion of this phase of the lesson. Encourage discussion that looks at the reasons for the replacements as well as the correct answers. (You may use this book again during independent practice when you ask students to conclude the story using their own pronouns.)

5. During independent practice, select additional books in which the authors use pronouns to replace other words in the stories. The following books include numerous pronouns:

Eve Bunting's *The Mother's Day Mice*
Eve Bunting's *The Man Who Could Call Down Owls*

Mary Calhoun's *High-Wire Henry*
Rachel Isadora's *At the Crossroads*

6. Continue this independent practice phase of the activity by asking students to locate additional examples of literature in which pronouns are used and to read and identify the meanings of the pronouns.

7. Students may write their own stories using pronouns correctly. They may finish the story of *Matthew's Dragon* by writing the story from the place left off in the earlier example.

REFERENCES

Baumann, J., & Stevenson, J. (1986). Teaching students to comprehend anaphoric relations. In J. W. Irwin (Ed.), *Understanding and teaching cohesion comprehension.* Newark, DE: International Reading Association.

Chomsky, C. (1970, May). Reading, writing, and phonology. *Harvard Educational Review,* 287–309.

Finnie, B. (1972). *The stages of English.* Boston: Houghton Mifflin.

Harris, K., Graham, S., Reid, R., McElroy, K., & Hamby, R. S. (1994, Spring). Self-monitoring of performance: Replication and cross-task comparison studies. *Learning Disability Quarterly, 17,* 121–139.

Hinman, C. (1968). *The First Folio of Shakespeare.* New York: W. W. Norton.

Mathews, M. M. (1951). *Dictionary of Americanisms on historical principles.* Chicago: University of Chicago Press.

McCrum, R., Cran, W., & MacNeil, R. (1986). *The story of English.* New York: Viking Penguin.

McKnight, G. H. (1956). *The evolution of the English language, from Chaucer to the twentieth century.* New York: Dover.

Norton, D. E. (1997). *The effective teaching of language arts.* (5th ed.). Upper Saddle River, NJ: Merrill/Prentice Hall.

Strong, W. (1986). *Creative approaches to sentence combining.* Urbana, IL: National Council of Teachers of English.

Struthers, J. P., Bartlamay, H., Bell, S., & McLaughlin, T. E. (1994, Spring). An analysis of the Add-A-Word Spelling Program and public posting across three categories of children with special needs. *Reading Improvement, 31,* 28–36.

CHILDREN'S LITERATURE REFERENCES

Bunting, Eve. *The Man Who Could Call Down Owls.* Illustrated by Charles Mikolaycak. New York: Macmillan, 1984.

Bunting, Eve. *The Mother's Day Mice.* Illustrated by Jan Brett. New York: Clarion, 1986.

Calhoun, Mary. *High-Wire Henry.* Illustrated by Erick Ingraham. New York: Morrow, 1991.

Cole, Joanna, and Calmenson, Stephanie (compiled by). *Ready . . . Set . . . Read!: The Beginning Reader's Treasury.* New York: Doubleday, 1990.

Cooper, Susan. *Matthew's Dragon.* Illustrated by Jos. A. Smith. New York: Macmillan, 1991.

Isadora, Rachel. *At the Crossroads.* New York: Greenwillow, 1991.

Potter, Beatrix. *The Tale of Mrs. Tiggy-Winkle.* London: Frederick Warne, 1905.

Van Leeuwen, Jean. *Oliver, Amanda, and Grandmother Pig.* Illustrated by Ann Schweninger. New York: Dial, 1987.

Van Leeuwen, Jean. *Oliver Pig at School.* Illustrated by Ann Schweninger. New York: Dial, 1990.

6

Activities
for Literature

Literature activities encourage children to develop their imaginations and creativity, provide vicarious experiences, afford insights into human behavior, stimulate literary awareness and growth, and develop higher thought processes. A national trend toward literature-based instruction encourages teachers to use literature throughout the curriculum. For example, when asked to respond to curriculum changes, California State Superintendent of Education William Honig stated, "We need to revamp the curriculum toward more writing, more problem solving, and more literature" (Putka, 1990, p. 1). According to *Reading Today* (Miller & Luskay, 1988), the newspaper of the International Reading Association, "Everywhere you look, there seems to be a renewed interest in the use of children's literature in the school reading program. This trend is evident in increased coverage of the topic in conference presentations, journal articles, and books" (p. 1).

Educators who use and recommend literature-based instruction emphasize the dynamic nature of the environment and the desirability of developing both understanding of and appreciation for literature. For example, Taxel (1988) describes the literature-based classroom "as fluid and dynamic, . . . a place where educators see literature as central to the curriculum, not as an occasional bit of enrichment undertaken when the real work is completed" (p. 74). Five (1988) uses minilessons that focus on such literary elements as characterization, setting, flashbacks, and book selection. After each lesson, the students read related literature, discuss the books, and complete writing activities. Five emphasizes that the program dramatically increases independent reading, peer discussion of literature, and student evaluation of areas such as believable characters and effective language and dialogue. The sequence of these minilessons followed by reading, discussing, and writing is similar to that recommended by Hiebert and Colt (1989) for effective literature-based programs. The sequence also has characteristics similar to Zarrillo's (1989) recommended use of core books, literature units, and self-selected literature. (For a detailed development of activities associated with core books, literature units, and self-selected literature, see Norton's *The Impact of Literature-Based Reading,* 1992.)

The literature activities developed in this chapter include a wide range of activities designed to increase students' knowledge of and appreciation for the various literary elements and literary genres (Norton, 1999, 1997). Some activities emphasize both efferent and aesthetic responses to literature. Rosenblatt (1985) distinguishes between the two when she states that *efferent reading* focuses attention on "actions to be performed, information to be retained, conclusions to be drawn, solutions to be arrived at, analytic concepts to be applied, propositions to be tested" (p. 70). *Aesthetic reading,* according to Rosenblatt, focuses on "what we are seeing and feeling and thinking, on what is aroused within us by the very sound of the words, and by what they point to in the human and natural world" (p. 70). Purves and Monson (1984) emphasize that students need both the efferent and the aesthetic responses to literature:

> It would seem therefore that students should be exposed to a variety of critical questions, including those which are personal and affective, those which are analytic, those which are interpretive, and those which are evaluative. Each of these questions can be answered intelligently and answering each can help a student learn to read and think and feel. And you can teach students how to answer them. (p. 189)

Activity 6–1:
INVESTIGATING CHILDREN'S INTERESTS

TYPE	TERM
○ CLASS	● STA
○ GROUP	○ LTA
● IND	○ LC

Purpose:　　　　　To take an interest inventory to determine interests

Materials:　　　　Interest inventory.

Grade level:　　　All grades—the inventory is read to young children; older children may complete it independently

Procedures:　　　**a.** Administer the following inventory:

(1)　What do you like to do when you get home from school?

_____

(2)　What do you like to do on Saturday? _____

_____

(3)　Do you like to watch television? _____
If you do, what are the names of your favorite programs?

_____

(4)　Do you have a hobby? _____
If you do, what is your hobby? _____

_____

(5)　Do you like to make or collect things? _____
If you do, what have you made or collected? _____

_____

_____

(6)　What is your favorite sport? _____

(7)　What games do you like best? _____

_____

(8)　Do you like to go to the movies?_____
If you do, what was your favorite movie? _____

(9)　Do you have a pet? _____

(10)　Where have you spent your summer vacations? _____

_____

_____

(11)　Have you ever made a special study?

rocks _____　　　space _____
plants _____　　　animals _____
travel _____　　　dinosaurs _____
other _____

(12)　What are your favorite subjects in school?

art_____　　　　　　handwriting _____
social studies _____　　　reading _____

physical education _____   science_____
spelling _____   arithmetic _____
creative writing _____   English _____
other_____

(13) What subject is hardest for you?_____

(14) What kinds of books do you like to have someone read to you?

animal stories _____   fairy tales _____
true stories _____   science fiction _____
adventures _____   mysteries _____
sports stories _____   poems _____
humorous stories _____
other_____

(15) What is your favorite book that someone has read to you?

_____

(16) What kinds of books do you like to read by yourself?

animal stories _____   picture books _____
fairy tales _____   true stories_____
science fiction _____   adventures _____
mysteries _____   sports stories _____
poems _____   funny stories _____
other_____

(17) What is your favorite book that you read by yourself? _____

_____

(18) Would you rather read a book by yourself or have someone read to you?

_____

(19) Name a book you have read this week. _____

_____

(20) What books or magazines do you have at home? _____

_____

(21) Do you ever go to the library? _____
How often? _____
Do you have a library card? _____

b. Tabulate your group's interests. Use the results to choose books to read aloud to
the group and to suggest books for students to read individually.

Activity 6–2:
THE FANTASY OF MOTHER GOOSE

TYPE	TERM
● CLASS	● STA
○ GROUP	○ LTA
○ IND	○ LC

Purpose:
1. To appreciate literature
2. To dramatize nursery rhymes creatively
3. To develop choral speaking with nursery rhymes
4. To write creatively a story stimulated by nursery rhymes
5. To interpret Mother Goose rhymes through art

Materials:
Mother Goose books and pictures; large sheets of cardboard or large boxes for humanette puppets; language experience charts; materials for puppet construction.

Grade level:
Kindergarten, first grade

Procedures:
1. Young children love the happy rhymes and nonsense in Mother Goose rhymes. Give them many opportunities to listen to and recite Mother Goose rhymes.
2. Pantomime—As you recite a Mother Goose rhyme to the children, have them act out each part of the rhyme.
3. Pantomime—Allow children to take turns pantomiming their favorite Mother Goose rhymes while the class guesses their identity.
4. Choral Speaking—Because most rhymes are easily memorized, children do not need to be able to read to perform choral speaking activities with nursery rhymes. Practice different choral speaking arrangements and try accompanying some of them with rhythm instruments or a bongo drum.

5. Creative Drama—Nursery rhymes provide an excellent introduction to the concept that a drama has several parts—a beginning, middle, and ending. Have children listen to a nursery rhyme that has obvious parts such as "Jack and Jill":

Jack and Jill went up the hill to get a pail of water.
Jack fell down and broke his crown,
And Jill came tumbling after.

Ask the children to identify the first, second, and final act in the rhyme. Divide the class into groups and have each group act out what the members think would happen during the first part, the second part, or the final part. Encourage them to extend their parts by adding dialogue to each part or pretending to be objects such as trees, flowers, or other creatures that might be on the hill. After each group has an opportunity to act out its part, put the parts of the nursery rhyme back together and have each group play its own part.

6. Role-Playing—Put pictures of nursery rhyme characters into a pail (symbol for Jack and Jill). Provide a picture for each character in a nursery rhyme. Have the children select a character from the pail, form a group with the other characters in the rhyme, and role-play their part in the jingle.

7. Humanette Puppets—A child can be transformed into a human-size puppet by making a cardboard figure large enough to cover the front of the child or by using a box large enough to cover the body. Have students select nursery rhyme characters they would like to be and design humanette puppets. After they make the puppets, have students act out the rhymes.

8. Creative Writing (Language Experience Chart Stories)—After reading nursery rhymes, allow the children to select a nursery rhyme they would like to write a story about. This activity may be done many times, with different rhymes for stimulation. For example, after reading "Jack and Jill," ask students: "What do you think happened after Jack and Jill fell down the hill? What do you think their mother might have done? Would they go back and get more water?" After reading "The Old Woman and the Shoe," you might ask: "What would you do if you were the Old Woman in the Shoe? How would you take care of your children? What would it be like living in a shoe?" Or after reading "Peter, Peter Pumpkin Eater," you might say: "Imagine that you lived in a pumpkin like Peter." (Provide a pumpkin for students to see and feel.) "How would you decorate your room? What could you do inside the shell? Would a pumpkin make a good home? Why or why not? What do you think your neighbors would think of your home?"

Draw a large object that symbolizes the nursery rhyme. Have the children dictate a story, which you write inside the shape. Display the stories on the bulletin board. Encourage children to read their stories.

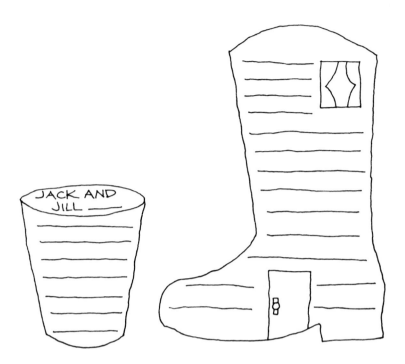

9. Art Interpretation—Create a Mother Goose Land bulletin board illustrating the homes and people who live in Mother Goose Land. The center of the board might contain a large figure of Mother Goose carrying a wand and riding on her goose. The children could paint a large mural depicting this land. Place the chart stories below the bulletin board.

10. Creative Drama (Puppetry)—After the children have listened to, pantomimed, and drawn pictures of many rhymes, allow them to select several rhymes to present as puppet shows. They might add to the puppet show by including their own language experience stories as part of the rhyme. Encourage them to make simple puppets showing their favorite rhymes. Invite another class to the festival to

see the puppet plays, hear choral speaking, look at pictures, and read the children's chart stories. Write invitations to the Mother Goose festival on figures, drawn by the children, depicting nursery rhyme characters.

Activity 6–3:
PERSON VERSUS PERSON PLOT STRUCTURE

Purpose:
1. To develop an understanding of and appreciation for person versus person plot structure
2. To draw and discuss person versus person plot structures

Materials:
Eric Kimmel's *Hershel and the Hanukkah Goblins* (1989; a Caldecott Honor Award winner, 1990).

Grade level:
Lower and middle elementary

Book summary:
Hershel and the Hanukkah Goblins is a literary folktale similar to many Jewish folktales. The story is set in a village during Hanukkah. Hershel, the main character, enters the village and discovers that the people are unable to celebrate Hanukkah because wicked goblins haunt the synagogue. To rid the village of goblins, someone must spend eight nights in the old synagogue, light the Hanukkah candles each night, and convince the king of the goblins to light the candles on the eighth night. Hershel declares that he is not afraid of the goblins and offers to rid the village of them. The plot develops as Hershel uses his wits and common materials to trick increasingly fearsome goblins and light the candles. The story progresses until on the eighth night Hershel tricks the king of the goblins into lighting the Hanukkah candles. At this point the spell is broken and all of the households celebrate Hanukkah in their homes. The author develops the theme that even common materials, when used in uncommon ways by a person with wit and intelligence, can bring about heroic outcomes.

Procedures:
1. Plots in stories frequently follow Freitag's triangle, a structure in which the beginning of the story identifies the problem, introduces the characters, and describes the setting. Increasing conflict is then developed until the story reaches a climax. Following the climax there is usually a turning point incident, followed quite rapidly by an end of the conflict or a resolution of the problem. To show this conflict, draw the following plot diagram on the board:

2. Ask the students to think about some stories they know that follow this type of plot structure. For example, they can retell "The Three Billy Goats Gruff" or "Goldilocks and the Three Bears" and decide how the story follows this diagram. Asking students to act out one of these stories will help them understand and appreciate the developing conflict. After students have retold or acted out a familiar story, have them place the incidents from the story on the plot diagram.

3. Introduce *Hershel and the Hanukkah Goblins* to students. Show the illustrations and ask the students to respond to the mood of the story and to consider what type of problem or conflict might be in the story. If desired, you may read the author's endnote, in which he provides information about the Hanukkah celebration.

4. Read the story aloud to the students. Before placing the incidents on the plot diagram, encourage the students to provide their personal responses to the story. Next, draw a new plot diagram on the chalkboard and ask the students to identify elements from the story that can be placed on the plot diagram. For example, a group of third-grade students identified the following information:

Hershel tricks King of the goblins into lighting the Hanukkah candles

Hershel fools 4th through 6th goblins

Hershel plays game with 3rd goblin and goblin loses gold

Hershel makes greedy goblin believe he has cast a spell

Hershel enters synagogue, lights candles, and tricks little goblin

Hershel arrives in village and offers to outwit goblins

Hershel breaks the spell

The village celebrates Hanukkah

Problem: Goblins haunt Synagogue
Characters: Witty Hershel, Evil goblins
Setting: Country village during winter. Time of Hanukkah

5. After the students complete the plot diagram, ask them to consider what they think is the theme or the message that the author is trying to get across. The third-grade students who completed this activity decided that the themes were (a) it is important to use one's wits and intelligence and (b) even common objects may be used to outwit the enemy if they are used with intelligence. Have the students defend their choice of themes by identifying what happened in the story to make the ideas important. For example, all of Hershel's actions show the importance of

wit and intelligence. In the search for common objects that are used to outwit the enemy, Hershel crushes a hard-boiled egg, which is part of his lunch, to make the little goblin believe that he can crush rock. He uses pickles and the second goblin's greed to make the goblin believe that he has cast a spell on the pickle jar that has caught the goblin's fist. He uses a dreidl and his wits to play a game with the third goblin and force the goblin to lose the goblin's gold. He uses the Hanukkah candles to trick the king of the goblins into lighting some candles that provide light that make Hershel believe that the goblin really is fierce and king of the goblins.

6. Additional books that may be used in studying person versus person plot structure include Diane Stanley's *Rumpelstiltskin's Daughter* (1997), Janet Stevens's *Tops and Bottoms* (1995; a Caldecott Honor Award winner, 1996), and Eugene Trivizas's *The Three Little Wolves and the Big Bad Pig* (1993).

Activity 6–4:

PERSON VERSUS SELF PLOT STRUCTURE

TYPE	TERM
● CLASS	○ STA
● GROUP	● LTA
● IND	○ LC

Purpose:
1. To develop an understanding of person versus self plot structure
2. To respond to a story in which a girl with a physical handicap discovers her true worth
3. To trace the comparisons between the weakest eagle's struggle for survival and the girl's struggle against her physical handicap
4. To draw and discuss person versus self plot structures

Materials: Ian Strachan's *The Flawed Glass* (1990).

Grade level: Upper elementary, middle school

Book summary: *The Flawed Glass* is set on an island off the coast of Scotland. The main character, Shona MacLeod, has a physical handicap that makes it difficult for her to walk and to speak. When Shona befriends the American son of the owner of the island, she discovers that she has a great deal to share with another person. Her introduction to computers makes it possible for her to communicate as well as save her family from disgrace. A parallel plot development showing the struggle of the weakest eagle to survive on the island provides interesting insights into the person versus self conflict. The author develops strong themes that show the positive power of persistence and the negative results when people judge others on the basis of their physical appearance.

Procedures:
1. Story structures in books for older students frequently develop plots through person versus self conflict. Students can use the same plot structure as in the lesson for person versus person plot structure. Only the terminology changes; the major components in the development of person versus self plot structures include problem, struggle, realization, and achievement of peace or truth. To show this conflict, draw the following plot diagram on the board:

Struggle with self → Struggle with self → Struggle with self → Self-realization

Problems, characters, and setting introduced

Achievement of peace and truth

Discuss the meaning of *problem, struggle, realization,* and *achievement of peace or truth.* Ask students to identify conflicts in their own lives that might include each of these elements.

2. Introduce *The Flawed Glass* and ask students to speculate about the characters on the cover and to consider what they might be looking at, the location of the story, and the meaning of the title of the book. To provide a better understanding of the possible meaning of the title, ask students to look through a piece of colored glass, discuss what they see, and consider how their vision changes because of the glass. Ask the students to think about what the main character, Shona, means when she compares herself to an old piece of colored glass. As an introduction to Shona's difficulties, read the following quote and discuss its possible meanings: "In many ways she felt that she had much in common with that old piece of glass. Just as the images that entered the glass were changed, not always for the better, by the time they got through it, so it was with her. Capable of receiving the most complex information, she could not make use of it to the point that she could tell anyone what she knew or felt" (p. 64).

   To introduce the setting for the book, show and discuss pictures of a Scottish island, a crofter's cabin, and birds and other wildlife that would inhabit the island. Read the following quote and ask students to close their eyes and visualize the book's setting from the viewpoint of a golden eagle soaring high above the island: "He watched the fishermen out in their boats trying their lobster pots, the crofters scything their hay, and the tractor hauling a cartload of rich, wet seaweed along the narrow road. He took in the high mountains, their shoulders peppered with white and purple heather, as easily as the lowlands, where the hundreds of tiny lochs lay scattered like fragments of a smashed mirror, each reflecting the intense blue of the sky" (p. 12). Ask the students to describe what they visualized. It may be necessary to show them pictures of a farmer using a scythe, land covered with heather, and lochs. After they see pictures, ask students to visualize the setting as you read the passage again. Does it make a difference when they know that a scythe is a tool with a long handle and a curved blade on the end used to cut hay or grass? Does it make a difference after they see the small, bell-shaped, purple plant that covers so much of the ground in Scotland? Does it make a difference when they know that a loch is another name for a lake or for a portion of the sea that is nearly surrounded by land?

3. As you either read the book to the students or have them read the book independently, ask them to identify incidents from the book that reveal the problem, Shona's increasing struggle with herself, her self-realization, and her achievement of peace or truth. The following plot diagram shows several of these major incidents from the book:

Shona
struggles
to make
her fingers
use the
computer
keys

Shona success-
fully uses computer,
compares it to a
piece of glass, and
is able to be
understood

Shona
struggles
to warn
Carl about
quicksand

Shona
compares
herself
to flawed
glass

Shona
fears leaving
the island

Shona feels
she is trapped
in her body

Shona happily
discovers that
Carl did not
desert her. She
can still
communicate
with Carl even
though he is in
America.

Shona, a girl with
a severe physical
handicap, tries
to overcome her
fear and problems.
Shona's family, the
Laird's son, Carl.
An island off the
coast of Scotland

4. After they complete the diagram, ask students to identify the themes found in the book and to discuss how each of the themes is related to the increasing struggle, the moment of self-realization, and the achievement of peace and truth. For example, students usually identify the following themes: (1) Persistence is important if we are to gain our dreams; (2) there is pleasure in discovering that we have a talent and sharing it with someone else; and (3) people should not judge others and find them wanting on the basis of a handicap or their physical appearance.

5. Ask the students to develop a plot structure for the weakest eagle as he struggles for survival and finally wins his own ability to fly. Ask them to consider why the author would develop parallel stories for both Shona and the eagle.

6. Toward the end of the book, Shona compares the green screen on the computer to a modern version of her piece of flawed glass. Ask the students to consider how a computer screen could be similar to the piece of colored glass. How does this modern piece of glass change Shona's future and her perception of herself?

7. Students could write a continuation to this story. Ask them to write their own story about what happens to Shona after she discovers that she can communicate through the computer.

8. Additional books that may be used in studying person versus self plot structure include Russell Freedman's *Out of Darkness: The Story of Louis Braille* (1997), Mary Downing Hahn's *Stepping on the Crack* (1991), and Ruth Whites *Belle Prater's Boy* (1996; a Newbery Honor Award winner, 1997).

Activity 6–5:

RESPONDING TO CHARACTERS
AND CONFLICTS IN LITERATURE—PART I

TYPE	TERM
● CLASS	● STA
● GROUP	○ LTA
● IND	○ LC

Purpose:
1. To develop an aesthetic response to literature
2. To respond to the characters and conflicts in literature
3. To enjoy a good story that relates to the needs of many young children
4. To write a story about a favorite toy

Materials:
Shirley Hughes's *Dogger* (1977).

Grade level:
Lower elementary

Book summary:
Dogger is the story of a young boy who has a close attachment to his toy. When the toy is lost and sold at a fair, his sister performs an unselfish act that makes it possible for the boy to regain his toy.

Procedures:
1. Introduce the book in a way that will increase interest and encourage students' responses. For example, ask students the following: "Have you ever had a special toy that was so important to you that the toy went everywhere with you? Imagine how you would feel if one day you lost your toy. How would you feel if you saw the toy for sale at a school fair? Now, how would you feel if you did not have any money to buy back the toy? Do you think that there is any way you could get that toy? How would you feel if someone helped you get the toy? The book *Dogger* is a story about a boy who loses his special toy and then tries to regain it. As you read (or listen to) *Dogger* pretend that you are that boy and you are feeling all of his emotions. How do you respond to playing with Dogger, the loss of Dogger, and the regaining of Dogger?"

2. Encourage the students to read or listen to *Dogger* and to write or tell their own personal responses to the character and the conflict.

3. This book may be used to motivate creative writing as students write their own stories about close relationships with toys.

4. Additional books that encourage children to respond to characters and conflict include Kevin Henkes's *Lilly's Purple Plastic Purse* (1996), Amy Hest's *In the Rain with Baby Duck* (1995), and Kathryn Lasky's *Lunch Bunnies* (1996).

Activity 6–6:

RESPONDING TO CHARACTERS AND CONFLICTS IN LITERATURE—PART II

TYPE	TERM
● CLASS	○ STA
● GROUP	● LTA
● IND	○ LC

Purpose:

1. To develop an aesthetic response to literature
2. To respond to the characters and conflict in a good realistic animal story
3. To respond to the setting that creates the conflict
4. To write a pet survival story

Materials:

Sheila Burnford's *The Incredible Journey* (1960) and Juster Esbensen's *Great Northern Diver: The Loon* (1990).

Grade level:

Middle elementary

Book summaries:

The Incredible Journey is a contemporary realistic novel set in the Canadian wilderness. The story accompanies three animals as they cross 250 miles of wilderness on their journey to find their family. *The Great Northern Diver: The Loon* is a nonfictional information book that includes numerous illustrations of the wilderness.

Procedures:

1. Understanding of these books and the quality of students' responses to them will improve if students are first introduced to the location and characteristics of the Canadian wilderness. They can identify the location of the wilderness on maps. Photographs will help them picture a vast area of forests and lakes. This is an area inhabited by numerous animals, some of which are quite dangerous and might even consider the three pets to be respectable meals. Pictures such as those in *Great Northern Diver: The Loon* help students to visualize this great expanse of wilderness.

2. After discussing the setting for this book, present students with an introduction that increases interest and encourages students to provide personal responses to the book. For example, say to students: "Close your eyes and try to picture the Canadian wilderness. This is a great tract of land covered with forests and lakes and inhabited by more wild animals than people. Now try to imagine that you are a lost dog or cat and that you must travel on foot 250 miles across this wilderness if you are to find your family. What would you do? How would you live? How would you find your way through the wilderness and eventually to your home? Do you think you would succeed? This is the adventure three animals face in *The Incredible Journey*. On this journey are a trained hunting dog, an English bulldog that is a cherished family pet, and a Siamese cat that has always shown a great deal of independence. As you read this story imagine that you are one of these animals or that one of these animals is your special pet. How would you respond if attacked by wild animals? How would you react if you faced dangerous areas in the wilderness? How would you feel if people wanted to keep you from continuing on your journey?"

3. As students read or listen to this book, they may write personal responses to the characters, the plot, and the setting. If students have pets, they may closely relate

to the needs of the animals. As students write their responses, help them to consider why they are responding in certain ways.

4. Students may write and illustrate their own stories in which their pets are faced with a survival adventure. Before they do this activity, students should think about how Burnford created believable settings for and actions of the pet characters.

Activity 6–7:

RESPONDING TO CHARACTERS AND CONFLICTS IN LITERATURE—PART III

TYPE	TERM
● CLASS	○ STA
● GROUP	● LTA
● IND	○ LC

Purpose:

1. To develop an aesthetic response to literature
2. To evaluate an author's ability to create a believable person versus nature conflict
3. To respond to the characters and conflict in a survival story
4. To discover the experiences a writer or a photographer needs to write or photograph believable stories that deal with nature
5. To write a story that requires higher thought processes and problem-solving abilities
6. To write a survival story from the perspective of one of the animals identified in *Hatchet* or *Think Like an Eagle: At Work·with a Wildlife Photographer*
7. To integrate a study of animal behavior with language arts
8. To create a northwoods alphabet book from the perspective of Brian in *Hatchet*

Materials:

The core book, Gary Paulsen's *Hatchet* (1987), and books that provide background or extension experiences, such as Betsy Bowen's *Antler, Bear, Canoe: A Northwoods Alphabet Year* (1991), Holling Clancy Holling's *Paddle to the Sea* (1941), Kathryn Lasky's *Think Like an Eagle: At Work with a Wildlife Photographer* (1992), and Gary Paulsen's *Woodsong* (1990).

Grade level:

Upper elementary through middle school for the activities associated with *Hatchet* and *Woodsong*. For middle elementary students, this activity will enrich the understanding gained from completing activity 6–6. These younger students may use *Antler, Bear, Canoe: A Northwoods Alphabet Year* and *Paddle to the Sea*.

Book summaries:

Hatchet is a realistic fictional survival story set in the Canadian wilderness. The main character expresses a strong will to survive as he is able to live for fifty-four days in the wilderness with only a hatchet and his problem-solving abilities to help him. *Antler, Bear, Canoe: A Northwoods Alphabet Year* is a picture book set in the northwoods of Minnesota. *Paddle to the Sea* follows a carved miniature canoe after it is placed in the water in the Canadian wilderness and travels through the Great Lakes to the Atlantic Ocean. *Think Like an Eagle: At Work with a Wildlife Photographer* is a nonfictional information book that follows a wildlife photographer as he photographs eagles, beavers, and deer in various wilderness areas. *Woodsong* is an autobiography in which the author reveals how he learned lessons from nature, especially from working with his dogs in the northwoods and across Alaska.

Procedures:

1. Develop an introduction to *Hatchet* that increases students' interest in the story and the conflict and provides stimulus for discussion. For example, you might say to students: "Have you ever seen or been in a wilderness that stretches for thousands of miles? This is a wilderness that has many trees, lakes, and animals but few people. What would you do if you were flying over such a wilderness in a small plane and all of a sudden the pilot had a heart attack and died? You are the

only one in the plane and do not know how to pilot the plane. How would you react as you look out of the window, see only lakes and forests, and have no idea where you are? How would you fly the plane, land the plane, and then live in this wilderness? This is the exciting story of survival that you will read about in Gary Paulsen's *Hatchet*. As you follow Brian's adventure, try to place yourself in his position as he spends fifty-four days in the wilderness with only a hatchet and his clear thinking and problem-solving skills for help. Do you think that you would have the ability to last for fifty-four days without stores and normal shelter? Why or why not?" Encourage the students to discuss their reactions to being lost in a wilderness and their potential for survival.

2. If students have completed activity 6–6, using *The Incredible Journey* and *The Great Northern Diver: The Loon,* they may review their knowledge of the wilderness and consider how a human would survive in this same setting. If students have not completed this activity, they will benefit from an introduction to the wilderness setting. They can find the Canadian wilderness on maps and globes. They can look at and discuss photographs and illustrations in nonfictional sources that show the Canadian wilderness. As students look at the illustrations, they can describe nature and consider how dangerous that setting might be if a person were caught there. They can also increase their understanding of person versus nature settings by describing the environments in the illustrations in such a way that readers understand the possible dangers found in them. Two additional picture books—*Antler, Bear, Canoe: A Northwoods Alphabet Year* and *Paddle to the Sea*—may be read and discussed to provide additional knowledge about rural northern settings. (See also activity 4–5 for a writing activity using *Paddle to the Sea*.)

3. Before reading *Hatchet,* explain to the students that this is a survival-in-nature story in which a boy must make correct decisions if he is to survive alone in the Canadian wilderness. Ask the students to look at the illustration on the jacket cover. Have them note and discuss the importance of the wilderness, the wolf, the hatchet, and the lone boy.

4. Explain to the students that Paulsen's techniques for developing and showing his character's problem-solving abilities are especially noteworthy. Ask the students to consider their own responses when Paulsen reveals Brian's reasoning processes as he tries to survive in nature. The following examples are especially good for stimulating discussions and responses: Brian considers the actions he should take after the pilot dies (pp. 17–39), Brian thinks about the reasons he should return to the raspberry patch even though he has seen a bear in that location (p. 75), Brian analyzes the way to create a means of catching fish (pp. 111–115), Brian thinks about ways to capture birds for meat (pp. 140–141), and Brian considers how to make a raft and reach the plane (pp. 166–183). Students can offer their own responses to each of these situations. They should also be aware of how Paulsen encourages readers to understand the gravity and the consequences of many of the problems. As they are giving their personal responses to Brian's situation students can also evaluate what makes them believe in the person versus nature conflict.

5. Students can also speculate about the types of experiences the author, Gary Paulsen, must have had for him to write such vivid descriptions of nature and survival in the wilderness. To answer this question, students may read Paulsen's autobiography, *Woodsong*. Paulsen's introduction to *Woodsong* provides a source for interesting discussions. For example, read and encourage students to discuss possible meanings for the following: "I understood almost nothing about the woods until it was nearly too late. And that is strange because my ignorance was based on knowledge. Most of my life it seems I've been in the forest or on the sea. Most of my time, sleeping and waking, has been spent outside, in close contact with what we now call the environment. . . . I spent virtually all my time hunting. And

learning nothing. Perhaps the greatest paradox about understanding 'the woods' is that so many who enjoy it, or seem to enjoy it, spend most of their time trying to kill parts of it" (p. 1). Students can speculate about what they think Paulsen means by this statement. They can read his autobiography and discover how and what he finally learned about nature. They can also relate Paulsen's learning about nature as revealed in his autobiography with the descriptions of survival in nature developed in *Hatchet*.

6. In addition, students may consider the experiences and techniques a wildlife photographer requires to photograph believable and accurate pictures of wild animals in wilderness settings. *Think Like an Eagle: At Work with a Wildlife Photographer* provides an excellent source for learning more about the requirements for being a wildlife photographer. The text also stimulates interesting science projects and writing assignments. For example, the author describes the work of one wildlife photographer as follows: "In fact, just getting an animal into the viewfinder was the most difficult challenge of all. During long hours of hiking, he saw deer that ran off, beavers that submerged, and foxes that disappeared into their dens. He was still on the other side of the invisible wall. He had to figure out how to move through it without shattering it, so he could be with the animals quietly and unnoticed. To become a great wildlife photographer, Jack had to become a student of animal behavior and figure out how to be at the right place at the right time, without being detected by the animals" (p. 9). The remainder of the book describes how and what the photographer learned about animal behavior. After students have read the book, ask them to consider the following: "What would a photographer of _____ need to know about the animal's behavior?" Ask students to investigate the animal and then write a story in which they use their own problem-solving abilities to photograph the animal.

7. *Hatchet* is written from the point of view of a person surviving in nature. Ask the students to choose one of the animals that Brian sees, hears, or interacts with in the story. Have the students write a survival story from the point of view of the wild animal.

8. *Antler, Bear, Canoe: A Northwoods Alphabet Year* may be used to motivate students to create their own illustrated alphabet books. Ask the students to create an alphabet book that Brian might have made to illustrate his experiences in the northwoods.

9. Additional books that have survival-in-nature themes and may be used to encourage students to respond to characters and conflicts include Alden R. Carter's *Between a Rock and a Hard Place* (1995), set in Minnesota lake country; Nancy Farmer's *A Girl Named Disaster* (1996; a Newbery Honor Award winner, 1997), set in Mozambique and Zimbabwe; and Jean Craighead George's *Julie of the Wolves* (1972; a Newbery Medal Award winner, 1973).

Activity 6–8:
RESPONDING TO CHARACTERS AND CONFLICTS IN LITERATURE—PART IV

TYPE	TERM
● CLASS	○ STA
● GROUP	● LTA
● IND	○ LC

Purpose:
1. To develop an aesthetic response to literature
2. To relate history and literature

Materials:
Ida Vos's *Hide and Seek* (1991), Lois Lowry's *Number the Stars* (1989), and Milton Meltzer's *Rescue: The Story of How Gentiles Saved Jews in the Holocaust* (1988).

Grade level:
Middle elementary through middle school

Book summaries:
Hide and Seek is a historical novel set in the Netherlands during World War II. This is the story of a Jewish family who experiences both the German occupation and the kindness and courage of the Dutch people who risk their own lives to hide the Jewish residents of Holland. *Number the Stars* is a historical novel set in Denmark during World War II. It is a story of bravery as members of the Danish Resistance smuggle the Jewish population across the sea to Sweden. *Rescue: The Story of How Gentiles Saved Jews in the Holocaust* is a nonfictional account of World War II.

Procedures:

1. Introduce this response activity by providing some background information so that students will understand the setting and the conflicts that develop in *Hide and Seek*. Sources such as *Rescue: The Story of How Gentiles Saved Jews in the Holocaust* illustrate the human decency and courage shown by people who tried to save the Jewish people. These stories authenticate the fact that thousands of European families tried to help the Jewish people.

2. After discussing the background for the Holocaust and the Resistance Movement, introduce *Hide and Seek* in such a way that students will be interested in providing their personal responses to the book. For example, in this introduction you might say: "Imagine that the year is 1940 and you are a Jewish student living in the Netherlands. You have a normal life in which you go to school, do activities with friends, swim in the pool, and visit family and friends. All of a sudden something happens, and you are forbidden to attend school, go to the movies, and even swim in the pool. Life for you becomes so bad and so threatening that you and your family are afraid for your lives and must go into hiding. This is what happens to Rachel and many other people in *Hide and Seek*. As you read (or listen to) this story, which is based on the author's family's life during World War II, try to imagine how you would work things out if you were living during this time in Europe. Remember the author's words when she asks you, 'Imagine what it would be like not ever to be allowed to go outside, year after year. Imagine being able to do your shopping only between three and five o'clock. Imagine . . .' (p. ix, foreword)."

3. As students read or listen to this book ask them to write their own responses to the various characters, the changing situations, and the conclusion. Students are usually especially responsive to actions such as having bicycles confiscated, not being allowed to attend school or go to the swimming pool, being forced to wear

yellow stars on clothing, being in hiding and not going outside for years, and discovering that loved ones have disappeared and died.

4. A similar response activity may accompany *Number the Stars.*

5. Older students may respond to the nonfictional accounts in *Rescue: The Story of How Gentiles Saved Jews in the Holocaust.* This book may also be used to help older students authenticate the information in either *Hide and Seek* or *Number the Stars.*

6. Additional books that relate to the topic of the Holocaust include Livia Bitton-Jackson's *I Have Lived a Thousand Years: Growing Up in the Holocaust* (1997), Anne Frank's *The Diary of a Young Girl: The Definitive Edition* (1995), Uri Orlev's *The Island on Bird Street* (1984), and Johanna Reiss's *The Upstairs Room* (1972).

Activity 6–9:
DEVELOPING UNDERSTANDING
OF CHARACTERIZATION

TYPE	TERM
● CLASS	● STA
● GROUP	○ LTA
● IND	○ LC

Purpose:
1. To develop an understanding and appreciation for characterization in illustrated books
2. To observe characterization as revealed through illustrations
3. To write character descriptions to accompany characters in wordless books
4. To draw illustrations that accompany character descriptions in literature

Materials:
Provide wordless books in which students can describe and write characterizations for the major characters, such as Emily Arnold McCully's *Picnic* (1984), *School* (1987), and *New Baby* (1988) and Peter Collington's *The Angel and the Soldier Boy* (1987) and *On Christmas Eve* (1990).

Grade level:
These books are usually used in lower elementary grades, although all students can prepare characterizations to accompany the books. These characterizations can be more complex when developed with older students.

Book summaries:
Picnic, School, and *New Baby* are stories about a mouse family. The major emphasis is on the littlest mouse, who is lost on a picnic, attends school, and adjusts to a new baby in the family. *The Angel and the Soldier Boy* and *On Christmas Eve* tell, through the illustrations, an adventure in which two toys protect a young girl's piggy bank and a plot in which an angel makes it possible for Santa Claus to find the home of a young girl who does not have a fireplace, respectively.

Procedures:
1. Lead a discussion with students in which they identify favorite characters in literature. Ask them the following: "Why are these characters among your favorites? Why do you remember these characters?" Make a list of favorite characters and the reasons why they are favorites.
2. Share with the students some of the ways that authors make their characters seem real. For example, authors can create dialogue between characters so that readers know not only what characters are saying to each other but also how the characters say it. They can tell readers about a character so that the readers know important information about the character such as where the character lives, what the character looks like, and information about the character's likes and dislikes. Authors can describe the thoughts of the character or the thoughts of others about the character. Authors can also present considerable information about characters by showing their actions. Using creative dramatics, encourage students to try each of these ways of developing characterization. For example, after they have created a dialogue between two characters, ask them to think about what they learned about each character as a result of the dialogue. Did they notice that the way the characters said something may have been just as important as the actual words?

3. Introduce one of the wordless books to students. Ask them to consider how they know information about the characters even though there are no words provided. For example, if the first book introduced is *Picnic,* students may suggest that the illustrations describe the characters, show the actions of the characters, and even develop emotions through the characters' facial expressions. Continue sharing and discussing the totally wordless book.

4. Next challenge the students to create their own vivid characterizations for one of the characters in the story. They might choose the littlest mouse and describe actions, feelings, and inner thoughts as the mouse becomes lost, solves problems, and is reunited with the family. They might create dialogues between grandfather mouse and one of the mouse children when the young mouse's disappearance is discovered. They might create inner thoughts, dialogues, and descriptions of mother mouse as she faces the fact that her young child is lost. After the students have created their characterizations, ask them to share the characterizations within their groups.

5. Students may create additional characterizations using the other wordless books. Because the books by each illustrator include the same characters, students could use several books to create more detailed portrayals of the same character.

6. Place the character portrayals in the library next to the appropriate wordless books.

7. This activity may be reversed by asking students to draw illustrations that depict characterization after they read vivid written descriptions of characters. Ask the students to identify some of their favorite characterizations in books. Then ask them to develop these characterizations through their own illustrations.

Activity 6–10:

CHARACTERIZATION AND PLOT DEVELOPMENT IN THE WRITINGS OF BEVERLY CLEARY

TYPE	TERM
● CLASS	○ STA
● GROUP	● LTA
● IND	○ LC

Purpose:

1. To identify the characteristics of the characters in Beverly Cleary's popular books and to write personal responses to chosen characters
2. To compare the characterization of Leigh Botts in *Dear Mr. Henshaw* with the characterization of Leigh Botts in the sequel, *Strider*
3. To compare the plot development and conflict in *Dear Mr. Henshaw* and *Strider*
4. To choose other characters from Cleary's numerous books and to analyze what the students believe makes the characters and the books so popular
5. To write a short sequel to one of the books other than *Dear Mr. Henshaw* and *Strider*
6. To read Cleary's autobiography, *A Girl from Yamhill: A Memoir,* and to identify any reasons the students find for Cleary's choosing to write for children and any evidence that suggests why she will become a popular writer
7. To write letters to favorite authors

Materials:

Beverly Cleary's *Dear Mr. Henshaw* (1983; Newbery Medal award winner, 1984), *Strider* (1991), and *A Girl from Yamhill: A Memoir* (1988); an additional selection of Cleary's books, including *Henry and Beezus* (1952), *Muggie Maggie* (1952), *Mitch and Amy* (1967), *Ramona and Her Father* (1977), *Ramona and Her Mother* (1979), *Ramona the Brave* (1975), *Ramona the Pest* (1968), and *Ramona Quimby, Age 8* (1981).

Grade level:

Middle elementary through middle school, depending on the books chosen

Book summaries:

In *Dear Mr. Henshaw,* Cleary uses correspondence with an author to help Leigh, a sixth-grade boy, overcome problems related to his parents' divorce. In *Strider,* Leigh, now 14 years old, discovers that his life has changed a great deal. This time a dog helps him overcome his problems. *Strider* is written in diary format. *A Girl from Yamhill: A Memoir* is Beverly Cleary's autobiography, in which she tells about her early life through high school. In *Henry and Beezus,* Henry and the girl he finds least obnoxious have a humorously good time. In *Muggie Maggie,* a third grader decides that she does not want to learn cursive writing. In *Mitch and Amy,* Cleary provides a humorous story about everyday experiences. In *Ramona and Her Father,* Ramona tries to help her father through a trying period after he loses his job. In *Ramona and Her Mother,* Ramona's mother goes to work. In *Ramona the Brave,* Ramona has many difficulties until she finally wins a truce with her first-grade teacher. In *Ramona the Pest,* Ramona enters kindergarten and spreads exasperation into a wider sphere. In *Ramona Quimby, Age 8,* Ramona faces new challenges when her father returns to college.

Procedures:

1. This series of activities, designed to accompany the works of one author, differs depending on the grade level of students. For example, after younger students have read or listened to the appropriate books, they may write responses to such

characters as Henry and Beezus, Muggie Maggie, Mitch and Amy, and Ramona. Younger students may consider why these characters do or do not appeal to them, write or tell personal responses about these characters, and write their own stories about friendships and other interesting characters.

2. Students in upper elementary and middle grades should first be introduced to the character of Leigh Botts in *Dear Mr. Henshaw*. As they read or listen to the book they should look for evidence of both Leigh's character and the changes that take place as he writes. For example, they can consider how Leigh views himself in comparison with the other children in his school and his attitudes toward his mother and father. They should look for evidence that reveals Leigh's self-image and changing character as he writes his first letter to Mr. Henshaw, continues writing his pretend letters to Mr. Henshaw, and finally discovers that he can write what he thinks on a piece of paper without pretending to be writing to an author. Students can respond to any of the characters in *Dear Mr. Henshaw*. For example, you might ask the following: "Who was your favorite character in the story? What caused you to respond to this character in a favorable way? Who was your least favorite character? What caused you to respond to this character in an unfavorable way? What did the author do to make these characters real for you? Do you know any people who remind you of these characters?"

3. *Dear Mr. Henshaw* may be used to motivate students to write their own letters to their favorite authors.

4. After completing activities with *Dear Mr. Henshaw*, students may summarize what they have learned about the characters of Leigh Botts and his mother and father. They may also draw a person versus self plot diagram that shows Leigh's various struggles as he finally comes to the realization that he can write without addressing letters to an author.

Dear Mr. Henshaw

Struggles with lunch box thief and lack of friends.

"I don't have to pretend to write to Mr. Henshaw anymore."

Struggles with thoughts that he hates his father.

Divorce — Father doesn't call or write.

Leigh Botts and his need to face both a new school and his parents' divorce.

Leigh begins to feel a sense of peace when his dad comes to visit.

5. Next, introduce *Strider* by asking students what they think has happened to Leigh Botts and his mother and father since they read about him in *Dear Mr. Henshaw*. What information would they want to know about the characters and their lives? List some of the thoughts of the students. Keep these thoughts and predictions available so that students can make comparisons with their predictions after they read *Strider*.

6. As students read or listen to *Strider*, ask them to note characterizations, especially similarities and differences in characters between the close of the first book and the opening of *Strider*. Ask students to identify and respond to particularly revealing instances of character development in the book. For example, they might identify and discuss the reasons for Leigh's thoughts when he finds

the abandoned dog: "Barry and I slogged through the dry sand to the wet sand, both of us hoping the dog would follow, but he didn't. I couldn't forget the look on that dog's face. I know what it feels like to be left behind, so I probably have the same look on my face when Dad and Bandit drop in to see me and then drive off, leaving me behind" (p. 14). Students might identify and discuss the importance of Leigh's thoughts when he states, "Writing all this, I don't feel so lonely at night, and when I am busy, I forget to listen for funny noises" (p. 17). Or they might trace and discuss the significance of the joint custody for the dog developed by Leigh and his friend Barry: " 'We could have joint custody,' said Barry. 'You keep him nights, we both have him days, and when school starts, we can leave him at our house because we have a fenced yard. After school, he would belong to both of us.' 'And we can split the cost of dog support!' " (p. 20). The development and outcomes of this joint custody are of particular interest because there are parallels between the family experiences of the boys and their experiences with the dog.

7. Ask the students to summarize the changes in Leigh's character between the two books. They can also identify the plot structure in the second book and consider the similarities and differences in Leigh's character that brought the changes in the second book.

8. Older students may read Cleary's autobiography, *A Girl from Yamhill: A Memoir,* and try to find experiences, beliefs, and attitudes in Cleary's real life that might have motivated her to write her books for children.

9. Ask students to choose another Cleary book and write a sequel to that book.

10. Older students can do a historical analysis of the changes in the types of stories, plots, conflicts, and characters that Cleary writes about in her books. Her books show publication dates ranging from the early 1950s into the 1990s. Are there changes in these books that might reflect changes in American society? If so, what are those changes? How are the changes reflected in the plots, conflicts, and characters?

Activity 6–11:

APPRECIATING SETTINGS THAT EXPLORE THE IMAGINATION

TYPE	TERM
● CLASS	● STA
● GROUP	○ LTA
● IND	○ LC

Purpose:
1. To respond to illustrations that depict the imaginative settings created in children's minds
2. To create and illustrate stories that develop imaginative settings
3. To expand the imagination

Materials:
Books that have illustrated texts in which children's imaginations go beyond the simple settings and create new settings, plots, and experiences, such as Joanne Ryder's *White Bear, Ice Bear* (1989), Rafe Martin's *Will's Mammoth* (1989), Karen Ackerman's *Song and Dance Man* (1988), Paul Fleischman's *Shadow Play* (1990), and David Wiesner's *Free Fall* (1988).

Grade level:
Lower and middle elementary

Book summaries:
White Bear, Ice Bear develops as a boy imagines that he changes into a polar bear and explores the pack ice of the far north. *Will's Mammoth* follows the creative imagination of a boy as he turns a snow pile into a large mammoth, rides the mammoth through adventures, and views the world of this mammoth. *Song and Dance Man* turns an attic setting into a dazzling vaudeville stage for a grandfather and his three grandchildren. *Shadow Play* shows how simple shadow puppets and the puppeteers create a vivid adventure for two children. *Free Fall,* a wordless book, develops an imaginative story through a boy's dreams.

Procedures:
1. Read each story to students as they look at the illustrations. Allow the students to respond with their own feelings and imaginations. Students can share any experiences they have had in which they create worlds and stories in their imaginations.
2. After they have responded to *White Bear, Ice Bear* and *Will's Mammoth* ask students to think of settings that they know about and to use their imaginations to create their own stories. Students might select common settings such as parks, playgrounds, swimming pools, backyards, or even kitchen tables. If they used their imaginations, what could happen in these settings? Ask the students to place themselves in a setting of their choice and to consider what they would do in that setting if they could become anything or do anything that their imaginations can create. After they create their stories, ask students to illustrate them. These illustrations should reveal the creativity of their imaginations.
3. As in *Free Fall,* students may choose to develop their own imaginative dream sequences and illustrate their imaginative stories as wordless books. *Free Fall* also shows that imagination is stimulated by the books that children read. Students can create their own imaginative stories as they consider what could happen if their books become part of their dreams.

Activity 6–12:
CREATIVE SETTINGS FOR
IMAGINATIVE WORLDS

TYPE	TERM
● CLASS	○ STA
● GROUP	● LTA
● IND	○ LC

Purpose:

1. To create maps and illustrations depicting well-defined settings in literature
2. To evaluate the effectiveness of an author's textual description by using the description to create a map or other illustration
3. To defend the depiction on the map through the textual descriptions
4. To write travel brochures that introduce and accompany imaginative worlds

Materials:

Books in which the authors create new and imaginative worlds, such as Lloyd Alexander's *The Book of Three* (1964), James Barrie's *Peter Pan* (1911, 1950), L. Frank Baum's *The Wizard of Oz* (1900, 1956), Lewis Carroll's *Alice's Adventures in Wonderland* (1865, 1963), Ursula K. LeGuin's *A Wizard of Earthsea* (1968), C. S. Lewis's *The Lion, the Witch, and the Wardrobe* (1950), Robin McKinley's *The Hero and the Crown* (1984), J. R. R. Tolkien's *The Hobbit* (1938), Brian Jacques's *Pearls of Lutra: A Tale from Redwall* (1997), and Philip Pullman's *The Golden Compass* (1996) and *The Subtle Knife* (1997).

Grade level:

All grades—the grade level depends on the books chosen. *Peter Pan, The Wizard of Oz,* and *Alice's Adventures in Wonderland* are appropriate for younger students. The remainder of the books are more appropriate for students in upper elementary and middle school.

Book summaries:

The Book of Three develops the land of Prydain. *Peter Pan* creates Never Land. *The Wizard of Oz* develops the land of Oz. *Alice's Adventures in Wonderland* follows a rabbit down a hole into Wonderland. *A Wizard of Earthsea* provides detailed descriptions of Earthsea. *The Lion, the Witch, and the Wardrobe* creates the land of Narnia. *The Hero and the Crown* develops a far distant planet. *The Hobbit* creates the world of Middle Earth. *Pearls of Lutra: A Tale from Redwall* creates the Kingdom of Redwall inhabited by talking animals. *The Golden Compass* and *The Subtle Knife* develop parallel worlds.

Procedures:

1. Share several heavily illustrated books with students in which Oz or Wonderland is clearly developed through the illustrations. Ask the students to describe these worlds and to speculate whether they could find these worlds on the earth as we know it.
2. Explain to students that when authors create new worlds they must describe those worlds so carefully that readers can see and feel the worlds. If these descriptions are very good the readers should almost believe that the worlds are possible and be able to draw illustrations and maps that show the major places in those worlds.
3. This activity may be approached in several ways. Students may all read or listen to the same book and then divide into groups and develop a map of the imaginary world. The students should support where they draw specific features by providing quotes from the book. Interesting comparisons can be developed

among the groups as they defend their reasons for placing landmarks in certain locations. Some groups might want to change their maps after they hear the arguments of other students. After they have completed and defended their maps, ask students to evaluate the author's ability to create a believable fantasy world with a carefully developed geographical background. Or individuals or groups may each select a different book, draw the maps, and defend their placements.

4. After students have developed and shared their maps, ask them to create travel brochures that could entice visitors to travel to a particular land. It is helpful if students first look at travel brochures to help them identify what types of information and illustrations are included in the brochures. Students should present their travel brochures to the rest of the group. The resulting maps and travel brochures provide interesting materials for bulletin boards.

5. Select a book, such as Tolkien's *The Hobbit* or Jacques's *Pearls of Lutra: A Tale from Redwall,* that contains a map of the imaginary world in the story.

   a. Have students read the book and verify whether the map correctly illustrates the world of the story.
   b. Have students draw maps based on their own reading and then compare these maps with the one provided in the book. If any maps differ in detail from the printed maps, ask the students to identify and discuss the textual basis for these differences.

6. This activity may extend into creative writing as students draw their own maps of new imaginary worlds and then create the characters and conflicts that would take place in these worlds. Other students can evaluate the descriptions of the new worlds by trying to draw maps of the worlds. As they try to draw their maps, they should consider whether the student author has provided enough detail and description to allow them to draw the maps.

AUTHOR'S STYLE: APPRECIATING AND IDENTIFYING HUMOR—PART I

TYPE	TERM
● CLASS	○ STA
● GROUP	● LTA
● IND	○ LC

Purpose:
1. To develop an appreciation for humor in texts and illustrations
2. To provide individual responses to the humor in texts and illustrations
3. To analyze recent Caldecott Medal or Caldecott Honor books for humor in both the texts and illustrations

Materials:
A selection of Caldecott Medal and Honor books published during the previous twenty years. The following books are especially good for analyzing humor in illustrations and/or texts: 1996—Peggy Rathman's *Officer Buckle and Gloria* (1995), 1993—Jon Scieszka's *Stinky Cheese Man and Other Fairly Stupid Tales* (1992), 1992—David Wiesner's *Tuesday* (1991), 1991—David Macaulay's *Black and White* (1990), 1990—Eric Kimmel's *Hershel and the Hanukkah Goblins* (1989), 1987—Arthur Yorinks's *Hey, Al* (1986), 1986—Audrey Wood's *King Bidgood's in the Bathtub* (1985), 1986—Cynthia Rylant's *The Relatives Came* (1985), and 1982—Chris Van Allsburg's *Jumanji* (1981).

Grade level:
All grades—the type of response and analysis differs with the grade level of the students

Book summaries:
These books are all award-winning texts that were granted the Caldecott Medal or Honor Award for their illustrations. *Officer Buckle and Gloria* presents humor through unexpected dog behaviors. *Stinky Cheese Man and Other Fairly Stupid Tales* retells tales using ridiculous situations and illustrations. *Tuesday* is a wordless book that creates humor through surprise and unexpected situations. *Black and White* creates humor through ridiculous situations and caricature and through exaggeration. *Hershel and the Hanukkah Goblins* develops humor through the superiority of wit and also surprise and the unexpected. *Hey, Al* develops humor through surprise, the unexpected, and exaggeration. *King Bidgood's in the Bathtub* creates humor through surprise, the unexpected, and ridiculous situations. *The Relatives Came* develops humor through exaggeration. *Jumanji* develops humor through surprise and the unexpected.

Procedures:
1. When sharing these books with younger students, you may choose to read the books aloud and ask the students to provide personal responses that reflect their reactions to the books. Younger children may consider what appeals to them in both the illustrations and the text. For example, they may consider how they reacted when they heard the stories and viewed the illustrations. If they laughed at any of the situations or illustrations, they may consider the elements that make these books humorous.

2. After reading or listening to the books and providing their initial reactions, older students may critically evaluate the features that make them humorous. You may, for example, share with older students a study by Sue Anne Martin (1969) in which she analyzed Caldecott Medal Award books published between 1938 and 1968. In her study, Martin concluded that humor in books awarded the Caldecott

Medal had five general sources: (1) word play and nonsense, (2) surprise and the unexpected, (3) exaggeration, (4) the ridiculous and caricature, and (5) superiority. Explore each of these terms with the students and encourage them to discuss the meanings of each of the terms.

3. Next, ask students to critically evaluate each of the more recent Caldecott Medal and Honor Award books. Ask the students to analyze the humor developed in the illustrations and the texts and to categorize that humor, when possible, into the types of humor identified by Martin. If they find different kinds of humor, they should also identify these types. Ask the students to validate their conclusions by providing examples from the illustrations and the texts that support their conclusions.

4. Finally, ask the students to draw their own conclusions about Caldecott Medal and Honor Award books published after Martin's study. Do they believe that the books still illustrate Martin's different types of humor? Why or why not?

5. Students can develop a bulletin board titled "Humor in Illustrations and Texts." They can identify different types of humor and place examples of that humor in each of the categories. The bulletin board could be divided between humor in published books and humor in students' own writings.

Activity 6–14:

AUTHOR'S STYLE: APPRECIATING AND IDENTIFYING HUMOR—PART II

TYPE	TERM
● CLASS	○ STA
● GROUP	● LTA
● IND	○ LC

Purpose:

1. To develop an appreciation for humor in texts and illustrations
2. To provide individual responses to the humor in texts and illustrations
3. To analyze and categorize humor in illustrations and texts
4. To compare humor in books written for younger readers with humor in books written for older readers

Materials:

A selection of humorous picture story books written for younger readers, such as Jan Brett's *Berlioz the Bear* (1991), Grace Chetwin's *Box and Cox* (1990), Lisa Campbell Ernst's *Miss Penny and Mr. Grubbs* (1991), William Joyce's *Dinosaur Bob and His Adventures with the Family Lazardo* (1988), Eric Kimmel's *The Chanukkah Tree* (1988), Reeve Lindbergh's *The Day the Goose Got Loose* (1990), and Patricia Polacco's *Appelemando's Dreams* (1991); a selection of humorous stories written for middle elementary through middle school students, such as Pamela Pollack's edited text *The Random House Book of Humor* (1988), Judy Blume's *The One in the Middle Is the Green Kangaroo* (1981), Betsy Byars's *The Cybil War* (1981), Beverly Cleary's *Ramona Quimby, Age 8* (1981), and Anne Fine's *Alias Madame Doubtfire* (1988).

Grade level:

Middle elementary through middle school, depending on the books chosen

Book summaries:

Berlioz the Bear creates humor through an ending that develops surprise and the unexpected. *Box and Cox* develops humor through a ridiculous situation. *Miss Penny and Mr. Grubbs* develops a plot that concludes with an unexpected, ironic situation. *Dinosaur Bob and His Adventures with the Family Lazardo* develops humor through ridiculous situations. *The Chanukkah Tree* describes a very ridiculous situation. *The Day the Goose Got Loose* creates exaggeration and ridiculous situations. *Appelemando's Dreams* relies on surprise and the unexpected. *The Random House Book of Humor* is a collection of 34 humorous stories by authors such as Mark Twain, Garrison Keillor, James Thurber, and Roald Dahl. *The One in the Middle Is the Green Kangaroo* uses humorous situations and analogies to clarify feelings. *The Cybil War* explores problems caused by misinterpretation. *Ramona Quimby, Age 8* uses exaggerated situations and plays on words to develop humor. *Alias Madame Doubtfire* uses unexpected and often ridiculous situations when an ex-husband disguises himself as a cleaning woman and babysitter in his ex-wife's house.

Procedures:

1. Begin this lesson in a similar way as you did activity 6–13. Encourage students to respond to both the illustrations and texts in the books for younger readers. Ask the students to identify the types of humor that they find in the picture storybooks and compare the humor to the humor found in the Caldecott books discussed in activity 6–13. Ask the students to develop a summary statement about the types of humor that they find in books for younger students, supporting their statements with evidence from the books.

2. After the students have read and discussed the picture storybooks, introduce the books for older readers. This activity may be a small-group or individual project. Ask the students to read several of these selections and to analyze the types of humor developed in books for older readers. Ask the following: "Is the type of humor similar to or different from the humor developed in books for younger readers? What examples of humor are found in the literature? If you find similarities, why do you believe that there are similarities? If you find differences, why do you believe that there are differences?"

3. Ask the students to develop a chart in which they identify examples of humor in books for younger readers and in books for older readers:

EXAMPLES OF HUMOR FOUND IN BOOKS

	Humor in Books for Younger Readers	Humor in Books for Older Readers
Book: Quote: Sources of Humor:		
Book: Quote: Sources of Humor:		

4. Divide the students into groups of writers and editors. Ask the writers to pretend that they are writing and illustrating a humorous book for younger students. Ask them to bring their ideas in the form of book outlines to the editors' group. Tell the writers that they must be specific in how they will develop humorous situations in their stories. Ask the editors to respond to the humorous ideas of the writers and to tell the writers if they believe that the ideas are worthy of a story for younger readers. After this activity has been completed, ask the students to change roles. The writers now become editors for humorous books for older readers; the editors become writers and must bring their ideas for humorous books to the new editors. Following this activity, the students may choose to complete their humorous stories.

Activity 6–15:
DEVELOPING UNDERSTANDING OF THEME

TYPE	TERM
● CLASS	● STA
● GROUP	○ LTA
○ IND	○ LC

Purpose:

1. To develop an understanding of theme
2. To identify evidence in a story that supports a theme
3. To develop higher thought processes

Materials:

Patricia Polacco's *Appelemando's Dreams* (1991).

Grade level:

Lower and middle elementary

Book summary:

Appelemando's Dreams is the story of a boy who teaches the people in his village the importance of dreaming. At the beginning of the story, the villagers criticize him for dreaming and even call him slow. The book develops the theme that it is important to retain one's dreams.

Procedures:

1. Introduce or review the concept of *theme* by sharing with students that the theme of the story is an important message (or messages) that an author is trying to tell us through the story. As we read stories we can try to identify theme by asking ourselves the following: "What is the author trying to tell us that would make a difference in our lives?"

2. Ask the students to think about a story that they know, such as the folktale "Cinderella." Ask the students to review the story and try to identify a message or theme that the storyteller is trying to tell them. Students will usually identify two contrasting themes: kindness is good and cruelty is bad. Then ask them what happens in the story to help them understand that these are the themes. They will usually review Cinderella's character and identify that Cinderella is rewarded at the end of the story. Likewise, they can review the stepsisters' characters and identify that they are punished as a consequence of their behavior.

3. Remind the students that they can make discoveries about theme through such things as the character's actions, the character's thoughts, and how the story ends. Sometimes the author tells us the theme of the story. Even the illustrations may add to or support the theme.

4. Next, introduce the book *Appelemando's Dreams*. Tell the students that they are first going to listen to the story to try to identify the message or theme that the author is stating in the story. As they listen to the story they should ask themselves the following: "What is the author trying to tell us that would make a difference in our lives?" Read the story to the students and ask them to identify the possible theme or themes. Write the theme or themes on the board. For example, students may tell you that the theme is "Dreams are important," or they might decide it is that "Real friendship is very important." Then read the story a second time and ask the students to find proof that one of these is the theme of the story. List the proofs under each theme.

5. For example, a group of third-grade students identified the following proof to support "Dreams are important":
    a. The boy who did not have anything to do in this drab village made his life interesting by dreaming about colorful things.

   b. His four good friends tell him not to listen to the villagers.

   c. The boy shares his colorful dreams with his friends and makes them happy.

   d. The boy enjoys dreaming with his friends.

   e. His friends try to keep his dreams.

   f. His friends are afraid they will lose Appelemando's dreams after the angry villagers make them wash the dreams off of the village walls.

   g. The children are lost, but the dreams make it possible for people to see and find them.

   h. The villagers follow the dreams and are glad to find the lost children.

   i. The villagers agree, "Never again would they question the importance of dreams."

   j. The village becomes a colorful place that people enjoy visiting.

6. Additional books that may be used for this activity include Ann Grifalconi's *Darkness and the Butterfly* (1987) and John Steptoe's *Mufaro's Beautiful Daughters* (1987; a Caldecott Honor Award winner, 1988).

WEBBING LITERARY ELEMENTS

TYPE	TERM
● CLASS	○ STA
● GROUP	● LTA
● IND	○ LC

Purpose:
1. To develop an understanding of the integrated nature of literary elements in a book
2. To develop a literary web that includes setting, characterization, conflicts, and themes
3. To discuss the importance of each of the literary elements in a book
4. To write journal entries that could be the background for the book

Materials: Avi's *The True Confessions of Charlotte Doyle* (1990; Newbery Honor Award winner, 1991).

Grade level: Upper elementary, middle school

Book summary: *The True Confessions of Charlotte Doyle* is a historical novel set in 1832 aboard the *Seahawk* as it sails from England to America. The only passenger on the ship, thirteen-year-old Charlotte Doyle, is caught between the cruelty of the captain and the mutinous actions of the crew. Details develop the historical accuracy of the time period and a carefully constructed plot creates considerable action as the heroine faces and overcomes charges of murder on the high seas. The heroine shares with the readers the information that she would not have been able to recreate her story if she had not kept a detailed journal of her experiences.

Procedures:
1. Introduce the book by reading and discussing the introduction, "An Important Warning." Ask the students to think about what the author is revealing about the story and the character in the first paragraph: "Not every thirteen-year-old girl is accused of murder, brought to trial, and found guilty. But I was just such a girl, and my story is worth relating even if it did happen years ago. Be warned, however, this is no *Story of a Bad Boy*, no *What Katy Did*. If strong ideas and action offend you, read no more. Find another companion to share your idle hours. For my part I intend to tell the truth as I lived it" (p. 1). Also, ask the students to respond to the impact of this first paragraph on readers.

   To introduce the setting for the book, show and discuss pictures of smaller merchant sailing ships that would have crossed the Atlantic in 1832. You can also discuss the author's references to the two books in the first paragraph. For example, *The Story of a Bad Boy* was written by Thomas Bailey Aldrich in 1870. The types of exploits described in the book are common for Victorian heroes during the late 1800s: boys practiced the "manly arts," formed clubs, and played pranks. These activities are very different from the exploits of Charlotte Doyle. Students can compare what they believe Charlotte's exploits will be with those in *The Story of a Bad Boy.*

2. Place a literary elements web on the board. As you write setting, characters, conflicts, and themes on the board, ask the students to consider what they might expect to find under each element in this book after they have listened to and discussed the introduction. Ask the students to fill in the details on the web as they

either listen to or read *The True Confessions of Charlotte Doyle*. After the web has been completed, discuss the interactions and importance of each of the details under the literary elements. The following is a partial example of this literary web:

3. After completing the web, ask students to consider the importance of the journal entries in the following quote: "Keeping that journal then is what enables me to relate now in perfect detail everything that transpired during that fateful voyage across the Atlantic Ocean in the summer of 1832" (p. 3). Ask the students to select one of the chapters in *The True Confessions of Charlotte Doyle* and write the journal entry that may have motivated the writing of and provided the details for the incidents described in the chapter.

4. Another writing activity may be developed around point of view. Ask students to consider and discuss why they think Avi wrote this story from Charlotte Doyle's point of view. Ask them to look again at the web to identify each of the instances on the web in which the heroine's point of view is extremely important in developing the various literary elements. Then ask the students to consider how the story might change if told through the point of view of Captain Jaggery, Zachariah, or one of the other crew members. They could also choose to write a response to Charlotte Doyle's journal from the point of view of her father.

5. Although this webbing activity may be used with any well-written book, you may want students to web additional historical novels such as Karen Cushman's *Catherine, Called Birdy* (1994; a Newbery Honor Award winner, 1995) and *The Midwife's Apprentice* (1995; a Newbery Medal winner, 1996), Patricia Reilly Giff's *Lily's Crossing* (1997; a Newbery Honor Award winner, 1998), Karen Hesse's *Out of the Dust,* a Newbery Medal winner, 1998), and Laurence Yep's *Dragon's Gate* (1993; a Newbery Honor Award winner, 1994).

Activity 6–17:

ACTIVITIES AROUND *CALL IT COURAGE*

	TYPE		TERM
	● CLASS		○ STA
	● GROUP		● LTA
	● IND		○ LC

Purpose:

1. To develop an understanding of the setting and culture associated with a Polynesian book set in the South Seas
2. To develop an appreciation for the language used by the author
3. To develop an understanding of person versus nature and person versus self conflict
4. To draw plot diagrams showing conflict
5. To develop a literary web to accompany a book
6. To write a response to literature
7. To compare courage as developed in books from various cultures
8. To write cinquain and diamante poems that develop an understanding of characterization and courage
9. To develop an understanding of and an appreciation for the use of chants to tell stories of the people
10. To relate books to the five themes of geography
11. To develop an appreciation for Polynesian music
12. To conduct research into the influence of Europeans on the native peoples in a culture

Materials:

The core book, Armstrong Sperry's *Call It Courage* (1940); books that provide background information, such as Kiri Te Kanawa's *Land of the Long White Cloud: Maori Myths, Tales, and Legends* (1989), Marcia Brown's *Backbone of the King: The Story of Paka'a and His Son Ku* (1984), and Rhoda Blumberg's *The Remarkable Voyages of Captain Cook* (1991); books that show other peoples who worship courage, such as Padraic Colum's retelling of Greek mythology in *The Golden Fleece* (1921, 1949), Harold Courlander's retelling of African legends in *The Crest and the Hide* (1982), Kevin Crossley-Holland's retelling of the epic *Beowulf* (1982), Terry Jones's retelling of *The Saga of Erik the Viking* (1983), and Rosemary Sutcliff's historical fiction, *The Shining Company* (1990); books that depict chants and songs that tell stories of various peoples, such as John Bierhorst's *A Cry from the Earth: Music of the North American Indians* (1979) and *The Sacred Path: Spells, Prayers, and Power Songs of the American Indians* (1983) and J. R. R. Tolkien's fantasy *The Hobbit* (1938); books that show the influence of Europeans on native peoples, such as Jane Yolen's *Encounter* (1992) and Francine Jacobs's *The Tainos: The People Who Welcomed Columbus* (1992); more contemporary literature that shows how the traders and missionaries might have affected the Polynesians, such as Fay Stanley's *The Last Princess: The Story of Princess Ka'iulani of Hawai'i* (1991); maps of the South Seas and the Pacific; pictures of early sailing canoes that sailed across the Pacific before the dawn of recorded history; records of Polynesian music; Norton's web of a hero unit (*The Impact of Literature-Based Reading*, 1992).

Grade level:

Middle elementary through middle school, depending on the literature selected

Book summaries:

The core book, *Call It Courage,* is a story of survival as the main character overcomes both his fear of the sea and his person versus self conflict. The author also develops a strong person versus nature conflict as Mafatu, a Polynesian boy who lives in a culture that worships courage and loves the sea, faces his enemy, the sea, and works out his own fears. *Land of the Long White Cloud: Maori Myths, Tales, and Legends* is a collection of ancient folklore told by the Polynesian sailors who discovered New Zealand—the Land of the Long White Cloud. *Backbone of the King: The Story of Paka'a and His Son Ku* is an ancient Hawaiian legend about bravery, courage, and honor among people who live by the sea. *The Remarkable Voyages of Captain Cook* describes early ideas about the South Seas and chronicles Cook's exploration of the Pacific Ocean and his interactions with the people. *The Golden Fleece* includes stories about Jason and the Greek heroes who search for the Golden Fleece. *The Crest and the Hide* includes twenty traditional tales of heroes, chiefs, and bards from Africa. *Beowulf* is a legend of the Norse hero who is strong, loyal, courageous, and willing to take vengeance. *The Saga of Erik the Viking* includes numerous stories of courage and adventures at sea. *The Shining Company,* set in 600 A.D. Britain, is a historical fiction about three hundred warriors who courageously fight the Saxon invaders. *A Cry from the Earth: Music of the North American Indians* includes a discussion of Indian music, dance, and instruments. The text includes musical scores and interpretations. *The Sacred Path: Spells, Prayers, and Power Songs of the American Indians* is an anthology of poetry, chants, and songs that deals with important instances in life such as birth, growing up, love songs, traveling, illness, hunting, and planting. *The Hobbit* includes the words to numerous songs that reveal the history, culture, and beliefs of the dwarfs whom Bilbo Baggins joins in their quest to travel over the Misty Mountains and claim their long-forgotten gold from Smaug, the fire-breathing dragon. *Encounter* presents a hypothetical interaction between a Taino Indian boy and Columbus and his men on the island of San Salvador in 1492. *The Tainos: The People Who Welcomed Columbus* provides anthropological material about the people and describes the interactions between the Tainos and the Spaniards who enslaved and murdered the native people. *The Last Princess: The Story of Princess Ka'iulani of Hawai'i* is a highly illustrated biography.

Procedures:

1. Develop an introduction to *Call It Courage* that encourages students to be interested in the text and to understand the importance of a certain type of courage in the lives of ancient peoples. For example, ask students the following: "Can you imagine living on an island surrounded by water and being terribly afraid of the sea? What would the people of the island think about you if they all earned their living from the sea? What would you think of yourself as you discovered your fear and decided that you had to do something about that fear? This is the problem that Mafatu faces and overcomes in *Call It Courage.* Although his name means Stout Heart, he is considered a coward by the people on the island. As you read this exciting story, imagine that you are Mafatu as you face a hurricane alone in a small boat in the ocean. Imagine that you are alone on another island and you are facing the dangers that are on that island. Finally, imagine that you are Mafatu as he goes proudly home to reveal his new self to his father and the people of the island. Try to decide at what point you believe that Stout Heart is a good meaning for Mafatu." Encourage students to discuss the importance of showing courage and overcoming fear and to consider environments in which overcoming fear of the sea would be especially important.

2. Develop an introduction to the setting in *Call It Courage* that includes an understanding of time and place. Read and discuss the first page in chapter 1: "It happened many years ago, before the traders and missionaries first came into the South Seas, while the Polynesians were still great in numbers and fierce of heart. But even today the people of Hikueru sing this story in their chants and tell it over the evening fires. It is the story of Mafatu, The Boy Who Was Afraid. They

worshiped courage, those early Polynesians. The spirit which had urged them across the Pacific in their sailing canoes, before the dawn of recorded history, not knowing where they were going nor caring what their fate might be, still sang its song of danger in their blood" (p. 1).

Encourage students to speculate about how long ago this story might have taken place and to try to find information about when the traders and missionaries came to the South Seas. For this research they may read and discuss *The Remarkable Voyages of Captain Cook*. The first chapter, "An Unknown Continent," provides insights into the time and place and into the beliefs of the Europeans about the South Seas. For example, read and discuss the following quotation: "There were tales about miserable brutes, ugly giants, and man-eating monsters who lived in the southern part of our globe. There were also stories about kind, beautiful people who dwelled there in luxury on lush, treasure-laden lands. In the eighteenth century, when King George III ruled England, government officials wanted to know the truth about people and places in the 'South Seas,' a term used to mean 'Pacific Ocean' " (p. 2). Later chapters discuss Cook's journeys in the 1700s and his interactions with the Polynesian people.

To provide additional background information about the location and the people, show a map of the Pacific Ocean and the South Seas. Tell students that it is believed that Polynesian men spent considerable time at sea and often remained at sea for weeks at a time. It is also believed that the Polynesians voyaged long distances on their sea travels, including such long trips as from Hawaii to New Zealand. Show the students pictures of early sailing canoes and ask them to speculate about the dangers and adventures these people must have experienced. Ask the students to think about why courage would be so important to the Polynesians. To provide additional background information about the people, share some folklore of the Polynesians, such as the tales found in *Land of the Long White Cloud: Maori Myths, Tales, and Legends*. After students read or listen to some of these tales, they can identify the beliefs and values of the people as reflected in their folklore. (Several tales are especially appropriate. In chapter 2 of *Call It Courage,* Mafatu prays to Maui, God of the Fishermen. Several of the tales in the folklore collection refer to Maui.) The legend *Backbone of the King: The Story of Paka'a and His Son Ku* provides information about the ancient cultures of the Pacific regions.

3. As students read or listen to *Call It Courage,* encourage them to notice and discuss the techniques that Armstrong Sperry uses to develop a person versus nature conflict. The language and vivid descriptions of the hurricane in chapter 2, "The Sea," are especially appropriate to emphasize the techniques that Sperry uses to make readers believe that the sea is a real antagonist. It is helpful to read this chapter out loud and to ask students to listen for and identify the techniques that Sperry uses to make them believe that Mafatu is in extreme danger from the sea. During a first reading, students can respond to Sperry's vivid descriptions and develop an understanding that nature is a harsh antagonist. During a second reading, they can listen for techniques that the author uses to make readers believe that nature is dangerous and that the boy is in conflict with nature. For example, students can identify that Mafatu's actions reveal how frightened he is. He grips the paddle with hands that are white at the knuckles, desperately prays to Maui, remembers that the sea had claimed his mother's life and would someday claim him, tries to cry out but cannot, winds his arms around the midthwart, and concludes that it is the end of the world. The author uses personification to help readers understand the dangerous nature of the storm as the storm is compared with the dangerous advance scouts of an oncoming army and is referred to as a hungry and livid monster. The author also manipulates the length of the sentences as the conflict increases. As the storm reaches a climax, the sentences become shorter and shorter as the crest approaches until the au-

thor uses only one word, "Chaos!" Students may illustrate this vivid setting and show through their illustrations just how dangerous the sea is in *Call It Courage*.

4. To help students develop a further understanding of person versus nature and person versus self conflict, ask them to trace the various incidents in the book that reveal how Mafatu is overcoming his person versus self conflict as he also overcomes his fear of nature. On plot diagrams ask the students to identify the problem and Mafatu's characteristics at the beginning of the book. They can then identify the incidents that show Mafatu's increasing struggle with himself until he reaches the point of self-realization and faces his own inner conflict. Finally, they can identify the moment in which he achieves a feeling of peace and truth. Students can compare Mafatu's character at the beginning of the book, and especially in the chapter "The Sea," with his character at the end of the book. They may consider what happened so that Mafatu could respond to the sea with these words: " 'Moana, you Sea God!' he shouted violently. 'You! You destroyed my mother. Always you have tried to destroy me. Fear of you has haunted my sleep. Fear of you turned my people against me. But now—!' he choked; his hands gripped his throat to stop its hot burning, 'now I no longer fear you, Sea!' His voice rose to a wild note. He sprang to his feet, flung back his head, spread wide his arms in defiance. 'Do you hear me, Moana? I am not afraid of you! Destroy me—but I laugh at you. Do you hear? I laugh!' " (p. 112).

5. Either while reading the book or after completing the book, students can develop a literary web to accompany the book. On their literary webs they should identify details related to setting, characterization, conflict, and themes.

6. *Call It Courage* may be used to stimulate various writing experiences. For example, Mafatu's character and conflict provide numerous opportunities for students to write personal responses to Mafatu's actions, feelings, and conflict. Students may pretend that they are having a dialogue with Mafatu and provide their reactions to some of the most moving chapters. The vivid descriptions of nature and the techniques that Sperry uses to make nature believable may also be used to stimulate descriptive writing in which students identify other harsh environments and make readers visualize the nature of those environments. If they have analyzed and discussed Sperry's techniques, they can use some of these techniques such as vivid language, forceful verbs, personification, characters' actions, and changing sentence lengths to create their own descriptions of nature as an antagonist.

7. Lead a discussion in which students provide their own definitions of courage and then identify some of the characteristics of people who develop or show courage. Ask the students to identify people whom they believe are courageous and to explain why they believe them to be courageous. Provide books that represent other cultures in which courage is considered very important. This selection might include *The Golden Fleece, The Crest and the Hide, Beowulf, The Saga of Erik the Viking,* and *The Shining Company.* Encourage each student to select one of the books. After they have read the books allow students to share instances of courage and to compare how courage is expressed in various cultures.

8. Ask the students to select either Mafatu from *Call It Courage* or one of the main characters in one of the other books in which the characters show courage. Encourage the students to write a cinquain or a diamante poem about the character or about courage. Before students write their poems, review the requirements for each form of poetry. A *cinquain* is a five-line poem with the following characteristics: the first line has one word for a title, the second line has two words to describe the title, the third line has three words to express action, the fourth line has four words to express feeling, and the fifth line is either the title repeated again or a word like the title. A *diamante* is a seven-line poem with the following characteristics: the first line is a noun; the second line has two adjectives related

to the first-line noun; the third line has three participles or verbs ending in *-ing, -ed,* or *-en;* the fourth line has four nouns or a phrase that contrasts with the first noun so that readers' thoughts move from the subject of the first noun to the subject of the contrasting noun in line seven; the fifth line has three participles that correspond with the noun on the seventh line; the sixth line contains two adjectives that correspond with the final noun; and the seventh line contains one noun that contrasts with the noun in the first line. The following examples are cinquains that depict Mafatu at the beginning and the end of the novel:

<table>
<tr><td>Mafatu</td><td>Mafatu</td></tr>
<tr><td>Cowardly, frightened</td><td>Bold, fearless</td></tr>
<tr><td>Gripping, praying, remembering</td><td>Daring, shouting, hunting</td></tr>
<tr><td>Fears the sea's actions</td><td>Now called Stout Heart</td></tr>
<tr><td>Fainthearted</td><td>Courageous</td></tr>
</table>

The next example is a diamante that shows the changes in Mafatu as he progresses from cowardly to courageous:

Mafatu

Cowardly, frightened

Shaking, trembling, shuddering

Faces challenges on island

Shouting, stabbing, trapping

Brave, bold

Courageous

9. In *Call It Courage,* Sperry states that "even today the people of Hikueru sing this story in their chants and tell it over the evening fires. It is the story of Mafatu, the Boy Who Was Afraid" (p. 1). The students may do research in which they investigate other cultures that use chants and songs to tell stories about important instances in their lives. For example, they can investigate the use of chants and songs in Native American cultures through books such as *A Cry from the Earth: Music of the North American Indians* and *The Sacred Paths: Spells, Prayers, and Power Songs of the American Indians.* They may discover the importance of chants and songs that tell the history of a people by reading *The Hobbit,* a fantasy that has its foundations in mythology. After reading *The Hobbit,* ask students to discuss what they learned about the history of the dwarfs through the songs and chants.

10. Sperry emphasizes that *Call It Courage* takes place before the traders and missionaries came to the South Seas. Students may explore the possible influence of explorers, traders, and missionaries on the lives of various native peoples. Books that show the influence of Europeans on other native peoples may be used to develop an understanding of the impact of the Age of Exploration and the Age of Colonization. Both *Encounter* and *The Tainos: The People Who Welcomed Columbus* chronicle the impact of explorers on the Native peoples of North America. (Activity 8–10 in this text may be used to integrate literature and geography using *Encounter.*) After reading either of these books, students can do additional research on the impact of outside forces on the lives of the people and speculate about what might have happened to Mafatu's people. Students could write a continuation of *Call It Courage* but place the story at the time of the missionaries and traders mentioned by Sperry. For a later influence, students may read *The Last Princess: The Story of Princess Ka'iulani of Hawai'i.* This is a story of personal courage and loss of power as the last heir to the throne is denied her right to rule when Hawaii is annexed to the United States in 1897.

11. Polynesian music may be used to stimulate numerous activities. For example, students could read selections of Polynesian folklore and accompany the folklore with appropriate music. Dramatic readings from *Call It Courage* could be accompanied by music. The music could be used to stimulate artistic interpretations.

12. If desired, students may extend their study of courage with a study of heroes and heroines. A listing of appropriate books and a web showing characteristics of heroes and heroines is found in Norton's *The Impact of Literature-Based Reading* (1992, pp. 87–88).

Activity 6–18:

MAURICE SENDAK AND HIS LITERATURE—
AN INTEREST CENTER

TYPE	TERM
○ CLASS	○ STA
○ GROUP	○ LTA
● IND	● LC

Purpose:

1. To be able to explain why Sendak became interested in books and in writing his own stories, how he developed his artistic talents, and how he gathered ideas for writing and drawing
2. To write a creative story motivated by sketches of children
3. To write a creative story motivated by cartoons
4. To write a creative story motivated by music
5. To write a creative story motivated by *Where the Wild Things Are*
6. To react to music that motivates Maurice Sendak
7. To design a bulletin board with ideas for Sendak's books
8. To give an oral presentation comparing the illustrations and writings of Lewis Carroll, Edward Lear, and Maurice Sendak
9. To experiment with the art medium Sendak uses and discuss the effectiveness of his illustrations
10. To interpret a character through the use of papier-mâché
11. To develop and perform a creative drama activity motivated by *Where the Wild Things Are*
12. To develop literature appreciation and interpret poetry through choral speaking
13. To create a poster that might accompany one of Maurice Sendak's books
14. To create three-dimensional stage-set models for an opera or a play that might be produced from one of Sendak's books
15. To create compact disc covers to accompany music that might be used to motivate a story

Materials:

A selection of books illustrated by Maurice Sendak such as those listed. (Selma G. Lanes's *The Art of Maurice Sendak*, 1984, includes a chronology of 78 books illustrated by Sendak, additional information about Sendak that may be used to develop ideas for this interest center and to motivate activities, and examples of Sendak's art.)

Marcel Ayme's *The Wonderful Farm* (1951)
Ruth Krauss's *A Hole Is to Dig* (1951)
Ruth Krauss's *A Very Special House* (1953)
Sesyle Joslin's *What Do You Say, Dear?* (1958)
Janice May Udry's *The Moon Jumpers* (1959)
Else Holmelund Minarik's *Little Bear's Visit* (1961)
Charlotte Zolotow's *Mr. Rabbit and the Lovely Present* (1962)
Isaac Bashevis Singer's *Zlateh the Goat and Other Stories* (1966)
Wilhelm Grimm's *Dear Mili* (1988)

Books illustrated and written by Maurice Sendak:

> *Kenny's Window* (1956)
> *Pierre: A Cautionary Tale* (1962)
> *Where the Wild Things Are* (1963)
> *Higglety Pigglety Pop* (1967)
> *Seven Little Monsters* (1977)
> *Outside Over There* (1981)
> *We Are All in the Dumps with Jack and Guy* (1993)

Additional examples of Sendak's art, found in Maurice Sendak's *Posters By Maurice Sendak* (1986); books by Lewis Carroll and Edward Lear.

Grade level: Lower elementary; middle elementary; many of the activities are also appropriate for older students

Procedures:

1. Place information about Sendak's professional background on a tape or type the information on cards or paper. Sendak's background is interesting and provides insights into the motivational processes of a successful author and illustrator. The dialogue for this exercise might read as follows:

   As you listen to this tape [or read this paper], I want you to think about three questions: How did Mr. Sendak become interested in books and in writing his own stories? How did Mr. Sendak develop his artistic talents? How does Mr. Sendak gather ideas for writing and drawing?

   Maurice Sendak, a favorite children's author, was born in Brooklyn, New York, on June 10, 1928. He is so popular with children that he has been called the "Picasso of children's books." He was given this title because he has drawn the illustrations for more than sixty books. One of his books, *Where the Wild Things Are,* won the Caldecott Medal in 1964 for the best picture book.

   Maurice Sendak's father got him interested in stories when Mr. Sendak was a young child. His father told him bedtime stories from Eastern European Jewish folktales. He loved books and even wrote his own books and drew the pictures for them. By the time he became a teenager, he was so interested in stories and writing that he decided he would be a writer and illustrator.

   While Mr. Sendak was growing up, he drew pictures of kids playing and later used many of these ideas in his books. When he was in high school, he took numerous art courses. One of his favorite pastimes was drawing comic strip adventures about the other kids in school. He even had a part-time job working on the Mutt and Jeff characters for comic books. After he graduated from high school, he worked for a window display company and made papier-mâché models of storybook characters. He designed window displays for both books and toys.

   Mr. Sendak became an illustrator for children's books when he was asked to draw the pictures for Marcel Ayme's book *The Wonderful Farm* in 1951. The next year, he illustrated Ruth Krauss's book *A Hole Is to Dig.* These books started his rapidly growing career as an illustrator and author of his own books. Mr. Sendak uses the sketches he made of children to give him ideas for his many books. He also listens to music while he works.

2. Creative Writing—When Maurice Sendak was a boy, he drew pictures of kids playing. Later, he used these pictures to get ideas for his books. Have the children draw pictures of kids on their own sketch pads; then have them use their drawings to motivate their own illustrated stories.

3. Creative Writing—Maurice Sendak drew cartoons about the adventures of children who got into trouble at school. Have students pick a comical situation and draw cartoon characters to illustrate the story. Write the dialogue in comic strip form.

4. Creative Writing, Appreciative Listening—Maurice Sendak listens to music while he works. Some of his favorite composers are Mozart, Beethoven, and Wagner. Have students listen to a recording by one of these composers. Ask them to describe what they visualize while they listen. Then have them draw a series of pictures motivated by the music, listen to the music again, and write a story to accompany the pictures.

5. Art Interpretation of Literature—Maurice Sendak designed window displays for new books. Have a group of children select one of Sendak's books and design a bulletin board as if it were a window display in a department or bookstore.

6. Oral Language: Comparisons of Writing, Styles, and Illustrations—Maurice Sendak's books have been compared with the writings of Lewis Carroll and Edward Lear. These writers also use both fantasy and reality. Have older students read a selection by each of these authors and then give an oral presentation comparing the authors' use of pictures, content of stories, and writing styles.

7. Comparisons of Illustrations and Art Media—Maurice Sendak's illustrations vary from black-and-white pen-and-ink drawings to full-color illustrations. Have children look carefully at the illustrations in each book. Ask them to explain why they feel each type of drawing is effective. (*The Moon Jumpers* uses both black-and-white ink drawings and full-page illustrations that develop the greens and blues of a moonlit summer's evening.) After they have examined the author's use of color or black-and-white drawings, have the students experiment with Sendak's art techniques.

8. Art Interpretation—Maurice Sendak constructed papier-mâché models of storybook characters. Ask the students to select their favorite Sendak character and make a papier-mâché model of that character.

9. Creative Drama—After reading *Where the Wild Things Are,* discuss how we often daydream and make ourselves the hero of the story. What kinds of activities do you dream about when you are the hero? Talk about how you would feel if you were sent to your room, what makes you fantasize, and what you would fantasize about. Have the children act out their dreams in a creative play session.

10. Creative Drama—Have the students make masks depicting the wild things in *Where The Wild Things Are.* Let them be the wild things by wearing the masks. Perform a creative drama of this story and other adventures Max might have during another visit with the wild things.

11. Creative Writing—Have the children pick one of their favorite monsters in *Where the Wild Things Are.* Ask what the monster's name is, what it likes to do, whether it is a good or bad monster, what it thinks about Max, and what the child and the monster would do if they met. Have students write stories about their special monsters.

12. Choral Speaking—Read *Pierre: A Cautionary Tale* to the class. Develop a choral arrangement by having the class join in whenever the repeated line is stated.

13. Posters—Ask the students to select a story and draw a poster that might be used to advertise the book.

14. Three-Dimensional Stage-Set Models—Ask the students to choose one of Sendak's illustrated books and to create a three-dimensional stage-set model for a presentation of the book as a play or an opera.

15. Art and Music Interpretation—Sendak has created record album covers for music such as Gustav Mahler's "Third Symphony." (The cover illustration is shown in Lanes's *The Art of Maurice Sendak,* 1984, p. 259.) Ask the students to create a compact disc cover for one of the musical selections that motivated Sendak's writing.

Activity 6–19:

CAROL RYRIE BRINK'S *CADDIE WOODLAWN*—
AN INTEREST CENTER FOR HISTORICAL FICTION

TYPE	TERM
○ CLASS	○ STA
● GROUP	○ LTA
● IND	● LC

Purpose:

1. To listen to a tape about the author Carol Ryrie Brink and answer questions about her
2. To develop the oral language skill of interviewing
3. To interpret a literature character
4. To develop reference skills
5. To interpret a scene through creative writing
6. To write a creative story motivated by literature
7. To read for comprehension of detail
8. To read for the purpose of evaluation
9. To interpret literature through an art medium
10. To develop discussion skills through value clarification activities
11. To develop math skills

Materials:

Carol Ryrie Brink's *Caddie Woodlawn* (1935, 1963, 1973, 1975); reference books describing samplers, candle making, early transportation, and Native American villages; tape and tape recorder; writing materials, construction paper, and art materials for modeling a Native American camp; several catalogues showing prices of candy, tops, combs, and handkerchiefs.

Grade level:

Third through fifth grades

Book summary:

Caddie Woodlawn is a story of a pioneer family set in Wisconsin during the last half of the nineteenth century. In this narrative the author tells a story that is similar to the experiences of her grandmother. It is a story of a warm-hearted, brave, rambunctious girl who loves to play in the woods and along the river with her brothers. She is also a friend of Native Americans in the area.

Procedures:

1. Record information about the author Carol Ryrie Brink on a tape or type the information on cards or paper. Tell the students that, after listening to this tape, they should be able to answer the following questions: (1) How is Carol Ryrie Brink related to Caddie Woodlawn? (2) How did Mrs. Brink gain her knowledge about Caddie's adventures? (3) Why did Mrs. Brink write *Caddie Woodlawn*? (4) Is *Caddie Woodlawn* a true story? The dialogue for this tape might read as follows:

    Carol Ryrie Brink had a very special reason for writing *Caddie Woodlawn*. The heroine of the book was Mrs. Brink's grandmother. When Mrs. Brink was eight years old, she went to live with her grandmother. Her grandmother Caddie told her many stories about growing up in Wisconsin in the 1800s. During Mrs. Brink's childhood, she amused herself by drawing, writing, reading, and telling herself long stories.

When Mrs. Brink was an adult, she remembered the stories of Caddie's childhood and thought other children would also like to read them. She wrote *Caddie Woodlawn* while her grandmother was still alive. She wrote letters to her grandmother to ask questions about details she could not remember.

Carol Ryrie Brink says the facts in *Caddie Woodlawn* are mostly true. Some of the facts are changed slightly to fit the story. *Caddie Woodlawn* won the Newbery Medal for the best children's book in 1936.

2. Oral Language, Interviewing, Writing—Carol Ryrie Brink wrote *Caddie Woodlawn* because she enjoyed her grandmother's stories. Ask the children to interview older relatives or other older people in the community. In their interviews, they should ask people to retell experiences they remember from childhood or stories they heard from their grandparents. During the interviews, the students can also gather information about what these people did for entertainment, how they traveled, where they got their food, how they dressed, and what toys they played with. Have the children share their information orally with the rest of the class or ask them to write stories using the information. Develop a bulletin board to display the stories.

3. Oral Characterization—Ask the students to choose a character from *Caddie Woodlawn* and tell about that character as if they were that person. Allow other children to guess the identity of the character. Some of the characters in the book are Caddie, Mr. Woodlawn, Minnie, Indian John, Hetty, Tom, Mr. Tanner, Mrs. Woodlawn, Warren, and Uncle Edmund.

4. Reference Skills, Oral Language—Caddie played in the woods with her brothers, Tom and Warren, rather than making samplers or dipping candles like the other girls did. Have the children investigate how a sampler is made or the process for dipping candles. Ask a research group to explain the process to the rest of the class.

5. Creative Drama—Allow a group of students to choose a scene from *Caddie Woodlawn* to dramatize for the rest of the class. Allow students to work in groups so they will experience the roles of both player and audience. Some scenes for this activity might include Caddie dropping the nuts on the floor in front of the Circuit Rider, Caddie riding to the Indian camp to warn the Indians of an intended attack, the prairie fire that almost destroys the school house, and Uncle Edmund talking the family into taking Nero to St. Louis.

6. Creative Writing—Caddie was frightened when she rode through the night to warn Indian John about the men who were going to attack the Indians. Ask the children to think about a time when they were frightened. How did they feel? What were their thoughts? How did they overcome their fear? Have the children write a story about a frightening experience they have had.

7. Creative Writing—Have the students choose a favorite chapter from *Caddie Woodlawn*. Ask them to pretend they are Caddie and write a diary entry for that chapter.

8. Reading for Details—After reading *Caddie Woodlawn,* have students complete the following chart with drawings that show details for each category:

LIFE IN WISCONSIN IN 1864
Clothing   Transportation   Home Furnishings
Entertainment   Education   Food

9. Evaluative Reading—Place in the learning center several reference and history books that give factual descriptions of the 1860s. Ask students to compare their readings about the historical period with the picture of daily life presented in the book. Are the historical facts accurate in *Caddie Woodlawn?* Make a list of accurate facts and a list of any inaccurate information.

10. Reference and Art—Caddie has a special friend named Indian Joe. Caddie even visits the Indian camp. Provide several reference books describing the Native Americans who lived in that part of Wisconsin. Students can read reference material about these peoples and then design and build a model of an authentic Native American camp.

11. Map Skills—Nero, the Woodlawn's dog, goes on a long trip with Uncle Edmund. They travel in a steamship all the way from Downsville to St. Louis. Nero runs away after he reaches St. Louis and finally reaches his home in Wisconsin.
    a. Look at a map of the United States. Draw in the route Nero and Uncle Edmund followed to reach St. Louis.
    b. Page 53 of the Scholastic Book Services edition cites a river that is not near Downsville. What is the current name of the river on which Nero and Uncle Edmund started their journey?

NERO'S JOURNEY

   c. Now look at the map again. Imagine the route that Nero traveled on his lonely trip back to Wisconsin. What states did he go through? What was the country like? Draw in the route you think he followed.

12. Several types of transportation characteristic of the 1860s are mentioned in *Caddie Woodlawn:* canoes, horses, steamships, horse-drawn wagons, and rafts. Provide reference pictures and books describing these forms of transportation. Ask children to construct a mobile illustrating these early means of travel.

13. Discussion, Values Clarification—Caddie makes some major decisions in the process of growing up. The following experiences can be used for discussion. The children should also relate personal experiences they have had in similar circumstances.

   a. Do you believe it would have been all right for the settlers to attack the Native Americans because the settlers thought that they would be attacked? Why or why not? Did Caddie do the right thing when she warned Indian Joe? Who do you believe showed the most courage, Caddie or the settlers? Why? What would you have done if you had been Caddie? Have you ever had an experience in which someone thought you were going to do something harmful? What would happen if we always acted out of fear or believed everything we heard?

   b. Caddie spent her valued dollar on gifts for three Native American children because she wanted to "drive that awful lonesome look out of their eyes." Do you believe Caddie acted correctly when she bought the gifts for the Indian boys? Why or why not? What would you have done if you were Caddie?

14. Math, Comparison of Values—Caddie spent her dollar for candy and other gifts for the Native American boys. List the gifts on a card and ask the children to investigate the cost of buying similar items today.

CADDIE'S GIFTS	1864	199__
Horehound sticks (enough for three children)	?	
Striped peppermint sticks (enough for three children)	?	
Pink wintergreens (enough for three children)	?	
Three tops	?	
Three combs (good quality)	30¢	
Three large turkey-red handkerchiefs	30¢	
Total	$1.00	

Activity 6–20:
THE SALEM WITCH HUNTS—
A HISTORICAL FICTION UNIT

TYPE	TERM
● CLASS	○ STA
● GROUP	● LTA
○ IND	○ LC

Purpose:

1. To compare and discuss two pieces of historical fiction on the New England witch hunts
2. To write a diary from the viewpoint of an accused witch
3. To write a comparison of the facts in a fictional story and a factual account
4. To write a creative article for a classroom newspaper
5. To orally interpret and present a character from the witch hunts
6. To investigate, create, and act out a Salem witch trial
7. To create a puppet show that demonstrates fear of an unusual person
8. To investigate superstition versus scientific facts
9. To interpret folk literature through an art medium
10. To debate the position that physical characteristics do or do not determine character
11. To write a business letter
12. To critically evaluate and compare two periods in history characterized by a mania for persecution

Materials:

Historical fiction: Ann Petry's *Tituba of Salem Village* (1964) and Elizabeth George Speare's *The Witch of Blackbird Pond* (1958); references that provide details of the witch hunts and the beliefs of the time period.

Grade level:

Upper elementary, middle school

Book summaries:

Tituba of Salem Village is the story of a slave who is sold by a fairly permissive owner in Barbados to a solemn, dark-clothed minister from Boston. The book develops a person versus society conflict as Tituba is accused of witchcraft. *The Witch of Blackbird Pond* has a similar setting, except the main character is a free white girl who moves from Barbados to New England. She also raises the suspicions of the townspeople and is eventually arrested for practicing witchcraft.

Motivation for the unit:

Elizabeth George Speare's fictional story *The Witch of Blackbird Pond* could provide motivation for a unit on the Salem witch hunts. This book describes Kit Tyler's experiences when she comes to live with her Puritan cousins in Connecticut. Kit befriends an old woman who is suspected of being the witch of Blackbird Pond. Kit is finally arrested and tried for practicing witchcraft; she is saved, following an exciting climax.

In addition to this historical fiction, you can provide related facts to provoke interest in the subject, among them:

1. During the late 1600s, many people were accused of practicing witchcraft in Massachusetts and Connecticut.
2. The famous witch hunt that took place in Salem in 1692 started when a doctor stated that several hysterical teenage girls' behavior was due to the "evil eye."

Within six month of this accusation, 20 persons were sentenced to death and 150 were sent to prison.

3. The Boston minister Cotton Mather spread interest in trials when he wrote *Wonders of the Invisible World* (1693).

4. Judge Samuel Sewall finally became conscience stricken and asked forgiveness for his mistakes.

5. Belief in witchcraft faded in the 1700s when people gained more scientific understanding of previously frightening phenomena.

Introduction of the unit: A "time tunnel" can be made from a large box and placed at the door of the classroom. As the children enter the room, they are told they are entering Salem Village during the year 1693. There should be several props in the room to remind students of Puritan days (more props can be added during the unit). Numerous pictures and reference books should be on display.

Procedures: **Language Arts**

1. Creative Writing—Tell students the following: "Read several accounts of witch hunts in both fictional books and factual references. Write a diary, pretending you are being accused of practicing witchcraft. Include descriptions of the people and the surroundings, events leading up to the accusation, the trial proceedings, your personal feelings, and the conclusion of your experience."

2. Written Composition—Tell students the following: "Read a fictional story about the witch trials. Then read about the witch trials in a history book and an encyclopedia. Write a two-page paper comparing the facts presented in the fictional story with those in the encyclopedia and the history book."

3. Creative Writing—Develop a class newspaper titled *The Salem Post* or *The Salem Times*. Some of the students may play the reporter's role and interview classmates who are accused persons, jury members, eyewitnesses to strange happenings, or judges. Students may write editorials concerning the witch hunts and factual stories based on reference materials. Other sections of the paper might include a foods section with recipes from Puritan times, a home section that describes the interiors of Puritan homes, or a fashion section that illustrates the dress of the Puritan period.

4. Oral Language—Tell students the following: "Choose a character from research in the Salem witch hunts. Dress as that character and tell his or her story to the class from that character's point of view." Possible characters for this activity include Kit Tyler from *The Witch of Blackbird Pond;* Hannah Typper, the suspected witch from the same book; Cotton Mather, the Boston minister; and Judge Samuel Sewall, the Massachusetts judge who eventually begs forgiveness for his mistakes.

5. Creative Drama—After reading about the Salem witch trials, have the students perform a mock trial with the accused, the judge, the jury, and the witnesses.

6. Creative Drama—The Salem witch hunts emphasized people's fear of those who are different or unusual. Develop a puppet show about what might happen when people do not understand someone who is different and show how fear of an unusual person is overcome.

7. Critical Thinking and Discussion—The subject of *The Witch of Blackbird Pond* is similar to that of *Tituba of Salem Village*. The two stories, however, have a very different tone. Kit is a high-spirited cousin who comes to live with relatives, whereas Tituba is a black slave who belongs to a pious minister and lives under constant suspicion. Have students read these two stories dealing with the persecution of people who do not follow Puritan beliefs; then lead a discussion comparing the

two books. Topics for discussion include the causes and effects of persecution in each story, a comparison of the authors' styles, a comparison of each story's effect on the reader, and a discussion of the results of persecution in more modern times.

Science-Related Language Arts

Many of the medical "cures" or charms used in Puritan days were based on superstition. Some of the people accused of practicing witchcraft engaged in this type of medical practice or developed charms for various reasons. A study of these cures provides opportunities for verifying scientific facts versus superstition, developing oral language skills, and developing written composition skills.

1. Reference Skills—An early cure for a cough required shaving the patient's head and placing the hair in a bush where birds would carry the hair away. When the birds took the hair, they were also believed to take the cough away from the patient. Have students investigate how a cough is cured today. Which method is more realistic? Why?

2. Interpreting Folk Literature, Oral Expression—Folk medicine used the numbers three and nine. A child with whooping cough was passed under a three-year-old donkey three times and over the donkey three times for nine successive mornings. Have students investigate the significance of the numbers three and nine in folklore and present their findings to the class.

3. Interpreting Folk Literature—The phases of the moon were believed to influence health. A cure for asthma required the patient to walk three times around the house at midnight during a full moon. To cure rickets, a lock of a child's hair was buried at a crossroad when the full moon was shining. Read several stories from folk literature that have themes about superstitions related to the moon. Develop a bulletin board about superstitions and health cures related to the moon.

4. Using References, Developing a Journal—Have the students develop a medical journal, listing the folk cure for the ailment on one page and describing the recommended modern cure on the facing page. For example:

FOLK CURE

Toothache: To prevent a toothache, put your right sock on first.

Warts: Tie the hair from a gray stallion's tail around a wart to strangle the wart.

MODERN MEDICINE CURE

Toothache: Wart:

---

5. Written Composition—Girls went to witches to seek love charms or to learn the identity of their future husbands. Have students investigate folklore to discover love charms. Make a class love charm booklet. These examples may be used for a beginning:
   a. When a girl eats salt herring, walks backward, and goes to bed immediately, she will dream about her future husband.
   b. When a snail is placed on the cold ashes in a fireplace, the snail will write the initials of the future husband.
   c. If a girl eats an apple on Halloween while looking in a mirror, she will see her future husband over her shoulder.

6. Oral Language, Debate—Superstitions are often related to physical characteristics. For example, teeth were considered an index to a person's character. Large teeth were believed to be a sign of strength, and small, regular teeth showed a perfectionist. If teeth were set apart, the person was prosperous. Eyebrows were also thought to relate to character. If a person had eyebrows that met across the nose, the person was considered unlucky and deceitful. Have the students find examples of other physical characteristics that have been used to describe personality. Ask if they believe they are justified. Why or why not? Have them present their findings during a class debate. One team of debaters will take the position that physical characteristics show a person's character; the other team will argue that physical characteristics do not determine character.

Social Studies–Related Language Arts

1. Letter Writing, Oral Language—Have students write a letter to the Salem Chamber of Commerce asking for information about restoration of the historic section of this city and points of interest. Have a small group of students prepare an oral report illustrating the points of interest the class should see if it were to visit historic Salem.

2. Critical Thinking, Reference, Oral Discussion—The Salem witch hunts illustrate the effects of persecution, fear, and lack of understanding. Choose another period in history, such as the persecution of Jews in Nazi Germany, and ask the students to read a book of historical fiction from that period, verifying the facts in an encyclopedia or history book. Compare causes of the persecution, personal reactions to the persecution, and how the persecution or conditions were resolved. (Uri Orlev's *The Island on Bird Street* and *The Man from the Other Side* and Lois Lowry's *Number the Stars* are useful for this activity.)

Activity 6–21:
STORYTELLING

TYPE	TERM
● CLASS	● STA
● GROUP	○ LTA
○ IND	○ LC

Purpose:

1. To select an appropriate story for storytelling
2. To prepare a story for telling
3. To tell a story to an appreciative audience

Materials:

Stories suitable for storytelling.

Grade level:

Upper elementary, middle school

Procedures:

1. After you have told several stories to the class, discuss possible advantages of telling a story rather than reading a story.

2. Discuss the selection of a story for telling with the children. List several characteristics of good stories for oral telling, including the following:
   a. Folktales are good because they were originally told orally.
   b. The story should have a strong beginning that will quickly interest your listeners.
   c. The story should contain action.
   d. The story should contain only a few characters.
   e. The story should have a definite climax.
   f. The story should have a satisfactory ending.

3. Discuss with the students the procedures storytellers use to prepare a story. They do not memorize their story but instead go through the following steps:
   a. Read the story completely about three times.
   b. List mentally the sequence of events in the story.
   c. Reread the story, taking note of forgotten events.
   d. Go over the main events again and add the details; then think about the meaning of the events.
   e. Tell the story before a mirror.
   f. Practice two or three more times; then try using vocal pitch changes to show changes in characters.
   g. Use changes in posture or hand gestures to represent different characters
   h. Use pauses to separate scenes.

4. Discuss with the students the ways they can introduce their stories:
   a. Ask a question.
   b. Tell why you chose that story.
   c. Tell something interesting about the author.
   d. Provide background information about a country or a period in history.
   e. Display objects related to the book or story.

5. Have the students practice telling their stories to each other in small groups. When they feel confident, ask them to tell their stories to a group of younger children. (Teachers of lower elementary children are usually cooperative, and the older students enjoy such an attentive and appreciative audience.)

REFERENCES

Five, C. L. (1988). From workbook to workshop: Increasing children's involvement in the reading process. *The New Advocate, 1,* 103–113.

Hiebert, A., & Colt, J. (1989). Patterns of literature-based reading instruction. *The Reading Teacher, 43,* 14–20.

Lanes, S. G. (1984). *The art of Maurice Sendak.* New York: Abradale Press/Abrams.

Martin, S. A. G. (1969). *The Caldecott Medal Award books, 1938–1968: Their literary and oral characteristics as they relate to storytelling.* Detroit, MI: Wayne State University. University Microfilm No. 72-16.

Miller, M., & Luskay, J. (1988). School libraries and reading programs establish closer ties. *Reading Today, 5,* 1, 18.

Norton, D. E. *The impact of literature-based reading.* New York: Merrill/Macmillan, 1992.

Norton, D. E. (1997). *The effective teaching of language arts* (5th ed.). Upper Saddle River, NJ: Merrill/Prentice Hall.

Norton, D. E. (1999). *Through the eyes of a child: An introduction to children's literature* (5th ed.). Upper Saddle River, NJ: Merrill/Prentice Hall.

Purves, A., & Monson, D. (1984). *Experiencing children's literature.* Glenview, IL: Scott, Foresman.

Putka, G. (1990, August 28). Verbal skills slip as SAT scores fall. *The Wall Street Journal,* pp. B1, B4.

Rosenblatt, L. (1985). Language, literature, and values. In S. N. Tchudi (Ed.), *Language, schooling, and society* (pp. 64–80). Upper Montclair, NJ: Boyton/Cook.

Sendak, M. (1986). *Posters by Maurice Sendak.* New York: Harmony Books.

Taxel, J. (1988). Notes from the editor. *The New Advocate, 1,* 73–74.

Zarrillo, J. (1989). Teachers' interpretations of literature-based reading. *The Reading Teacher, 43,* 22–28.

CHILDREN'S LITERATURE REFERENCES

Ackerman, Karen. *Song and Dance Man.* New York: Alfred Knopf, 1988.

Aldrich, Thomas Bailey. *The Story of a Bad Boy.* London: Sampson Low, 1870.

Alexander, Lloyd. *The Book of Three.* Orlando: Holt, Rinehart & Winston, 1964.

Avi. *The True Confessions of Charlotte Doyle.* New York: Orchard, 1990.

Ayme, Marcel. *The Wonderful Farm.* Illustrated by Maurice Sendak. New York: Harper & Row, 1951.

Barrie, James. *Peter Pan.* New York: Scribner's, 1911, 1950.

Baum, L. Frank. *The Wizard of Oz.* Orlando: Holt, Rinehart & Winston, 1900, 1956.

Bierhorst, John. *A Cry from the Earth: Music of the North American Indians.* New York: Four Winds, 1979.

Bierhorst, John. *The Sacred Path: Spells, Prayers, and Power Songs of the American Indians.* New York: Morrow, 1983.

Bitton-Jackson, Livia. *I Have Lived a Thousand Years: Growing Up in the Holocaust.* New York: Simon & Schuster, 1997.

Blumberg, Rhoda. *The Remarkable Voyages of Captain Cook.* New York: Bradbury, 1991.

Blume, Judy. *The One in the Middle Is the Green Kangaroo.* New York: Bradbury, 1981.

Bowen, Betsy. *Antler, Bear, Canoe: A Northwoods Alphabet Year.* Boston: Little, Brown, 1991.

Brett, Jan. *Berlioz the Bear.* New York: Putnam's, 1991.

Brink, Carol Ryrie. *Caddie Woodlawn.* New York: Macmillan, 1935, 1963, 1973; Scholastic, 1975.

Brown, Marcia. *Backbone of the King: The Story of Paka'a and His Son Ku.* Honolulu: University of Hawaii Press, 1984.

Burnford, Sheila. *The Incredible Journey.* Boston: Little, Brown, 1960.

Byars, Betsy. *The Cybil War.* New York: Viking, 1981.

Carroll, Lewis. *Alice's Adventures in Wonderland.* New York: Macmillan, 1865, 1963.

Carter, Alden R. *Between a Rock and a Hard Place.* New York: Scholastic, 1995.

Chetwin, Grace. *Box and Cox.* New York: Bradbury, 1990.

Cleary, Beverly. *Henry and Beezus.* New York: Morrow, 1952.

Cleary, Beverly. *Muggie Maggie.* New York: Morrow, 1952.

Cleary, Beverly. *Mitch and Amy.* New York: Morrow, 1967.

Cleary, Beverly. *Ramona the Pest.* New York: Morrow, 1968.

Cleary, Beverly. *Ramona the Brave.* New York: Morrow, 1975.

Cleary, Beverly. *Ramona and Her Father.* New York: Morrow, 1977.

Cleary, Beverly. *Ramona and Her Mother.* New York: Morrow, 1979.

Cleary, Beverly. *Ramona Quimby, Age 8.* New York: Morrow, 1981.

Cleary, Beverly. *Dear Mr. Henshaw.* New York: Morrow, 1983.

Cleary, Beverly. *A Girl from Yamhill: A Memoir.* New York: Morrow, 1988.

Cleary, Beverly. *Strider.* New York: Morrow, 1991.

Collington, Peter. *The Angel and the Soldier Boy.* New York: Alfred Knopf, 1987.

Collington, Peter. *On Christmas Eve.* New York: Alfred Knopf, 1990.

Colum, Padraic (retold by). *The Golden Fleece.* Illustrated by Willy Pogany. New York: Macmillan, 1921, 1949.

Courlander, Harold (retold by). *The Crest and the Hide.* Illustrated by Monica Vachula. New York: Coward, McCann & Geoghegan, 1982.

Crossley-Holland, Kevin (retold by). *Beowulf.* Illustrated by Charles Keeping. Oxford: Oxford University Press, 1982.

Cushman, Karen. *Catherine, Called Birdy.* New York: Clarion, 1994.

Cushman, Karen. *The Midwife's Apprentice.* New York: Clarion, 1995.

Ernst, Lisa Campbell. *Miss Penny and Mr. Grubbs.* New York: Bradbury, 1991.

Esbensen, Juster. *Great Northern Diver: The Loon.* Boston: Little, Brown, 1990.

Farmer, Nancy. *A Girl Named Disaster.* New York: Orchard, 1996.

Fine, Anne. *Alias Madame Doubtfire.* Boston: Little, Brown, 1988.

Fleischman, Paul. *Shadow Play.* New York: Harper & Row, 1990.

Frank, Anne. *The Diary of a Young Girl: The Definitive Edition.* Edited by Otto H. Frank and Mirjam Pressler. Translated by Susan Massotty. New York: Doubleday, 1995.

Freedman, Russell. *Out of Darkness: The Story of Louis Braille.* Illustrated by Kate Kiesler. New York: Clarion, 1997.

George, Jean Craighead. *Julie of the Wolves.* Illustrated by John Schoenherr. New York: Harper & Row, 1972.

Giff, Patricia Reilly. *Lily's Crossing.* New York: Delacorte, 1997.

Grifalconi, Ann. *Darkness and the Butterfly.* Boston: Little, Brown, 1987.

Grimm, Wilhelm. *Dear Mili.* Illustrated by Maurice Sendak. New York: Farrar, Straus & Giroux, 1988.

Hahn, Mary Downing. *Stepping on the Cracks.* New York: Clarion, 1991.

Henkes, Kevin. *Lilly's Purple Plastic Purse.* New York: Greenwillow, 1996.

Hesse, Karen. *Out of the Dust.* New York: Scholastic, 1997.

Hest, Amy. *In the Rain with Baby Duck.* Candlewick, 1995.

Holling, Holling Clancy. *Paddle to the Sea.* Boston: Houghton Mifflin, 1941.

Hughes, Shirley. *Dogger.* London: Bodley Head, 1977.

Jacobs, Francine. *The Tainos: The People Who Welcomed Columbus.* New York: Putnam's, 1992.

Jacques, Brian. *Pearls of Lutra: A Tale from Redwall.* New York: Philomel, 1997.

Jones, Terry (retold by). *The Saga of Erik the Viking.* Illustrated by Michael Foreman. London: Pavilion, 1983.

Joyce, William. *Dinosaur Bob and His Adventures with the Family Lazardo.* New York: Harper & Row, 1988.

Kimmel, Eric. *The Chanukkah Tree.* New York: Holiday, 1988.

Kimmel, Eric. *Hershel and the Hanukkah Goblins.* Illustrated by Trina Schart Hyman. New York: Holiday, 1989.

Krauss, Ruth. *A Hole Is to Dig.* Illustrated by Maurice Sendak. New York: Harper & Row, 1951.

Krauss, Ruth. *A Very Special House.* Illustrated by Maurice Sendak. New York: Harper & Row, 1953.

Lasky, Kathryn. *Think Like an Eagle: At Work with a Wildlife Photographer.* Photographs by Christopher G. Knight and Jack Swedberg. Boston: Little, Brown, 1992.

Lasky, Kathryn. *Lunch Bunnies.* Boston: Little, Brown, 1996.

LeGuin, Ursula K. *A Wizard of Earthsea.* New York: Parnassus, 1968.

Lewis, C. S. *The Lion, the Witch, and the Wardrobe.* New York: Macmillan, 1950.

Lindbergh, Reeve. *The Day the Goose Got Loose.* New York: Dial, 1990.

Lowry, Lois. *Number the Stars.* Boston: Houghton Mifflin, 1989.

Macaulay, David. *Black and White.* Boston: Houghton Mifflin, 1990.

Martin, Rafe. *Will's Mammoth.* New York: Putnam's, 1989.

McCully, Emily Arnold. *Picnic*. New York: Harper & Row, 1984.

McCully, Emily Arnold. *School*. New York: Harper & Row, 1987.

McCully, Emily Arnold. *New Baby*. New York: Harper & Row, 1988.

McKinley, Robin. *The Hero and the Crown*. New York: Greenwillow, 1984.

Meltzer, Milton. *Rescue: The Story of How Gentiles Saved Jews in the Holocaust*. New York: Harper & Row, 1988.

Minarik, Else Holmelund. *Little Bear's Visit*. Illustrated by Maurice Sendak, 1961.

Orlev, Uri. *The Island on Bird Street*. Boston: Houghton Mifflin, 1984.

Orlev, Uri. *The Man from the Other Side*. Boston: Houghton Mifflin, 1991.

Paulsen, Gary. *Hatchet*. New York: Bradbury, 1987.

Paulsen, Gary. *Woodsong*. New York: Bradbury, 1990.

Petry, Ann. *Tituba of Salem Village*. New York: Cromwell, 1964.

Polacco, Patricia. *Appelemando's Dreams*. New York: Philomel, 1991.

Pollack, Pamela (ed.). *The Random House Book of Humor*. New York: Random House, 1988.

Pullman, Philip. *The Golden Compass*. New York: Alfred Knopf, 1996.

Pullman, Philip. *The Subtle Knife*. New York: Alfred Knopf, 1997.

Rathman, Peggy. *Officer Buckle and Gloria*. New York: Putnam's, 1995.

Reiss, Johanna. *The Upstairs Room*. New York: Crowell, 1972.

Ryder, Joanne. *White Bear, Ice Bear*. New York: Morrow, 1989.

Rylant, Cynthia. *The Relatives Came*. New York: Bradbury, 1985.

Scieszka, Jon. *Stinky Cheese Man and Other Fairly Stupid Tales*. Illustrated by Lane Smith. New York: Viking, 1992.

Sendak, Maurice. *Kenny's Window*. New York: Harper & Row, 1956.

Sendak, Maurice. *Pierre: A Cautionary Tale*. New York: Harper & Row, 1962.

Sendak, Maurice. *Where the Wild Things Are*. New York: Harper & Row, 1963.

Sendak, Maurice. *Higglety Pigglety Pop*. New York: Harper & Row, 1967.

Sendak, Maurice. *Seven Little Monsters*. New York: Harper & Row, 1977.

Sendak, Maurice. *Outside Over There*. New York: Harper & Row, 1981.

Sendak, Maurice. *We Are All in the Dumps with Jack and Guy*. New York: HarperCollins, 1993.

Singer, Isaac Bashevis. *Zlateh the Goat and Other Stories*. Illustrated by Maurice Sendak. New York: Harper & Row, 1966.

Speare, Elizabeth George. *The Witch of Blackbird Pond*. Boston: Houghton Mifflin, 1958.

Sperry, Armstrong. *Call It Courage*. New York: Macmillan, 1940.

Stanley, Diane. *Rumpelstiltskin's Daughter*. New York: Morrow, 1997.

Stanley, Fay. *The Last Princess: The Story of Princess Ka'iulani of Hawai'i*. Illustrated by Diane Stanley. New York: Four Winds, 1991.

Stevens, Janet. *Tops and Bottoms*. San Diego: Harcourt Brace, 1995.

Steptoe, John. *Mufaro's Beautiful Daughters*. New York: Lothrop, Lee & Shepard, 1987.

Strachan, Ian. *The Flawed Glass*. Boston: Little, Brown, 1990.

Sutcliff, Rosemary (retold by). *The Shining Company*. New York: Farrar, Straus & Giroux, 1990.

Te Kanawa, Kiri (retold by). *Land of the Long White Cloud: Maori Myths, Tales, and Legends*. Illustrated by Michael Foreman. New York: Arcade, 1989.

Tolkien, J. R. R. *The Hobbit*. Boston: Houghton Mifflin, 1938.

Trivizas, Eugene. *The Three Little Wolves and the Big Bad Pig*. Illustrated by Helen Oxenbury. New York: Macmillan, 1993.

Udry, Janice May. *The Moon Jumpers*. Illustrated by Maurice Sendak. New York: Harper & Row, 1959.

Van Allsburg, Chris. *Jumanji*. Boston: Houghton Mifflin, 1981.

Vos, Ida. *Hide and Seek*. Translated by Terese Edelstein and Inez Smidt. Boston: Houghton Mifflin, 1991.

White, Ruth. *Belle Prater's Boy*. New York: Farrar, Straus & Giroux, 1996.

Wiesner, David. *Free Fall*. New York: Lothrop, Lee & Shepard, 1988.

Wiesner, David. *Tuesday*. New York: Clarion, 1991.

Wood, Audrey. *King Bidgood's in the Bathtub*. San Diego: Harcourt Brace Jovanovich, 1985.

Yep, Laurence. *Dragon's Gate*. New York: HarperCollins, 1993.

Yolen, Jane. *Encounter*. Illustrated by David Shannon. San Diego: Harcourt Brace Jovanovich, 1992.

Yorinks, Arthur. *Hey, Al*. New York: Farrar, Straus & Giroux, 1986.

Zolotow, Charlotte. *Mr. Rabbit and the Lovely Present*. Illustrated by Maurice Sendak. New York: Harper & Row, 1962.

7

Media Activities

It has been estimated that by the time most students graduate from high school, they will have spent 11,000 hours in class and 15,000 hours watching television. Shanker (1993, p. E7) states, "In 1990, one in four 9-year-olds spent six or more hours, seven days a week, watching TV. That's more than most adults spend at work and certainly more than these kids spent in school. It's also true that kids who watch lots of TV have poor test scores." Growing criticism of television programs for children reflects much concern over declining achievement scores, the model presented by television, and the passive nature of the television viewer.

However, we do not need to consider the existence of television as entirely negative. A responsible teacher can present children with activities that utilize their television viewing habits to motivate reading, creative drama, and creative writing. Media activities can help children develop selective viewing habits and critically evaluate what they see. Analysis of television commercials, in particular, can provide children with instruction in critical listening and can help them identify the persuasive techniques that bombard the viewing public. Television programs and commercials can be powerful tools for instruction.

The television-related activities in this chapter investigate children's television interests; survey the actual time they spend watching television; instruct them in selective viewing; motivate reading; and help them evaluate fantasy and factual presentations, identify commercials, and evaluate persuasive techniques used in public interest commercials.

Films can also stimulate language arts activities such as creative drama, creative writing, discussion, and reading. Experimentation with film and film production provides students with opportunities to communicate in this medium as well as in writing and oral expression. The film-related activities in this chapter utilize cartoons and other films to help students to develop skills such as appreciative listening, listening comprehension, art interpretation, oral discussion, creative writing, creative movement, media interpretation through filmmaking, group investigations and oral reporting, critical evaluation of cartoon versions and original book versions of stories, creative dramatizations, and character analysis.

A third extremely influential medium that can be used as an educational aid is the newspaper. Newspapers provide dynamic, up-to-date instructional materials. A newspaper covers a wide variety of interests—news, editorials, business, society, sports, fashions, and entertainment. Newspapers include factual material as well as material classified as opinion or propaganda. A newspaper thus provides material not only for functional reading activities but also for critical evaluation activities. The activities in the newspaper section of this chapter develop categorizing skills, introduce students to the newspaper, develop vocabulary and thinking skills through a study of the significance of newspaper and magazine names, interpret a book through newspaper format, study headlines as main ideas and relate them to fairy tales, develop critical evaluation through comparative shopping, study advertising techniques designed to appeal to a specific population, critically evaluate fact versus fiction and fact versus opinion, and study and survey the newspaper- and magazine-reading habits of adults and students.

Activity 7–1:
INVESTIGATING VIEWING
INTERESTS AND HABITS

TYPE	TERM
● CLASS	● STA
○ GROUP	○ LTA
○ IND	○ LC

Purpose: To take an interest inventory to determine television viewing interests and habits

Materials: Television interest inventory.

Grade level: All grades—the inventory should be read individually to young children, whose answers are written down by the teacher; students who can read and write their own answers may complete their own inventories

Procedures: a. Administer the following interest inventory to the class:
    (1) Do you watch television? Yes _____ No _____
    (2) If you do, what kinds of programs do you like to watch?
        cartoons _____
        news _____
        game shows _____
        mysteries _____
        comedies _____
        science fiction _____
        music _____
        sports _____
        specials _____
        detective shows _____
        police shows _____
        westerns _____
        science shows _____
        stories about families _____
        animal programs _____
        educational TV _____
        other _____
        _____

    (3) What are your favorite television shows? _____
        _____

    (4) Who are your favorite characters on television? _____
        _____

    (5) Do you watch any educational television programs?
        Yes _____ No _____
    (6) If you watch educational television, how often do you watch it?
        _____

    (7) What are your favorite educational television programs?
        _____
        _____

(8)   How many hours do you watch television after school? _____

(9)   How many hours do you watch television on Saturday? _____

(10) When you watch television, do you watch the programs with your parents?
      Yes _____ No _____

(11) Have you ever read a book about a television show?
      Yes _____ No _____
      Which ones? _____
      _____

(12) Have you seen any television programs about subjects you would like to
      learn more about? Yes _____ No _____

(13) If your answer is yes, which subjects would you like to know more about?
      _____

(14) How do you choose the programs you are going to watch?
      _____

(15) Are there any kinds of programs you do not like? _____
      Which kind? _____
      _____

b. Compile the information to obtain an overview of the television interests of your
   class. This information can be used to motivate individual children's reading and
   writing, to stimulate creative activities with the group, and to develop critical evaluation activities.

Activity 7–2:

SURVEY OF TIME SPENT WATCHING TELEVISION AND PROGRAMS WATCHED

TYPE	TERM
● CLASS	○ STA
○ GROUP	● LTA
○ IND	○ LC

Purpose:

1. To compute time spent watching television during one week
2. To compute time spent watching different kinds of television programs
3. To compare time actually spent watching television with previously stated interest

Materials:

Photocopied sheets for listing television programs that students watch and the time the students spend watching each program.

Grade level:

All grades

Procedures:

1. Discuss with the students how they could become more aware of what programs they watch during the week and how much time they spend watching television.
2. Develop a photocopied sheet the children can fill in easily with the programs they watch and the time they spend watching each program. The log might look like this:

Television Programs Watched on Weekday after School

Time	Name of Program	Minutes Spent Watching	Kind of Show
4:00	_____	_____	_____
4:30	_____	_____	_____
5:00	_____	_____	_____
5:30	_____	_____	_____
6:00	_____	_____	_____
6:30	_____	_____	_____
7:00	_____	_____	_____
7:30	_____	_____	_____
8:00	_____	_____	_____
8:30	_____	_____	_____

Total Time Spent Watching Television: _____

Another worksheet should be developed for the weekends because possible viewing times cover a more extensive period.

3. As a group activity, compose a letter to the children's parents explaining the purpose of the television viewing survey and the procedures the children should follow for keeping the daily logs. Younger children who cannot write the names of the programs independently will need to ask their parents to help them complete their surveys.
4. Have students fill out the daily viewing survey.

5. After the students have completed the week's survey, determine the total number of hours of each child's television viewing, average the number of television hours watched by the entire class, determine the number of hours spent by each child in viewing specific types of television, and average the number of television hours spent watching specific types of television shows for the entire class. For example:

_____*Grade Television Viewing*

a. Average number of hours watched each week _____

b. Average number of hours (minutes) spent watching each kind of television program:

cartoons _____
news_____
game shows _____
mysteries _____
comedies _____
science fiction _____
music _____
sports _____
specials _____
detective shows _____
police shows _____
westerns _____
science shows _____
stories about families _____
animal programs _____
educational TV _____
other _____

_____

c. Television shows watched by the greatest number in the class.

1st _____
2nd _____
3rd _____
4th _____
5th _____

6. Finally, compare the number of hours actually spent in viewing specific types of programs with the information obtained on the television interest inventory. Do the stated interests on the inventory match the viewing habits of the children? If they do not, discuss possible reasons for these discrepancies.

Activity 7–3:
USING A GUIDE FOR SELECTIVE VIEWING

TYPE	TERM
● CLASS	○ STA
○ GROUP	● LTA
○ IND	○ LC

Purpose:

1. To understand that planning can help a viewer find programs of interest or merit
2. To understand that television viewing should be selective
3. To locate specific information using a television guide

Materials:

Weekly television guide from the local Sunday newspaper or *TV Guide* magazine; photocopied viewing suggestions and scheduling worksheet.

Grade level:

Second grade through middle school

Procedures:

1. Introduce the television guide to the children. Discuss the purposes for printing and reading a television guide. Ask the following: "What information can you learn from the television guide? Why would you want to use the guide?"

2. Look at the different sections of the television guide. You might ask: "Is there a table of contents? How would the table of contents help us to locate information? How is the television guide arranged?" Ask children to find the table of contents and then use it to find the programs scheduled for Tuesday (or some other day). After they find a specific day, ask questions demanding that they locate information on the schedule for that day: "At what time do the television stations start broadcasting? What is the first program shown in our area? What is the last program shown in our area? How does the television guide indicate the number of the television channel?" (Find an example of this number.) "How many different channels are listed in the television guide?" (Have students find examples of each channel.) "How is the daily television guide divided so that it is easier to find programs?" (The twenty-four-hour day is divided into half-hour time segments.) Ask specific questions that require students to use both the television station number and the time period: "What programs are on at 8:30 on Tuesday evening? What channel is each program on? Find a comedy show listed on Tuesday evening. Find a science program about the planet Mars. When could you watch a news program on Tuesday?" Have the children ask each other questions about the time or subject matter for specific programs.

3. Ask the students if any information in the television guide will help them find programs of special interest or merit. Discuss sections that describe recommended programs for the week, special sports programs, special children's programs, and so forth. Discuss how this information can help a family choose the best television programs to watch during the week.

4. Discuss the fact that many people fear that children watch too many poorly selected programs. Develop with the children a list of positive reasons for watching television and a list of negative results of too much television viewing. For example:

Watching Television Is Good Because
a. TV provides entertainment.
b. TV shows us pictures of places we have never been.
c. We can learn about new subjects on TV.
d. We can learn about what is happening in the world.

e. We can see and hear famous people.

f. We can talk about what we see on television.

Watching Too Much Television Is Bad Because

a. If we do not spend enough time studying, our grades will not be good.

b. We may not have time to read if we watch television all of the time.

c. We will not do things with our families such as play games, go on trips, and talk.

d. Some programs are too violent.

e. We will not play outside with our friends and family.

5. With the students, develop several recommendations for appropriate television viewing that give them opportunities to see the best shows but still leave them with plenty of time for activities with family and friends, as well as time for homework and other chores.

Our Television Viewing Suggestions

Do: a. Select good shows your whole family wants to watch.

b. Read the television guide and plan your viewing.

c. Turn the TV off when you are not watching a selected show.

d. Learn more about a TV subject by reading a book about it.

e. Talk about the good programs you see with your family.

f. Read a book about your favorite TV character.

Don't: a. Leave the TV on during a program that has not been personally selected.

b. Become a TV addict.

c. Always watch TV alone.

d. Watch TV when you are studying.

e. Choose TV instead of a book, game, or other family activity.

6. After selecting several television viewing suggestions, have the students discuss their television viewing recommendations with their parents. (Compose a class letter explaining the purpose of this activity and asking for parental cooperation.) Then, ask the children to develop a TV viewing schedule with their parents for the week. This schedule should allow them to see special programs of interest but still leave time for schoolwork, sports, playing with friends, and the like. These television scheduling forms may be photocopied and presented to each child.

My Special Television Schedule for the Week

Name _____

Title of Program	Day	Time	Station
_____	_____	_____	_____
_____	_____	_____	_____
_____	_____	_____	_____
_____	_____	_____	_____
_____	_____	_____	_____
_____	_____	_____	_____
_____	_____	_____	_____

_____

Parent's Signature

7. During class discussion, talk about the children's impressions of and reactions to some of the television programs selected by a majority of the class. Allow individual children to explain why they and their families chose a certain program. Did they have special interests? Did they read a book about the story? Did they visit a special location? If they could have chosen just one television program to watch during that week, which one would they have chosen? Why?

Activity 7–4:
USING TELEVISION TO MOTIVATE READING—PART I

TYPE	TERM
● CLASS	○ STA
● GROUP	●LTA
○ IND	○ LC

Purpose:
1. To enjoy listening to television-related stories
2. To enjoy reading television-related stories
3. To compare a television presentation with a book presentation
4. To create a dramatic presentation of a television production and related stories
5. To write creatively after seeing a television production and reading related stories

Materials:
Television-related picture books such as those adapted from A. A. Milne's *Winnie-the-Pooh* (1926, 1973) and *The House at Pooh Corner* (1928, 1973), the Dr. Seuss stories, *Charlie Brown,* and books about *Sesame Street* characters; box cut to show a roll story; roll of paper for the story; puppet theater and material for puppets.

Grade level:
Lower elementary

Procedures:
1. This activity may be used with any book-related television special or series; be aware of television programs to be shown in the area and of what programs are available on videotape.

2. Create an attractive display of television-related stories or a display of books relating to a specific television program. As part of the display, design a bulletin board with spaces the children can fill in after seeing the television presentation and reading the story. A bulletin board might be developed before a television production of Winnie-the-Pooh.

3. Introduce the book display table and the bulletin board to the children. Show them that the handmade television screen does not have anything drawn on the roll of paper. Ask them what they think is missing. Explain to the students that they will make their own television show and will draw pictures to fill in the rest of the bulletin board after they have seen the television production and have read or listened to other stories about Winnie-the-Pooh.

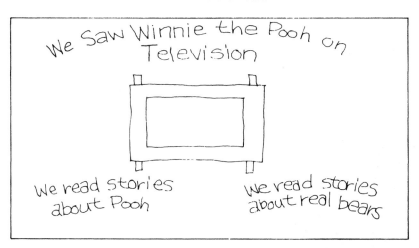

4. Ask children to watch the television presentation of the book. Tell them to watch carefully so that they can make their own television shows after watching.

5. After students have viewed the television production, discuss the story with the children. Allow them to describe the characters, the settings, the action, and their reactions to the program. After they have all had an opportunity to respond, ask students to relate the sequence of the story: what happened first, second, and so forth. Divide the children into groups and assign each group a portion of the story to illustrate. Divide the roll of paper into sections so that each group has a manageable length of paper to work with. Measure and mark the space for each picture. Have each group determine what illustrations its members will draw.

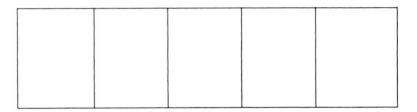

After the sections are completed, tape them together to form a continuous roll story. Place the roll in the box and allow children to retell the story using the roll story.

6. Read aloud the picture book or story that was shown on television. Discuss differences and similarities between the two presentations—setting, characters, illustrations, descriptions, dialogue, and so forth. Ask the children what they consider the advantages of each type of presentation.

Why I Like to Watch the TV Story	*Why I Like to Read the Book*
1. The animals and people look alive.	1. I can read the book when I want to.
2. I like the colors and music.	2. I can learn more about the people in the story.
3. The TV shows me what characters look like.	3. I can use my imagination and think about what the story looks like.
4. I don't have to ask anyone for help with words.	4. I can ask someone to read the story to me.
5. I like the action on TV.	5. I can read the story to my little brother. This makes me feel good.

7. Read aloud and allow children to read other stories about the television presentation. For example, there are numerous Winnie-the-Pooh stories other than those that have been shown on television. Allow groups of children to select their favorite Pooh stories. Ask them to make puppets of the characters so that they can present the story to the rest of the class. A dismantled television set can become a puppet theater for television tie-ins—when the back and inside of the set are removed, the shell forms a box with an opening in the front. Children enjoy acting out and viewing their own television shows. One class of first graders named its own classroom television station and set the dial on that number.

8. After the children have seen the TV show, listened to oral presentations of books, and read related stories, give them an opportunity to write creative stories. Several motivational methods may be used. For example, you can read a portion of a story they have not read. Stop at an exciting place and allow the children to finish the story. Or you can ask them to pretend they are going to meet one of the main characters and have an adventure together. Where will they go? Whom will they meet? Will they have problems? What will they do? Share their finished stories orally with a group of children.

Activity 7–5:

FANTASY AND FACT ON TELEVISION AND IN TELEVISION-RELATED BOOKS

TYPE	TERM
● CLASS	○ STA
● GROUP	● LTA
○ IND	○ LC

Purpose:

1. To identify characteristics of television and television-related books that are fantasy and those that are factual
2. To compare factual presentations with fantasy
3. To do further reading to evaluate fantasy and factual writing and viewing
4. To write factual paragraphs and compare them with an enjoyable television story

Materials:

Television-related picture storybooks (e.g., those about Winnie-the-Pooh); factual picture books and magazines depicting real bears, rabbits, tigers, pigs, owls, and so on; film of real animals or a zoo trip to see real animals.

Grade level:

Lower elementary

Procedures:

1. This activity is an extension of activity 7–4, in which children read television-related stories. The example, Winnie-the-Pooh, is a fantasy and can be used to stimulate an interest in real animals and in the realization that fantasy stories are quite different from factual stories.

2. Provide factual picture books about the animals seen in the television fantasy. Ask children if they think real animals could do all of the things the animals in the television show could do. Ask them to think about the television show, the books they read, and their own creative dramas and stories: "Which parts were real and which parts were make believe?" Ask them to think about a real pet they have at home: "How is that pet different from the animals in our story? Why can the television show and the stories show animals talking, living in their own furnished houses, and wearing clothes?" Ask the children to list the animals they saw and read about in their stories. Explain to the children that they will be learning more about the exciting real lives of these animals. Have them compile a list of questions they would like to have answered about each animal. Put their questions on a chart.

What I Would Like to Know about Real Bears

1. Where do real bears live?
2. What do real bears eat—do they like honey?
3. How big are real bears?
4. Are real bears friendly like Pooh?

What I Would Like to Know about Real Tigers

1. Where do real tigers live?
2. What do real tigers eat?
3. Do tigers climb trees?
4. How big are real tigers?
5. Would I want a real tiger for a pet?

3. Ask the children how they might find answers to their questions. Discuss information found in books and television shows about real animals (*Animals, Animals, Animals; National Geographic; Wild Kingdom;* and so forth) as well as information obtained from observing real animals in a zoo or on a farm. Show the available books to the students. Allow each child to choose an animal as a subject for further reading and research.

4. Create a bulletin board showing the fantasy and real worlds of the animals:

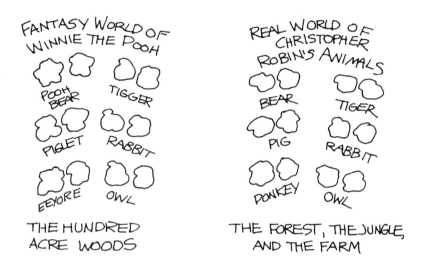

5. Write factual paragraphs about the specific animal. Place the factual paragraphs and the fantasy stories on a table below the fantasy and real-world bulletin board. Include related books on this table.

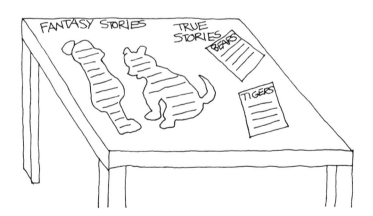

Activity 7–6:

USING TELEVISION TO
MOTIVATE READING—PART II

TYPE	TERM
● CLASS	○ STA
● GROUP	● LTA
○ IND	○ LC

Purpose:

1. To enjoy reading television-related stories
2. To compare the strengths and weaknesses of a television presentation with the same story in book form
3. To compare the setting, main idea, character development, writing style, and illustrations of television presentations with the same stories in book form
4. To create an original drama after seeing a television presentation

Materials:

Books from which various television series originated, such as Laura Ingalls Wilder's *Little House on the Prairie* (1941); books written as a result of a television series; books, such as E. B. White's *Charlotte's Web* (1952), Johanna Spyri's *Heidi* (1884, 1962), Robert Louis Stevenson's *Treasure Island* (1911), Mark Twain's *The Adventures of Tom Sawyer* (1876, 1962), and Howard Pyle's *The Merry Adventures of Robin Hood* (1883, 1946), that are repeated yearly as specials or that may appear as a short series on educational or cable television. (Many are also available on videotape.)

Grade level:

Middle and upper elementary

Procedures:

1. Create a library display of television-related books. Introduce the books to the students and describe the connection between the book and the television program. (In some cases, a television show is an adaptation of a book; some books are written because of interest in a television series.)

2. Ask the students to watch a book-related television program. Before they view the show, discuss with students any comparisons they could make between the television presentation and the book and list the items they can look for.

THINGS TO LOOK FOR	TELEVISION	BOOK
1. Where did the story take place?	_____	_____
2. Did this setting seem real to me? Why or why not?	_____	_____
3. Who was the main character in the story?	_____	_____
4. Who were the supporting characters in the story?	_____	_____
5. Did these characters seem real to me? Why or why not?	_____	_____
6. What was the main idea of the story?	_____	_____
7. How was the dialogue presented?	_____	_____
8. What did I like best about this presentation?	_____	_____
9. What did I like least about this presentation?	_____	_____

3. After viewing the television story, discuss the list of things to look for. What were the particular strengths and weaknesses of this presentation?

4. Make comparisons between the television presentation and the book. Allow students to read the book and answer the same questions they discussed after they viewed the television presentation. Find examples in the book of setting, characters, and dialogue. Ask the following: "Are there differences in interpretation? Do we know more about the character, setting, or plot after reading the book? Are there differences in picture interpretation?"

5. Allow students to divide into groups and ask them to choose a television-related book. After they have read the book, ask the students to present a book report as if it were a television presentation. Ask them to present the report to the rest of the class or to a group of classmates. Encourage students to use any techniques that are effectively used on television (e.g., costumes, music, and sound effects).

Activity 7–7:

IDENTIFYING COMMERCIALS ON CHILDREN'S TV SHOWS

	TYPE		TERM
	● CLASS		● STA
	● GROUP		○ LTA
	○ IND		○ LC

Purpose:

1. To identify products advertised during programs designed specifically for children
2. To understand that companies advertise different products depending on audience

Materials:

Tapes of commercials played on several children's programs; photocopied worksheets for listing products advertised during specific time periods.

Grade level:

Lower and middle elementary

Procedures:

1. Videotape or tape-record the audio for the commercials shown during a Saturday morning cartoon show designed specifically for children.

2. Discuss with the children the expenses connected with paying actors, directors, film crews, and the like. Ask them to think about how the television networks pay for the shows they see. Through discussion, develop the understanding that networks charge advertisers a certain amount of money per minute for commercial time. These commercials pay for the production, allowing the networks to present the programs to the viewer without charge.

3. Continue the discussion by talking about what the children believe the advertisers receive in return for their money: "If you were going to spend thousands of dollars for a short commercial, what would you want in return?" Discuss the products advertisers want us to buy.

4. Play recordings of the commercials seen during Saturday morning cartoons. Before playing the tape, ask the children the following: "Who is the audience for Saturday morning cartoons? Who are the advertisers trying to persuade? What kinds of products would this audience want to buy?" Ask the children to watch and listen to a tape of the advertisements heard during a half-hour cartoon show on Saturday morning. Ask them to listen for the products sold, who is talking during the commercial (the main characters), and what persuasive words they hear on the commercials. Develop a chart of this information:

**COMMERCIALS SEEN ON SATURDAY
CARTOONS, CHANNEL _____ , 9:00–9:30**

Product Advertised	*Main Characters*	*Persuasive Words*
1. breakfast cereal	animated cartoon	mm-mm, delicious
2. a toy	two boys playing wth toy	high-speed, great action
3. _____	_____	_____
4. _____	_____	_____
5. _____	_____	_____
6. _____	_____	_____

5. After compiling the chart, discuss why these specific products might be included in a children's show, why the advertisers would use animated cartoons and children in the commercials, and why some of the persuasive words might appeal to children.

6. Assign children (with parental permission) to watch various segments of the Saturday morning children's shows. Divide the assignment to include the major broadcast and cable channels seen in your area; for example:

	ABC John	CBS Mary	NBC Susan	Nickelodeon Letitia	TNT Jamal
8:00–8:30	_____	_____	_____	_____	_____
8:30–9:00	_____	_____	_____	_____	_____
9:00–9:30	_____	_____	_____	_____	_____
9:30–10:00	_____	_____	_____	_____	_____
10:00–10:30	_____	_____	_____	_____	_____
10:30–11:00	_____	_____	_____	_____	_____
11:00–11:30	_____	_____	_____	_____	_____
11:30–12:00	_____	_____	_____	_____	_____

7. Provide the children with photocopied worksheets for listing the commercials they viewed for their assignment. The worksheet should be similar to the following:

Commercials heard on _____
                                            (Program)

Saturday morning at _____
                                            (Time)

On channel _____
                                  (Network and number)

My name is _____

	Product Advertised	Main Characters	Persuasive Words
1.	_____	_____	_____
2.	_____	_____	_____
3.	_____	_____	_____
4.	_____	_____	_____
5.	_____	_____	_____
6.	_____	_____	_____

---

8. After the students have filled out this worksheet, have them tabulate the number of different products advertised on Saturday cartoons and the frequency of such advertising. For example:

Kinds of Products Advertised	Number of Advertisements
breakfast cereals	_____
candy	_____
fast food stores	_____
toys, games	_____
bicycles	_____
soda	_____
other	_____

9. Have the children tabulate data on the kinds of main characters used in the ads or the kind of ad presentation. For example:

Who Presented the Ad	*Number of Advertisements*
animal cartoon	_____
people cartoon	_____
live animals	_____
children	_____
sports heroes	_____
famous actors	_____
other	_____

10. Have students list the persuasive vocabulary words they heard. Discuss the meaning of each word. Ask the children whether they believe all of these words really describe that product. Why or why not?

11. Create a bulletin board that illustrates Saturday morning commercials for children. Have the children draw pictures of some of the commercials. Include on the bulletin board some of the facts learned from the commercial survey and tapes of some of the commercials.

Activity 7-8:
THE POWER OF PERSUASION—UNIT OF STUDY

	TYPE	TERM
	● CLASS	○ STA
	● GROUP	● LTA
	○ IND	○ LC

Purpose:

1. To identify propaganda techniques used in commercials shown during children's television programs
2. To critically evaluate propaganda techniques used in television commercials
3. To write original television commercials
4. To dramatize television commercials

Materials:

Transparencies illustrating each type of propaganda technique; tapes of commercials heard during Saturday morning cartoon shows; videotapes of commercials seen during Saturday morning cartoons; worksheet for surveying propaganda techniques found in commercials; questions for team participation; lists of statements that use propaganda techniques and statements that do not.

Grade level:

Middle and upper elementary

Procedures:

1. These activities would be a logical extension of activity 7–7, in which children identified the products advertised, the type of presentation, and the persuasive words in Saturday morning commercials.
2. Ask children the following: "Have you ever had an experience in which you bought or sent for a product that was advertised on television?" (Sending for a toy advertised by a cereal sponsor and buying games, toys, or cereals are examples.) "Did the toy or the item always do what the advertisement led you to believe it could do? Were you ever disappointed because you believed you would get something better than what you actually received? What made you believe the product was something you really wanted or needed?" Allow each child to share his experience with the class.
3. Writers and producers of television commercials use various approaches to persuade the viewer to buy products. Through inductive questioning lead children into identification of specific propaganda techniques:

Bandwagon Technique

a. Place the following statements on the chalkboard or on a transparency (fill in the blanks with current names and places):

All of the kids on our block chew _____ gum.
Every boy and girl wants this new game for Christmas._____
Don't eat any more dull meals; join the gang at the _____.
Everyone who wants to win the race wears _____shoes.
---

b. Read each statement with the children and ask them if they can identify any similarities among all of the statements: "What is each statement trying to lead us to believe?" (Everyone is doing something, and we should too.) "What are some key words that help persuade us that everyone is doing something?"

All the kids
Every boy and girl
Join the gang
Everyone

c. Ask the group if anyone knows what this type of persuasive technique is called. If no one knows, introduce the term *bandwagon*. Discuss the reasons why *bandwagon* is a good term for this kind of advertising. Ask the students if they see any bias or falsehood in this kind of advertising: "Does everyone really do what the ad suggests? Even if they did, should you do it too?"

d. Ask students to supply other examples of statements that use the bandwagon approach. Ask them to suggest commercials they think use this approach.

e. Listen to or view tapes of several television commercials that use the bandwagon technique. Ask children to identify which part of the commercials uses bandwagon statements or pictures: "Are these statements all true? Why or why not?"

f. Ask students to draw a picture illustrating a bandwagon commercial. (These pictures may be used to develop a bulletin board or a book on propaganda techniques.) Ask them to write their own definitions of *bandwagon* under their pictures.

Everyone is doing or buying something.
You should do it too.

Testimonials

a. Place the following statements on the chalkboard or on a transparency (fill in the blanks with current names and products):

> _____ _____, the great Olympic swimmer, eats _____ for breakfast every morning.
>
> _____ _____, the tennis pro, wears _____ tennis shoes.
>
> _____ _____, the child film star, uses _____ toothpaste.
>
> _____ _____ gets his energy by eating a _____ bar between meals.
>
> _____ _____ rides a _____ motorcycle.

b. Read these statements with the children and ask them to identify what technique is used in each statement to persuade them to buy something. Ask students the following: "What is the advertiser trying to make us believe by telling us that so-and-so eats Greebie cereal for breakfast? Do you believe eating this cereal would make you a great swimmer? Why or why not? Why would the advertiser for tennis shoes choose so-and-so to sell her product? What does this suggest to us? Why do you believe so-and-so might be asked to do a toothpaste commercial? What is the advertiser suggesting might happen if we also use that toothpaste?" Continue asking similar questions about each statement. Stress the connection between the well-known personality, the type of product, and the intended implication to the consumer. Discuss what facts may have been left out of the statements. Then ask: "Would we need to know all of these facts before we could decide about the worthiness of the product?"

c. Ask the students if anyone knows the name for this persuasive advertising technique. Introduce the term *testimonial.* Ask the students to give you a definition for the term *testimonial.* (A respected or well-known person tries to influence the buyer by saying he or she uses something. It is often suggested that we will have some of the same benefits if we also use the product.)

d. List testimonials suggested by the class.

e. Listen to or view tapes of several television commercials that use a testimonial approach. Ask the students to identify the person giving the testimonial, to identify the relationship (if any) between the product and the person, and to identify the benefit suggested by the commercial.

f. Ask the students to draw a picture of a testimonial commercial to add to the bulletin board or book on propaganda. Have them write a definition for *testimonial* under their pictures.

Testimonial
A well-known person tries to persuade the buyer by saying that he or she uses the product.

Glittering Generalities

a. Place the following statements on the chalkboard or a transparency:

For the greatest time of your life, visit the _____ amusement park.

For a wow taste, chew _____ gum.

Don't eat at another ho-hum restaurant, eat at _____, the most magical place in town.

Have hours of excitement with your friends after you buy the new fantastic _____ game by _____.

---

b. Read the statements with the children and ask if they see any similarities among the statements: "What words are used to try to persuade us to buy a product or to visit some place?" List these terms or have the children underline them in each statement:

greatest time of your life
a wow taste

most magical place in town
hours of excitement
fantastic

c. Ask the students to close their eyes and visualize each statement as you read it. Allow students to share their imagined pictures for each statement. Ask them if anyone knows the name for this persuasive technique. If they do not, tell them the term is *glittering generalities*. Discuss the meaning of this term and why advertisers might use this technique. Ask the students to give you a list of other words they would also call glittering generalities. Finally, ask them to provide a definition for the term *glittering generalities*. (These are terms that cause the listener to accept something because of the association with the words. The exact meaning is not always clear.)

d. Ask the students to list any commercials they can think of that use glittering generalities.

e. Listen to or view tapes of television commercials that use glittering generalities. Ask the students to identify these terms and to describe what they would expect the product to be after they heard the commercials. Discuss with the students their feelings about the accuracy of each of these terms. If possible, have them try some of the products and decide whether the term is appropriate.

f. Ask the students to illustrate the glittering generality persuasive technique for the bulletin board or for their booklets. Write a definition for the term below the picture.

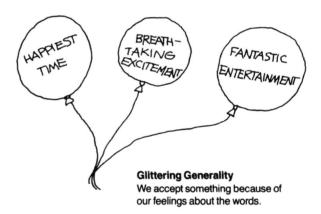

Glittering Generality
We accept something because of
our feelings about the words.

Persuading with Humor

Many commercials shown during children's programs use visual or sound techniques to create humor. Cartoons, jingles, exaggerated incidents, or preposterous situations appeal to the viewer's sense of humor. (Certain humorous symbols are readily associated with specific products—a clown advertising a fast food chain or a dancing cat singing the praises of a brand of cat food.)

a. Select several humorous advertisements from magazines. Ask the students to look at them and tell you what approach the advertisers used. Ask children to identify the humorous or exaggerated incident in each ad. You might ask the following: "How do you feel when you look at these advertisements? Why do you think the advertiser might want you to feel that way?"

b. Have the students list several TV commercials that use humor to sell a product. Ask how each commercial shows humor.

c. Listen to or view tapes of several television commercials that rely on humor to persuade the viewer to buy a product. Ask the students to identify the type of humor.

d. You can experiment with your class to demonstrate how successfully some types of humor or exaggeration help people to retain information. Memory authorities often suggest that, to remember a list of items or names, people should associate each item with something funny or place it in an exaggerated context.

For this experiment, provide the class with two lists of items to remember. Present the first list of items and give students one minute to memorize them:

cat	wagon
boy	lamp
tree	chair
fence	horse
car	fly

After one minute, have students write as many items as they can remember. Tally the number of items they retained. Allow the students to do something else for a while; then test them again on their words. How many items do they remember now?

Continue with the second experiment. This time, show the students how to associate the items on a list using an exaggerated or humorous connection. For example, if they want to remember from a list of words "wagon" and "fly," they could visualize the wagon actually flying. Now, ask them to memorize the following words.

wagon
fly
cloud
oranges
apples
house
face
plant
man
tub

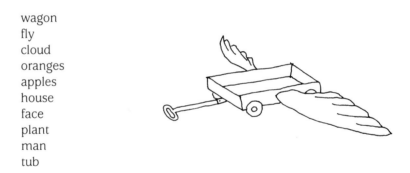

We could visualize our list of words as a wagon flying near a cloud of oranges and apples, which is over a house with a smiling face, next to a man planted in a tub.

After students have rapidly made their associations and visualized their results, ask them to list the items in this second group of ten words. Have them tally the number of words they remember. Compare the number of words remembered in the two approaches. If more of the children remember the second list, why do they think their memories improved? Do they also remember commercials for a longer time if they are humorous or exaggerated? Later in the day, ask the children again to visualize their second word list and have them write down the words they remember. Are they still able to remember most of the words, even though considerable time has passed?

e. Have the students illustrate a humorous commercial for the bulletin board or the propaganda booklet. Write a definition for a humorous commercial under the picture. For example:

The cheapest flight to Hawaii takes you into the beautiful clouds.

4. Now that the children have identified and experienced many of the persuasive techniques used in commercials, they can survey propaganda techniques in children's programming. Older children can be introduced to other propaganda techniques such as name calling, plain folks, snob appeal, and transfer. Use the procedures already mentioned for this activity but take most examples from commercials aimed at adults. Give the children a photocopied sheet for surveying television commercials during a specific time. (Divide the class so that the networks and different time periods are surveyed.) A photocopied commercial survey might resemble the following:

PERSUASION TECHNIQUES USED IN COMMERCIALS

Commercials seen from _____ to _____
                              (beginning time)   (end time)

on _____, channel _____
        (date)

Name of surveyor _____

	Name of Product	Propaganda Techniques	Key Words
1.	_____	_____	_____
2.	_____	_____	_____
3.	_____	_____	_____
4.	_____	_____	_____
5.	_____	_____	_____
6.	_____	_____	_____
7.	_____	_____	_____
8.	_____	_____	_____
9.	_____	_____	_____
10.	_____	_____	_____

Discuss the results of the survey and tabulate the findings. Ask questions such as the following: "What types of persuasive techniques are most widely used in advertisements aimed at children? What does this mean to us as viewers? Did you believe everything you heard and saw on the commercials? Which commercials did you feel were the most accurate? Why? Which commercials did you feel might not be telling the whole truth? Why? How can we check the accuracy of the commercial before we buy a product? If you watch television with a younger brother or sister, what could you tell him or her about commercials?"

5. Mock Television Game Show—Divide the class into teams. On slips of paper write questions about the propaganda devices students have studied and examples of different kinds of propaganda to identify. Allow the teams to take turns selecting the items from a container. Give one point for each correct answer. Examples of items could include the following:

What is the definition of a bandwagon commercial?	What is the definition of a testimonial?
Define a glittering generality.	Why does a sponsor use humor in a commercial?
Name three terms often used in glittering generalities.	Name three terms often used in bandwagon commercials.
Name three people who might do a testimonial commercial for athletic socks.	Name three famous dogs who might do testimonials for a dog food commercial.
What kind of a commercial is this? "Most people prefer Swiggley Hair Shampoo. Try it, and you'll know why."	What kind of a commercial is this? "Swift Eagle, the fastest runner in the world, always wears Blue Dot Tennis Shoes."
What kind of a commercial is this? "Let your dreams come true. Visit the fabulous Ten Flags over the Hudson."	

6. Reinforcement Worksheet—On a worksheet, list statements that use propaganda techniques and statements that do not. Have the students read the randomly organized statements and ask them to underline those they think use propaganda techniques.

IDENTIFYING PROPAGANDA TECHNIQUES

Some of these statements use propaganda devices to persuade us to do something. Some of the statements do not. Underline the sentences that use propaganda devices. If you underline the sentence, write the name of the propaganda device it uses on the blank provided.

_____ 1. Dr. and Mrs. Jerald Norris are leaving Sunday for a three-week tour of England and Scotland.

_____ 2. The newly crowned Miss America says her beautiful smile is due to Dazzle toothpaste. She wants you to have this beautiful smile too.

_____ 3. Jo-Jo the clown flips with joy every time he takes a bite of a foot-long hot dog.

_____ 4. The new cars were shown for the first time today. Studies show these cars get better gas mileage than last year's models.

_____ 5. The members of the Saturday Jogging Club all buy their jogging shorts at the Coaches' Corner.

_____ 6. The falls at the State Park drop over a 400-foot gorge and will be used to generate electricity.

_____ 7. Stay at the new, elegant State Falls Park Hotel. The gourmet dining room will thrill you with its fabulous new menu.

---

7. As a culminating activity for a unit of study on propaganda techniques, divide the class into small groups. Ask each group to develop a television commercial. They may use as many propaganda devices as they wish. If possible, videotape the commercials and play them back to the class.

Activity 7-9:

IDENTIFYING PERSUASIVE TECHNIQUES

TYPE	TERM
● CLASS	● STA
● GROUP	○ LTA
○ IND	○ LC

Purpose:

1. To identify television and radio commercials designed to sway public opinion (public interest commercials)
2. To identify visual and auditory techniques that commercial writers use to attract attention
3. To write creative public interest commercials

Materials:

Tapes of radio and television commercials illustrating public interest concerns; television—live or videotaped public interest commercial; worksheet for surveying public interest commercials.

Grade level:

Middle and upper elementary

Procedures:

1. Discuss with children the fact that television and radio commercials use various techniques to persuade us to buy something or act in a certain way for the good of the companies that aim the ads at us. Their purpose is to reach as many people as possible. Sometimes, however, television or radio tries to influence us to do something for our own good or safety. Ask the children to think of examples of commercials that do not try to make us buy something but instead attempt to get us to act in a certain way for our own good (e.g., spot ads about vaccinations, safe driving in school zones, prevention of forest fires, pollution, and zip codes). Ask students the following: "Why do you think these commercials are called public interest commercials? Who do you think would want to sponsor these commercials?"

2. The writers and producers of public interest commercials hope to attract our attention and persuade us to do something. Play a video- or audiotape recording of several public interest commercials. Ask the children to identify the techniques the commercial writer uses to attract our attention. List the auditory techniques illustrated in the commercial:

   ### This Attracted Our Listening Attention
   Music
   Jingles, rhymes
   Persuasive words:
       "Protect our children"
       "Save the forest for these families"
   A famous personality's voice
   Sound effects: a fire burning, a horn, an ambulance

3. Television commercials use not only sound but also sight to attract our attention. Discuss the following: "Do you remember seeing these commercials on television? Would you like to listen to these commercials on radio or would you rather see them on television? Why? What advantages do sponsors of commercials have when they show the commercials to us?"

4. Play a public interest television commercial or a videotape of several commercials. Ask the children to identify the visual techniques each commercial uses to attract attention. List the visual techniques:

This Attracted Our Visual Attention

Colors
Patterns
Cartoons
Dancing animals
Puppets
Famous personalities
Beautiful scenery
Picture of a disaster
Children

5. Assign students the task of viewing public interest television commercials during a specific time period. Divide the task so that all of the networks will be surveyed. Ask the students to identify the purpose of the public interest commercial, the sponsor, and the visual and auditory techniques used to attract the viewer's attention. The following worksheet will help students in this survey:

SURVEY OF PUBLIC INTEREST TELEVISION COMMERCIALS

Channel _____   Time _____
Day _____   Name _____

Public interest commercial subject:
_____
What does the sponsor want me to do? _____
_____

What might happen if I do not do it? _____
_____

Who sponsors the commercial? _____
_____

What visual techniques are used to attract my attention? _____
_____

What sound techniques are used to attract my attention? _____
_____

Draw a picture illustrating this commercial.

6. Divide the class into smaller groups and allow each group to select a subject of public or school interest. Ask each group to write and present a public interest commercial to the rest of the class using the visual and sound techniques found in commercial advertising.

Activity 7–10:
THE PARTS OF A NEWSPAPER

TYPE	TERM
● CLASS	● STA
● GROUP	○ LTA
○ IND	○ LC

Purpose:
1. To name major sections of the newspaper
2. To identify the primary purpose for reading each section of the newspaper
3. To identify the proposed audience for each section of the newspaper
4. To locate newspaper features using the index

Materials: Duplicate copies of a local newspaper; copies of several different newspapers.

Grade level: Middle and upper elementary

Procedures:
1. Ask each child to bring a copy of a local newspaper or have them obtain copies from other sources.
2. Introduce the various sections of the newspaper as a group activity.
   a. Identify and underline the name of the newspaper. Ask students the following: "Is there any reason for that particular name? Does the newspaper use any technique to make the name more visual? Why would the newspaper want to be visual? The top portion that contains the name of the newspaper is called a *masthead.* Find the term in a dictionary. Why do you think the term is used by newspapers? What information do you gain by looking quickly at the masthead of your newspaper?" (Name of paper, date, location, edition.) On a large sheet of newsprint, paste the masthead from your newspaper. Label this portion *masthead.*

   b. Look at the front page of the newspaper. Ask the students to read the front page for one minute. Instruct them to acquire as much information as they can in that minute. Then have them cover or fold the paper so they cannot see it. Lead a brainstorming session in which as much information as possible is written on the chalkboard. Ask the students how they learned so much information in one minute. (Some students will try to read an article, whereas others will scan the headlines. Learning to scan the headlines is the point you want to stress.) Ask students the following: "What attracted your attention as you tried to identify the contents of the front page?" (Headlines and pictures.) "How does the newspaper indicate that one story may be more important than another story?" (Size of headline.) "Which story do you think is the most important on the front page of your paper? Where is that story located?" (The top story on the page.) "What two ways did your newspaper use to indicate the importance of the story?" (Size of headline and location of story.) Ask the students to look again at their list of information on the chalkboard and the headlines in the newspaper. "What kinds of stories are included on the front page?" (Important news stories from around the world or the United States.) "What does the headline tell us about the story?" (The main idea of the story.) "Look at the headlines again. Which stories would you want to read? Why? What words attracted your attention? Why is the front page of the paper so important?" Cut out the headlines from the front page of the paper and place them on the newsprint sheet containing the masthead. Label the headlines.

```
+-------------------------------------------------------------+
|               (Main Story Headline — Largest Type)          |
|             President Signs Tax                             |
|                       Cut                                   |
|                                                             |
|                                  (Secondary Headlines)      |
|                               JUDGE CITES SMITH             |
|                                                             |
|  (Secondary Headlines)                                      |
|  ZOO GAINS MONKEY                                           |
+-------------------------------------------------------------+
```

c. Ask students what parts of the newspaper they like to read. When a student mentions a section, ask the class to find that section. During this first experience, observe the techniques students use to locate information. Do they browse through the paper page by page, or do they use the index? Ask the students to look carefully at the front page. Ask the following: "Is there anything on the front page that would help you find the comics or the television section?" Help them identify and locate the index. While they look at the index discuss the fact that newspapers are divided into sections. Ask the students to locate the section numbers in the newspaper: "Where are section numbers found?" (Top right-hand corner of each page.) Provide an opportunity for students to identify the number and location of sections in their newspapers. Allow the students to use the index to identify specific features located in the newspaper. While one student names a feature, the remainder of the class can locate the item. This activity can be used as a game, with teams of students competing.

	Team 1	Team 2	Team 3	Team 4
Obituaries	_____	_____	_____	_____
Horoscopes	_____	_____	_____	_____
Classified Ads	_____	_____	_____	_____
Sports Section	_____	_____	_____	_____
Weather	_____	_____	_____	_____
Television	_____	_____	_____	_____
Editorials	_____	_____	_____	_____

d. Continue your introduction to the newspaper by looking at each section of the paper listed in the index. Ask students what information is found in each section. Why would they want to read that section? Cut out examples of articles in each section of the paper. Make a newsprint page for each section of the newspaper.

3. Reinforcement Game—After introducing students to the newspaper, divide the class into teams. Have the teams write specific types of articles on slips of paper. These slips are then drawn, and the teams, using the index and their knowledge of feature locations, compete to see which team will be first to find each story or feature.

	Team 1	Team 2	Team 3	Team 4
An editorial cartoon	——	——	——	——
A report of an NFL football game	——	——	——	——
The 7 P.M. TV show on channel 3	——	——	——	——
A house listed for sale	——	——	——	——
Forecast for today's weather	——	——	——	——
A hero in the comics	——	——	——	——
A letter to the editor	——	——	——	——
A recipe for children	——	——	——	——
The temperature in Moscow	——	——	——	——
Report from the New York Stock Exchange	——	——	——	——
The movie at the _____	——	——	——	——
A pet for sale	——	——	——	——
The latest hairstyle	——	——	——	——
A lost poodle	——	——	——	——

Activity 7-11:
SIGNIFICANCE OF NEWSPAPERS AND PERIODICAL NAMES

TYPE	TERM
● CLASS	● STA
● GROUP	○ LTA
○ IND	○ LC

Purpose:
1. To expand vocabulary
2. To study inferred meaning from newspaper and magazine names
3. To study audience appeal and newspaper and magazine names

Materials:
Titles of many newspapers in the United States and other parts of the world; copies of newspapers, if possible; copies of a variety of magazines; dictionaries.

Grade level:
Middle and upper elementary

Procedures:
1. Look at a number of the newspapers the class is reading and studying.
2. Discuss the fact that newspapers use many different names. Have children offer reasons they think a newspaper might choose a specific name.
3. List the names of some major newspapers. Discuss the significance of the name. Use a dictionary to learn the meaning of each title. Why is it appropriate for a newspaper?
4. Create a bulletin board showing the titles of U.S. and foreign newspapers. On the bulletin board, illustrate the meanings of the newspaper names and provide a written meaning for each title. Following are some examples of newspaper names:

American Newspapers

Los Angeles Times	*Arkansas Gazette*
New York Times	*Indianapolis Star*
Chicago Tribune	*Desert News*—Salt Lake City
Milwaukee Journal	*Minneapolis Star*
Denver Post	*Gulfport Daily Herald*
Idaho Statesman	*Star Telegram*—Fort Worth
Des Moines Register	*Wall Street Journal*

Foreign Newspapers

London Times—England	*Guardian*—Rangoon, Burma
Manchester Guardian—England	*Daily Mail*—London
Ottawa Citizen—Ottawa, Canada	*Pravda*—Russia (means *truth*)
Globe and Mail—Toronto, Canada	*Izvestia*—Russia (means *news*)

5. Discuss the fact that magazines use many different names. Look at several magazines and discuss the meaning of the names, the appropriateness of the names for the subject matter, and the appeal of the names for the desired audiences.

6. Ask students to select a magazine. Have them investigate the subject matter, the appropriateness of the title, and the appeal of the title for the desired audience. Put this information on a poster. Following are some examples of magazine names:

Fortune	*American Home*
Business Week	*House Beautiful*
Time	*Changing Times*
Newsweek	*Life*
U.S. News and World Report	*Seventeen*
Ladies Home Journal	*Spin*

7. Choose a name for a classroom newspaper or magazine. Why would that name be appropriate?

Activity 7–12:

RELATING PARTS OF A NEWSPAPER
TO A BOOK OR STORY

TYPE	TERM
● CLASS	○ STA
● GROUP	● LTA
● IND	○ LC

Purpose:
1. To study parts of a newspaper
2. To write a book report
3. To refine creative writing skills

Materials:
William Pene du Bois's *The 21 Balloons* (1947, 1975); sections of the newspaper—editorial, news, women's, home, sports, entertainment, weather, and so forth.

Grade level:
Middle and upper elementary; this activity is focused on a specific book but would be equally appropriate for many other books or stories

Book summary:
The 21 Balloons is a fantasy story set on the island of Krakatoa before and during the violent volcanic eruption. The time period is between 1860 and 1890, when balloons were the most popular. According to the introduction, "Half of this story is true and the other half might very well have happened. Some of the balloon inventions in this book were actually built with success, some were designed by famous balloonists who didn't have enough money to build them and try them out. The others might easily have happened too. The part about the Pacific Island of Krakatoa is true. There is a volcanic island of that name in the Pacific and it did blow up with the biggest explosion of all time so that it is now half as big as it was in 1883" (p. 6).

Procedures:
1. After studying different parts of a newspaper, the class can try many creative writing activities that use a newspaper format. Read the Newbery Award winner *The 21 Balloons.*
2. Students can select the newspaper approach they would like to use for reporting information from this book. Suggestions include the following:
   a. Write a front-page news story describing Professor William Sherman's unusual voyage in his balloon.
   b. Write a front-page news story relating the true incidents of the volcanic explosion on the island of Krakatoa in Java. Include a worthy headline for this disaster, such as the following:

   "Volcanic Matter Thrown 23 Miles in the Air"
   "Most Terrible Volcanic Explosion in History"
   "Ocean Bed Sinks 900 Feet"
   "50- to 135-Foot Tidal Waves Sweep Coasts"
   "Explosion Heard 3,000 Miles Away"
   "36,000 Perish in Holocaust"

   c. Write a feature article for the home section of the newspaper. Describe a room in the Moroccan House of Marvels. Illustrate your article.

    d. Write an editorial expressing an opinion about the "Gourmet Government," "The Selection of Citizens for Krakatoa," or "Secrecy and Diamonds."

    e. Write a feature article for the fashion section of the newspaper. Illustrate the fashions worn by the citizens of Krakatoa in the 1880s.

    f. Write a feature article for the travel section of the newspaper. Describe and illustrate the wonders of visiting a tropical island in the Pacific Ocean.

    g. Write a feature science article describing the scientific reasons for the eruption of the volcano on Krakatoa or write an article describing the history of ballooning.

    h. Write a story for the recreation section of the paper describing the Airy-Go-Round or write a story about a good place to eat.

    i. Write an article for the sports page, describing ballooning as a sport.

    j. Design advertisements for the paper that relate to the book, such as a furniture ad for a fantastic invention, a restaurant ad for one of the family restaurants, or a travel ad selling a voyage in a balloon.

3. Choose a title for the newspaper. Combine the articles for the newspaper and duplicate the newspaper so that all students have their own copies.

Activity 7–13:
HEADLINES SHOW THE MAIN IDEA

TYPE	TERM
○ CLASS	● STA
● GROUP	○ LTA
● IND	○ LC

Purpose:
1. To understand that a headline shows the main idea of a story
2. To practice writing headlines
3. To learn to identify the main idea of a fairy tale

Materials:
List of headlines describing familiar folk stories; collection of familiar folktales.

Grade level:
Lower and middle elementary

Procedures:
1. Provide a list of headlines that a newspaper might write to introduce familiar folk stories or fairy tales:

> Goat Destroys Troll ("Three Billy Goats Gruff")
> Pigs Finally Defeat Wolf ("Three Little Pigs")
> Prince Overcomes 100-Year Curse ("Sleeping Beauty")
> Cinderwench Hit of the Ball ("Cinderella")
> Animals Terrify Criminals, Capture Jewels ("Bremen Town Musicians")
> Cat Wins Kingdom for Poor Master ("Puss in Boots")
> Ruler Parades in Underwear ("Emperor's New Clothes")
> Old Lamp Has Unbelievable Powers ("Aladdin and the Wonderful Lamp")
> Space Travel Possible with Beanstalk ("Jack and the Beanstalk")

2. Ask children to identify fairy tales represented by the headlines.
3. Ask children to write their own headlines for a group of fairy tales. Use, perhaps, "Rumpelstiltskin," "Tom Thumb," "The Three Bears," "Henny Penny," "The Gingerbread Boy," "Hansel and Gretel," "Little Red Riding Hood," "Dick Whittington and His Cat," "Thumbelina," and "Fat Cat."
4. Allow children to read their headlines to a group so that the group can identify the story described by the headline.

Activity 7–14:

ADVERTISERS TRY TO APPEAL
TO A SPECIFIC POPULATION

TYPE	TERM
o CLASS	● STA
● GROUP	o LTA
o IND	o LC

Purpose:

1. To identify advertisements designed to appeal to a specific population
2. To find words that might appeal to a specific population
3. To write advertisements designed for a specific population

Materials:

Ads from newspapers and magazines that appeal to different age groups and segments of the population; magazines aimed at specific segments of the population.

Grade level:

Middle and upper elementary

Procedures:

1. Discuss the following: "Do all of the people who read advertisements want to buy the same things? How do you think advertisers reach the people who are most likely to buy their products? Are there any differences between readers that allow the advertisers to write a more appealing ad? Who are the groups that advertisers wish to reach?" (Children, sports enthusiasts, teenagers, men, women, home owners, campers, car owners, farmers, ranchers, boat owners, and hobbyists.) "How can each of these groups be reached most efficiently? What are some items each group might want to buy? What would they want to know about the items? What might make the items more appealing to this buyer?"

2. Supply newspapers and magazines. Have students search for advertisements that appeal to specific populations. Find an advertisement designed to appeal to each of the following: a home owner, a child, a car buyer, a man, a teenager, a hobbyist, a sports enthusiast, and a woman. Label each advertisement according to its appeal.

3. Underline any words in the advertisement that might have special appeal to that population.

4. Supply several magazines written for a specific population, such as *Sports Illustrated, Field and Stream, Motorboating and Sailing, Modern Photography, McCall's, Fortune, Business Week, Popular Mechanics, Architectural Digest,* and *Daisy* (Girl Scout magazine). Have the students look at the ads in the magazines. Ask them to identify the advertisers and discuss the relationship between the advertisements and the content of the magazines. The class may divide into groups and create a chart for each type of magazine. For example:

MAGAZINE: *BUSINESS WEEK*

Articles in Magazine

1. Economics
2. Finance
3. Government
4. International outlook

5. Management
6. Marketing
7. Accounting
8. Corporate strategies

Advertisers in Magazine

1. Las Vegas Convention Center
2. Diners' Club
3. 3M—data recording products
4. Western—temporary business help services
5. Lyon Office products—office furniture

6. IBM Computers
7. Xerox Compact Copiers
8. Swissair
9. Apple Computers
10. RCA Communications

Examples of advertisements with key words underlined:

850,000 <u>square feet</u> 4 <u>exhibit halls</u> 50 <u>meeting rooms</u> <u>boost attendance</u> and <u>profits</u>	<u>double</u> <u>sales</u> and <u>production</u>	<u>reduce</u> <u>costs</u> $5,000 per month $60,00 <u>annual</u> savings

---

PEOPLE WHO PROBABLY READ *BUSINESS WEEK*

1. People who work for large businesses
2. People in business management
3. People who make buying decisions for businesses
4. People who own their own businesses
5. White-collar workers (the ads show businesspeople in suits)
6. People who earn high salaries (they fly to Europe; they are looking for investments)

---

5. Ask the students to select a particular population, to consider its needs, and to write an advertisement to sell something to that group. Tell them to make their ads as appealing as possible.

Activity 7–15:

CRITICAL READING—FACT VERSUS FICTION

TYPE	TERM
o CLASS	o STA
● GROUP	● LTA
o IND	o LC

Purpose:
1. To define the difference between fact and fiction
2. To identify factual sections of the newspaper
3. To identify fictional sections of the newspaper
4. To identify factual magazine articles
5. To identify fictional magazine articles

Materials:
Examples of factual and fictional materials; newspaper articles that illustrate fact and fiction (*My Weekly Reader* and the like); magazine articles that illustrate fact and fiction (*Jack and Jill, Highlights for Children,* and the like); dictionary and thesaurus.

Grade level:
Lower and middle elementary

Procedures:
1. Discuss with children their viewpoint of what is fact and what is fiction. Make a list of characteristics for fact and fiction.

2. Ask the students to find the words *fact* and *fiction* in their classroom dictionary and thesaurus. Write a definition and synonyms for *fact* and *fiction* on the chalkboard. Compare this list with the children's previous list. Ask the students the following: "Are the two lists similar? Did we give an accurate definition for fact and fiction? What new information do we have now?"

Fact
Meaning: Something that has happened or is true. Synonyms: truth, reality, certainty, accuracy

Fiction
Meaning: Something that has been made up; something that did not happen. Synonyms: story, tale, yarn, invention, fantasy, falsehood, lie, fib

3. Some articles containing fact or fiction are easy to identify. Ask the following: "How do we know for sure which of two articles is fact and which is fiction?" Then read articles such as the following:

Man's Best Friend

Dogs have been helping humans for thousands of years. Early humans tamed and trained dogs to go hunting and protect their camps. Later, dogs were trained to guard and herd flocks of sheep. The Egyptians may have been the earliest people to keep dogs as pets. If you are looking for a dog today, you have six different groups of dogs to choose from. The first group includes the sporting dogs such as the pointers and spaniels used for hunting birds. The second kind are the hounds, including bassetts and elkhounds, which are often used for hunting fur-bearing animals such as raccoons or squirrels. The third group includes the working dogs such as German shepherds and huskies. Terriers are the fourth group of dogs and are very good at catching rats. The fifth kind of dog is the toy dog including chihuahuas and the smallest poodles. The final group is the non-sporting dog such as the standard poodle. At one time, these dogs were used for hunting, but now they are owned as house pets.

The Three Poodle Puppies

Three poodle puppies named Raja, Tooto, and Samantha lived in a pretty house on the edge of a large woods. They were happy puppies and spent their days chasing butterflies in the meadow, eating their mother's delicious dinners, and sleeping in their own baskets by the fireplace. This ideal life continued until one day when mother poodle walked out to the meadow and said, "Raja, Tooto, and Samantha, you are big dogs now, and you must learn a trade so you can get a job." Mother poodle told Raja, "You are very good with your hands. You will help your father carve toys for boys and girls." Then she turned to Tooto and said, "Tooto, you jump so high when you chase butterflies and land so gracefully on your feet that we will send you to Madam Fifi to learn to be a ballerina." Finally, she turned to Samantha and said, "Samantha, you like to bring home little animals so we will send you to the Woods Veterinary College so you can take care of the woodland animals when they are hurt or sick."

The next morning, Raja, Tooto, and Samantha dressed in their very best clothes, said goodbye to their mother, and started out to learn their new jobs. As time passed, they learned to be a very good wood carver, ballerina, and veterinarian. But they never forgot those happy days they spent chasing butterflies.

4. Have the students identify which story is fact and which is fiction. Compare the two stories with the list of information compiled about fact and fiction. Ask students the following: "When did you decide the second story was fiction? What things in the story could not happen? How can you be positive that the first story is fact?"

Fact	*Fiction*
"Man's Best Friend"	"Three Poodle Puppies"
1. Listed information about dogs that can be checked.	1. Mother poodles cannot talk.
2. Named six real groupings of dogs that can be checked.	2. Poodles cannot carve toys or go to school.
	3. Poodles do not wear clothes.

5. The two stories contain elements that are easy to identify as fact or fiction. Other stories and articles, however, are not as easy to classify. Children often have difficulty telling the difference between stories that actually happened and stories that did not happen but seem lifelike. Read several realistic selections to children and discuss the differences between fact and fiction and how to identify them.

6. Allow students to look through newspapers and magazines (include *My Weekly Reader* and children's magazines such as *Jack and Jill* and *Highlights* for the younger elementary child). Select articles that really happened and others that did not really happen. Create a bulletin board of fact and fiction. Draw pictures to illustrate the stories and articles.

7. Motivate children to write or dictate both factual and fictional stories about a specific subject. For example, bring into the classroom a small animal such as a baby chick, rabbit, kitten, or hamster. Allow the children to look at the animal, to touch it, and to observe its habits. Discuss the care of the animal, why people would own it, its characteristics, and any personal experiences the children have had with that kind of animal. Then have them write a factual account of the animal, perhaps inside a large drawing of the animal. Next, have the children think of an imaginary experience their animal might have. Ask them the following: "Does your animal have a secret wish? What would it want to do? Where would it want to go? What special things can it do? Who are its friends? Does it have any prob-

lems? If you could talk to it, what would you talk about?" Ask students to write these fantasy stories inside a fanciful representation of the animal or in comic strip format using bubbles for speech.

THE "TALL TALE" CHICK

Activity 7–16:

CRITICAL READING—FACT VERSUS OPINION

	TYPE	TERM
	○ CLASS	○ STA
	● GROUP	● LTA
	○ IND	○ LC

Purpose:

1. To define the difference between fact and opinion
2. To identify factual sections of the newspaper
3. To identify opinion sections of the newspaper
4. To identify vocabulary terms related to factual writing and to opinion

Grade level:

Middle and upper elementary

Procedures:

1. Read the following three statements or write them on cards for students to read independently:

   a. The Model T Ford was built in 1908 by Henry Ford. In 1912 the Model T was the first car to be mass-produced. Mass production reduced the price of cars and allowed more people to buy them. There have been many changes since these early cars. In 1915 tops and windshields became standard equipment on cars. Rear-view mirrors, brake lights, and windshield wipers were added in 1916. Four-wheel brakes were added in 1923, and automobile heaters were introduced in 1926. Car radios were added in 1929. The first automatic transmission was placed in a car in 1937.

   b. The automobile may be one of the most dangerous machines invented by humans. Fumes from gasoline engines cause damage to plants, animals, and people. Bands of highways cover the green grass with cement and destroy the forests. Billboards block out the beauty of the countryside. The automobile kills many pedestrians and drivers every year. It would be better to go back to the simpler life people lived before this dangerous invention.

   c. The automobile affects all of our lives. It may be one of humanity's greatest helpers. Instead of walking or riding in a horse-drawn carriage, you can now use the car to buy groceries, take a trip, or go to work. Distances that would once have taken hours are now covered in minutes. Cars also provide many jobs. Men and women work in factories to build cars. They also work on highway crews to build roads for the cars. The oil industry provides many jobs so that cars can travel. People would not live well without the car for transportation.

2. After the students read the three paragraphs, discuss the differences between them. Ask students the following: "Which statements are factual? Why do you believe they are factual? How can you check to make sure the statements are factual? Why are the other paragraphs not factual?" (Help students identify the final two paragraphs as someone's opinion.) "Are the opinions expressed in these two paragraphs similar?" (Help students develop the understanding that the second paragraph has a negative opinion or bias and the third paragraph has a positive opinion.)

3. The same article may contain both fact and opinion. Ask students to underline facts that can be checked in the preceding paragraphs with red pen or pencil; tell them to circle statements that are someone's belief with a blue pen or pencil.

4. Then have students look through various sections of the newspaper. Ask them to locate factual articles and opinion articles. Tell them to underline factual state-

ments with red and have them circle opinion statements with blue. Place the predominantly factual articles in one group and the predominantly opinion articles in another group. Compile a list of the types of newspaper articles that are usually factual and those that are usually opinion.

5. Create a bulletin board of factual versus opinion newspaper articles.

Fact		*Opinion*	
Statements can be checked for proof.		Statements include beliefs.	
World news	Local and state news	Editorials	Editorial cartoons
Obituaries	Births	Letters to the editor	
Sports news	TV	Horoscopes	Advice columns

6. Choose a subject to write about as a factual news article and as an article containing considerable personal opinion. Possible subjects are a Little League baseball game, the Girl Scout cookie sale, the school lunch program, and Saturday morning children's television.

REFERENCES

Shanker, A. (1993, March 7). Where we stand. *New York Times,* p. E7.

CHILDREN'S LITERATURE REFERENCES

Milne, A. A. *Winnie-the-Pooh.* Decorations by Ernest H. Shepard. New York: E. P. Dutton, 1926; Dell, 1973.

Milne, A. A. *The House at Pooh Corner.* Decorations by Ernest H. Shepard. New York: E. P. Dutton, 1928; Dell, 1973.

Pene du Bois, William. *The 21 Balloons.* New York: Viking, 1947, 1975.

Pyle, Howard. *The Merry Adventures of Robin Hood.* n.p., 1883; New York: Scribner's, 1946.

Spyri, Johanna. *Heidi.* Illustrated by Greta Elgaard. n.p., 1884; New York, Macmillan, 1962.

Stevenson, Robert Louis. *Treasure Island.* New York: Scribner's, 1911.

Twain, Mark. *The Adventures of Tom Sawyer.* Illustrated by John Falter. n.p., 1876; New York: Macmillan, 1962.

White, E. B. *Charlotte's Web.* Illustrated by Garth Williams. New York: Harper & Row, 1952.

Wilder, Laura Ingalls. *Little House on the Prairie.* Illustrated by Garth Williams. New York: Harper & Row, 1941.

8

Multicultural Activities

Meeting the needs of all students in a multicultural nation is an important challenge for educators. Sensitivity to the needs of children from European, Native American, African-American, Asian, and Hispanic backgrounds has led to the realization that the language arts program should heighten self-esteem and create a respect for the individuals, contributions, and values of all cultures.

The language arts teacher can use positive multicultural literature and related activities to achieve these goals. Multicultural activities can help children to identify a multicultural heritage, understand sociological change, respect the values of minority groups, raise aspirations, and expand an understanding of the products of imagination and creativity (Norton, 1999).

Folklore is not only enjoyable literature but also one of the best sources for discovering the traditional values of a cultural group. Research by Franchot Ballinger (1984), Michael Dorris (1979), and Donna Norton (1990) recommends a sequence of study of Native American literature that begins with studying broad oral traditions, narrows to specific tribal experiences as expressed in mythology, continues with biographical and autobiographical study of specific cultural areas, and concludes with a study of contemporary literature. Many of the activities developed in this chapter begin with a study of the values of a specific culture as revealed by the folklore of that culture.

Students can be taught language arts skills while learning to respect different ethnic cultures. Because the activities in this chapter are designed to develop specific language arts objectives, such as literature appreciation, fluency in oral language, evaluative comprehension, creative writing, plot and character development, author's point of view, symbolic language, fact versus fiction, and aesthetic development, multicultural education also provides the objectives of the basic language arts education.

Comparative literature activities are excellent resources for multicultural education because they encourage students to identify and appreciate similarities and differences across cultures. This chapter concludes with several activities that encourage students to compare the various plot developments of traditional folktales from different cultures; to appreciate the assimilation of folktale elements and plots into different cultures; to analyze the content of music, understand the historical context of a people, and understand a common need for music across cultures; to develop an understanding that discovering one's own heritage brings pride to individuals from all backgrounds; to develop an understanding that people from all backgrounds have similar needs and feelings; and to develop an understanding that people from all backgrounds have desires and dreams and that they may work very hard to reach their goals.

The criteria for evaluating the multicultural literature used in this section are from Norton's *The Effective Teaching of Language Arts,* 5th edition (1997).

Activity 8–1:

TRADITIONAL VALUES—AFRICAN FOLKLORE

TYPE	TERM
● CLASS	● STA
● GROUP	● LTA
○ IND	○ LC

Purpose:

1. To develop an appreciation for a cultural heritage that values storytelling, verbal ability, wit, intelligence, beauty, and imagination
2. To listen for and to identify traditional values found in African folktales

Materials:

Gail Haley's *A Story, A Story* (1970) and Walter Dean Myers's *The Story of Three Kingdoms* (1995); values chart for African folklore.

Grade level:

Middle and upper elementary

Book summaries:

A Story, A Story is a folktale that reveals how Ananse, the spider man, outwitted various animals and brought stories from the sky god down to the people. *The Story of the Three Kingdoms* reveals the power of sharing and knowledge.

Procedures:

1. Discuss various ways in which students can identify traditional values found in folktales. For example, they can read the folktale to discover answers to each of the following questions:
   a. What reward or rewards are desired?
   b. What actions are rewarded or admired?
   c. What actions are punished or despised?
   d. What rewards are given to the heroes, heroines, or great people in the stories?
   e. What are the personal characteristics of the heroes, heroines, or great people in the stories?
2. Print each of these questions on a chart. Allow room to include several African folktales. When students read various African folktales, they may use the chart to identify and discuss traditional values. The following chart identifies two books that teachers could use for this activity:

VALUES IDENTIFIED IN AFRICAN FOLKTALES

Questions for Values	A Story, A Story	The Story of the Three Kingdoms
What reward is desired?	stories from powerful sky god	ability to share forest with powerful elephant, sea with shark, and air with hawk
What actions are rewarded or admired?	outwitting the leopard, the hornet, and the fairy	learning from stories that encourage the people to work together and conquer powerful animals

VALUES IDENTIFIED IN AFRICAN FOLKTALES

Questions for Values	A Story, A Story	The Story of the Three Kingdoms
What actions are punished or despised?		
What rewards are given to the heroes, heroines, or great people?	oral stories to delight the people	understanding that in oral stories can be found wisdom and in wisdom knowledge
What are the personal characteristics of the heroes, heroines, or great people?	small old man, intelligence, verbal ability	humans with the gift of stories who can learn from the stories ability to share wisdom

3. Introduce Haley's *A Story, A Story.* Ask students to listen carefully so that they will be able to answer the questions and identify the values that will be printed on the chart.

4. After reading *A Story, A Story* aloud, ask the students to identify and place the values in the proper location on the chart. Discuss the importance of the value in the traditional tale. (This approach may be used to identify, discuss, and compare the values in folktales found in any culture.)

5. During other reading sessions share *The Story of the Three Kingdoms.* Follow the previously developed listening, listing, and discussing procedures. After students have identified the answers to the questions, ask them to compare their findings. Do they believe that *The Story of the Three Kingdoms* is based on values that are similar to those found in the oral traditional tales? Why or why not? Make sure that they understand that both stories reflect the value of oral stories and the need for wisdom and knowledge.

6. Additional African folktales may be used for this activity. The following books may be read aloud or silently before the identification of traditional African values:

> Ashley Bryan's *Beat the Story-Drum, Pum-Pum* (1980)
> Tololwa Mollel's *A Promise to the Sun: An African Story* (1992)
> Verna Aardema's *What's So Funny, Ketu? A Nuer Tale* (1982)
> Harold Courlander's *The Crest and the Hide: And Other African Stories of Heroes, Chiefs, Bards, Hunters, Sorcerers, and Common People* (1982)
> Nancy Raines Day's *The Lion's Whiskers: An Ethiopian Folktale* (1995)
> Dianne Stewart's *Gift of the Sun: A Tale from South Africa* (1996)

Activity 8–2:
STORYTELLING—AFRICAN FOLKLORE

TYPE	TERM
● CLASS	○ STA
● GROUP	● LTA
○ IND	○ LC

Purpose:
1. To develop an appreciation for a cultural heritage that values storytelling, verbal ability, wit, intelligence, beauty, and imagination
2. To recognize literary traditions of African storytellers
3. To develop fluency in using oral language to communicate effectively
4. To follow the plot and the character development in a story and to retell the story using traditional storytelling techniques

Materials:
African folklore suitable for storytelling; examples include Gail Haley's *A Story, A Story* (1970), Verna Aardema's *Who's in Rabbit's House?* (1977) and *Why Mosquitoes Buzz in People's Ears* (1975), and Ashley Bryan's *Beat the Story-Drum, Pum-Pum* (1980) and *The Ox of the Wonderful Horns and Other African Folktales* (1971); examples of story openers and story endings used by traditional African storytellers.

Grade level:
All grades

Book summaries:
A Story, A Story is a folktale that reveals how Ananse, the spider man, outwitted various animals and brought stories from the sky god down to the people. *Who's in Rabbit's House?* presents a folktale in the form of a play that features players wearing masks to represent the various animals in the story. *Why Mosquitoes Buzz in People's Ears* is a cumulative tale that reveals why mosquitoes make their specific noise. *Beat the Story-Drum, Pum-Pum* and *The Ox of the Wonderful Horns and Other African Folktales* are both collections of folktales that are very appropriate for storytelling.

Procedures:
1. After you have told several stories to the class, discuss possible advantages of telling a story rather than reading a story.
2. Share information with the class about how traditional folktales were handed down from one generation to the next by oral storytellers. Tell the class that the art of traditional storytelling, cultivated in every culture by people from every level of society, reflects the culture, the nature of the land, the social contacts, and the traditional values of the people. African folktales, for example, are characterized by a highly developed oral tradition. The influence of this oral language is shown in the repetitive language and interaction between the audience and the storyteller.
3. Ask the children to identify the ways in which a storyteller may begin a story. (Most children will probably identify "Once upon a time.") If they cannot identify any common story openings, read them several examples from folktales. Tell the students that storytellers from many cultures used a beginning that introduced their listeners to an earlier time. African storytellers might begin a story with the following introduction:

Storyteller:	Listen to a tale! Listen to a tale!
Audience:	A tale for fun, for fun,
	Your throat is a gong,
	Your body a locust;
	bring it here for me to roast!
Storyteller:	Children, listen to a tale,
	A tale for fun, for fun.

Another common story introduction was

"Once upon a time, a very good time
Not my time, nor your time, old people's time."

Read several introductions aloud and discuss what each one means. Explore the similarities between the introductions and identify the traditional values found in African folktales.

4. Search the folktales listed in the materials to discover how interpreters and translators of traditional folklore introduced their stories. Are there differences in the type of tale or the people who told the stories? For example, students can find these story openers in Bryan's *The Ox of the Wonderful Horns and Other African Folktales:*

"We do not mean, we do not really mean, that what we are going to say is true."
"Listen, let me tell the story of . . ."
"I never tire of telling the tale of . . ."
"Listen, brothers and sisters, to this story of . . ."
"There are those who enjoy telling of . . ."

Bryan's *Beat the Story-Drum, Pum-Pum* includes the following openings:

"I've told one tale, here's another.
Call your sister, call your brother."
"Beat the story-drum, pum-pum! Tell us a big story, brum-brum!"
"If you're talking about the beginning of things, you've got to go back, way, way back, back to the time when the animals had no tails."

Develop a comparative chart showing the locations of the stories and include examples of the story openers.

5. Ask students to identify any endings that storytellers may use. (They will probably identify some form of "And they lived happily ever after.") Tell the students that African storytellers also used certain types of endings. For example, if the story was dramatic it might end with one of the following:

Hausa Suka zona ("they remained")
Mahezu ("finished")

An exaggerated story might end in the following way:

"Chase the rooster and catch the hen
I'll never tell a lie like that again."

If the story was humorous it might end in this way:

"They lived in peace, they died in peace
And they were buried in a pot of candle grease."

Read the endings aloud and discuss what they mean. Consider why each ending might be appropriate for a dramatic tale, an exaggerated tale, or a humorous tale (see activity 8–3).

6. Model a storytelling experience for the students by telling an African folktale with a traditional introduction and ending.

7. Allow the students to select African folktales and develop their own stories to share with the group. Encourage them to plan their stories using the steps recommended in activity 6–21, "Storytelling." Also encourage them to use appropriate opening and closing phrases. (Activity 8–3 encourages students to evaluate whether the stories are dramatic, exaggerated, or humorous.)

8. Develop a chart on which students identify general openings and endings found in folktales from various African countries.

Activity 8–3:
DRAMA, EXAGGERATION, AND HUMOR IN AFRICAN FOLKTALES

TYPE	TERM
● CLASS	○ STA
● GROUP	● LTA
○ IND	○ LC

Purpose:

1. To evaluate if African folktales are dramatic tales, exaggerated tales, or humorous tales
2. To develop appreciation for a culture that created a variety of literary forms and for people who created tales that could depict a sense of justice as well as rollicking humor

Materials:

Examples of storytelling closings that were used for dramatic, exaggerated, and humorous tales; collections of African folktales including Ashley Bryan's *Beat the Story-Drum, Pum-Pum* (1980) and *The Ox of the Wonderful Horns and Other African Folktales* (1971), Harold Courlander's *The Crest and the Hide: And Other African Stories of Heroes, Chiefs, Bards, Hunters, Sorcerers, and Common People* (1982), Verna Aardema's *Tales from the Story Hat* (1960), and Barbara K. Walker's *The Dancing Palm Tree and Other Nigerian Folktales* (1990); collections of African-American folktales, including Mary E. Lyons's *Raw Head, Bloody Bones: African-American Tales of the Supernatural* (1991) and Virginia Hamilton's *When Birds Could Talk and Bats Could Sing: The Adventures of Bruh Sparrow, Sis Wren, and Their Friends* (1996).

Grade level:

Middle and upper elementary

Book summaries:

Beat the Story-Drum, Pum-Pum and *The Ox of the Wonderful Horns and Other African Folktales* include many stories that have both humor and exaggeration. *The Crest and the Hide* includes tales of drama and exaggeration. *Tales from the Story Hat* is a collection of stories selected for oral storytelling. *The Dancing Palm Tree and Other Nigerian Folktales* includes tales from Nigeria selected for their ability to reveal morals or human truths. *Raw Head, Bloody Bones: African-American Tales of the Supernatural* includes folktales about goblins, ghosts, monsters, and superhumans. *When Birds Could Talk and Bats Could Sing* includes eight African-American tales.

Procedures:

1. Review the story endings identified and discussed in activity 8–2, "Storytelling—African Folklore." Discuss the meanings of each of the following terms: *dramatic, exaggerated,* and *humorous.* Ask the students to describe the characteristics and content of stories that might be considered under each category. For example, dramatic folktales contain considerable conflict and are characterized as having strong, highly emotional themes; exaggerated folktales increase or enlarge an action or a character beyond what is normally possible; and humorous folktales are simply funny, comical, and amusing.

2. Print each of the categories on a chart. Leave space for the titles, sources, and characteristics of each folktale that make the story dramatic, exaggerated, and/or humorous. This chart may be used on successive days when various African tales are read, discussed, and evaluated. The following chart identifies a few of the stories that might be read, discussed, and evaluated:

DRAMA, EXAGGERATION, AND HUMOR IN AFRICAN FOLKTALES

African Folktale	Source	Examples of Drama	Examples of Exaggeration	Examples of Humor
The Third Gift	Juba			
"Elephant and Frog Go Courting" (*The Ox of the Wonderful Horns*)	Angola			
"The Husband That Counted Spoonfuls" (*Beat the Story-Drum, Pum-Pum*)	Hausa			
"How Spider Got a Thin Waist" (*The Adventures of Spider*)	Liberia			
"All Things Are Linked" (*The Crest and the Hide*)	Lega			

3. Choose and read a folktale aloud to the students while they listen for examples of dramatic, exaggerated, or humorous incidents or characterizations. After reading the folktale, ask students to identify these characteristics. Discuss their reasons for selecting that category and write the examples on the appropriate place on the chart. (A story may have more than one type of characteristic.) When the examples are finished, ask the students to decide whether they believe the story is predominantly dramatic, exaggerated, or humorous. Ask individual students to justify the selections. Discuss which story ending students believe would be the most appropriate for the story and why.

4. On subsequent days read additional books to the class or have students read the books silently. Fill in the chart characteristics and discuss the reasons for the selections.

Activity 8–4:
TALES FROM THE STORY HAT

TYPE	TERM
● CLASS	● STA
● GROUP	○ LTA
○ IND	○ LC

Purpose:

1. To develop appreciation for African folklore
2. To listen to or read African folklore and to identify objects that represent main ideas or characters
3. To identify the relationship between an object and the main idea or character that the object represents

Materials:

Picture books that are appropriate for reading aloud to lower elementary children include Verna Aardema's *Who's in Rabbit's House?* (1977), *Why Mosquitoes Buzz in People's Ears* (1975), *Tales from the Story Hat* (1960), and *Bringing the Rain to Kapiti Plain: A Nandi Tale* (1981); Virginia Hamilton's *The Time-Ago Tales of Jahdu* (1969); Gail Haley's *A Story, A Story* (1970); Gerald McDermott's *Anansi the Spider: A Tale from the Ashanti* (1972), and *Zomo the Rabbit: A Trickster Tale from West Africa* (1992); and Robert D. San Souci's *Sukey and the Mermaid* (1992); cutouts or objects representing the main idea or character from each story.

Grade level:

Lower elementary

Book summaries:

Who's in Rabbit's House is a humorous story about animals that are outwitted by one of the smaller animals. *Why Mosquitoes Buzz in People's Ears* is a "why" tale about the actions of the mosquito. *Tales from the Story Hat* is a collection of tales that are appropriate for storytelling. *The Time-Ago Tales of Jahdu* includes four stories about a mischievous being. *A Story, A Story* tells about the spider man's bargain with the sky god; through this bargain, stories are brought to the people. *Anansi the Spider: A Tale from the Ashanti* is a tale of a spider who has sons with special powers. *Zomo the Rabbit* is a trickster tale that shows the importance of courage, sense, and caution. *Sukey and the Mermaid,* a story transported from West Africa to the Sea Islands of South Carolina, presents the story of a girl and a mermaid.

Procedures:

1. This activity is based on the actions of story minstrels in Africa who carried nets containing small objects or wore hats with articles suspended from the brim. When a listener selected an item, the storyteller responded with an appropriate story.
2. Create a story hat like the one shown on the cover of *Tales from the Story Hat* or create objects for a story net by cutting symbolic objects from cardboard, using miniature objects, or locating real objects that suggest the main idea, plot, or characters from a story. Examples of objects include a hut or a rabbit (*Who's in Rabbit's House?*), a mosquito (*Why Mosquitoes Buzz in People's Ears*), a gum tupelo tree (*The Time-Ago Tales of Jahdu*), an old man or a box containing stories (*A Story, A Story*), a cloud or a bow and arrow (*Bringing the Rain to Kapiti Plain*), a large spider (*Anansi the Spider*), and a rabbit (*Zomo the Rabbit*).
3. Allow the children to select an object from the story hat or the story net. Discuss the object and encourage the students to form hypotheses about the meaning of

the object in the story. Ask them to listen to the story and consider how the object is used in the story.

4. Read the story to the students and discuss the meaning of the object as it was used in the story. How closely did their predictions match the story?

5. After you have read all of the stories, use the same story hat or story net to motivate children to retell the stories. Allow students to select an item and then retell the related story.

POETRY EXPRESSES FEELINGS

TYPE	TERM
● CLASS	● STA
● GROUP	○ LTA
○ IND	○ LC

Purpose:
1. To participate in a creative writing activity
2. To improve creative writing through a processing activity that includes brainstorming and word webbing
3. To listen for examples of feeling happy and unhappy and liking, waiting for, and loving someone
4. To interpret feelings as expressed in illustrations
5. To develop an understanding that children from all backgrounds have similar needs and feelings

Materials: Nikki Grimes's *Something on My Mind* (1978).

Grade level: Early and middle elementary

Book summary: *Something on My Mind* is a collection of contemporary poems that reveal the joys, hopes, fears, and sorrows of children. The black-and-white illustrations add to the feelings reflected in the poems.

Procedures:
1. Share with children the information that poets frequently express their hopes, joys, sorrows, and fears through their poetry. Tell the children that you will read poems in which the poet expresses emotions about feeling happy, feeling unhappy, liking someone, waiting for someone, and loving someone. Encourage the students to discuss the importance of these feelings in their own lives.
2. Before reading the poems, draw a semantic map or web in which the title of the book is at the center and the feelings are drawn out from the web. Leave the next level of webbing blank until the poems are read. The following semantic map is an example:

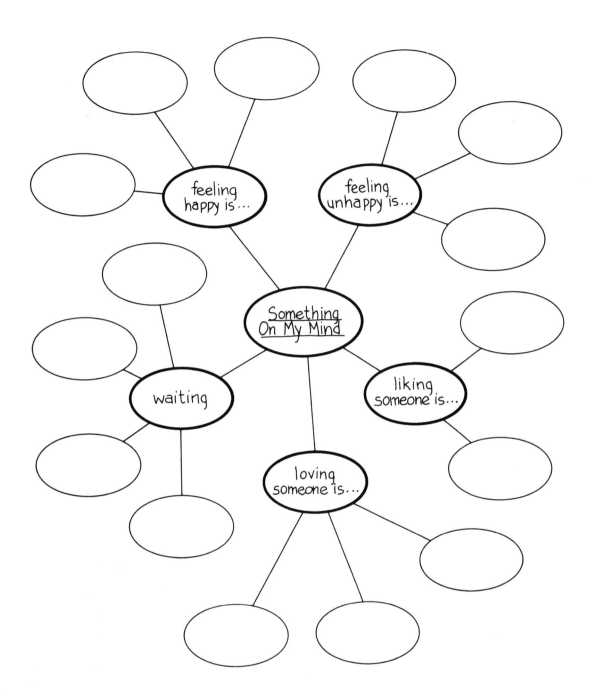

3. Read *Something on My Mind* aloud. Ask the children to listen carefully for examples that will complete the web.

4. Following the oral reading of *Something on My Mind,* ask the children to fill in the missing examples. The web will look like the following example:

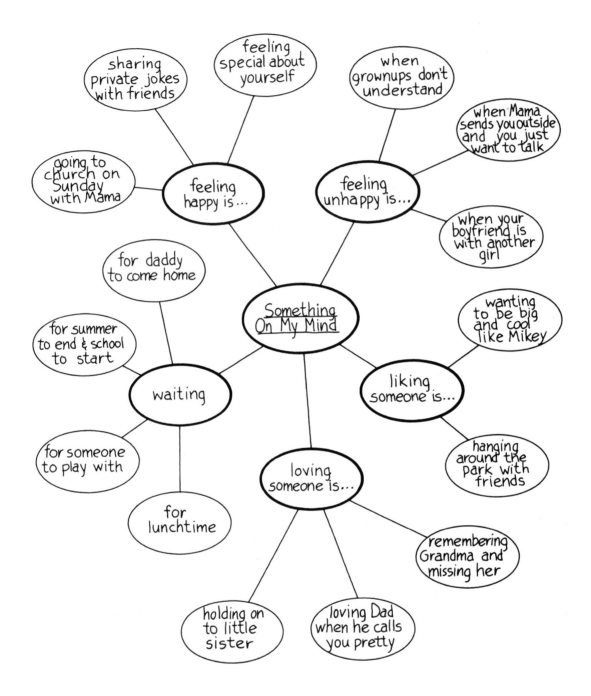

5. Have the children look at the illustrations and discuss how the artist used the illustrations to create the moods of the poems.

6. Use the original categories to draw another web. Ask the students to consider their own feelings and fill in what feeling happy is and so forth. Ask them to think about what makes them feel happy, what makes them feel unhappy, what liking someone is, what waiting feels like, and what loving someone means to them. Have them complete the web during an individual or group activity.

7. Have the students write poems of their own. Begin the poems with phrases such as "Love is . . . ," "Feeling happy is . . . ," or "Feeling sad is . . . ."

8. Have the students illustrate their poems and display them for others to read and enjoy.

Activity 8-6:

TRADITIONAL VALUES—
NATIVE AMERICAN FOLKLORE

TYPE	TERM
● CLASS	● STA
● GROUP	● LTA
○ IND	○ LC

Purpose:
1. To develop an appreciation for a cultural heritage that places importance on oral tradition; respect for nature; understanding between animals and humans; the knowledge of elderly people; folklore as a means of passing on cultural and tribal beliefs; and diversity of Native American folktales, cultures, and customs
2. To listen for and identify traditional values found in Native American folklore

Materials:
Tomie dePaola's *The Legend of the Bluebonnet* (1983); Paul Goble's *Star Boy* (1983); values chart for Native American folklore.

Grade level:
Middle and upper elementary

Book summaries:
The Legend of the Bluebonnet is a Comanche tale that shows how unselfish actions are rewarded. *Star Boy* is a Blackfoot tale that reveals the importance of courageous and wise actions.

Procedures:
1. Use the same questions listed in activity 8-1, "Traditional Values—African Folklore." Develop a chart with the questions and books that include various values. (Using the same chart for different cultures will help students compare the traditional values.) The following chart identifies two books that could be used for this activity:

VALUES IDENTIFIED IN NATIVE AMERICAN FOLKLORE

Questions for Values	The Legend of the Bluebonnet (Comanche Indian)	Star Boy (Blackfoot Indian)
What reward is desired?	to end the drought and famine to save the land and the people	to remove a scar to marry the chief's daughter
What actions are rewarded or admired?	sacrifice of a loved object to save the tribe obedience to the will of the Great Spirit	courage obedience to the Creator
What actions are punished or despised?	selfishness taking from the earth without giving	disobedience cast out of Sky World and made unhappy

VALUES IDENTIFIED IN NATIVE AMERICAN FOLKLORE

Questions for Values	The Legend of the Bluebonnet (Comanche Indian)	Star Boy (Blackfoot Indian)
What rewards are given to the heroes, heroines, or great people?	bluebonnets beautiful flowers a sign of forgiveness rain honored name change	scar removed married chief's daughter happiness life in Sky World after death
What are the personal characteristics of the heroes, heroines, or great people?	unselfishly loved her people willing to give her most prized possession	poor courageous respect for wisdom of animals wisdom purity honoring the Creator

2. Introduce dePaola's *The Legend of the Bluebonnet*. Ask the students to listen for answers to the questions printed on the chart.

3. After reading *The Legend of the Bluebonnet* aloud, have the students identify and place the values in the proper location on the chart and discuss the importance of the values to the traditional tale.

4. During another class time, follow the same procedures with Goble's *Star Boy*.

5. Additional Native American folktales may be used for this activity. The following books may be read aloud or silently before the identification of traditional Native American values:

> Terri Cohlene's *Turquoise Boy: A Navajo Legend* (1990)
> Lois Duncan's *The Magic of Spider Woman* (1996)
> Paul Goble's *The Gift of the Sacred Dog* (1980)
> Olaf Baker's *Where the Buffaloes Begin* (1981)
> Penny Pollock's *The Turkey Girl: A Zuni Cinderella Story* (1996)
> Michael Rosen's *Crow and Hawk: A Traditional Pueblo Indian Story* (1995)

Activity 8–7:

STORYTELLING—NATIVE AMERICAN FOLKLORE

TYPE	TERM
● CLASS	○ STA
● GROUP	● LTA
○ IND	○ LC

Purpose:

1. To develop an appreciation for a cultural heritage that places importance on oral tradition; respect for nature; understanding between animals and humans; the knowledge of elderly people; folklore as a means of passing on cultural and tribal beliefs; and diversity of Native American folklore, cultures, and customs

2. To recognize literary traditions of Native American storytellers

3. To develop fluency in using oral language to communicate effectively

4. To follow plot and character development in a story and to retell the story using appropriate storytelling techniques

Materials:

Native American folklore suitable for storytelling. The following texts contain collections of folklore from various locations: Michael J. Caduto and Joseph Bruchac's *Keepers of the Animals: Native American Stories and Wildlife Activities for Children* (1991), Christine Normandin's *Echoes of the Elders: The Stories and Paintings of Chief Lalooska* (1997), Maurice Metayer's *Tales from the Igloo* (1972), and Jean Guard Monroe and Ray A. Williamson's *They Dance in the Sky: Native American Star Myths* (1987); examples of individual stories that are appropriate for storytelling, such as Barbara Juster Esbensen's *The Star Maiden* (1988) and Paul Goble's *Iktomi and the Berries* (1989) and *Iktomi and the Boulder* (1988).

Grade level:

All grades

Book summaries:

Keepers of the Animals is a large collection of tales from numerous North American tribal areas. *Echoes of the Elders: The Stories and Paintings of Chief Lelooska* is a collection of tales from the Indians of the Northwest Coast of North America. *Tales from the Igloo* is a collection of Copper Eskimo tales. *They Dance in the Sky: Native American Star Myths* is a collection of stories from various tribes developed around the theme of star myths. *The Star Maiden* is an Ojibway tale that tells about the creation of water lilies. *Iktomi and the Berries* and *Iktomi and the Boulder* are trickster tales from the Lakota Sioux.

Procedures:

1. After you have told several stories to the class, discuss possible advantages of telling a story rather than reading a story.

2. To develop background information about the oral tradition in folklore, follow the discussion suggestions for activity 8–2, "Storytelling—African Folklore."

3. Explain to the students that African and Native American storytellers developed styles of telling stories over centuries of oral tradition. Storytelling was an important part of earlier Indian life, and stories were carefully passed down from one generation to the next. It was quite common for Indians to gather around a fire or sit around their homes and listen to stories. Each tribesman told a story, and the storytelling sessions frequently continued for long periods. Several collectors of tales and observers of storytellers have identified opening sentences, storytelling styles, and endings that characterize the storytelling of various tribes. These techniques may be used to make the storytelling experience more authentic.

4. Write the following story openings on the chalkboard or on a chart where the class may read them.

Navaho storytellers frequently began their stories with one of these openings:

> "In the beginning, when the world was new . . ."
> "At the time when men and animals were all the same and spoke the same language . . ."

White Mountain Apache frequently opened their stories with

> "Long, long ago, they say . . ."

Discuss the meanings of each introduction and consider how the introduction relates to traditional Indian values.

5. Use the folktales listed in the materials section to discover how interpreters and translators of traditional folklore introduced their stories. Are there differences according to tribe or region? For example, students can find the following examples in Normandin's *Echoes of the Elders: The Stories and Paintings of Chief Lalooska* (Kwakiutle, Northwest Coast):

> "Once there was a beautiful village."
> "Many generations ago, there lived . . ."
> "One day Sea Gull became jealous of the daylight."
> "Our ancestors believed there were . . ."

Develop a comparative chart showing tribes and listing examples of story openers.

6. Share with the students information about the Native American storytelling style. For example, storytellers from the Northwest used a terse, staccato, and rapid style to tell their stories. The Coeur d'Alenes used gestures to increase the drama of their tales. Hopi children responded to the story by repeating the last word of the sentence, and Crow children responded with "E!" ("yes") following every few sentences. Jicarilla Apache storytellers gave kernels of corn to children during story time. (It was believed that if children ate corn during the storytelling, they would remember the content and the importance of the stories.) Kiowans did not tell Trickster tales during daylight hours because when Trickster was about ready to leave our world, he told the people never to tell stories about him in the daytime.

7. Write the following story endings on the chalkboard or on a chart where the class may read them:

> Clackama storytellers ended many of their stories with words that meant "myth, myth" or "story, story."
> The Kiowa ended many of their stories with "That's the way it was—and is—down to this very day."

8. Search Native American folklore to discover how interpreters and translators ended their stories. For example, the following examples are from Normandin's *Echoes of the Elders: The Stories and Paintings of Chief Lalooska:*

> "Each night just as the sun disappears into the sea . . ."
> ". . . the people would feel kin to all the beings within the sea forever."
> ". . . and she lived a long and happy life."

Discuss the meaning of each ending and consider how the ending might relate to Native American traditional values.

9. Model a storytelling experience for the students by introducing a Native American folktale using an appropriate introduction, style, and ending.

10. Divide the class into groups according to a Native American tribe or a region of the country. Have the students develop appropriate storytelling techniques for that tribe and ask them to practice and present their stories to the rest of the class.

Activity 8–8:

MY BROTHER THE HAWK—
THE WRITER'S POINT OF VIEW

TYPE	TERM
● CLASS	● STA
● GROUP	○ LTA
○ IND	○ LC

Purpose:

1. To participate in a creative writing activity
2. To recognize differences in literature depending on the author's point of view
3. To identify the sequence in plot development
4. To infer the symbolic significance of a book title
5. To develop an understanding that all people, from all backgrounds, have dreams and desires

Materials: Byrd Baylor's *Hawk, I'm Your Brother* (1976).

Grade level: Middle and upper elementary

Book summary: *Hawk, I'm Your Brother* is the story of Rudy Soto, a Native American boy who lives in the southwestern part of the United States. Rudy's dream is to glide through the air like a hawk. To realize his dream, he captures a young hawk from his nest on the mountain and tries to learn to fly from the hawk. By the end of the book, Rudy realizes that if he truly loves the hawk he cannot keep the hawk chained. Consequently, he lets the hawk go free and enjoys the experience as he sees the hawk, for the first time, soaring through the air.

Procedures:

1. Ask the students if they have ever wanted to do something very, very much. How did they feel if they could not do it? Allow them to share times when they have really wanted something. Tell them that you are going to read a story about Rudy Soto, a Native American boy who wants more than anything else to fly. Ask students to listen to the way the author describes and develops Rudy Soto's dream so that the reader can understand it. Ask them to also consider how they would feel if they were Rudy Soto and what they would have done if they were in his place. Finally, ask them to consider the feelings and desires of the hawk.

2. After reading *Hawk, I'm Your Brother,* lead a discussion in which the students identify the major sequence of events leading up to Rudy's decision to release the hawk. The following sequence of events is listed for your assistance:

   a. Rudy Soto dreams of soaring over canyons, floating on the wind, and wrapping himself in the wind while facing the sun.

   b. Rudy's desires are emphasized by his decision to capture a young hawk, learn the hawk's secret of flying, and become his brother.

   c. The captured hawk shows his resistance by pulling against the restraining string, beating his wings against the cage, and calling to his free brothers soaring in the canyon.

   d. Rudy loves the hawk; he does not wish to see him unhappy. Rudy shows his love and understanding by returning the hawk to Santos Mountain.

e. The freed hawk reacts by rising in splendor and circling the mountains above Rudy. For the remainder of the day, the boy and his hawk brother call back and forth to each other.

f. Although Rudy is on the ground, he feels as if he is soaring through the air with his friend.

g. Rudy does not talk about his hawk brother, but people know he has changed. His eyes flash like the eyes of a young hawk; the sky is reflected in his eyes.

3. Following your discussion and the identification of major events in the story, ask the students to consider the significance of the author's title. Why did Baylor choose *Hawk, I'm Your Brother* for the title? What does the word *brother* imply? Is it an accurate description of Rudy Soto's relationship to the hawk? How are Rudy and the hawk alike? How are they different? Why did Rudy release the hawk? How do you think Rudy felt after releasing the hawk? How do you think the hawk felt after being released? What would you have done if you were Rudy Soto? How would you react if you were the hawk?

4. Share with the students that an incident may be described in different ways by several people who have the same experience. The details they choose to describe, the feelings they experience, and their beliefs in the right or wrong of an incident may vary depending on whom the author chooses to tell the story. Consequently, the same story could change drastically depending on the point of view of the storyteller. For example, Beatrix Potter tells her popular story of a rabbit who invades a garden through the point of view of Peter Rabbit. The story would be very different if it were told through the point of view of Mr. McGregor. (Ask the students to tell you how the story might change if it were written from a gardener's point of view.) Next, ask the students to tell you whose point of view Baylor develops in *Hawk, I'm Your Brother*. How did they know that the story was told from Rudy's point of view? Then ask students to consider how the story might be written if the author chose the hawk's point of view.

5. Ask the students to imagine that they are the hawk that Rudy captured. Have them write a story about what happened to them, beginning from the time that Rudy Soto captured the hawk from the nest high on Santos Mountain.

Activity 8–9:

FINDING NATIVE AMERICAN SYMBOLS
IN THE ILLUSTRATIONS OF PAUL GOBLE

TYPE	TERM
● CLASS	○ STA
● GROUP	● LTA
● IND	○ LC

Purpose:

1. To develop an appreciation for illustrations
2. To discover that illustrations may reinforce various Native American symbols
3. To develop observational abilities
4. To develop understanding of the Native American culture by discussing the importance of these symbols as they relate to the culture

Materials:

Various books illustrated by Paul Goble, including *Dream Wolf* (1990), *The Girl Who Loved Wild Horses* (1978), *The Gift of the Sacred Dog* (1980), *Star Boy* (1983), *Buffalo Woman* (1984), and *Beyond the Ridge* (1989); a list of common Native American symbols.

Grade level:

All grades

Book summaries:

Dream Wolf tells the story of two lost children who are helped to return to safety by a wolf. *The Girl Who Loved Wild Horses* tells about a Native American girl's attachment to horses. *The Gift of the Sacred Dog* reveals how horses were given to the Native American people. *Star Boy* is a story about a Native American who proves his bravery. *Buffalo Woman* reveals why the Native Americans and the buffalo are closely related. *Beyond the Ridge* follows an older Native American woman after she dies and goes to a new land.

Procedures:

1. Introduce the idea of visual symbols by showing and discussing several symbols that are familiar to the students. For example, show an American flag and ask the students to share the meanings, feelings, and emotions that are associated with the flag. Continue this introduction by sharing and discussing illustrations of symbols such as doves representing peace, valentines representing love, and eagles representing the American spirit.

2. Explain to the students that various cultures have symbols that mean a great deal to those cultures. Present a list of important symbols that are common in Native American traditional literature. Explain to the students that they will be searching illustrated books that depict the Native American culture to identify whether illustrators also use those symbols. Introduce and discuss the importance of the symbols shown in the following chart. As the students search for the symbols they should consider what the symbols represent in each illustration and within the story.

3. The following chart lists common Native American symbols and their usual meanings and provides space for students to give examples from texts in which that symbol is shown in the illustrations:

Symbols	Meanings	Literature Examples
Beaver	Tenacity, dependability	
Braids	Experience	
Butterfly	Life, child's toy	
Circle	Wholeness	
Coyote	Gentle trickster, teacher	
Evening	Rest, dreams	
Eyes	Perception	
Fire	Spirit of the people, children	
Fox and kits	Peers	
Grandmother or grandfather	Teacher	
Hawk	One who has no enemies	
Lake	Mirror or wholeness	
Prairie	Everyday life	
Rainbow	Myths, strengths, connection of the spiritual and physical	
River	Spirit of life	
Stone	Power	
Sweetgrass	Earth's purification	
Thunderbird	Thunder and lightning, part of creation story	
Touching ground	Being in contact with nature, laws of Mother Earth	
Turtle	Traditions, old symbol	

4. As a class activity, you may choose to identify and discuss the symbols located in one book before the students search independently for symbols. For example, ask students to listen to the story and view the illustrations in *The Girl Who Loved Wild Horses.* The text includes illustrations that show butterflies, braids, lake as a mirror reflection, girl lying on the ground, turtles, prairie, stone, rainbow, and circles.

5. After the students have observed and discussed the symbols and illustrations in one book, ask them to search for possible symbols in other illustrated books. Divide the class into groups and ask them to identify and discuss possible symbols found in other illustrations. Ask the students to discuss the possible meanings and the appropriateness of these symbols in the illustrations.

6. Students may draw their own illustrations in which they use these symbols. They can write stories that include the symbols as well.

Activity 8–10:
INTEGRATING LITERATURE AND GEOGRAPHY

	TYPE		TERM
	● CLASS	○ STA	
	● GROUP	● LTA	
	○ IND	○ LC	

Purpose:

1. To analyze literature according to the five themes of geography
2. To integrate the study of literature and geography
3. To develop higher thinking skills
4. To increase understanding of the Native American people before and at the time of Columbus
5. To motivate discussions related to geography and nonfictional literature and to compare geography themes from two different locations.

Materials:

Marcia Sewall's *People of the Breaking Day* (1990), Jane Yolen's *Encounter* (1992), and John S. Major's *The Silk Route: 7,000 Miles of History* (1995).

Grade level:

Lower elementary for *Encounter;* middle elementary and above for *People of the Breaking Day* and *The Silk Route: 7,000 Miles of History.*

Book summaries:

People of the Breaking Day is a nonfictional story about the Wampanoag nation of southeastern Massachusetts before the English settlers arrived. *Encounter* presents a hypothetical interaction between a Taino Indian boy and Columbus and his men on the island of San Salvador in 1492. The text is developed on the premise that dreams forewarn the boy about the disastrous consequences of interacting with the explorers. *The Silk Route: 7,000 Miles of History* is a nonfictional text that discusses the history of the route between China and Byzantium.

Procedures:

1. Before reading the books, provide some historical background about the time period and the locations. For *People of the Breaking Day,* explain to students that this story takes place before the English settlers arrived and changed the lives of the native people. Using a map or globe, show and discuss the location of the story. For *Encounter,* explain to the students that this is a story about what might have happened when the Taino Indians of the West Indies met Christopher Columbus and his Spanish explorers for the first time. Also show and discuss the location of San Salvador in the West Indies. For *The Silk Route: 7,000 Miles of History,* show and discuss the map at the beginning of the book on which the Silk Route is traced from Chang'an, China, to Byzantium during the Tang Dynasty (A.D. 618–906). Discuss the geographical locations through which the Silk Route extends as well as the importance of trade routes during this time period.

2. Introduce the five themes of geography that will be used to analyze and discuss the information in these books. Tell the students that geographers have developed a procedure that allows students to inquire about places on the earth and to analyze their relationships to the people who live there. Discuss these themes with language that is appropriate for the grade level and understanding of the students. The following five fundamental themes in geography were developed by the Committee on Geographic Education (1983) and are also discussed in the *GEO News Handbook* (1990):

a. *Location,* including where and why: Where does the story take place as far as city, country, continent, longitude, latitude, and so forth? Why does the story take place in this location?

b. *Place,* including physical and human characteristics: What are the physical features and characteristics? What are the characteristics of the people, including distinctive cultural traditions?

c. *Relationships within places,* including cultural and physical interactions and how relationships develop: How do human-environmental relationships develop and what are the consequences? What is the primary use of land? How have the people altered the environment? Where do most people live?

d. *Movement,* including people, ideas, and materials: How are the movements of people, ideas, and materials influenced and accomplished? What are the consequences of such movements?

e. *Regions,* including how they form and change: What are the major languages? What are the vegetation regions? What are the country's political divisions? How do the regions change?

3. Develop a chart for each of the books. On this chart place the five themes of geography. As students read or listen to each book, ask them to identify and discuss information that would be appropriate for each of the categories.

4. The following chart shows examples that were identified, discussed, and analyzed around *People of the Breaking Day:*

BOOK TITLE: *PEOPLE OF THE BREAKING DAY*

Location	Place	Relationships	Movement	Regions
East Coast	Climate has	Great Sachem, or	Paths bind villages	Vegetation: woods,
Small	four seasons	leader, knows	Trade with	fields, and
settlement	Plentiful food	fields, forests,	Narragansetts for	forests
"Where the sun	Cold winters	and water; he	soapstone, pipes,	Regions divided
rises"	Wampanoag tribe	decides just	bowls, and	according to
Close to the sea	Hunt, fish, plant	punishments	beads	hunting grounds
Away from	Father is teacher	Council decides	Trade pipes, bowls,	May fight over
Mohawks,	Ceremonies for	issues of war	beads, and corn	fishing and
Penacooks,	war and death	Men make arrows	with Abanakis	hunting grounds
and Abanakis	Animals: foxes,	and build fences	for birch bark	
	bears, deer, and	and canoes	Make birch bark	
	hawks	Women garden,	into canoes	
		tend fields, and	Play games with	
		care for needs	other nations	
		Relationships with	Move for survival	
		Mother Earth		

5. The following chart shows examples that were identified, discussed, and analyzed around *Encounter:*

BOOK TITLE: *ENCOUNTER*

Location	Place	Relationships	Movement	Regions
West Indies, 1492 San Salvador Bay on which ships anchor	Taino people believed in welcoming strangers Illustrations and text contrast Taino and Spaniards Illustrations show physical features of place	Taino lifestyles were changed forever Originally 300,000 natives; 50 years later, 500 remained Lost language, religion, and culture	Tainos gave cotton thread, spears, and balls Spaniards gave beads and hats Tainos wanted weapons from Spaniards Spanish ideas prevailed	Emphasizes that regions were changed forever because Spaniards took everything from the Tainos

6. The following chart shows examples that were identified, discussed, and analyzed around *The Silk Route: 7,000 Miles of History*:

7. If students have read and analyzed all of the books they may make comparisons related to the five themes of geography and to the locations.

8. Additional books that may be used for this type of activity include Jean Fritz's *The Double Life of Pocahontas* (1983), Francine Jacobs's *The Tainos: The People Who Welcomed Columbus* (1992), and George DeLucenay Leon's *Explorers of the Americas before Columbus* (1989).

BOOK TITLE: *THE SILK ROUTE: 7,000 MILES OF HISTORY*

Location	Place	Relationships	Movement	Regions
Chang'an, China, the largest city in the world in A.D. 700 Silk Route— ancient trade route between China and Byzantium Oasis town of Dunhuang is an important trading and supply center Transoxiana is a wild area in which bandits attack caravans Baghdad is the greatest city in the Islamic world and a hub of world trade	Network of caravan tracks cross the steppes and deserts of central Asia Conditions on caravan route include heat, hunger, thirst, and bandit raids Buddhist temples are seen in China Each different city includes goods that are created and traded	Emperors of Tang Dynasty brought China to high point of power and culture Importance of Silk to ancient Western world brought trade with China China: Men grow grain; women produce silk Trade goods from China include porcelain, herbal medicines, and silk cloth desired by Islamic and Byzantine worlds	Expanding world of Islam following founding by Muhammad in A.D. 622 Silk used as money Materials brought to trade changed hands several times along the way Buddhist religion came to China from India along the Silk Route about A.D. 100	China: Farmlands suitable for growing grains China has groves of mulberry trees Taklimakan is one of the world's driest deserts, with sand dunes, rocky flats, and dry riverbeds

Activity 8–11:

TRADITIONAL VALUES—HISPANIC FOLKLORE

	TYPE		TERM
●	CLASS	●	STA
●	GROUP	●	LTA
○	IND	○	LC

Purpose:

1. To develop an appreciation for a cultural heritage that values wisdom and understanding and places importance on the relationship between the people and their faith
2. To listen for and identify values in Hispanic folklore

Materials:

Folktales from Mexico and other Latin American countries; the example lesson uses two Mexican folktales, "The Sacred Drum of Tepozteco" and "Pancho Villa and the Devil," found in Zena Sutherland and Myra Cohn Livingston's *The Scott, Foresman Anthology of Children's Literature* (1984) and M. A. Jagendorf and R. S. Boggs's *The King of the Mountains: A Treasury of Latin American Folk Stories* (1960); values chart for Hispanic folklore.

Grade level:

Middle and upper elementary

Book summary:

The King of the Mountains: A Treasury of Latin American Folk Stories is a large collection of folktales. The stories are divided according to countries, including Argentina, the Bahamas, Barbados, Bolivia, Brazil, Chile, Colombia, Costa Rica, Cuba, Dominican Republic, Ecuador, El Salvador, Guatemala, the Guianas, Haiti, Honduras, Jamaica, Mexico, Nicaragua, Panama, Paraguay, Peru, Puerto Rico, Trinidad, Uruguay, and Venezuela. The anthology provides many examples that may be used for comparing values in the folklore of the various countries.

Procedures:

1. Review the questions used to identify traditional values listed in activity 8–1, "Traditional Values—African Folklore."
2. Print each of these questions on a chart. Identify several folktales that will be used for initial study. Allow the students to add additional stories. The following chart identifies two folktales and provides examples for values identified in the literature:

VALUES IDENTIFIED IN HISPANIC FOLKLORE

Questions for Values	"The Sacred Drum of Tepozteco" (Mexico)	"Pancho Villa and the Devil" (Mexico)
What reward is desired:	protection of the people wisdom destiny to be a god	to fool the devil to show the devil that Pancho Villa is smarter than the devil fearlessness
What actions are rewarded or admired?	wise counseling and understanding virtues	extreme observation going to church wearing a cross

Questions for Values	"The Sacred Drum of Tepozteco" (Mexico)	"Pancho Villa and the Devil" (Mexico)
What actions are punished or despised?	outward show does not demand respect gathering an army and attacking the revered king and his people	selling one's soul
What rewards are given to the heroes, heroines, or great people?	worshiped by the people people made him king and worshiped him as a god love and respect	going to heaven after death
What are the personal characteristics of the heroes, heroines, or great people?	rich in wisdom and understanding great strength great speed great hunter successful counsel rich in virtues	stronger than others knows everything understands all things about humans and animals fearless

3. Introduce "The Sacred Drum of Tepozteco." Ask the students to listen for the answers to the questions printed on the chart.

4. After reading "The Sacred Drum of Tepozteco" aloud, have the students identify and place the values in the proper location on the chart. Discuss the importance of the values in the traditional tale.

5. Follow the same procedure with "Pancho Villa and the Devil." (This folktale has universal characteristics often given to national heroes in folklore. See activity 8–12, "Folk Heroes across Cultures—Comparing a Traditional Hispanic Folktale with American Tall Tales" for an identification of tall tale characteristics.)

6. Additional Hispanic folktales may be used for this activity. You may choose several tales from a specific Latin American country and then compare the values expressed in the tales. Examples of folktales include Tomie dePaola's *The Lady of Guadalupe* (1980, Mexico), Verna Aardema's *The Riddle of the Drum: A Tale from Tizapan, Mexico* (1979); Lois Ehlert's *Cuckoo: A Mexican Folktale* (1997), Pura Belpré's *The Rainbow-Colored Horse* (1978, Puerto Rico), Harriet Rohmer and Dorminster Wilson's *Mother Scorpion Country* (1987, Nicaragua), and Jane Anne Volkmer's *Song of the Chirimia: A Guatemalan Folktale* (1990).

Activity 8–12:

FOLK HEROES ACROSS CULTURES— COMPARING A TRADITIONAL HISPANIC FOLKTALE WITH AMERICAN TALL TALES

TYPE	TERM
● CLASS	○ STA
● GROUP	● LTA
○ IND	○ LC

Purpose:

1. To identify characteristics of tall tales
2. To develop the understanding that various story types and motifs are found among stories told by people from different cultures
3. To distinguish between fact and fiction and exaggeration and nonexaggeration
4. To distinguish between real and fictional characters
5. To enjoy a humorous tale
6. To develop an understanding that humor is multicultural

Materials:

"Pancho Villa and the Devil," found in Sutherland and Livingston's *The Scott, Foresman Anthology of Children's Literature* (1984); texts that contain American tall tales, such as Walter Blair's *Tall Tale America: A Legendary History of Our Humorous Heroes* (1944), Edward C. Day's *John Tabor's Ride* (1989), and Steven Kellogg's *Paul Bunyan* (1984).

Grade level:

Middle and upper elementary

Book summaries:

Tall Tale America: A Legendary History of Our Humorous Heroes is a collection of exaggerated tales. *John Tabor's Ride* is a highly illustrated version of the whaler who journeyed around the globe on the back of a whale. *Paul Bunyan* is a highly illustrated version of the legendary lumberjack and his blue ox, Babe.

Procedures:

1. Read several tall tales to students. Ask them to listen for and distinguish between experiences that could and could not happen to people. Ask them to listen for characteristics of the main characters.

2. After reading the tall tales, have the students compile a list of experiences that could happen, experiences that could not happen (e.g., riding a cyclone, stirring molten iron with an arm, and creating the Grand Canyon), and characteristics of the main characters (e.g., bragging about accomplishments and personal strength, exaggerating claims, and inventing stories). From this list, develop a list of tall tale characteristics including humorous stories; exaggerated claims; and swaggering, boisterous, courageous, and strong characters. Discuss the differences between factual and nonfactual experiences and between exaggerated and nonexaggerated experiences and characteristics. Emphasize that tall tale stories may be about real or fictional heroes.

3. Read "Pancho Villa and the Devil" aloud. Have the students listen for the location of the story and identify examples of experiences that could happen, exaggerations, and character traits. Have the students list their findings on a chart similar to the following:

CHARACTERISTICS OF NATIONAL HEROES—REAL AND FICTIONAL

Name	Location	Real or Fictional Character	Personal Characteristics	Examples of Exaggeration
Pancho Villa	Mexico	Real	Fearless Strong	Stronger than any other Mexican who ever lived Knew everything Rode a devil-horse
Davy Crockett	Frontier America	Real	Boisterous Conquered mountains and wild animals	Tamed and rode a bear Battled a comet
Daniel Boone	Frontier America	Real		
Mike Fink	Ohio and Mississippi Rivers	Fictional		
Pecos Bill	Texas, Southwest	Fictional		

4. Ask students if Pancho Villa was a real or fictitious character. (They may need to do some research to answer this question.) Then read several tall tales about real American heroes such as Davy Crockett and Daniel Boone whose exploits have been exaggerated. Ask the students to identify exaggerations and character traits. Have them discuss any similarities among the tall tales about Pancho Villa, Davy Crockett, and Daniel Boone. Ask the students to form hypotheses that explain why real characters became subjects for tall tales.

5. Read several tall tales about the exploits of fictional characters. Identify the exaggerated exploits and characters' traits. Compare the stories about fictional and nonfictional characters.

6. A research lesson could follow this activity. Students could compare nonfictionalized biographical stories about Pancho Villa, Davy Crockett, and Daniel Boone with the plots and characterization in the tall tale versions.

7. Encourage students to write their own tall tales about real or fictional people. They should use the characteristics of the tall tales identified in this activity.

Activity 8–13:
NURSERY RHYMES AND
AESTHETIC DEVELOPMENT

TYPE	TERM
● CLASS	● STA
● GROUP	● LTA
○ IND	○ LC

Purpose:

1. To foster the self-esteem of Hispanic children

2. To develop an understanding that oral language, as characterized in nursery rhymes, is an important part of the Hispanic cultural heritage as well as the heritage of other cultural groups

3. To develop an understanding that nursery rhymes have universal appeal for all children

4. To stimulate oral language development, listening appreciation, and aesthetic development

Materials:

Margot Griego et al.'s *Tortillitas Para Mama and Other Nursery Rhymes/Spanish and English* (1981); Mother Goose rhymes from other cultures, including Robert Wyndham's *Chinese Mother Goose Rhymes* (1982), Charlotte De Forest's *The Prancing Pony: Nursery Rhymes from Japan* (1968), N. M. Bodecker's *It's Raining, Said John Twaining* (1973), Marguerite De Angeli's *Marguerite De Angeli's Book of Nursery and Mother Goose Rhymes* (1954), Demi's *Dragon Kites and Dragonflies: A Collection of Chinese Nursery Rhymes* (1986).

Grade level:

Lower elementary students dramatize the characteristics of the rhymes; middle and upper elementary students compare rhymes

Book summaries:

Each of these Mother Goose collections is a highly illustrated version of the rhymes. The illustrations also reinforce the culture depicted in the rhymes.

Procedures:

1. Read various rhymes to lower elementary students. Encourage them to dramatize the language of the nursery rhymes by doing the finger plays and the counting rhymes, clapping along with appropriate rhymes, acting out the turning and twirling rhymes, and joining in with the nonsense words. If possible, also read the Spanish versions of the nursery rhymes in *Tortillitas Para Mama*.

2. Read the rhymes to middle and upper elementary students. Ask them to analyze how the rhymes are similar and different. What are the universal appeals of Mother Goose rhymes? What do these universal themes imply about children from around the world? What are the differences in the rhymes (consider content, style, and subject matter)? What do these differences imply about cultural influences?

3. Stimulate older children's aesthetic development and appreciation for the cultural relationships between the illustrations and the rhymes. After sharing the nursery rhymes with children, have them look at the illustrations and discuss the relationships among the illustrations, the cultural content of the illustrations, and the literary content of the nursery rhymes. Older students may consider how effectively the illustrator creates the setting for the rhymes and uses colors or artistic

technique to support the cultural motif. Are the illustrations and text placed effectively within the pages of the book?

For example, in *Tortillitas Para Mama,* illustrator Barbara Cooney recreates the varied settings associated with Spanish nursery rhymes. Warm browns depict the interior of a Mexican home, cool blues warmed by the shining moon suggest a village by the water, and warm fuchsias reflect the emotional tone of a mother and father sharing quiet time with their baby.

Ed Young's illustrations for *Chinese Mother Goose Rhymes* are simple, colorful drawings representing such Chinese symbols as the dragon. The Chinese impact is increased by printing the rhymes in both English and Chinese orthography.

Keiko Hida, illustrator of *The Prancing Pony,* used a form of Japanese collage called *kusa-e* to depict a Japanese setting. The colors of the handmade textured rice paper used in the collage were made from natural Japanese plant dyes.

Bodecker's colorful full-page illustrations in *It's Raining, Said John Twaining* show settings with wooden shoes, kings, queens, princes, and princesses, which are common characteristics of Danish verse.

Marguerite De Angeli's illustrations in her *Book of Nursery and Mother Goose Rhymes* have an early English setting. There are flowering fields, blossoming hedgerows, stone walls, castles, cobblestone streets, and the chalky cliffs of Dover. Ask the students to use the illustrations of the nineteenth-century English illustrator Kate Greenaway to make additional English comparisons.

Demi's illustrations and rhymes included in *Dragon Kites and Dragonflies: A Collection of Chinese Nursery Rhymes* emphasize Chinese kites, camelback bridges, dragon boats, New Year lanterns, and Chinese architecture.

4. Stimulate older children's interest in the collection of nursery rhymes by having them analyze some of the collections edited by the British collectors Iona and Peter Opie. Examples of the Opies' collections include the following:

> *A Nursery Companion* (1980)
> *The Oxford Nursery Rhyme Book* (1955, 1984)
> *I Saw Esau: The Schoolchild's Pocket Book* (1992)
> *Tail Feathers from Mother Goose: The Opie Rhyme Book* (1988)

What do students believe is the appeal of nursery rhymes for these collectors?

Activity 8–14:

TRADITIONAL VALUES—ASIAN FOLKLORE

	TYPE	TERM
	● CLASS	● STA
	● GROUP	● LTA
	○ IND	○ LC

Purpose:

1. To develop an appreciation for a cultural heritage that values knowledge, wise ancestors, humility, kindness, compassion, and life free from persecution and oppression
2. To listen for and identify traditional values found in Asian folktales

Materials:

A collection of Chinese folktales, such as Catherine Edwards Sadler's *Treasure Mountain: Folktales from Southern China* (1982), Lafcadio Hearn's *The Voice of the Great Bell* (1989), Marilee Heyer's *The Weaving of a Dream* (1986), and He Liyi's *The Spring of Butterflies and Other Chinese Folktales* (1985).

Grade level:

Middle and upper elementary

Book summaries:

Treasure Mountain: Folktales from Southern China includes six folktales that reveal many of the beliefs and values of the people. *The Voice of the Great Bell* is a highly illustrated story about a girl who makes a sacrifice to cast a flawless bell. *The Weaving of a Dream* is a tale that develops the value of love and loyalty and the harmful results of greed. *The Spring of Butterflies and Other Chinese Folktales* is a collection of folklore from China's minority people.

Procedures:

1. Review the questions used to identify traditional values listed in activity 8–1, "Traditional Values—African Folklore."
2. Print each of these questions on a chart. Identify several folktales that will be used for the initial study. (Because there are so many folktales from various Asian countries, you should choose one country for the initial activity. Later you may choose other countries and then compare the results.) The following chart identifies Chinese folktales and provides examples for the values identified in the literature:

VALUES IDENTIFIED IN TRADITIONAL CHINESE FOLKLORE

Questions for Values	"Treasure Mountain" (*Treasure Mountain*)	"The Chuang Brocade" (*Treasure Mountain*)
What reward is desired:	to want a better life tools that make work easier and feed people	a beautiful estate the return of a brocade
What actions are rewarded or admired?	generosity kindness respect for elders honesty	courage bravery respect for parent artistic ability
What actions are punished or despised?	greed dishonesty cruelty	greed disrespect for parent

VALUES IDENTIFIED IN TRADITIONAL CHINESE FOLKLORE

Questions for Values	"Treasure Mountain" (*Treasure Mountain*)	"The Chuang Brocade" (*Treasure Mountain*)
What rewards are given to the heroes, heroines, or great people?	a magical key that opens Treasure Mountain magic stone grinder magic mortar magic hoe	return of the brocade a grand estate
What are the personal characteristics of the heroes, heroines, or great people?	honesty generosity respectful kind	believing courageous bravery compassion respectful to elderly parent

3. Introduce "Treasure Mountain" from Sadler's *Treasure Mountain.* Read the story while the students listen for answers to the questions. Place the answers on the chart and discuss the identified values.

4. Introduce "The Chuang Brocade" from Sadler's *Treasure Mountain.* Read the story while students listen for answers to the questions. Write the answers on the chart and discuss and compare the values found in the two tales. Have students read additional Chinese tales and identify the values.

5. Select other Asian countries, read folktales, and identify traditional values. Choices might include the following collections or single stories:

> Jane Hori Ike and Baruch Zimmerman's *A Japanese Fairy Tale* (1982)
> Patricia Montgomery Newton's *The Five Sparrows: A Japanese Folktale* (1982)
> Katherine Paterson's *The Tale of the Mandarin Ducks* (1990)
> Claus Stamm's *Three Strong Women: A Tall Tale from Japan* (1990)
> Sumiko Yagawa's *The Crane Wife* (1981)
> Peter Hyun's *Korea's Favorite Tales and Lyrics* (1986) and Laurence Yep's *The Rainbow People* (1989), which contains Chinese folktales collected from Asian-Americans

Activity 8–15:

RED RIDING HOOD ACROSS CULTURES— COMPARING A CHINESE AND A GERMAN VERSION

	TYPE	TERM
	● CLASS	● STA
	● GROUP	○ LTA
	○ IND	○ LC

Purpose:

1. To diagram the plot development in a folktale
2. To compare Chinese and German variations of a common folktale
3. To appreciate the assimilation of folktale elements and plots into different cultures

Materials:

Diagrams of plot development and folktales that have variations found in more than one culture, such as "The Chinese Red Riding Hoods" found in Sutherland and Livingston's *The Scott, Foresman Anthology of Children's Literature* (1984) and Isabelle Chang's *Chinese Fairy Tales* (1965); the Grimms' *Little Red Riding Hood* retold and illustrated by Trina Schart Hyman (1983); Ed Young's *Lon Po Po: A Red-Riding Hood Story from China* (1989) may also be used for this comparison.

Grade level:

Middle and upper elementary

Book summaries:

"The Chinese Red Riding Hoods" is a folktale that develops strong female characters who are able to trick the wolf. *Little Red Riding Hood* is the traditional German version of the tale recorded by the Brothers Grimm. In the German version the wolf eats both the grandmother and the girl. They are then saved by the huntsman who attacks the wolf. *Lon Po Po: A Red-Riding Hood Story from China* is an ancient tale in which three girls trick the wolf.

Procedures:

1. Introduce the concept that a plot includes characters trying to overcome a conflict. Explain that a plot has beginning, middle, and ending incidents. Draw a diagram like the following to show the progress of a plot:

2. Introduce the popular and well-known Grimm Brothers' folktale *Little Red Riding Hood.* Ask the students to listen to the story so that they can identify the series of incidents that develop the plot and then diagram the plot. Students will probably identify the following incidents:

   a. Little Red Riding Hood takes a basket of food to her sick grandmother who lives in the forest.
   b. Little Red Riding Hood meets and talks to the wolf.
   c. The wicked wolf runs straight to grandmother's cottage and deceives her by impersonating Little Red Riding Hood.
   d. Grandmother invites the wolf inside, and the wolf eats her.
   e. The wolf dresses as grandmother and gets into her bed.
   f. The wolf deceives Little Red Riding Hood.
   g. The wicked wolf jumps out of bed and eats Little Red Riding Hood.
   h. The huntsman is attracted to the cottage and kills the wolf.
   i. Little Red Riding Hood and her grandmother are rescued from the wolf's stomach.

3. Place the incidents from the Grimms' version of *Little Red Riding Hood* on the plot development diagram:

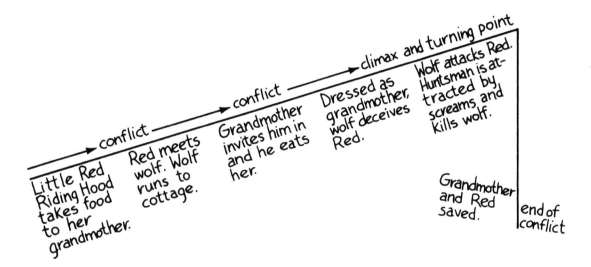

4. Introduce the Chinese variation, "The Chinese Red Riding Hoods." Ask the students to listen to the story and identify the series of incidents that develop this plot. Students will probably identify the following incidents:

   a. A mother of three girls goes to visit grandmother on her birthday.
   b. A crafty wolf disguises himself as grandmother and deceives the children.
   c. The children invite the wolf into the house.
   d. The wolf gets into bed with the children.
   e. Felice discovers the wolf's identity.
   f. The girls trick the greedy wolf into trying to climb the tree.
   g. The girls get him to climb into a basket and then drop the basket.
   h. The wolf is killed; the children are saved.

5. Place the incidents from "The Chinese Red Riding Hood" on the plot development diagram:

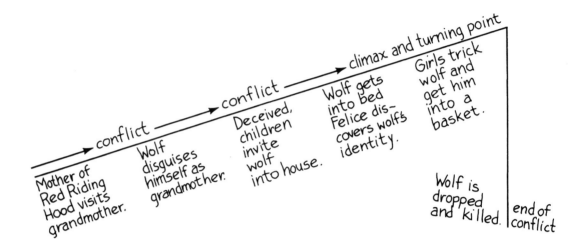

6. Discuss the similarities and differences in the two folktales.

7. Compare the two Red Riding Hood versions from China.

8. Compare the illustrations in the two Caldecott Award–winning books: Hyman's illustrations for *Little Red Riding Hood* and Young's illustrations for *Lon Po Po: A Red-Riding Hood Story from China*. Discuss the cultural information that is provided through the illustrations.

Activity 8–16:

CROSS-CULTURAL MUSIC
APPRECIATION AND ANALYSIS

TYPE	TERM
● CLASS	● STA
● GROUP	● LTA
○ IND	○ LC

Purpose:

1. To encourage language development
2. To develop appreciation for music as part of a literary heritage
3. To stimulate the imagination by interpreting musical selections through art
4. To use African-American and Native American music to understand the history of these cultures
5. To analyze the content of work songs, folk songs, and favorite traditional songs and understand a common need for music across cultures
6. To research the historical significance of traditional music

Materials:

A collection of music depicting work songs, folk songs, and traditional songs of the cultures. Examples include Ashley Bryan's *Walk Together Children: Black American Spirituals,* Vol. 1 (1974), *I'm Going to Sing: Black American Spirituals,* Vol. 2 (1982), and *All Night, All Day: A Child's First Book of African-American Spirituals* (1991); John Bierhorst's *A Cry from the Earth: Music of the North American Indians* (1979); Edward Field's *Eskimo Songs and Stories* (1973); Dan Fox's *Go in and out the Window: An Illustrated Songbook for Young People* (1987); Jane Hart's *Singing Bee! A Collection of Favorite Children's Songs* (1982); and David Hom's *Literature of American Music in Books and Folk Music* (1977).

Grade level:

Students in all grades can learn to enjoy and participate in music activities and can use the visual arts to interpret music. Middle and upper elementary students can analyze the content and research the history of traditional music and relate the content to the history of a people.

Book summaries:

These materials were selected because students can sing the songs and discuss the content of the music. In addition, many of the selections include illustrations that reinforce the culture from which the songs originated. Illustrated texts such as Fox's *Go In and Out the Window: An Illustrated Songbook for Young People* also provide opportunities for studying the history of art. Each of the songs in this collection is accompanied by a reproduction of a work of art that is on display at the Metropolitan Museum of Art. According to the text, "The songs are drawn from American, British, and European traditions. The art spans more than five thousand years and comes from such diverse places as Japan, England, France, China, America, and Mexico. Running throughout the book are comments on the art, the songs, or the combination of the two" (front cover).

Procedures:

1. To encourage language development and appreciation for a literary heritage, share music from different countries with the children and encourage them to sing and discuss the music. You may wish to begin with traditional music that may be more familiar to your students. *Singing Bee! A Collection of Favorite Children's Songs* contains both piano and guitar accompaniment for lullabies, Mother

Goose rhymes, game songs, folk songs, and holiday songs. Artist Anita Lobel chose historical settings for the illustrations because many of the songs are traditional. She effectively used a little-theater concept, dressed her characters in eighteenth-century fashions, and placed the various characters and stage assistants against theater backdrops.

2. Share and discuss music from African-American, Native American, Hispanic, and Asian cultures. Also include other types of American folk songs.

3. To introduce an art activity and stimulate children's imaginations through music and art, read Ashley Bryan's introduction to *I'm Going to Sing: Black American Spirituals.* Bryan describes his childhood in which he listened to music, played various instruments, and drew pictures. Bryan states,

   > I cannot remember a time when I was not drawing and painting, and the spirituals played a role in that growth. I began to recognize images for these songs in almost everything I saw. Or they stimulated my efforts to draw pictures of what can only be seen through the imagination. I have often done drawings that came right out of these songs. It was natural, then, that I would one day begin work illustrating the spirituals. (p. viii)

   Discuss with children how their imaginations could be stimulated by music. Provide opportunities for them to listen to music and to use their imaginations to draw what they see and feel. Share the artwork and discuss the illustrations in the literature selections.

4. Develop a research activity with older students. Have them read the lyrics of African-American, Native American, and other American folk songs. Ask them to find background information in references and to analyze the significance of the words in the songs. Have them develop a traditional song timeline in which they identify the song, the period in history that might have influenced the music, the important characteristics of that period in history, and the traditional values identified in the music.

Activity 8–17:

DISCOVERING ONE'S OWN HERITAGE BRINGS PRIDE TO INDIVIDUALS FROM ALL BACKGROUNDS

TYPE	TERM
● CLASS	○ STA
● GROUP	● LTA
○ IND	○ LC

Purpose:
1. To develop an understanding that discovering one's own heritage brings pride to individuals from all backgrounds
2. To develop an understanding that people from all backgrounds have similar needs and feelings
3. To research one's own heritage

Materials:
Contemporary literature about children who are searching for information about their own heritage: examples include Evelyn Sibley Lampman's *The Potlatch Family* (1976, Native American), Virginia Hamilton's *Zeely* (1967, African-American), Laurence Yep's *Child of the Owl* (1977, Chinese-American), and Kathleen and Michael Lacapa's *Less than Half, More than Whole* (1994).

Grade level:
Middle and upper elementary

Book summaries:
Each of the books is summarized in the following procedures section.

Procedures:
1. Introduce the subject by allowing students to talk about their own heritage. Ask them to consider how important it is to them or to other people to understand their heritage.
2. Divide the students into groups according to the books that each group will read. As they read the books, have them search for examples of characterization that show the characters' need to know their heritage, how characters gain knowledge of their heritage, what the characters learn about their heritage, and personal reactions after the characters make discoveries about themselves and their heritage.
3. For example, the setting for *The Potlatch Family* is the northwestern United States, the home of the Chinook Indians. Although the heroine's ancestors were chiefs who were proud of their culture, she is not proud of her lineage. The author's characterization develops a girl who feels rejection because her classmates ridicule her. Her younger brother says that the only way Native Americans can make whites look up to them is to be superior in sports, and a conflict develops between the new and the old values. The older brother, Simon, however, is determined to revive knowledge of and pride in their Chinook heritage. After the older brother involves the family and neighboring Native Americans in research, they plan and perform a traditional Potlatch celebration to show the townspeople that their cultural heritage is worth preserving. The characters develop strong pride in their heritage and revive one of their ancient customs. The characters' personal conflicts are also resolved as they gain pride in themselves and in their heritage.
4. *Zeely* is the story of an imaginative girl, Geeder, who is intrigued by her uncle's neighbor who is the color of rich Ceylon ebony. She is thin and stately and more

than six feet tall, her expression is calm and filled with pride, and she has a very beautiful face. When Geeder discovers a photograph of a Watusi queen, she believes her neighbor is a queen or at least has royal blood. Geeder makes discoveries about herself as well as about her neighbor.

5. *The Child of the Owl* is a story of a girl who must look deep within herself to discover who she is. When she goes to live with her grandmother in San Francisco's Chinatown, she discovers that she knows little about her heritage. She attends a Chinese school, talks with her grandmother, goes to Chinese movies, and visits Chinatown. These experiences help her to understand and respect her heritage.

6. After reading the stories have each group report its findings to the rest of the class.

7. Have students identify their own cultural heritage (there may be more than one cultural heritage in their backgrounds, as there is in *Less than Half, More than Whole*), interview their relatives, and conduct research on important aspects of their own heritage. They should consider ancient customs; traditional celebrations, stories, and music; heroes; leaders; and other items that were important in several of the stories they read.

Activity 8-18:

RESPONDING TO AND DEBATING
ABOUT STEREOTYPES

TYPE	TERM
● CLASS	● STA
● GROUP	○ LTA
● IND	○ LC

Purpose:
1. To develop an understanding that stereotypes are harmful and frequently incorrect
2. To develop discussion skills as students debate the issues related to stereotypes
3. To respond to characters in literature

Materials: Laurence Yep's *Dragonwings* (1975).

Grade level: Upper elementary and middle school

Book summary: *Dragonwings* is set in San Francisco from 1903 to 1910. The story was motivated by a true incident in which a Chinese immigrant made a flying machine. The father and son, working together through a common bond, build an airplane and soar with it off the cliffs overlooking San Francisco Bay. After he fulfills this dream, the father returns to work to obtain his even greater dream—to earn money so that his wife can join him in America. There are two types of stereotypes developed in the book: the Chinese immigrants have stereotypes about the white Americans, and the white Americans have stereotypes about the Chinese. In the course of the book, both groups learn a great deal about each other. They also discover that their stereotypes are frequently incorrect.

Procedures:
1. Before reading this book, provide some historical background about the time period and the immigration of large numbers of Chinese to work in America. Students will also benefit from an introduction to the concept of stereotypes.
2. After introducing the time period and discussing the concept of stereotypes, introduce the book in such a way that students will be interested in searching for and responding to stereotypes. For example, in this introduction you might say: "Imagine that you are a Chinese boy in 1903. Your father has left China to work in America and to raise money for the family. You leave your mother in China to go to this strange land that some call 'Land of the Demons' and others call 'Land of the Golden Mountain.' Try to imagine your feelings, expectations, and fears as you find your father and become familiar with what to you is a very strange land. This is the adventure you will read about (or listen to) in Laurence Yep's *Dragonwings*. As you read this story imagine that you are Moon Shadow as you meet your father, become part of his dream to build a flying machine, and discover that your stereotypes of the "white demons" are not always accurate. Also imagine what it would be like to try to educate one of the Americans about the ways of your people. How do you feel when you discover that the American people also have stereotypes about you? If this experience were happening to you, how would you change those stereotypes?"
3. Before reading the book students can also compare "Land of the Demons" and "Land of the Golden Mountain." Ask what each title suggests and how these titles could be given to the same country.

4. As students read or listen to *Dragonwings* ask them to search for and identify two types of stereotypes: the Chinese immigrants' stereotypes about the white Americans and the white Americans' stereotypes about the Chinese. Ask students to identify the stereotypes and then trace how each group discovers that the stereotypes are incorrect.

5. Students can also provide written or oral responses to these stereotypes and consider how they would have responded to and changed those stereotypes.

6. This discovery about stereotypes can lead into a discussion about the harmful nature and the inaccuracy of stereotypes.

7. An additional response activity could ask students to respond to the importance of each of the characters' names: the son, Moon Shadow, and the father, Windrider.

TRADITIONAL VALUES—JEWISH LITERATURE

TYPE	TERM
● CLASS	○ STA
● GROUP	● LTA
● IND	○ LC

Purpose:
1. To develop an understanding that Jewish folklore transmits the essential values of the culture, provides a portrait of the people, and offers an understanding of the Jewish heritage
2. To read and analyze the literature to locate references to historical characters and to Jewish place and people and to identify values and beliefs of the people

Materials:
Folktales that reflect the Jewish culture including both single-volume texts and anthologies such as Joan Rothenberg's *Yettele's Feathers* (1995), Josepha Sherman's *Rachel the Clever and Other Jewish Folktales* (1993) and *Jewish American Folklore* (1992), Beatrice Silverman Weinreich's *Yiddish Folktales* (1988), Howard Schwartz and Barbara Rush's *The Sabbath Lion: A Jewish Folktale from Algeria* (1992) and *The Diamond Tree: Jewish Tales from Around the World* (1991), Steve Sanfield's *The Feather Merchants and Other Tales of the Fools of Chelm* (1991), Isaac Bashevis Singer's *When Shlemiel Went to Warsaw and Other Stories* (1968), Adele Geras's *My Grandmother's Stories: A Collection of Jewish Folk Tales* (1990), and David Wisniewski's *Golem* (1996; Newbery Medal winner, 1997).

Grade level:
Middle and upper elementary

Book summaries:
The listed books contain a variety of Jewish folk tales that provide students with opportunities to identify and analyze characteristics of Jewish folklore.

Procedures:
1. Remind the students that folklore refers to traditional literature that was passed from generation to generation by oral stories before the stories were written down.
2. If necessary, develop a definition of *Judaism* for the students. Rabbi Morris N. Kertzer's *What Is a Jew?* (1993) provides an excellent introduction to Judaism as well as answers to questions about rituals and customs, Jewish beliefs, and Jewish life. For example, Kertzer provides both a religious and a cultural definition. He states that Jews are not a race, but instead "A Jew is one who seeks a spiritual base in the modern world by living the life of study, prayer, and daily routine dedicated to the proposition that Jewish wisdom through the ages will answer the big questions of life. . . . A Jew is one who . . . regards the teachings of Judaism—its ethics, its folkways, its literature—as his or her own" (p. 7).
3. Remind the students that Jewish people live in almost all parts of the world. If desired, the students may study a timeline of Jewish history such as the one found in Kertzer's *What Is a Jew?* This timeline progresses from Abraham and Sarah in 2,000 B.C.E. to the birth of the state of Israel in 1948.
4. Place a web on the chalkboard or a transparency. Write *Jewish folklore* in the center of the web and draw the following subcategories on the web: *reference to Jewish place and people, important historical characters, values and beliefs,* and *despised characteristics.* Discuss the meaning of each of these categories.
5. This activity may proceed as a whole-group activity that becomes a group or individual activity. For example, choose one of the folk tales and read it to the class.

Lead a discussion in which you help the students identify values and beliefs or other areas on the web. Place these values, beliefs, and so forth on the web and identify the story that represents that category. After several books have been completed and discussed with the whole class, divide the class into groups or allow individual reading and analysis.

6. The following is a partial web that was developed with a group of students. The original web was much larger than the one shown in the drawing. The web will become larger as students add additional books and stories.

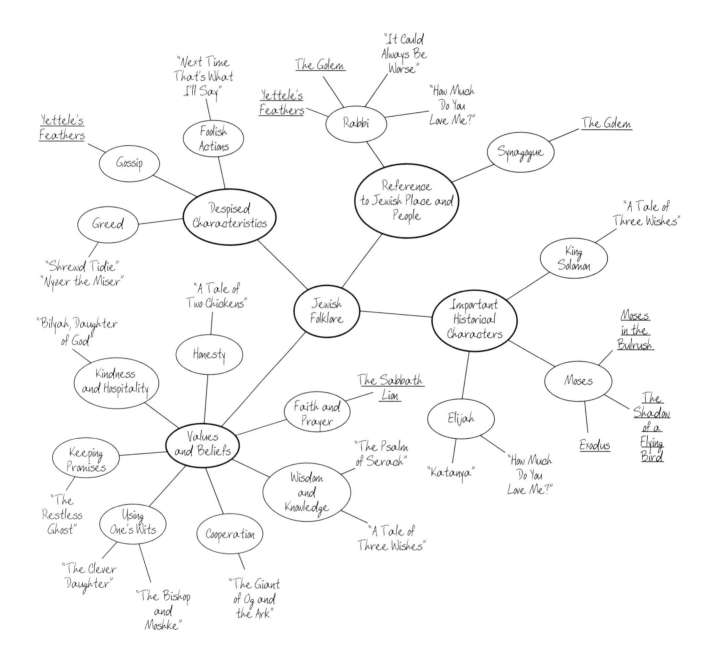

7. Students may summarize what they have discovered about the Jewish culture by placing their findings on a chart such as the following:

JEWISH CULTURE				
Cultural Knowledge	*Values and Beliefs*	*Historical Characters*	*Admired Characteristics*	*Despised Characteristics*
Example of story				
Proof from story				

8. Discuss the understandings gained from this study of Jewish folklore.

9. Students can take part in a culminating activity in which they prepare favorite folktales to be told orally or to be presented as a readers' theater production.

10. Students can also write their own literary folktales that follow the format of and develop the characteristics of traditional literature.

Activity 8–20:

TRADITIONAL VALUES— FOLKLORE FROM THE MIDDLE EAST

TYPE	TERM
● CLASS	○ STA
● GROUP	● LTA
● IND	○ LC

Purpose:

1. To develop an appreciation for the folk tales, myths, and legends from various countries of the Middle East
2. To identify and analyze the respected values, beliefs, and disliked qualities in folklore from the Middle East

Materials:

Collect numerous folktales, myths, and legends from countries of the Middle East. You may do one country at a time, if desired, later adding other countries and comparing the results. Examples of the books available include Inea Bushnaq's *Arab Folktales* (1986, an adult source), Lise Manniche's *The Prince Who Knew His Fate* (1981, Egypt), A. E. Jackson's *Ali Baba and the Forty Thieves and Other Stories* (1994), Eric A. Kimmel's *The Three Princes: A Tale from the Middle East* (1994) and *The Tale of Aladdin and the Wonderful Lamp: A Story from the Arabian Nights* (1992), Neil Philips's *The Arabian Nights* (1994), Diane Stanley's *Fortune* (1990), David Kherdian's *Feathers and Tales: Animal Fables from Around the World* (1992), Jules Cashford's *The Myth of Isis and Osiris* (1993, Egypt), Virginia Hamilton's *In the Beginning: Creation Stories from Around the World* (1988, Egyptian myth "The Sun-God and the Dragon: God Ra the Creator"), and Shulamith Levy Oppenheim's *Ibis* (1994, Islamic).

Grade level:

Middle and upper elementary, middle school

Book summaries:

The listed books contain a variety of folk tales from the Middle East that provide opportunities for students to identify and analyze characteristics of the folklore.

Procedures:

1. Introduce the Middle East by showing its location on a map. Tell the students that folklore from the Middle East includes literature from a wide range of countries, from Egypt and Turkey to Saudi Arabia, Yemen, and Iran. The literature may also include the influence of the Islamic faith. (Students in middle school may be studying the Middle East as part of the social studies or history curriculum. These curricular goals may be easily added to this study of traditional values.)
2. Remind the students that traditional literature was passed from generation to generation through the oral tradition before the stories were written.
3. Place a web on the chalkboard or on a transparency. Write *Folklore from the Middle East* in the center of the web. Then write *respected values, beliefs,* and *disliked qualities* on the web. Read several of the books as a group and include their characteristics on the web. You may continue the activity as a group or individual activity as students read additional stories. The following example is a partial web developed around the literature:

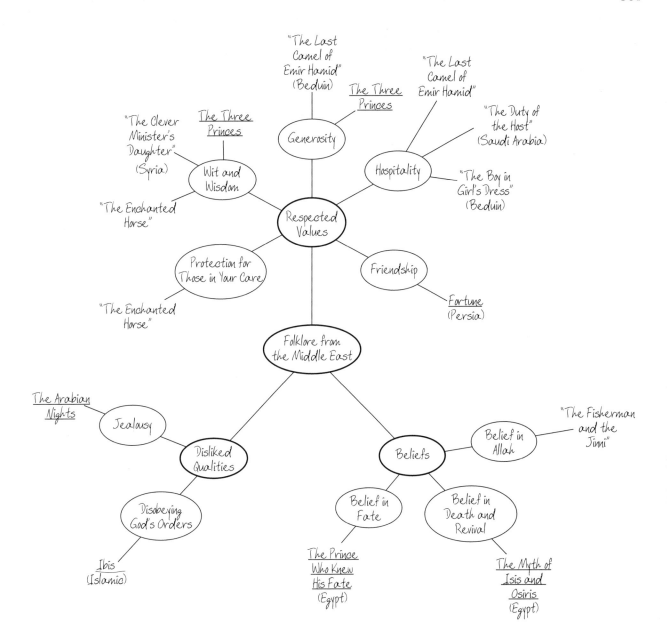

4. After completing the web, lead a discussion in which the students summarize their findings and compare values, beliefs, and disliked qualities from different countries in the Middle East. You may ask them to complete a chart similar to the one used to summarize the Jewish culture in activity 8–19.

5. Many of the books include beautiful illustrations. The cultural knowledge gained from the folklore may be expanded to an analysis of the cultural information included in the illustrations. Several adult sources add interest to such a study and encourage students to authenticate the illustrations found in the folklore. Excellent adult sources include *The Art and Architecture of Islam: 1250–1800* by Shelia S. Blair and Jonathan M. Bloom (1994) and *The Ancient Egyptian: Book of the Dead* translated by Raymond O. Faulkner (1985).

6. Tales such as the various versions of "The Arabian Nights" lend themselves to oral storytelling sessions in which students try to tell stories that will allow them, like Shahrazad, to save their lives. The introduction to the adult source, *Tales from the Arabian Nights: A Thousand Nights and a Night* by Sir Richard Burton (1985), states

that many of the stories were performed as pantomimes during the Christmas holidays. In keeping with this tradition, students could pantomime these stories.

7. The introduction to Burton's text also provides additional information about the tales that could be used for analysis: "The origins of *The Thousand Nights and a Night* are remote and obscure. Burton deduced that the tales were handed down from generation to generation of professional story tellers and that the oldest stories probably dated from the 8th century A.D. They are of three types. The classic fable; the Fairy tales, those based on some super-natural agency, (this was a favorite type of tale in old Persia and much deplored by the puritanical Mohammed); and the stories based on historical fact or anecdote" (p. vii). Older students could analyze some of the tales from "The Arabian Nights" and divide them into these three categories (classic fable, fairy tale, or historical story). In addition, they could investigate the teachings of Mohammad and identify how some of these tales might differ from Mohammad's beliefs and values.

Activity 8–21:

PEOPLE FROM ALL BACKGROUNDS HAVE DREAMS THAT INFLUENCE THEIR LIVES

TYPE	TERM
● CLASS	○ STA
● GROUP	● LTA
○ IND	LC

Purpose:

1. To develop an understanding that people from all backgrounds have dreams that influence their lives
2. To develop an understanding that people from all backgrounds have strong desires and that they may work very hard to reach their goals
3. To research a nonfictional person who has had a dream and to find out how the dream influenced his or her life
4. To write a story about one's own dream and how it may be accomplished

Materials:

Fictional and nonfictional literature about people who have dreams that influence their lives, including Judith Bentley's *Harriet Tubman* (1990, African-American), Carol Fenner's *Yolonda's Genius* (1995, African-American; a Newbery Honor Award winner, 1996), Virginia Hamilton's *Anthony Burns: The Defeat and Triumph of a Fugitive Slave* (1988, African-American), Gaye Hicyilmaz's *Against the Storm* (1992, Turkish), Joseph Krumgold's *. . . And Now Miguel* (1953, Hispanic), Robert Lipsyte's *The Brave* (1991, Native American), Michele Murray's *Nellie Cameron* (1971, African-American), Walter Dean Myers's *Now Is Your Time!: The African-American Struggle for Freedom* (1991, African-American), Gary Soto's *Taking Sides* (1991, Hispanic), Fay Stanley's *The Last Princess: The Story of Princess Ka'iulani of Hawai'i*(1991, Hawaiian), Tobi Tobias's *Maria Tallchief* (1970, Native American), Laurence Yep's *Dragonwings* (1975, Chinese-American), and *Sea Glass* (1979, Chinese-American), and Ruth Ashby and Deborah Gore Ohrn's *Herstory: Women Who Changed the World* (1995).

Grade level:

Middle and upper elementary and middle school—depending on the literature chosen

Book summaries:

The book summaries are provided in the following procedures section.

Procedures:

1. Introduce the subject by allowing students to talk about their own dreams and how those dreams have influenced their lives or will shape their lives in the future. Ask the students if they have ever known anyone whose life was influenced by a strong desire. What did he or she do to make the dream come true? Ask them if they have read any books about people who tried to make dreams come true. Encourage the students to list other people's dreams that could influence their lives. Have them consider some obstacles to those dreams and what a person might have to accomplish to overcome the obstacles.
2. Have each student read a different book about a real or fictional character who attained a dream after overcoming obstacles.
3. Provide a brief introduction to a book that your students would like to read. The listed materials are examples of books that develop characters who have attained their dreams:

> *Harriet Tubman:* Harriet Tubman is one of the great women of history; she escaped from slavery and then dedicated her life to helping others travel

north on the Underground Railroad. To fulfill her dreams she also became involved in a number of causes, including the women's suffrage movement.

Yolonda's Genius: Yolonda is determined that her brother is a musical genius and not a slow learner, as he has been labeled.

Anthony Burns: The Defeat and Triumph of a Fugitive Slave: Anthony Burns had a dream of freedom. The story shows what happens when a group of abolitionists, who also believe in the dream, and the Boston Vigilance Committee defend the rights of fugitive slaves.

Against the Storm: A boy in Turkey discovers that it is difficult to retain his dreams when his family moves from their rural home to the poverty of a large city. His experiences, however, allow him to become stronger in spirit and to return to his village, where he will be prepared to work for a better life.

. . . And Now Miguel: Miguel Chavez's family raises sheep. His great dream is to go with the older sheepherders to the Sangre de Cristo Mountains. Miguel strives to make everyone realize that he is ready for this difficult journey. When he is finally allowed to accompany his elders to the mountains, he feels pride in his family's traditions and his accomplishments.

The Brave: A Native American youth has a dream to become a heavyweight boxing contender. He must experience much more than rigorous training, however, if he is to reach his goal as a contender.

Nellie Cameron: Nellie is an unhappy child who experiences conflicting emotions. She feels confident during athletic activities but "too dumb to live" when she is in the classroom and must read. Although Nellie portrays a wistful determination to succeed, she considers reading to be a mountain that she cannot climb; she can see the top is beautiful, but she does not know how to reach it. Nellie finally feels proud of herself when she learns to read with the help of an understanding remedial reading teacher.

Now Is Your Time!: The African-American Struggle for Freedom: The author explores dreams of many people as he describes the lives of various people across time. Some of these people dream of freedom during slavery, while others continue their dreams and struggles during the Civil Rights movement of the 1960s and into contemporary times.

Taking Sides: Lincoln Mendoza is an aspiring basketball player. When he moves from the inner city to a white suburban neighborhood he tries to keep his dreams alive as he plays on the basketball team at his new school. He faces conflict when his new school faces his old school in a league game. Can he retain his loyalties to his old friends and still play for the new team?

The Last Princess: The Story of Princess Ka'iulani of Hawai'i: This biography is about a princess who fights bravely to preserve the rights of her people. Even though the monarchy was abolished, she gained the respect of her people.

Maria Tallchief: A talented prima ballerina studies piano and ballet with determination. After working very hard, she is asked to dance with the Paris Opera Ballet, the New York City Ballet, and the American Ballet Theatre.

Dragonwings: The setting for this book is based on a true incident that happened in San Francisco in 1903. A Chinese boy joins his father in America, where he discovers the problems that are associated with being a Chinese immigrant. However, he also discovers the powerful influence of his father's dream. Motivated by the early work of Orville and Wilbur

Wright, the father dreams of building a flying machine. After overcoming many obstacles, the father, with his son's assistance, builds an airplane and soars off the cliffs that overlook San Francisco Bay.

Sea Glass: Craig is an unhappy boy whose dream is in conflict with his father's dream for him. Craig tries unsuccessfully to fulfill his father's dreams of having a son with great athletic ability. With the help of an old Chinese uncle, Craig learns to respect himself and convinces his father that Craig's own dreams must be taken seriously.

Herstory: Women Who Changed the World: This book includes 120 biographical sketches about women from many cultural backgrounds. The sketches are divided into three time periods: "The Dawn—Prehistory to 1750," "From Revolution to Revolution, 1750 to 1850," and "The Global Community, 1890 to the Present."

4. After the students have read the books, ask them to share their discoveries about the influence of dreams and desires. Have them describe what actions their characters took to realize their dreams.

5. Have students select a nonfictional person who has had a dream. Have them do library research to discover how the dream influenced his or her life.

6. Ask the students to identify a dream that either influences their lives or that they would like to have influence their lives. Have them write a short story about their dream, describing how it might change their lives.

REFERENCES

Ballinger, F. (1984). A matter of emphasis: Teaching the "literature" in Native American literature courses. *American Indian Culture and Research Journal, 8,* 1–12.

Blair, S. S., & Bloom, J. M. (1994). *The art and architecture of Islam, 1250–1800.* New Haven, CT: Yale University Press.

Burton, R. (1985). *Tales from the Arabian nights: A thousand nights and a night.* New York: Excalibur.

Committee on Geographic Education. (1983). *Guidelines for geographic education: Elementary and secondary schools.* Washington, DC: National Council for Geographic Education and the Association of American Geographers.

Dorris, M. (1979, October). Native American literature in an ethnohistorical context. *College English, 41,* 147–162.

Faulkner, R. O. (1985). *The ancient Egyptian: Book of the dead.* New York: Macmillan.

GEO News Handbook. 1990, November 11–17, p. 7.

Kertzer, M. N. (1993). *What Is a Jew?* New York: Macmillan.

Norton, D. E. (1997). *The effective teaching of language arts* (5th ed.). New York: Merrill/Macmillan.

Norton, D. E. (1990, September). Teaching multicultural literature in the reading program. *The Reading Teacher, 44,* 28–40.

Norton, D. E. (1999). *Through the eyes of a child: An introduction to children's literature.* New York: Merrill/Macmillan.

Sutherland, Z., & Livingston, M. C. (1984). *The Scott, Foresman anthology of children's literature.* Glenview, IL: Scott, Foresman.

CHILDREN'S LITERATURE REFERENCES

Aardema, Verna. *Tales from the Story Hat.* New York: Coward, McCann, & Geoghegan, 1960.

Aardema, Verna. *Why Mosquitoes Buzz in People's Ears.* New York: Dial, 1975.

Aardema, Verna. *Who's in Rabbit's House?* New York: Dial, 1977.

Aardema, Verna. *The Riddle of the Drum: A Tale from Tizapan, Mexico.* New York: Four Winds, 1979.

Aardema, Verna. *Bringing the Rain to Kapiti Plain: A Nandi Tale.* New York: Dial, 1981.

Aardema, Verna. *What's So Funny, Ketu? A Nuer Tale.* New York: Dial, 1982.

Ashby, Ruth, and Ohrn, Deborah Gore (eds.). *Herstory: Women Who Changed the World.* New York: Viking, 1995.

Baker, Olaf. *Where the Buffaloes Begin.* Illustrated by Stephen Gammell. New York: Warne, 1981.

Baylor, Byrd. *Hawk, I'm Your Brother.* Illustrated by Peter Parnall. New York: Scribner's, 1976.

Belpré, Pura. *The Rainbow-Colored Horse.* Illustrated by Antonio Martorell. New York: Warne, 1978.

Bentley, Judith. *Harriet Tubman.* New York: Watts, 1990.

Bierhorst, John. *A Cry from the Earth: Music of the North American Indians.* New York: Four Winds, 1979.

Blair, Walter. *Tall Tale America: A Legendary History of Our Humorous Heroes.* Illustrated by Glen Rounds. New York: Coward, McCann, 1944.

Bodecker, N. M. *It's Raining, Said John Twaining.* New York: Atheneum, 1973.

Bryan, Ashley. *The Ox of the Wonderful Horns and Other African Folktales.* New York: Atheneum, 1971.

Bryan, Ashley. *Walk Together Children: Black American Spirituals,* Vol. 1. New York: Atheneum, 1974.

Bryan, Ashley. *Beat the Story-Drum, Pum-Pum.* New York: Atheneum, 1980.

Bryan, Ashley. *I'm Going to Sing: Black American Spirituals,* Vol. 2. New York: Atheneum, 1982.

Bryan, Ashley. *All Night, All Day: A Child's First Book of African-American Spirituals.* New York: Atheneum, 1991.

Bushnaq, Inea. *Arab Folktales.* New York: Pantheon, 1986.

Caduto, Michael J., and Bruchac, Joseph. *Keepers of the Animals: Native American Stories and Wildlife Activities for Children.* Illustrated by John Kahionhes Fadden. Golden, CO: Fulcrum, 1991.

Cashford, Jules. *The Myth of Isis and Osiris.* Boston: Barefoot Books, 1993.

Chang, Isabelle. *Chinese Fairy Tales.* New York: Barre, 1965.

Cohlene, Terri. *Turquoise Boy: A Navajo Legend.* Illustrated by Charles Reasoner. Mahwah, NJ: Watermill, 1990.

Courlander, Harold. *The Crest and the Hide: And Other African Stories of Heroes, Chiefs, Bards, Hunters, Sorcerers, and Common People.* Illustrated by Monica Vachula. New York: Coward, McCann, 1982.

Day, Edward C. *John Tabor's Ride*. Illustrated by Dirk Zimmer. New York: Alfred Knopf, 1989.

Day, Nancy Raines. *The Lion's Whiskers: An Ethiopian Folktale*. Illustrated by Ann Grifalconi. New York: Scholastic, 1995.

De Angeli, Marguerite. *Marguerite De Angeli's Book of Nursery and Mother Goose Rhymes*. New York: Doubleday, 1954.

De Forest, Charlotte B. *The Prancing Pony: Nursery Rhymes from Japan*. Illustrated by Keiko Hida. New York: Walker/Weatherhill, 1968.

Demi. *Dragon Kites and Dragonflies: A Collection of Chinese Nursery Rhymes*. San Diego: Harcourt Brace Jovanovich, 1986.

dePaola, Tomie. *The Lady of Guadalupe*. New York: Holiday, 1980.

dePaola, Tomie. *The Legend of the Bluebonnet*. New York: Putnam's, 1983.

Duncan, Lois. *The Magic of Spider Woman*. Illustrated by Shonto Begay. New York: Scholastic, 1996.

Ehlert, Lois. *Cuckoo: A Mexican Folktale*. San Diego: Harcourt Brace, 1997.

Esbensen, Barbara Juster. *The Star Maiden*. Illustrated by Helen K. Davie. Boston: Little, Brown, 1988.

Fenner, Carol. *Yolonda's Genius*. New York: Simon & Schuster, 1995.

Field, Edward. *Eskimo Songs and Stories*. New York: Delacorte, 1973.

Fox, Dan. *Go in and out the Window: An Illustrated Songbook for Young People*. New York: Metropolitan Museum of Art and Holt, 1987.

Fritz, Jean. *The Double Life of Pocahontas*. Illustrated by Ed Young. New York: Putnam's, 1983.

Geras, Adele. *My Grandmother's Stories: A Collection of Jewish Folk Tales*. Illustrated by Jael Jordon. New York: Alfred Knopf, 1990.

Goble, Paul. *The Girl Who Loved Wild Horses*. New York: Bradbury, 1978.

Goble, Paul. *The Gift of the Sacred Dog*. New York: Bradbury, 1980.

Goble, Paul. *Star Boy*. New York: Bradbury, 1983.

Goble, Paul. *Buffalo Woman*. New York: Bradbury, 1984.

Goble, Paul. *Iktomi and the Boulder*. New York: Watts, 1988.

Goble, Paul. *Beyond the Ridge*. New York: Bradbury, 1989.

Goble, Paul. *Iktomi and the Berries*. New York: Watts, 1989.

Goble, Paul. *Dream Wolf*. New York: Bradbury, 1990.

Griego, Margot C., Bucks, Betsy L., Gilbert, Sharon S., and Kimball, Laurel H. *Tortillitas Para Mama and Other Spanish Nursery Rhymes*. Illustrated by Barbara Cooney. New York: Holt, Rinehart & Winston, 1981.

Grimes, Nikki. *Something on My Mind*. Illustrated by Tom Feelings. New York: Dial, 1978.

Grimm, Brothers. *Little Red Riding Hood*. Retold and illustrated by Trina Schart Hyman. New York: Holiday, 1983.

Haley, Gail E. *A Story, A Story*. New York: Atheneum, 1970.

Hamilton, Virginia. *Zeely*. New York: Macmillan, 1967.

Hamilton, Virginia. *The Time-Ago Tales of Jahdu*. New York: Macmillan, 1969.

Hamilton, Virginia. *Anthony Burns: The Defeat and Triumph of a Fugitive Slave.* New York: Alfred Knopf, 1988.

Hamilton, Virginia. *In the Beginning: Creation Stories from Around the World.* Illustrated by Barry Moser. San Diego: Harcourt Brace, 1988.

Hamilton, Virginia. *When Birds Could Talk and Bats Could Sing: The Adventures of Bruh Sparrow, Sis Wren, and Their Friends.* Illustrated by Barry Moser. New York: Scholastic, 1996.

Hart, Jane. *Singing Bee! A Collection of Favorite Children's Songs.* Illustrated by Anita Lobel. New York: Lothrop, Lee & Shepard, 1982.

He Liyi. *The Spring of Butterflies and Other Chinese Folktales.* Edited by Neil Philip; illustrated by Pan Aiqing and Li Zhao. New York: Lothrop, Lee & Shepard, 1985.

Hearn, Lafcadio. *The Voice of the Great Bell.* Retold by Margaret Hodges; illustrated by Ed Young. Boston: Little, Brown, 1989.

Heyer, Marilee. *The Weaving of a Dream.* New York: Viking Kestrel, 1986.

Hicyilmaz, Gaye. *Against the Storm.* Boston: Little, Brown, 1992.

Hom, David. *Literature of American Music in Books and Folk Music.* Metuchen, NJ: Scarecrow Press, 1977.

Hyun, Peter. *Korea's Favorite Tales and Lyrics.* Illustrated by Dong-il Park. Seoul, Korea & Rutland, Vermont: Tuttle/Seoul International, 1986.

Ike, Jane Hori, and Zimmerman, Baruch. *A Japanese Fairy Tale.* New York: Warne, 1982.

Jackson, A. E. *Ali Baba and the Forty Thieves and Other Stories.* New York: Derrydale, 1994.

Jacobs, Francine. *The Tainos: The People Who Welcomed Columbus.* New York: Putnam's, 1992.

Jagendorf, M. A., and Boggs, R. S. *The King of the Mountains: A Treasury of Latin American Folk Stories.* New York: Vanguard, 1960.

Kellogg, Steven. *Paul Bunyan.* New York: Morrow, 1984.

Kherdian, David. *Feathers and Tails: Animal Fables from Around the World.* Illustrated by Nonny Hogrogian. New York: Philomel, 1992.

Kimmel, Eric A. *The Tale of Aladdin and the Wonderful Lamp: A Story from the Arabian Nights.* Illustrated by Ju-Hong Chen. New York: Holiday, 1992.

Kimmel, Eric. *The Three Princes: A Tale from the Middle East.* Illustrated by Everett Fisher. New York: Holiday, 1994.

Krumgold, Joseph. *. . . And Now Miguel.* New York: Crowell, 1953.

Lampman, Evelyn Sibley. *The Potlatch Family.* New York: Atheneum, 1976.

Lacapa, Kathleen, and Lacapa, Michael. *Less than Half, More than Whole.* Flagstaff, AZ: Northland, 1994.

Leon, George DeLucenay. *Explorers of the Americas before Columbus.* New York: Watts, 1989.

Lipsyte, Robert. *The Brave.* New York: HarperCollins, 1991.

Lyons, Mary E. *Raw Head, Bloody Bones: African-American Tales of the Supernatural.* New York: Scribner's, 1991.

Major, John S. *The Silk Route: 7,000 Miles of History.* Illustrated by Stephen Fieser. New York: HarperCollins, 1995.

Manniche, Lise. *The Prince Who Knew His Fate.* New York: Philomel, 1981.

McDermott, Gerald. *Anansi the Spider: A Tale from the Ashanti.* New York: Holt, Rinehart & Winston, 1972.

McDermott, Gerald. *Zomo the Rabbit: A Trickster Tale from West Africa.* San Diego: Harcourt Brace, 1992.

Metayer, Maurice. *Tales from the Igloo.* Illustrated by Agnes Nanogak. Edmonton, Alberta: Hurtig, 1972.

Mollel, Tololwa M. *A Promise to the Sun: An African Story.* Illustrated by Beatriz Vidal. Boston: Little, Brown, 1992.

Monroe, Jean Guard, and Williamson, Ray A. *They Dance in the Sky: Native American Star Myths.* Illustrated by Edgar Stewart. Boston: Houghton Mifflin, 1987.

Murray, Michele. *Nellie Cameron.* Seabury, 1971.

Myers, Walter Dean. *Now Is Your Time!: The African-American Struggle for Freedom.* New York: HarperCollins, 1991.

Myers, Walter Dean. *The Story of Three Kingdoms.* Illustrated by Ashley Bryan. New York: HarperCollins, 1995.

Newton, Patricia Montgomery. *The Five Sparrows: A Japanese Folktale.* New York: Atheneum, 1982.

Normandin, Christine, ed. *Echoes of the Elders: The Stories and Paintings of Chief Lalooska.* New York: DK, 1997.

Opie, Iona, and Opie, Peter. *A Nursery Companion.* New York: Oxford, 1980.

Opie, Iona, and Opie, Peter. *The Oxford Nursery Rhyme Book.* Illustrated by Joan Hassall. New York: Oxford, 1955, 1984.

Opie, Iona, and Opie, Peter. *Tail Feathers from Mother Goose: The Opie Rhyme Book.* Boston: Little, Brown, 1988.

Opie, Iona, and Opie, Peter. *I Saw Esau: The Schoolchild's Pocket Book.* Illustrated by Maurice Sendak. Cambridge, MA: Candlewick, 1992.

Oppenheim, Shulamith Levy. *Ibis.* Illustrated by Ed Young. San Diego: Harcourt Brace, 1994.

Paterson, Katherine. *The Tale of the Mandarin Ducks.* Illustrated by Leo and Diane Dillon. New York: Lodestar, 1990.

Philips, Neil. *The Arabian Nights.* Illustrated by Sheila Moxley. New York: Oxford, 1992.

Pollock, Penny. *The Turkey Girl: A Zuni Cinderella Story.* Boston: Little, Brown, 1996.

Rohmer, Harriet, and Wilson, Dorminster. *Mother Scorpion Country.* Illustrated by Virginia Stearns. San Francisco: Children's Book Press, 1987.

Rosen, Michael. *Crow and Hawk: A Traditional Pueblo Indian Story.* San Diego: Harcourt Brace, 1995.

Rothenberg, Joan. *Yettele's Feathers.* New York: Hyperion, 1995.

Sadler, Catherine Edwards. *Treasure Mountain: Folktales from Southern China.* Illustrated by Cheng Mung Yun. New York: Atheneum, 1982.

Sanfield, Steve. *The Feather Merchants and Other Tales of the Fools of Chelm*. Illustrated by Mikhail Magaril. New York: Orchard, 1991.

San Souci, Robert D. *Sukey and the Mermaid*. Illustrated by Brian Pinkney. New York: Four Winds, 1992.

Schwartz, Howard, and Rush, Barbara. *The Diamond Tree: Jewish Tales from Around the World*. Illustrated by Uri Shulevitz. New York: HarperCollins, 1991.

Schwartz, Howard, and Rush, Barbara. *The Sabbath Lion: A Jewish Folktale from Algeria*. Illustrated by Stephen Fieser. New York: HarperCollins, 1992.

Sewall, Marcia. *People of the Breaking Day*. New York: Atheneum, 1990.

Sherman, Josepha. *Jewish American Folklore*. Little Rock, AR: August House, 1992.

Sherman, Josepha. *Rachel the Clever and Other Jewish Folktales*. Little Rock, AR: August House, 1993.

Singer, Isaac Bashevis. *When Shlemiel Went to Warsaw and Other Stories*. Illustrated by Margot Zemach. New York: Farrar, Straus & Giroux, 1968.

Soto, Gary. *Taking Sides*. San Diego: Harcourt Brace Jovanovich, 1991.

Stamm, Claus. *Three Strong Women: A Tall Tale from Japan*. Illustrated by Jean and Mou-sien Tseng. New York: Viking, 1990.

Stanley, Diane. *Fortune*. New York: Morrow, 1990.

Stanley, Fay. *The Last Princess: The Story of Princess Ka'iulani of Hawai'i*. Illustrated by Diane Stanley. New York: Four Winds, 1991.

Stewart, Dianne. *Gift of the Sun: A Tale from South Africa*. Illustrated by Jude Daly. New York: Farrar, Straus & Giroux, 1996.

Tobias, Tobi. *Maria Tallchief*. New York: Crowell, 1970.

Volkmer, Jane Anne. *Song of the Chirimia: A Guatemalan Folktale*. Minneapolis: Carolrhoda, 1990.

Walker, Barbara K. *The Dancing Palm Tree and Other Nigerian Folktales*. Illustrated by Helen Siegl. Lubbock: Texas Tech University Press, 1990.

Weinreich, Beatrice Silverman. *Yiddish Folktales*. New York: Pantheon, 1988.

Wisniewski, David. *Golem*. New York: Clarion, 1996.

Wyndham, Robert. *Chinese Mother Goose Rhymes*. Illustrated by Ed Young. New York: Philomel, 1982.

Yagawa, Sumiko. *The Crane Wife*. Translated by Katherine Paterson; illustrated by Suekichi Akaba. New York: Morrow, 1981.

Yep, Laurence. *Dragonwings*. New York: Harper & Row, 1975.

Yep, Laurence. *Child of the Owl*. New York: Harper & Row, 1977.

Yep, Laurence. *Sea Glass*. New York: Harper & Row, 1979.

Yep, Laurence. *The Rainbow People*. Illustrated by David Wiesner. New York: Harper & Row, 1989.

Yolen, Jane. *Encounter*. Illustrated by David Shannon. San Diego: Harcourt Brace Jovanovich, 1992.

Young, Ed. *Lon Po Po: A Red-Riding Hood Story from China*. New York: Philomel, 1989.

9

Technology and the Language Arts

Activities that integrate technology and the language arts curriculum expand the boundaries of the traditional classroom. The Internet, which includes electronic mail (e-mail) and the World Wide Web, has become a global system for communication and information exchange. In using the Internet in the classroom, students are able to exchange ideas and communicate with schools from different geographical locations. In communicating with students from backgrounds that are different from their own, children are given the opportunity to understand a different culture and to become an active part of a global community. When compared with traditional classroom methods, the Internet offers students the most immediate opportunity to broaden their perspectives on global issues (U.S. Congress, 1995). The Internet also allows students to collaborate on writing and research projects with students, teachers, and field specialists from around the world.

Teachers and students who were once limited to the resources of their local school or library have more information available to them through the Internet. Because a seemingly unlimited amount of information is available on the Internet, the language arts classroom provides students the structure they need to help them learn to discriminate between the useful and irrelevant sources that can be found on the Internet. Activities that involve research and the Internet encourage students to collect and analyze source materials at a relatively rapid pace and thereby increase a student's research and analytical capabilities. As a result, students who learn to conduct research on the Internet are better prepared to adapt to the changing technologies that will continue to be part of their future (Leu, 1997).

Activities that involve process writing and publishing on the Internet provide students with more meaningful writing experiences because they encourage feedback from a distant audience and lead to more revision of student work. Studies show that when students write for a distant audience of their peers, they are more motivated to write and to share their knowledge and experiences (Cohen & Riel, 1989).

As the information superhighway meets the classroom, language arts educators confront the challenge of keeping up with constantly changing technologies. In the process, they must also guide their students and "become more knowledgeable in their roles as guides and facilitators of learning" (Kinzer & Leu, 1987, p. 134). In all likelihood, technology's role in the classroom will continue to increase. The number of K–12 classrooms connected to the Internet in the United States has been tripling every year (U.S. Congress, 1995). If this rate continues, every classroom will have an Internet connection within a few years, a widely publicized goal of the Clinton administration (Leu, 1997). Educators such as McGarvey (1997) believe strongly in the powers of the Internet to enrich the classroom. Hilts (1997) also maintains that computer technology and the Internet will have a tremendous influence in the future.

It is to an educator's advantage to explore the abundance of opportunities that are available when integrating technology into the language arts curriculum. This chapter includes a wide range of activities designed to increase students' knowledge of and appreciation for computer technology in the language arts classroom.

Activity 9–1:

TECHNOLOGY AND SOCIETY:
A HISTORY OF INFORMATION EXCHANGE

TYPE	TERM
● CLASS	● STA
● GROUP	● LTA
○ IND	○ LC

Purpose:
1. To develop an understanding of the changes in and chronological order of technology
2. To relate informational exchanges with history
3. To use prior knowledge to speculate about worlds without technology or worlds with a technological influence that is too powerful

Materials:
Steven Kroll's *Pony Express* (1996), Jennifer Erivitt and Rick Snolan's *24 Hours in Cyberspace: Painting on the Walls of the Digital Cave* (1996) (photographs may also be viewed on the book's web site at http://www.cyber24.com), Monica Hughes's *The Dream Catcher* (1987) and *Devil on My Back* (1987), and Virginia Hamilton's *The Gathering* (1981).

Grade level:
All grades, depending on the material used.

Book summaries:
Pony Express presents the history of the postal service. *24 Hours in Cyberspace: Painting on the Walls of the Digital Cave* documents the human side of technology through the eyes of photojournalists. *The Dream Catcher* speculates about social and political changes in A.D. 2147. *Devil on My Back* presents person versus society conflict in science fiction. *The Gathering* is a story of how survivors of a future world in which the earth supports only dust and mutant forms of animal and human life program a computer that helps rehabilitate the wasteland.

Procedures:
1. Have students consider the changes that have occurred in the world during the last one hundred years due to technological inventions such as airplanes, automobiles, calculators, and computers.
2. Read Steven Kroll's *Pony Express* to your class. Discuss the history of the postal service and information exchange as it is presented in the book. Have students pay particular attention to how the speed of information exchange increases as new technologies are created. For example, a letter traveling by ship took six months, a letter traveling by stagecoach took twenty-three days, the "horse express" took ten days, and a letter sent by a fax machine or e-mail takes only minutes to reach its destination.
3. Familiarize students with the current technologies of e-mail and the Internet. As already seen in *Pony Express,* e-mail is a form of exchanging letters and information through a computer. Ask students what they think about when you say the word *Internet.* Although some students have had very little exposure to the Internet and computers, others have already been introduced to both technologies at home. Have students brainstorm and list as many words as they can to describe the Internet. Ask students what images they think about when they hear phrases such as *information superhighway* and *surfing the net in cyberspace.*

4. Introduce students to the brief history of the Internet. Explain that it was created by the U.S. Department of Defense during the height of the cold war to provide authorities with a way to communicate in case of a nuclear attack. Previously, communications systems over the computer were connected point to point so that each place on the network was dependent on the link before it. If one point was destroyed, the whole network became useless. During the 1960s scientists designed a computer system set up more like a fishnet so that if one portion was destroyed, the system itself could still operate.

5. To generate discussion about how the Internet is used today, show students photographs from *24 Hours in Cyberspace: Painting the Walls of the Digital Cave.* For example, in one photograph an Inuit boy in Sachs Harbor, Canada, is shown in his parka sitting in front of a computer with friends. The narrative emphasizes that the boy spends his mornings on his father's dogsled traveling across the tundra, cutting ice blocks for water, and hunting caribou for dinner. During the evening, he surfs the Internet, sending digital pictures of his life to others around the world. In another photograph, a South African youth is shown carrying a computer on his head as he goes to the computer laboratory located in the Nelson Mandela Township Police Station in Port Alfred, South Africa. The narrative reveals that the youth uses the Internet to practice his English and correspond via e-mail about race relations and other subjects with students from all over the world.

6. Ask students to speculate about a world without technological inventions and a world in which these inventions could become too powerful. To generate discussion, have students read and discuss fictional books such as Monica Hughes's *The Dream Catcher* and *Devil on My Back,* in which rigid class systems are imposed on societies by the computer, and Virginia Hamilton's *The Gathering,* in which a computer programmed by survivors in a futuristic world helps rehabilitate a wasteland.

Activity 9–2:

INTRODUCING COMPUTER TECHNOLOGY THROUGH LITERATURE: SUSAN COOPER'S *THE BOGGART*

TYPE	TERM
● CLASS	● STA
● GROUP	● LTA
● IND	○ LC

Purpose:
1. To develop concepts related to computer technology through a discussion of literature
2. To compare characteristics of two different time periods
3. To analyze and evaluate information found in literature
4. To develop an understanding of computer-related vocabulary
5. To write a story related to personal experiences with a computer

Materials: Susan Cooper's *The Boggart* (1993).

Grade level: Upper elementary and middle school

Book summary: In Susan Cooper's *The Boggart,* Emily Volnik and her nine-year-old computer-genius brother, Jessup, inherit a Scottish castle and the mischievous spirit that comes with it. After they accidentally transport the Boggart back to Canada with them, they must use computer technology to help the Boggart return to Scotland.

Procedures:
1. Have students read Susan Cooper's *The Boggart.* Tell them to pay close attention to the role technology plays in the story. As they read, ask them to keep a record of the characters' various reactions and attitudes toward computer technology.

2. Using evidence from the text, have students contrast the ancient Scottish world where the Boggart comes from and the Volniks' modern-day world in Toronto. How does the ancient magic of the Boggart clash with modern technology? What evidence from the text shows that the Boggart knows very little about modern technology? For example, when Emily uses an eggbeater, the Boggart is surprised by the "magical whirring whisk that beat eggs," but soon finds that he "could make the lights flicker as if a bulb were about to burn out, or make the telephone ring even though nobody was calling" (p. 70). When he learns to manipulate lights from within the computer he realizes that "[b]y his own magic, he was using the magic of this new technological world in which he found himself—and the mixing of the two magics was a wonder" (p. 116).

3. What evidence from the text shows that Jessup is very comfortable with computer technology? For example, he is described as having a "cautious computer-trained mind" (p. 182). He and his friends from the Gang of Five are able to manipulate typefaces, develop computer games, and program their own computers.

4. Discuss the vocabulary words associated with computer technology that appear throughout the book. Ask students to help you find and define the terms. Computer-related vocabulary words that appear in the text include the following: keyboard, computer screen, megahertz, computer workstation, thirty-four inch color monitor, hard drive, bit, computer games, virus, antivirus program,

info-loop, lapsing into computalk, the computer will crash, voice synthesis, copy a file, and transferring files.

5. Have students write about their own experiences with computers. Ask them to respond to questions such as the following: "Do you identify yourself more with the Boggart or with Jessup and the Gang of Five? What would you do if you had the Boggart's powers? How would you manipulate technology?"

6. When Emily and Jessup lost the Boggart inside the computer, they "stared at the computer screen in horror. The dark whirlpool filled it, throbbing, like a living picture of death. Jessup jabbed frantically at different combinations of keys on the keyboard, but nothing changed" (p. 168). Ask students the following: "Have you ever 'stared at a screen in horror' or 'jabbed frantically at different keys' as Emily and Jessup did?"

7. The Boggart gets lost inside a computer game, and when Tommy tries to free the Boggart from the game, "Tommy could feel himself rushing through space as if it were really happening, as he fought to keep himself out of the illusion. In panic he stabbed at the keyboard, desperately trying to find some way to obey the computer" (p. 192). Ask students if they have ever felt like they were lost in a computer or computer game.

8. Tommy was also afraid "that his inexperience with the computer would lead him to make some terrible mistake" (p. 192). Ask students questions such as the following: "Do you ever feel this way with computers? Do computers ever scare you?"

9. When the Boggart sends his message from inside the computer, an image of Castle Keep and the Scottish Highlands appears on the screen: "a seagull swept across the screen," and Jessup could hear the "whine of the wind, and the lapping of the waves" (p. 179). Although the appearance of these images was explained as being the result of the Boggart's activity, discuss with students the possibilities of images appearing on a screen through computer technology.

10. Other books that could be used to introduce technology through literature include Elizabeth Levy's *The Creepy Computer Mystery* (1996) and Seymour Simon's *Einstein Anderson, Science Detective: The On-Line Spaceman and Other Stories* (1997).

Activity 9–3:
SAFETY ON THE INTERNET

TYPE	TERM
● CLASS	● STA
● GROUP	○ LTA
○ IND	○ LC

Purpose:
1. To make students aware of the safety rules they need to follow when using e-mail, the Internet, and the World Wide Web
2. To create a list of safety rules and post them where they can be easily accessed by students

Materials:
Articles about children's safety and the Internet such as Lawrence J. Magid's *Child Safety on the Information Highway* (1994), published by the National Center for Missing and Exploited Children and the Interactive Services Association. To report any inappropriate Internet behavior against children refer to http://www.missing kids.com/cybertip for additional information call 1-800-THE-LOST (1-800-843-5678).

Grade level:
All grades

Procedures:
1. Design a handout that lists safety rules students should review before exchanging information through e-mail or doing research on-line.
2. Go over these rules with your class. Emphasize that although most people who use on-line services have positive experiences, basic safety precautions must be taken when using the Internet. By practicing basic safety, children can learn how to protect themselves against potentially dangerous people or situations.
3. Explain to students that the Internet, like the rest of society, is made up of a wide range of people. Most are decent and respectful, but some may be rude, obnoxious, insulting, or mean.
4. Discuss these rules with your class and post a copy in your computer laboratory and next to each computer.

MY RULES FOR ON-LINE SAFETY

1. I will not give out personal information such as my home address, telephone number, parents' work address or telephone number, or the name and location of my school without the permission of my teacher and my parents.
2. I will tell my teacher and my parents immediately if I come across any information that makes me feel uncomfortable.
3. I will never share my password with anyone.
4. I will never agree to get together with someone I "meet" on-line without first checking with my parents. If my parents agree to the meeting, I will be sure that it is in a public place and I will bring along a trusted adult.
5. I will never send a person my picture or anything else without first checking with my parents or teacher.

6. I will not respond to any messages that are mean or in any way make me feel uncomfortable. If I find such messages, I will tell my parents or teacher right away so that they can report the problem to the on-line service provider.

7. I will talk to my parents and teacher to review rules for going on-line. We will decide on the time of day that I can be on-line, the length of time I can be on-line, and appropriate areas for me to visit. I will not access other areas or break these rules without adult permission.

5. Another article that could lead to discussions and lists of rules to accompany On-line activities is Frances F. Jacobson and Greg D. Smith's "Teaching Virtue in a Virtual World" in *School Library Journal,* March 1998. This article also includes a list of valuable resources and Internet addresses.

Activity 9–4:

HOW TO PARTICIPATE IN A COLLABORATIVE PROJECT OVER THE INTERNET: BECOMING PART OF THE GLOBAL CLASSROOM

TYPE		TERM	
● CLASS		○ STA	
● GROUP		● LTA	
○ IND		○ LC	

Purpose:
1. To collaborate on an Internet project with classrooms around the world
2. To develop international relationships
3. To recognize the design of a successful collaborative project
4. To learn how to participate in a collaborative Internet project with other classrooms around the world

Materials:
Computer(s) with e-mail and Internet access; articles that discuss guidelines to consider when creating Internet projects such as Al Rogers, Yvonne Andres, Mary Jacks, and Tom Clauset's article "Telecommunications in the Classroom: Keys to Successful Telecomputing" (1990).

Grade level:
All grades

Procedures:
1. With the help of e-mail and the World Wide Web, two or more classrooms located anywhere in the world can communicate with each other or study a common topic together and share what they are learning about the topic. Visit a Web site that hosts classroom information exchanges over the Internet. Examples of these sites include E-mail Classroom Exchange (http://ecemail.com/ece), Kidproject (http://www.kidlink.org.), The Global Schoolhouse (http://www.gsh.org), International Education and Resource Network I*EARN-US (http://www.iearn.org), and Classroom Connect (http://www.classroom.net).

2. Many classroom projects have already been created by other teachers who are looking for participants. Joining a project that is already posted allows your class to participate almost immediately in a collaborative project.

3. If you are looking for participation with a classroom in a particular state or region of the world and do not find a project posted on any of the existing message boards, you can search lists of schools that are on-line and make a request to individual schools. To find schools around the world and in your community with Web pages, visit a Web site such as Web 66 International School Registry (http://web66.coled.umn.edu).

4. If you do not find an existing project that you would like your class to join, you can create a new project for your class and post a request for participation, or a call for collaboration, on the message boards of Web sites such as those already mentioned.

5. When creating a new project consider the following guidelines based on Rogers, Andres, Jacks, and Clauset's article "Telecommunications in the Classroom: Keys to Successful Telecomputing" (1990):

GUIDELINES: HOW TO DESIGN A SUCCESSFUL PROJECT

1. Design a project with defined goals, tasks, and outcomes.
2. Include a time line for your project. The time line should include specific beginning and ending dates for your project and the precise deadlines for participant responses. Post your call for collaboration at least six weeks before the starting date. If necessary, repeat your call for collaboration again two weeks before the starting date.
3. In your call for collaboration include the following information:

   Contact person
   Contact addresses (e-mail and postal addresses)
   Grade levels of desired participants
   Time line
   Project goals and objectives
   Number of participants
   Complete project outline
   Examples of the kinds of writing or data collection students will submit
   Request of registration information from participants

4. At the conclusion of the project, share the results of the project with all participants. If the project involved the publication of any student writing, send a hard copy to all who participated. Have students collaborate on writing a summary of the project, describing the project, what they did, what they learned, and what changes they would make in the project. Send a copy of this summary to your principal, parent-teacher association president, superintendent, and board of education president. Have your students send a thank-you message to all contributors.

Activity 9–5:
CULTURAL EXCHANGE: KEY PALS

	TYPE	TERM
	● CLASS	○ STA
	● GROUP	● LTA
	○ IND	○ LC

Purpose:

1. To foster communication, technology, and cultural awareness
2. To develop word processing skills using communications technology
3. To increase awareness of different cultures
4. To develop an appreciation and understanding of the cultures and lifestyles of people living in countries outside of the United States
5. To collaborate with students from around the world
6. To develop oral and written language skills

Materials:

Computer(s) with e-mail connection.

Grade level:

All grades

Procedures:

1. In a key pal program, students communicate with children in other classrooms via e-mail. Enrich your teaching of another culture by developing a key pal program with a classroom in the country students are currently studying or have them choose a country they would like to learn more about.
2. Once your class has chosen a country to study, post a request for participation on the Internet.
3. To find lists of teachers and classrooms from different parts of the world who are interested in forming collaborative key pal relationships, visit Web sites such as Intercultural E-mail Classroom Connections (http://www.iecc.org), Kidlink (http://www.kidlink.org), Global Heinemann Keypals (http://www.reedbooks.com.au/heinemann/global/global.html), Pitsco's Launch to Keypals (http://www.keypals.com/p/keypals.html), or E-mail Classroom Exchange (http://ecemail.com/ece).
4. To request key pals from specific schools, visit Web 66 International School Registry (http://web66.coled.umn.edu) and explore the lists of classrooms around the world connected to the Internet. Send a message to several schools, inviting them to exchange e-mail messages with your class.
5. Post a request for participation at least six weeks before the project is scheduled to begin. Make sure you have participants lined up for each of your students before students begin composing their e-mail messages.
6. Have students conduct research about their chosen country before their e-mail exchanges begin. Divide the class into groups of three to five students. Each group could be responsible for researching different aspects of the country. For example, groups could focus their research on the geography, food, customs, history, or politics of their chosen country.
7. Ask each group to report its findings to the class.
8. Have students brainstorm about the kinds of questions they would like to ask their key pals and record these questions in a journal. Encourage them to also record their feelings about participating in an electronic exchange. Have them

write down their impressions of the country and culture before their exchange begins. Request that students in the corresponding school also record their impressions of the United States and their feelings about participating in an electronic exchange. A summary of these initial responses will be submitted along with their final e-mail exchange.

9. Discuss with students the concept of e-mail. Explain to them that millions of people around the world use computers to send messages to other people every day.

10. Before students begin corresponding with their key pals, have them review proper e-mail use. Remind students to always be respectful and tolerant of other people and other cultures. They should never type in all capital letters in their e-mail correspondence. This is the 'Net equivalent of shouting.

11. Exchanges can be open correspondence or directed by topic and time line. If directed by topic and time line, make sure that the classroom teacher of the corresponding country receives the same time line of topics. This time line of topics may be included as part of the original request for participation. The formal exchange might occur at least once a week, last for eight weeks, and include the following time line of topics:

Week 1	Students exchange biographical information.
Week 2	Students exchange information about their school and classroom environment.
Week 3	Students exchange political and historical information about their country.
Week 4	Students exchange information about their town and their family's history of living in their town.
Week 5	Students exchange information about social customs, foods, clothing, the arts, and holiday customs.
Week 6	Students exchange information about environmental, educational, and religious issues that affect their country.
Week 7	Students exchange remaining questions they may have about the other students' country and life.
Week 8	Students from both countries describe their experiences with the key pal exchange. They submit final e-mail messages that record responses to specific questions such as the following: "What were you most surprised to learn about your key pal and your key pal's country and culture? What was your favorite part of your electronic correspondence? In what ways does e-mail promote a global community?"

12. Have students compile a report that includes their impressions of the country and culture before the exchange and summarizes what they learned as a result of the exchange. Students can then share their reports with the rest of the class.

13. Collect the findings of all of the students and publish them in book form. Send a copy of the publication to the students in the participating class from the other country.

14. If this is the first of many key pal exchanges planned for your class, you could place a map of the world on the wall above your computer with pieces of yarn from your school's location running to each of the places from which you receive e-mail.

Activity 9–6:

BRINGING FIELD SPECIALISTS INTO THE CLASSROOM THROUGH ELECTRONIC MENTORING: A STUDY OF KING ARTHUR

TYPE	TERM
● CLASS	○ STA
● GROUP	● LTA
○ IND	○ LC

Purpose:
1. To structure a mentoring project
2. To share experiences with field experts and other students through e-mail
3. To explore information about King Arthur
4. To analyze the literary requirements for a legend
5. To develop a book that requires writing, editing, and organizing

Materials:
Abraham T. McLaughlin's "Mentors Log On to Help Students Make the Grade" (1997); various books on King Arthur, such as Howard Pyle's *The Story of King Arthur and His Knights* (1903); Rosemary Sutcliffe's *The Sword and the Circle: King Arthur and the Knights of the Round Table* (1981), *The Light Beyond the Forest* (1981), and *The Road to Camlann: The Death of King Arthur* (1982); and Susan Cooper's *Silver on the Tree* (1977); computer(s) with e-mail access.

Grade level:
Upper elementary and middle school

Book summaries:
In *Silver on the Tree* the author describes a final battle between good and evil. *The Story of King Arthur and His Knights* is a reissue of the classic story. *The Light Beyond the Forest* tells of the quest for the Holy Grail. In *The Road to Camlann: The Death of King Arthur,* Mordred attempts to destroy the kingdom by exposing Queen Guinevere and Sir Lancelot. *The Sword and the Circle: King Arthur and the Knights of the Round Table* contains thirteen stories associated with King Arthur.

Procedures:
1. Bring field experts into your classroom via e-mail. Field specialists from universities, businesses, government, or other schools can serve as electronic mentors to students wanting to explore specific topics of study. There are several ways to contact field experts. For example, useful lists of e-mail addresses for subject area experts can be found at Ask an Expert (http://www.askanexpert.com/askanexpert). You can also post a request for participation on the Internet or write or call individuals to request their participation. The Electronic Emissary Project (http://www.tapr.org/emissary/) is an on-line matching service that helps teachers locate experts in different disciplines who use the Internet and who are willing to engage in electronic exchanges with teachers and students. This service also helps volunteer experts, teachers, and students to structure a mentoring project and share what they learn with other students through e-mail.
2. Establish a time line and a plan of action for your class project. For example, your class could do a six-week study of the King Arthur legend. The first two weeks would be spent in the classroom reading and analyzing literature about King Arthur. The electronic exchanges would begin during the second week and continue for four more weeks.

3. Before the study begins, you might set up an electronic exchange with a literature professor whose specialty is Arthurian legend, a medieval history professor who can discuss what life was like during the middle ages, a children's literature author who has written about King Arthur, an anthropologist whose expertise is the role of legends in society, and a group of students from Wales and England. Because the Welsh version of the King Arthur legend places Arthur's resting place in a cave in Snowdonia, it would be particularly interesting to set up an electronic exchange with students from a classroom in Snowdonia.

4. Divide the class into five different groups. Each group can then exchange information with a different expert and report a summary of their findings to the class once a week. As a class, you might decide on a question that will direct the overall inquiry of each group. For example, the purpose of the exchange with the children's author might be to discover how he or she came to write a book about King Arthur and what research methods were used. The working title of the group's research could be "How one author came to write about King Arthur."

5. Before the electronic exchange begins, have students read several different books about King Arthur, such as those listed in the materials section.

6. Discuss the concept of *legend* with your students. Explain that legends are stories primarily about humans rather than supernatural beings. Historical tradition also maintains that King Arthur actually existed in fairly recent times.

7. Plan to have your students communicate with their field experts at least once a week on the same day of the week. For example, every Friday they might submit questions to their field experts and every Monday receive answers to their questions. Once a week students may brainstorm and plan the questions they will ask their field experts the following week.

8. Each group might have a specific overall question for its research during the course of the six-week study. For example, they might want to compare and contrast life in Wales and England during the Middle Ages and today.

9. At the end of the six-week study, have students compile their findings into a book. Each group presents its findings in a separate chapter of the book. Besides researching and compiling information about King Arthur, students include their own experiences with research and with the electronic exchanges.

10. Each group is responsible for writing, editing, and organizing the layout of its chapter. Once the book is complete, send a copy to each of the electronic exchange participants along with a letter of appreciation.

Activity 9–7:
SEQUENTIAL WRITING

	TYPE	TERM
	● CLASS	○ STA
	● GROUP	● LTA
	○ IND	○ LC

Purpose:
1. To discuss elements that make up a story
2. To create a beginning of a story that introduces characterization and setting
3. To develop the action for a story
4. To bring the story to a conclusion
5. To read and analyze the works of other students
6. To progressively create a common written text
7. To work collaboratively with a class to create one beginning of a story
8. To work collaboratively with other classes through e-mail to create a common written text
9. To encourage problem solving

Materials: Computer(s) with e-mail access.

Grade level: Lower and upper elementary, middle school

Procedures:

1. Before starting the writing activity, discuss with students the basic elements of a story including the setting, characters, plot, climax, and conclusion.
2. Ask each student to take out a clean piece of writing paper and a pencil. Do not have them write their names on these papers.
3. Direct students to write the beginning of a story. In this beginning, they should introduce the setting and characters. Students can write on any topic, or you could direct them with the opening line of a story. For example, "When I woke up this morning, I knew it was going to be a strange day, but nothing could have prepared me for what I found in my yard."
4. After ten minutes, direct students to pass their papers to the person sitting two desks behind them.
5. Have students read the story that has been started and continue it for the next ten minutes. Remind them that they should be developing the plot during this period.
6. After ten minutes, have the students pass the papers in the same pattern as before.
7. The students then read the new story, keeping in mind that it will be their job to write the conclusion for this story for ten minutes.
8. Have the students pass the paper again in the same direction. This time they read the story out loud to the class.
9. The stories could be used for an editing activity in which two or three students edit the same story. After the stories have been edited they could be compiled and published as a class book.
10. The next step in the writing exercise is to participate with other classes through e-mail.

11. Post a request for project participation on the Internet. Specify the details of the project and the date you would like to begin and end the project. For example, you could request participation from five classrooms from any location around the world; students in those classes will add to different parts of the story begun by children in your classroom. Each school will have one week to complete its portion of the project and e-mail its finished portion to the next class at the end of a week. The e-mail exchanges might take place every Friday.

Week 1	Classroom 1 begins a story by describing the setting and characters.
Week 2	Classroom 1 sends its beginning to classroom 2. Classroom 2 initiates an event or the action of the story to add to the setting and characters.
Week 3	Classroom 2 sends the story to classroom 3. Classroom 3 develops the plot.
Week 4	Classroom 3 sends the story to classroom 4. Classroom 4 writes the climax.
Week 5	Classroom 4 sends the story to classroom 5. Classroom 5 writes the conclusion and creates a title for the story.
Week 6	Classroom 5 sends the completed story back to classroom 1.
Week 7	Classroom 1 sends the story by e-mail and in paper form to all participating classes.

12. You could also request that each participating class include in its portion of the story at least one detail from its region of the world.

13. During the week before the beginning of the story is due to classroom 2, have students brainstorm ideas for possible beginnings of stories. Remind them that each beginning should include a description of the setting and introduce at least one character. Have each student complete at least one story beginning. Divide the class into small groups of three to five students. Ask the students to share their story ideas and then collaborate with their groups to decide on a common story.

14. When each group is finished collaborating, have the class come together. Ask student representatives from each group to read their groups' completed story beginnings. Of those beginnings, have your class choose which idea to use. If the choice is not unanimous, encourage students to put together their favorite details from the stories or have them vote by secret ballot to choose the story beginning to send to classroom 2.

15. After the sequential story has been completed and sent to all of the participating classes, encourage students to write down their impressions of the completed story. Ask them to respond to questions such as the following: "What did you like the most about the completed story? What did you think about collaborating with students from several different classrooms? How do you feel about having contributed to a major portion of the story? What part of the story's development surprised you the most?"

Activity 9–8:

A VIRTUAL FIELD TRIP TO THE WHITE HOUSE

	TYPE	TERM
	● CLASS	○ STA
	● GROUP	● LTA
	● IND	○ LC

Purpose:
1. To become familiar with and use a Web site
2. To work cooperatively with a group
3. To trace changes in technology
4. To develop and enhance basic research skills

Materials: Computer(s) with e-mail and World Wide Web access.

Grade level: Lower and upper elementary, middle school

Procedures:
1. Introduce students to the Internet and specifically to the World Wide Web by having them visit and research information that can be found on the White House Web site (http://www.whitehouse.gov). Because the specific information found on Web sites can change quickly, we recommend that teachers familiarize themselves with the White House Web site before they have students visit and conduct research at the Web site. It is also a good idea to bookmark the White House Web site ahead of time so that you can easily access the site for students (or give yourself a few minutes to access the Web page before the activity begins).

2. The White House Web site includes press releases and presidential speeches as well as history and information about past presidents and first ladies. It is basically user-friendly for students in upper elementary and middle school. The White House for Kids Web site (http://www.whitehouse.gov/WH/kids/html/kidhome. html) has been specifically designed for younger children and can be accessed from within the main White House Web site. The White House for Kids site includes a newsletter addressed to children. It also provides a virtual tour of the White House and links to information about U.S. history, the presidency, the first family, and the children and pets who have lived there. The kids' tour, which is led by the Clintons' cat, Socks, is easily traveled and contains information of interest to older and younger children.

3. Present students with a series of questions that can be answered by searching either the White House or White House for Kids Web site. Tell students that they are going to be detectives who will try to find answers based on certain clues they are given.

4. Divide the class into small groups. Have at least one person from each group be responsible for recording the group's research methods or the steps they take to find the answers to specific questions. The questions you present to the groups could include the following:
   a. In what city is the White House located? What is the street address of the White House? (1600 Pennsylvania Avenue, Washington, D.C.)
   b. Which president served the shortest term in office? How many days did he serve? (William Henry Harrison served only 32 days.)
   c. Which first lady had an uncle who was president before her husband and had the same last name? (Eleanor Roosevelt married her distant cousin, Franklin Delano Roosevelt. Her uncle was Teddy Roosevelt.)

    d. Which first child had a pony named Macaroni? (Caroline Kennedy.)

    e. Who was the only president's child to be born in the White House? (Esther Cleveland.)

    f. Who was the first president to live in the White House? (John Adams.)

    g. How many rooms does the White House have? How many bathrooms? (132 rooms; 32 bathrooms.)

5. Once one group finds the answers, and if students seem to need help, encourage the groups to help each other. Remind students that they cannot give each other the answers, but they can share their research methods of how to find the answers.

6. Once all groups are finished, discuss any difficulties students had with this exercise.

7. In another exercise, have students explore the history of the inaugural address. Have them find answers to another list of questions that you create and distribute.

8. Have students explore the history of technology in terms of the history of the inaugural address. For example, the spring 1997 issue of the newsletter for kids located on the White House for Kids Web site presents the following information:

> Only members of Congress heard Washington's first inaugural address on April 30, 1789.
>
> Thirty years later, James Madison's speech was the first to be published in the newspaper.
>
> In 1845 James K. Polk gave his speech while Samual Morse, inventor of the electric telegraph, sat near him and tapped out the speech.
>
> In 1857 James Buchanen was the first president to be photographed on Inauguration Day.
>
> Forty years later, movie cameras were used to record William McKinley's inaugural address.
>
> In 1925 Calvin Coolidge's inaugural address was the first to be heard by radio.
>
> In 1949 Harry Truman's inauguration was the first to be televised.
>
> In 1997 President Clinton's second inaugural address was the first to have an official Web site and be seen live on the Internet around the world.

9. Have students create and illustrate a time line of the technologies associated with the inaugural address.

10. Based on what they have learned about the White House and the first family, have students brainstorm questions they would like to ask the president, vice president, or first lady.

11. Have students compose and send an electronic message to the president, the vice president, or the first lady. Ask students to write individual letters or compose a letter as a class. If students write individual letters and include their home address on the e-mail form, they will receive a response through the mail.

12. Have students discuss what they have learned about the Internet through this project. Ask them questions such as the following: "What did you enjoy the most about this project? What did you enjoy the least? How do you feel knowing that so much information is available to you on the Internet? How do you feel about having sent an e-mail message to the White House?"

13. For further study of the White House, have students read any of the following books: Katherine Leiner's *First Children: Growing Up in the White House* (1996), Alice Provensen's *The Buck Stops Here: The Presidents of the United States* (1990), or Judith St. George's *The White House: Cornerstone of a Nation* (1990).

Activity 9–9:

THE LIBRARY OF CONGRESS ON-LINE:
USING AND EVALUATING PRIMARY SOURCES

TYPE		TERM	
● CLASS		○ STA	
● GROUP		● LTA	
● IND		○ LC	

Purpose:
1. To develop an understanding of the meaning of and use for primary sources
2. To evaluate the purposes for the creation of primary sources
3. To work cooperatively in a group
4. To analyze details in photographs
5. To compare the reliability and content of various primary sources

Materials: Computer(s) with World Wide Web access.

Grade level: Upper elementary and middle school

Procedures:
1. Introduce students to the idea of primary sources, which include the actual records, letters, photographs, and articles of clothing that have survived through history. Primary sources can also include historical documents, oral accounts, and direct quotes from people who were involved in historical events. Published primary sources such as newspapers, literature, pamphlets, posters, and court decisions are usually created to be read by the public. Unpublished primary sources such as journals, diaries, deeds, and personal letters are usually created to be read only by the person to whom they are addressed. Photographs and films are interesting primary sources because they capture people and moments in time.

2. Introduce students to the Library of Congress on-line (http://www.loc.gov). The special collection American Memory is particularly interesting because it includes documents, motion pictures, photographs, and sound recordings that trace different aspects of the American experience. One of the virtual exhibits in American Memory is called "Words and Deeds in American History: Selected Documents Celebrating the Manuscript Division's First 100 Years." This exhibit contains original works that have been copied and transferred into digitized images. Explain to students that although the original manuscripts are still housed in the Library of Congress, exact copies or the digitized images of the contents of the manuscripts can be viewed on-line.

3. Before viewing any of the manuscripts, encourage students to think critically whenever they read or view primary sources. Have them consider when and why a document was created. Was it created for public or private reasons? Was the document developed within a short time of the actual historical event, or does a significant amount of time separate the manuscript from the event? Was the document created for an objective or persuasive purpose?

4. Show students one of the digitized images of a document from the American Memory collection. For example, an interesting document is George Washington's first inaugural address, dated April 30, 1789 (George Washington Papers). Have students analyze this source by considering the questions presented in procedure 3.

5. After analyzing and discussing the document as a class, divide the class into small groups. Have groups search the collections to find specific documents and then analyze and consider the reliability of each document. If you prefer to have each group search for only one document, you could ask all of the groups to search for the same document so that they can compare research methods with one another. Have at least one person from each group write down the steps the group takes to find the answer. Ask groups to research one or more of the following questions:

   a. Locate the digitized image of the first telegraph message sent by Samuel Morse on May 24, 1844. What does the message say? (This document is located in the Samuel Finley Breese Morse Papers. The handwritten phrase "This sentence was written in Washington" appears on the top of the telegraph message "What hath God Wrought?")

   b. Find the digitized image of the letter and the illustrated fable that Theodore Roosevelt sent to his son on July 11, 1890. What is the fable about? (This document is located in the Theodore Roosevelt Jr. Papers. The first line of the fable is "A pony and a cow go out to see the world.")

   c. Find the digitized image of the letter Ralph Waldo Emerson addressed to Walt Whitman written July 21, 1855. Why is this letter considered to be the most famous letter in American literary history? (This document is located in the Charles E. Feinberg–Walt Whitman Collection. Emerson's praises launched the unknown poet's career. Although the letter was intended to be private, Whitman placed it on his book jacket and submitted it for publication in several newspapers, which contributed to the popularity of *Leaves of Grass*.)

6. Ask each group to summarize its search methods and analysis of the primary-source document. Have the groups present their conclusions to the class. Encourage supporting or refuting statements from the other groups. Have students share their research strategies and discuss difficulties they may have had in finding answers to the research questions.

7. Have each student choose a research topic that would encourage a search of the American Memory collection of the Library of Congress Web site. For example, topics could include the women's suffrage movement, immigration in America, or slavery in the United States.

8. Encourage students to analyze several primary-source documents including at least one photograph and one written manuscript for their chosen topic. For example, a student researching the women's suffrage movement could search the digitized documents located in the on-line collection entitled "The National American Woman Suffrage Association Collection, 1848–1921." From this collection they could choose a manuscript to analyze such as the November 1872 proceedings from Susan B. Anthony's trial when she was charged with illegal voting. To find photographs of suffrage leaders, suffrage parades, and picketing, students could search the " 'Votes for Women' Suffrage Pictures, 1850–1920" collection.

9. In analyzing a photograph, have students answer questions such as the following: "What details tell you the images in the photograph are from the past? What is the setting? How are people dressed? What are they doing?" Have students choose one image and write a detailed description that could establish the setting of a story.

10. Ask students to judge the quality and reliability of each of the primary sources they have chosen. Have them answer questions such as the following: "How reliable are the sources? How can you tell? What kind of information about your topic did each document provide? Did you find conflicting information in the sources? What overall statement can you make about primary sources based on your research with these documents? What additional sources would you like to investigate to expand your understanding of your topic?"

11. Have students explore other documents that are connected to their topic and analyze the reliability of each source.

12. After they have finished determining the reliability of different sources, encourage students to present their findings to the rest of the class. If several students have chosen the same research topic, have them give a collaborative presentation. Each student could then select and research different aspects of the same topic.

13. Have students pretend that they have just arrived in America. As an immigrant, as a new member of the suffrage movement, or as a slave or ex-slave, have students write a letter to their home country describing their experiences in America. What was their passage to America like? What are their living conditions like? What kinds of responsibilities do they now have in America? Have students share their letters with the rest of the class.

Activity 9–10:

DEBATE: PRINT-BASED CULTURE VERSUS VIRTUAL IMAGES CULTURE

TYPE	TERM
● CLASS	● STA
● GROUP	○ LTA
○ IND	○ LC

Purpose:
1. To investigate the strengths and weaknesses of a print-based culture
2. To investigate the strengths and weaknesses of a virtual images culture
3. To develop critical evaluation skills
4. To develop oral language ability through debate
5. To select and argue the most important points in a debate

Materials:
Articles from newspapers and journals; interviews with librarians and other users of both printed materials and various computer programs; personal experiences.

Grade level:
Middle and upper elementary, middle school

Procedures:
1. Ask the students if they believe there is currently more emphasis on technology, including computers and the Internet, or on printed books and newspapers. Ask the students to consider and to discuss the importance to them of both books and computers. Ask the following: "When and why do you use each one? What do you believe will be the future for both media?"
2. Tell the students that various newspapers and journals are currently debating the issue of printed materials versus virtual images. For example, you could share comments made in two *New York Times* editorials (May 25, 1997). Richard C. Hsu and William E. Mitchel argue that printed books are a 400 year-old technology. They hypothesize about what would have happened if books in print and books on computer had been produced at the same time. They compare topics such as cost, durability, portability, and quality, ultimately maintaining that books are superior. In contrast, Jack McGarvey (1997) argues that students today are the "generation of multimedia." He believes that the role of computers and software programs will increase and eventually change education. Another discussion about the role of technology is found in Paul Hilt's article in *Publishers Weekly,* "The Road Ahead: Publishing Visionaries Look at the Changes That Digital Technology Might Bring" (1997). Renee Olson's "When It Comes to Technology, The Postman Always Thinks Twice" (1996) presents some negative concerns related to technology.
3. After discussing with the students some of the concerns presented by people on both sides of this debate, divide the class according to pro–print-based and pro–computer-technology groups. Have them conduct additional research into the two types of media. In addition to articles, this research may include interviews and examples taken from personal experiences. After students have conducted their research, ask them to present it as a debate. Smaller teams may be selected for several debates so that every student has an opportunity to be part of both a debate experience and an audience that judges the quality of the debate.
4. Following this activity, students may discover advantages and disadvantages of both cultures. If they decide that the future of their education includes both books and technology, you may choose to complete activity 9–12 in which students make discoveries about evaluating the Internet.

Activity 9–11:

A VIRTUAL EXPEDITION TO THE ARCTIC

TYPE	TERM
● CLASS	○ STA
● GROUP	● LTA
● IND	○ LC

Purpose:

1. To interact with scientists and explorers through a Web site
2. To integrate language arts and geography
3. To create a time line of an expedition
4. To analyze the effectiveness of journal entries and to create fictional journals
5. To use knowledge gained about a location to respond to novels
6. To create an adventure story with an Arctic setting

Materials:

Computer(s) with e-mail and Internet access; nonfictional books about the Arctic such as Owen Beattie and John Geiger's *Buried in Ice: The Mystery of a Lost Arctic Expedition* (1992), Jim Brandemburg's *To the Top of the World: Adventures with Arctic Wolves* (1993), Will Steger and John Bowermaster's *Over the Top of the World: Explorer Will Steger's Trek across the Arctic* (1997), and Jean Craighead George's *Look to the North: A Wolf Pup Diary* (1997); fictional books about the Arctic such as John Bierhorst's *The Dancing Fox: Arctic Folktales* (1997), Jean Craighead George's *Julie of the Wolves* (1972), and Brian Heinz's *Kayuktuk, An Arctic Quest* (1996).

Grade level:

Upper elementary and middle school

Procedures:

1. Involve your class with a virtual expedition. Each year, the JASON Foundation for Education (http://www.jasonproject.org) embarks on a two-week scientific expedition to a remote location such as Iceland, Yellowstone National Park, or the Galapagos Islands. In addition to providing information about their scientific discoveries and posting it on their Web site, JASON scientists invite selected teachers and students to physically join each expedition and post their own experiences on the expedition's Web site. Goals: The Global OnLine Adventure Learning Site (http://www.goals.com) sponsors oceanic expeditions that are made by individuals. For example, Global recently followed Karen Thorndike in her attempts to become the first American woman to sail around the globe by herself. The National Aeronautics and Space Administration's (NASA's) Quest Project (http://quest.arc.nasa.gov) provides information for teachers and students to join shuttle missions via the Internet and to interact with NASA astronauts through e-mail and teleconferencing. Passport to Knowledge (http://passport.ivv.nasa.gov), sponsored by the National Science Foundation and NASA, invites teachers and students to join their scientists and explorers via the Internet as they explore remote locations such as Antarctica, the rain forests, the Arctic tundra, and the Amazon.

2. Once you have chosen an expedition and registered your class at the Web site, ask students to read nonfictional books about the region in which the expedition will take place. For example, if your class is going to join an expedition to the Arctic regions, they could read and discuss *Buried in Ice: The Mystery of a Lost Arctic Expedition*, which explores the tragedy of the people and ships that were lost as they tried to discover the Northwest Passage. The authors document the expedition that involved the search for the missing ships. In *To the Top of the World:*

Adventures with Arctic Wolves, a wildlife photographer describes his work in the Arctic. *Over the Top of the World: Explorer Will Steger's Trek across the Arctic* is a photojournalistic presentation of the authors' four-month-long 1995 expedition across the north pole by way of skis, dogsled, and canoe sled. It emphasizes the team's challenging, life-threatening, and awe-inspiring experiences. Interspersed with Steger's personalized accounts are background information and facts about the expedition, a brief history of Arctic exploration, a geographic description of the Arctic Ocean, minibiographies of the team members and the dogs, and a supply list. *Look to the North: A Wolf Pup Diary* is a yearlong chronicle that follows three wolf pups born in Alaska's alpine tundra. Although it is about work in Antarctica, *Braving the Frozen Frontier: Women Working in Antarctica* provides an interesting look at the women scientists who work in frozen tundra regions.

3. Once students have some knowledge of the geography, temperature, animal life, and possible dangers associated with expeditions to a particular location, encourage them to interact with the scientists and explorers involved. Have students respond to their expedition team at least once a week (or as often as is allowed on their particular expedition). Through e-mail, students are able to interact with and receive messages from scientists who are on-site. Through the expedition members' postings on the World Wide Web, students are able to follow the expedition, read journal entries about an explorer's day-to-day adventures and discoveries, view photographs of the expedition minutes after they have been taken, and participate in teleconferencing or real-time chat sessions set up by the scientists. The expeditions encourage students to interact with scientists and explorers who are on-site. Students usually receive answers to their e-mail questions within a few days, and their questions can influence the direction of the expedition.

4. Encourage students to make a time line of the expedition for the classroom and have them continue to update it as the expedition progresses. This time line could include the beginning date of the expedition, important discoveries that are made along the way, and a tracking of the physical progression of the expedition.

5. Have students read the scientists' and explorers' journal entries posted on the expedition's Web site. Encourage them to read journal entries of different people to get various perspectives of the same experience. Have students discuss their overall impressions of the journal entries. What can students learn from journals beyond scientific fact? Are some entries more scientific than others? Do some people focus more than others on animal life, cultural interactions, or their feelings about the expedition? Have students compare these on-line entries with Will Steger's journal entries published in *Over the Top of the World: Explorer Will Steger's Trek across the Arctic.* Discuss with students the different purposes people have for keeping journals. Ask students if any of them keep journals.

6. After students have read several of the journal entries from the on-line expedition, ask them to write a journal entry for their own imaginary journey through the Arctic. Tell them that they are explorers in the Arctic and they must record their observations, discoveries, and feelings for several days. Their audience will be students their own age. Provide a beginning sentence for students' first journal entries, such as the following:

> It is the end of October, and I watched as the sun slipped behind the horizon today for the last time. It will not appear again until February. It is dark and still and lonely, but in the distance, I can hear the children singing a farewell to the sun.

7. After students have finished their journal entries, divide the class into small groups. Have them read their fictional journals to their groups.

8. Encourage students to read fictional works that have an Arctic setting. For example, *Julie of the Wolves* is about an Eskimo girl who becomes lost on the north slope of Alaska and survives with the help of wolves. *Kayuktuk, An Arctic Quest* is about an Inupiat boy who wants to prove himself a man by showing his worth as a hunter. The book provides insight into the Inupiat culture as it follows the boy's personal development.

9. Have students write responses to one or both of the novels. They could respond to questions such as the following: "Using your knowledge of the Arctic region, what details do the authors use that make their settings seem realistic? What role does nature play in each novel? What is the main conflict of each novel? When does the conflict occur?"

10. Have students read and discuss stories from *The Dancing Fox: Arctic Folktales,* a compilation of eighteen Inuit traditional stories collected in the early twentieth century.

11. After reading *The Dancing Fox: Arctic Folktales,* have students write their own Arctic folktales. Remind them that in Arctic folktales, the natural world of the Arctic landscape is entwined with the narrative. Have them read their folktales to their small groups.

12. Using the knowledge they have gained about the Arctic regions through the online expedition and through book sources, have students create an adventure story with an Arctic setting. They can continue the narrative of their fictional journal entries or create a completely different story. Their main character could be an explorer, a scientist, an Eskimo, a wolf pup, or any other character, as long as students bring in details of the setting from their studies of the Arctic. Have them share their finished stories with the rest of the class.

13. Have students write a response to their research and writing experiences with the Arctic region. Ask them to respond to the following questions: "What was your favorite part of this project? How did interacting with scientists and explorers help you write your adventure story? How did this project change your perceptions of the Arctic?"

14. Have students create a class publication of their work. The publication could include a time line, a summary of the virtual expedition, a description of their involvement with the expedition, fictional journal entries, responses to the books about the Arctic, and completed adventure stories written by class members. Give the publication a title such as "Our Virtual Expedition to the Arctic."

Activity 9–12:
EVALUATING WEB SITES

TYPE	TERM
● CLASS	● STA
● GROUP	● LTA
● IND	○ LC

Purpose:

1. To develop critical evaluation skills
2. To discuss and analyze criteria for Web sites
3. To expand oral language capabilities
4. To identify effective and less effective Web sites

Materials:

Computer(s) with access to the World Wide Web; articles such as Patrick Jones's "A Cyber-Room of Their Own: How Libraries Use Web Pages to Attract Young Adults" (1997) and "Selection Criteria: How to Tell If You Are Looking at a Great Site," compiled by the Children and Technology Committee of the Association for Library Service for Children, a division of the American Library Association (http://www.ala.org/parentspage/greatsites/criteria.html).

Grade level:

Third grade and above

Procedures:

1. Before evaluating a Web site, discuss with students the American Library Association's selection criteria, which include the following:
   a. The name of the group or individual who created the site should be clearly stated. The Web site's address often indicates the nature of the site:

   > Commercial businesses usually include *.com*
   > Federal government sites end in *.gov*
   > K–12 school sites often include *k12* in the address
   > College and university sites often include *.edu*
   > Sites from nonprofit organizations often include *.org*
   > A site with a tilde (~) in the address usually indicates that the page is maintained or created by an individual rather than representing an organization, a business, or a school

   b. The Web site author should provide a way for users to make comments or ask questions.
   c. A site's purpose should be clear and its content and title should reflect its purpose: to entertain, to persuade, to educate, or to sell.
   d. Advertising should not overshadow the content.
   e. A good site should enrich the user's experience and expand the imagination.
   f. The information on the site should be easy to find and easy to use.
   g. The site design should be appealing to its intended audience.
   h. The text should be easy to read and not be cluttered with distracting graphics, fonts, and backgrounds.
   i. The page should load in a reasonable amount of time and without problems.
   j. The interactive features should be explained clearly.
   k. A user should not need to pay a fee or type in personal information (such as a name or e-mail address) before using the site.
   l. Spelling and grammar should be correct.
   m. Information should be current and accurate. A last-updated date should appear on the site.

2. Have students choose a Web site to critique. The Web site can be a lesson, a site about an author, or a site created by a school or student. For example, they could evaluate one of the Web sites listed in "Notable Films & Videos Recordings Computer Software Web Sites 1998" (*School Library Journal,* April 1998).

3. Ask students to provide an oral or written critique of the Web site based on the following questions:

   > What is the name of the site?
   > What is the purpose of the site?
   > Who are the intended viewers?
   > What can be learned at the site?
   > What is your favorite part of the site?
   > How would you improve the site?

4. Save the written review and place it in a "Reviews of Web Sites" notebook that can be made available for all students to read in your school's computer laboratory.

5. As a class, look at award-winning educational sites. What features make these sites effective? Students might also enjoy exploring the Web sites of several different schools listed in registries such as the Web 66 International School Registry (http://web66.coled.umn.edu).

6. As a class, look at a poorly created site. In your discussion emphasize the problems of the site and how it could be changed to be more effective.

7. Your students could develop a rating system to add to their reviews of Web sites. For example, a rating of four computer monitors could indicate their favorite sites, whereas a rating of one-half a computer monitor could indicate sites that are not worth a second visit.

8. Encourage students to evaluate and write reviews of Web sites on their own.

9. Discuss the elements of a good Web site. Have students consider ways they might create a Web site about their class, a project, or their own writing.

Activity 9–13:
ELECTRONIC PUBLISHING

TYPE	TERM
● CLASS	○ STA
● GROUP	● LTA
○ IND	○ LC

Purpose:
1. To develop creative writing that may be published on the Internet
2. To become involved in the writing process
3. To respond to the writing of other students
4. To create a student literary magazine

Materials:
Computer(s) with e-mail and World Wide Web access.

Grade level:
Lower and upper elementary, middle school

Procedures:

1. Encourage students to publish their writing on the Internet. Many current Web sites allow students to submit and electronically publish their short stories, poems, and essays. Each site provides on-line information about individual and class submissions. Locations include The Book Nook (http://i-site.on.ca/ booknook. html), which publishes student book reviews; Cyberkids (http://www.cyberkids. com), which invites submissions from students in grades two through six; Kids' Space Connection (http://www.KS-connection.com), which publishes the works of students in grades Kindergarten through eight; KidPub (http://www.kid-pub.org/kidpub/), which publishes all submitted work from children in grades four and above; and I*EARN-US (http://www.iearn.org), which publishes an electronic student news magazine called *The Contemporary.*

2. If your school has a Web site or you have the resources available for creating Web sites, encourage students to design their own Web page and publish their work directly on their Web page. Have them include a link to their e-mail address so that readers can send them messages about and respond to their work.

3. Encourage students to regularly post poems and stories on their Web page or to other Web sites so that other students can offer feedback in an electronic version of process writing sessions. Explain to them that the point of process writing is to give and receive constructive criticism for a work in progress. Electronic publishing encourages feedback from a distant audience. Because a link is usually provided to a writer's e-mail address, readers are able to respond immediately to a work they like and ask the writer questions. Many sites that support electronic publishing also show the number of people who have visited the work, so even if students do not get e-mail about their work, they can see that people have read their work. Encourage students to revise and edit their work before submitting them for electronic publication.

4. To introduce students to the idea of giving feedback to and receiving feedback from other students, have students participate in a process writing exercise in the classroom. Direct them to write a journal entry about what they think good writing entails. Have them include information about what they write, when they write, how their writing varies from genre to genre and medium to medium, and how writing makes them feel.

5. After they have finished writing their journal entries, have students pass their work to the person on their right. Direct students to write a response to the journal entry. Remind them to concentrate their feedback on the content of the writ-

ing rather than grammar and the like. Ask them to respond to questions such as the following: "What point about writing do you agree with the most in the journal entry? What image or phrase stands out the most to you or did you enjoy reading the most? What would you like to hear more about?"

6. After they have finished their responses, direct students to fold the response in half and attach it to the paper. Ask them to pass the paper and response in the same direction as before. Have the students write a response to the second paper, without reading the folded response. Encourage them to consider the questions listed in procedure 5.

7. Have students return the papers and responses to the original authors.

8. After students have had a chance to read the responses to their journal entries, have them write another journal entry describing their feelings about other students reading their papers. What did they like about it? What did they dislike about it? Encourage them to discuss these responses with the class.

9. Invite one or more distant classrooms to participate in the writing process with your class. The works and responses can be exchanged via e-mail. For example, you could involve two other classrooms in an eight-week-long process-writing exercise with the following schedule:

Week 1	Exchange essay about writing
Week 2	Exchange essay about favorite books
Week 3 and 4	Exchange poetry
Week 5 and 6	Exchange short stories
Week 7 and 8	Exchange personal essays or works of your choice

10. Each week, have students submit their work to at least three students for response. Have lists of students from each class and coordinate the schedule so that each student responds to three works and receives responses from three students. For example, a student could respond to the three names that appear directly below his name on the list.

11. As they read and respond to the writings of other children, remind students to address questions in their responses such as the following: "What do I like the most about this piece? What would I like to hear more about? What can the author do to make the work stronger?"

12. After students receive responses to their work, encourage them to consider the responses, revise their work, and send the revisions to other students.

13. After the eight-week writing project is completed, have each class discuss and summarize what it has learned from its experiences with electronic process writing. Have them send these summaries to your class via e-mail.

14. Using submissions from the distant classrooms and from your own classroom, have your class create a student literary magazine.

15. Have your class discuss the parameters for the submissions of the magazine:

> Will you publish one work from each student in each class?
> Will you limit the number of submissions to two from each student and choose the best one to publish?
> Will you have open and anonymous submissions and choose the best of these?
> Will you have each class choose the best works from its students and submit only those?
> Will you include the distant classes in the design and layout of the magazine? Or will this be a project completed within your classroom?

16. Ask each class to submit one piece that includes excerpts from the first writing exercise. This essay could be included in the magazine with a title such as "Overall Impressions of Writing and the Writing Process by *Class Name*."

17. Have your class discuss the design of your literary magazine. For example, have them consider the following:

The name of the magazine
The design and appearance of the banner or masthead
The number of pages to print
The sections to include such as poetry, short stories, essays, and book reviews
The general layout, including whether or not to have columns, the order of sections, and the amount of space devoted to each section
The kinds of graphics that will be included, such as photos, sketches, or clip art

18. Once the submissions guidelines and the overall design of the magazine have been considered, divide the class into groups. Each group is responsible for a different segment of the magazine. For example, there could be five groups, each responsible for one of the following areas: poetry, short stories, essays, book reviews, and artwork.

19. Assign roles for members of the group. For example, each group could have an editor responsible for the layout of its section of the magazine, a managing editor responsible for organizing the submissions for its area, and a copy editor responsible for the word processing and spelling check of the submissions for each group. Members of each group can then evaluate the submissions for their area.

20. Once submissions decisions have been made, have students create the layout of the magazine, using desktop publishing if possible.

21. Have students include an editorial or a letter in the preface of the magazine that describes the process, how telecommunications was used to create a magazine, and how they produced the magazine.

22. Send a paper copy of the magazine to each of the distant classes whose submissions were considered.

23. If your school has a Web site or you have the resources available for creating Web sites, have students create an electronic edition of the literary magazine. Make sure they include the e-mail address of each author in the bylines of the articles so that readers can respond to the works via e-mail.

REFERENCES

Association for Library Service to Children. (1998, April) "Notable Film & Videos Recordings Computer Software Web Sites 1998" *School Library Journal* 44(4) 36–41.

Children and Technology Committee of the Association for Library Service for Children, a division of the American Library Association. "Selection Criteria: How to Tell If You Are Looking at a Great Site" (http://www.ssdesign.com/parentspage/greatsites/criteria.html).

Cohen, M., & Riel, M. (1989). The effect of distant audiences on students' writing. *American Educational Research Journal, 26* (2), 143–159.

Erivitt, J., & Snolan, R. (1996). *24 Hours in Cyberspace: Painting on the Walls of the Digital Cave.* New York: an imprint of Macmillan Que Education and Training.

Hilts, P. (1997, July). The road ahead: Publishing visionaries look at the changes that digital technology might bring. *Publishers Weekly, 244,* 125–128.

Hsu, Richard C. and Mitchell, William E. (1997, May 25). "Books Have Endured for A Reason . . ." *New York Times* p. F12.

Jacobson, Frances F. and Smith, Greg D. (1998, March). "Teaching Virtue in a Virtual World." *School Library Journal* 44(3) 100–103.

Jones, Patrick. (1997, November). "A Cyber-Room of Their Own: How Libraries Use Web Pages to Attract Young Adults." *School Library Journal, 43,* 34–37.

Kinzer, C., & Leu, D. J., Jr. (1987, February). The challenge of change: Exploring literacy and learning in electronic environments. *Language Arts, 74,* 126–136.

Leu, D. J., Jr. (1997, September). Exploring literacy on the Internet. *The Reading Teacher, 51* (1), 62–67.

Magid, L. J. (1994). *Child safety on the information highway.* Arlington, Virginia National Center for Missing and Exploited Children and the Interactive Services Association.

McGarvey, J. (1997, May 25). . . . But computers are clearly the future. *New York Times,* p. F12.

McLaughlin, A. T. (1997, May 22). Mentors log on to help students make the grade. *Christian Science Monitor,* p. 1.

Olson, R. (1996, May). When it comes to technology, the postman always thinks twice. *School Library Journal, 42,* 19–22.

Rogers, A., Andres, Y., Jacks, M., & Clauset, T. (1990). Telecommunications in the classroom: Keys to successful telecomputing. *The Computing Teacher, 17* (8), 25–28.

U.S. Congress, Office of Congressional Assessment. (1995). *Teachers and technology: Making the connection.* Washington, D.C.: U.S. Government Printing Office.

CHILDREN'S LITERATURE REFERENCES

Beattie, Owen, and Geiger, John. *Buried in Ice: The Mystery of a Lost Arctic Expedition.* New York: Scholastic, 1992.

Bierhorst, John. *The Dancing Fox: Arctic Folktales* New York: Morrow, 1997.

Brandemburg, Jim. *To the Top of the World: Adventures with Arctic Wolves.* New York: Walker, 1993.

Cooper, Susan. *The Boggart.* New York: Macmillan, 1993.

Cooper, Susan. *Silver on the Tree.* New York: Atheneum, 1977.

George, Jean Craighead. *Julie of the Wolves.* Illustrated by John Schoenherr. New York: Harper & Row, 1972.

George, Jean Craighead. *Look to the North: A Wolf Pup Diary.* New York: HarperCollins, 1997.

Hamilton, Virginia. *The Gathering.* New York: Greenwillow, 1981.

Heinz, Brian. *Kayuktuk, An Arctic Quest.* Illustrated by John Van Zyle. San Francisco: Chronicle Books, 1996.

Hughes, Monica. *The Dream Catcher.* New York: Atheneum, 1987.

Hughes, Monica. *Devil on My Back.* New York: Atheneum, 1987.

Kroll, Steven. *Pony Express.* Illustrated by Dan Andreasen. New York: Scholastic, 1996.

Leiner, Katherine. *First Children: Growing Up in the White House.* Illustrated by Katie Keller. New York: Tambourine, 1996.

Levy, Elizabeth. *The Creepy Computer Mystery.* Illustrated by Denise Brunkus. New York: Scholastic, 1996.

Provensen, Alice. *The Buck Stops Here: The Presidents of the United States.* New York: HarperCollins, 1990.

Pyle, Howard. *The Story of King Arthur and His Knights.* New York: Scribner's, 1903; reissued, 1978.

Simon, Seymour. *Einstein Anderson, Science Detective: The On-Line Spaceman and Other Stories.* New York: Morrow, 1997.

St. George, Judith. *The White House: Cornerstone of a Nation.* New York: Putnam, 1990.

Steger, Will, and Bowermaster, John. *Over the Top of the World: Explorer Will Steger's Trek across the Arctic.* New York: Scholastic, 1997.

Sutcliffe, Rosemary. *The Light Beyond the Forest.* New York: Dutton, 1981.

Sutcliffe, Rosemary. *The Road to Camlann: The Death of King Arthur.* Illustrated by Shirley Felts. New York: Dutton, 1982.

Sutcliffe, Rosemary. *The Sword and the Circle: King Arthur and the Knights of the Round Table.* New York: Dutton, 1981.

Index

About the Authors

Following the completion of her doctorate at the University of Wisconsin, Madison, Donna E. Norton joined the College of Education faculty at Texas A&M University where she teaches courses in children's literature, language arts, and reading. Dr. Norton is the recipient of the Texas A&M Faculty Distinguished Achievement Award in Teaching. This award is given "in recognition and appreciation of ability, personality, and methods which have resulted in distinguished achievements in the teaching and the inspiration of students." She is also the recipient of the 1992 Virginia Hamilton Essay Award, which is presented by the Virginia Hamilton Conference Advisory Board at Kent State University. This annual award recognizes an article that "makes a significant contribution to the professional literature concerning multicultural literary experiences for youth." Dr. Norton is listed in *Who's Who of American Women*, *Who's Who in America*, and *Who's Who in the World*.

Dr. Norton is the author of three books in addition to this volume: *The Effective Teaching of Language Arts*, 5th ed., *Language Arts Activities for Children*, 4th ed., and *The Impact of Literature-Based Reading*. She is on the editorial board of several journals and is a frequent contributor to journals and presenter at professional conferences. The focus of her current research is multicultural literature, literature-based reading programs, and the literature and writing connection. The multicultural research includes a longitudinal study of multicultural literature in classroom settings. This research is supported by grants from the Meadows Foundation. She currently has grants from the King Foundation and the GTE Foundation to develop institutes in children's literature and

literacy. In conjunction with research in comparative education, she developed graduate courses that enable students to study children's literature and reading instruction in England and Scotland.

Prior to her college teaching experience, Dr. Norton was an elementary teacher in River Falls, Wisconsin and in Madison, Wisconsin. She was a Language Arts/Reading Consultant for federally funded kindergarten through adult basic education programs. In this capacity she developed, provided in-service instruction, and evaluated kindergarten programs, summer reading and library programs, remedial reading programs, learning disability programs for middle school children, elementary and secondary literature programs for the gifted, and diagnostic and intervention programs for reading-disabled adults. Dr. Norton's continuing concern for literature programs results in frequent consultations with educators from various disciplines, librarians, and school administrators and teachers.

Dr. Norton will present her most recent research, *Plot Structures and Archetypes in Recent Award-Winning Books*, at the invitational Conference on Children's Literature at Providence University in Taiwan. Dr. Norton has received a grant for bilingual education for doctoral students, which ties literature into bilingual programs.

Saundra Norton is completing doctoral studies at the University of South Carolina where she is a lecturer of literature in the English department. She completed her masters degree at Texas A&M University where she majored in literature with an emphasis in children's literature. Under the sponsorship of a Jordon Fellowship she studied language, culture, and folklore at the Goethe Institute in Germany. Her current research interests include biography, textual bibliography, and women's studies. She is a frequent participant at both national and international conferences. Her paper presented at the 15th International Ezra Pound Conference in Italy was presented the Bates Award for the best essay written by a graduate student at the University of South Carolina. Saundra is taking French studies at the Institute de Français. She has been accepted at the Paris Writer's Workshop in Paris, France.